THE SPIRI

MW01617155

Is it possible to see, hear, touch, smell and taste God? How do we understand the biblical promise that the 'pure in heart' will 'see God'? Christian thinkers as diverse as Origen of Alexandria, Bonaventure, Jonathan Edwards and Hans Urs von Balthasar have all approached these questions in distinctive ways by appealing to the concept of the 'spiritual senses'. In focusing on the Christian tradition of the spiritual senses, this book discusses how these senses relate to the physical senses and the body, and analyses their relationship to mind, heart, emotions, will, desire and judgement. The contributors illuminate the different ways in which classic Christian authors have treated this topic, and indicate the epistemological and spiritual import of these understandings. The concept of the spiritual senses is thereby recovered for contemporary theological anthropology and philosophy of religion.

PAUL L. GAVRILYUK is Associate Professor of Historical Theology at the University of St Thomas, Minnesota. He is the author of *The Suffering of the Impassible God: The Dialectics of Patristic Thought* (2004) and *Histoire du catéchuménat dans l'église ancienne* (2007).

SARAH COAKLEY is Norris-Hulse Professor of Divinity at the University of Cambridge. Her previous publications include *Powers and Submissions: Philosophy, Spirituality and Gender* (2002), and she is editor of *Re-Thinking Gregory of Nyssa* (2003) and co-editor (with Charles M. Stang) of *Re-Thinking Dionysius the Areopagite* (2009).

THE SPIRITUAL SENSES

Perceiving God in Western Christianity

PAUL L. GAVRILYUK

University of St Thomas, Minnesota

and

SARAH COAKLEY

University of Cambridge

CAMBRIDGE UNIVERSITY PRESS

CAMBRIDGE
UNIVERSITY PRESS

University Printing House, Cambridge CB2 8BS, United Kingdom

Published in the United States of America by Cambridge University Press, New York

Cambridge University Press is part of the University of Cambridge.

It furthers the University's mission by disseminating knowledge in the pursuit of education, learning and research at the highest international levels of excellence.

www.cambridge.org
Information on this title: www.cambridge.org/9781107685949

© Cambridge University Press 2012

First published 2012
First paperback edition 2013

A catalogue record for this publication is available from the British Library

Library of Congress Cataloguing in Publication data
The spiritual senses : perceiving God in Western Christianity / [edited by]
Paul L. Gavrilyuk and Sarah Coakley.
p.   cm.
Includes bibliographical references and index.
ISBN 978-0-521-76920-4 (hardback)
1. Senses and sensation – Religious aspects – Christianity.
I. Gavrilyuk, Paul L.   II. Coakley, Sarah, 1951–
BT741.3.S65   2012
231'.042 – dc23   2011035044

ISBN 978-0-521-76920-4 Hardback
ISBN 978-1-107-68594-9 Paperback

To the Eternal Memory of John

Contents

vii

Contributors

EDITORS

PAUL L. GAVRILYUK is University Scholar and Associate Professor of Historical Theology at the Theology Department of the University of St Thomas, St Paul, Minnesota. He is the author of *The Suffering of the Impassible God: The Dialectics of Patristic Thought* (2004) and *Histoire du catéchuménat dans l'église ancienne* (2007). He edited with Douglas M. Koskela and Jason E. Vickers *Immersed in the Life of God: The Healing Resources of the Christian Faith: Essays in Honor of William J. Abraham* (2008).

SARAH COAKLEY is Norris-Hulse Professor of Divinity at the University of Cambridge, and was previously Mallinckrodt Professor at Harvard Divinity School. Among her recent publications are: *Powers and Submissions: Philosophy, Spirituality and Gender* (2002); *Re-Thinking Gregory of Nyssa* (ed., 2003) and *Re-Thinking Dionysius the Areopagite* (ed. with Charles M. Stang, 2009). Forthcoming is the first volume of her systematics, *God, Sexuality and the Self: An Essay 'On the Trinity'* (Cambridge).

CONTRIBUTORS

WILLIAM J. ABRAHAM is the Albert Cook Outler Professor of Wesley Studies and Altshuler Distinguished Teaching Professor at Perkins School of Theology, Southern Methodist University, in Dallas, Texas. He is the author or editor of fifteen books, including the pioneering *Canon and Criterion in Christian Theology* (1998) and *Crossing the Threshold of Divine Revelation* (2006).

FREDERICK D. AQUINO is Professor of Theology and Philosophy in the Graduate School of Theology at Abilene Christian University. He is the author of *Communities of Informed Judgment: Newman's Illative Sense*

and Accounts of Rationality (2004) and *Unveiling Glory*, co-authored with
Jeff Childers (2004).

BOYD TAYLOR COOLMAN is Associate Professor of Theology at Boston
College in Chestnut Hill, Massachusetts. He is the author of *Knowing
God by Experience: The Spiritual Senses in the Theology of William of
Auxerre* (2004) and *The Theology of Hugh of St Victor: An Interpretation*
(Cambridge, 2010); he has also co-edited *Trinity and Creation* (*Victorine
Texts in Translation*, vol. 1, 2010). He is currently working on a book
on Thomas Gallus. He has also published articles in *Modern Theology*,
Theological Studies, *The Thomist* and *Traditio*.

RICHARD CROSS is John A. O'Brien Professor of Philosophy at the Uni-
versity of Notre Dame. He is the author of *The Metaphysics of the
Incarnation: Thomas Aquinas to Duns Scotus* (2002) and *Duns Scotus on
God* (2005).

GEORGE E. DEMACOPOULOS is Associate Professor of Historical Theology
and the Co-Founding Director of the Orthodox Christian Studies Pro-
gram at Fordham University. His books include *Five Models of Spiritual
Direction in the Early Church* (2007) and *Orthodox Readings of Augustine*
(ed. with Aristotle Papanikolaou, 2008).

GARTH W. GREEN is Associate Professor of Philosophy of Religion at
McGill University. He is the author of the book *The Aporia of Inner
Sense: The Self-Knowledge of Pure Reason and the Critique of Metaphysics
in Kant* (2010) and of articles in the areas of medieval theology, German
Idealism and contemporary phenomenology.

GREGORY F. LANAVE is Associate Professor of Systematic Theology in
the Pontifical Faculty of the Immaculate Conception at the Dominican
House of Studies in Washington, DC. He is the author of *Through
Holiness to Wisdom: The Nature of Theology According to St. Bonaventure*
(2005).

MATTHEW R. LOOTENS is a doctoral candidate in theology at Fordham
University, where he also has served as a senior teaching fellow in the
theology and medieval studies departments. He is writing a dissertation
on Gregory of Nyssa's *Contra Eunomium*.

BERNARD MCGINN is the Naomi Shenstone Donnelley Professor Emeritus
of Historical Theology and the History of Christianity at the Divinity
School of the University of Chicago. His current major project is a

multi-volume history of Western Christian mysticism under the general title *The Presence of God*.

MARK J. MCINROY is Assistant Professor of Systematic Theology at the University of St Thomas, Minnesota. He has published and presented academic examinations on Origen of Alexandria, Karl Barth and Hans Urs von Balthasar. He is currently expanding to a monograph his study of Balthasar's use of the spiritual senses tradition in his theological aesthetics.

MARK T. MEALEY is a professor of theology and the chair of Wesleyan Studies at Rocky Mountain College in Calgary, Alberta, where he teaches doctrinal and historical theology. He has published and presented studies on Augustine, Leontius of Jerusalem, Bernard Lonergan and John Wesley.

WILLIAM J. WAINWRIGHT is Distinguished Professor of Philosophy Emeritus at the University of Wisconsin-Milwaukee. He is the author or editor of nine books including *Mysticism* (1981), *Reason and the Heart* (1995), *Religion and Morality* (2005) and *The Oxford Handbook of Philosophy of Religion* (2005).

Foreword

This project began in a conversation between the editors of the present volume at an Italian restaurant in Leuven, Belgium, in November 2005. At the time both of us had developed an interest in the topic of spiritual perception: Sarah Coakley was exploring the importance of the patristic teaching on the spiritual senses for systematic theology and philosophy of religion, whereas Paul Gavrilyuk had discovered how little the topic had recently been explored in patristic scholarship in general. In spring 2007, Coakley, who was then teaching at Harvard Divinity School, gathered a reading group of scholars from the Boston area interested in the topic at her house in Watertown, Massachusetts, for a series of informal meetings on Friday afternoons. Besides the two editors, the initial Spiritual Senses Group included Boyd Taylor Coolman, Garth Green, Paul Kolbet, Mark McInroy and Cameron Partridge. We looked at the theme of spiritual perception in the writings of Origen, Gregory of Nyssa, Pseudo-Macarius, Pseudo-Dionysius, Symeon the New Theologian, Thomas Gallus, Bonaventure, Immanuel Kant and Michel Henry. We also identified the central role that the work of Karl Rahner and Hans Urs von Balthasar had had in the rediscovery of the topic of the spiritual senses in twentieth-century theology. Towards the end of our spring meetings, we decided to produce a jointly written volume, with mutual understanding that most editorial responsibilities would be carried out by Gavrilyuk.

In order to discuss the individual chapters and to forge a coherent vision of the future volume, Gavrilyuk organized three consultations. The first consultation was hosted at Boston College in May 2008. At this meeting the original group was joined by Frederick Aquino and Richard Cross. The second consultation was held in Chicago in November 2008, and the third and final consultation took place in Montreal in November 2009. The original group kept growing, as William Abraham, George Demacopoulos, Gregory LaNave, Matthew Lootens, Bernard McGinn, Mark Mealey and William Wainwright joined in the endeavour. During each of the three consultations, about a third of all essays that would make up the volume were discussed. Thus the volume grew as a cooperative endeavour, as the authors read and commented on each other's work and contributed constructively to the Introduction. Derek Michaud and Garth Green offered important bibliographic suggestions. The editorial work on the volume was conducted with the help of Gavrilyuk's graduate students Stephani Atkins, Kyle Sellnow and Ry Siggelkow. Gavrilyuk also wishes to thank his colleagues at the University of St Thomas – Philip Rolnick, Terence Nichols, Peter Feldmeier and David Penchansky – for their valuable comments on the Introduction and other parts of the book. The editors would also like to acknowledge the contributions of Brian Daley, Scot Bontrager, Philip Endean and Derek Neve to the consultation discussions. Mark McInroy, who contributed two chapters to the volume, is also principally responsible for the production of the indexes. Translations are by the contributors unless otherwise stated.

We are also profoundly grateful for the help that the editors at Cambridge University Press – Kate Brett, Laura Morris, Joanna Garbutt and Anna Lowe, as well as freelance copy-editor Fiona Little – have expertly offered at different stages of the volume's preparation.

PAUL L. GAVRILYUK AND SARAH COAKLEY

Abbreviations

Bibliographic information regarding less well-known primary sources is included in the footnotes.

Alexander of Hales, *Qu. disp.*	Alexander of Hales, *Questiones disputatae*
Aristotle, *De an.*	Aristotle, *De anima*
DMR	*De memoria et reminiscentia*
Met.	*Metaphysics*
NE	*Nichomachean Ethics*
Augustine, *Civ. Dei*	Augustine of Hippo, *De civitate Dei* (CCL 47–8)
Conf.	*Confessiones* (CCL 27)
De Gn. litt.	*De Genesi ad litteram* (CSEL 28.1)
De lib. arbit.	*De libero arbitrio* (CCL 29)
De q. an.	*De quantitate animae* (CSEL 89)
De trin.	*De trinitate* (CCL 50–50A)
En. Ps.	*Enarrationes in Psalmos* (CCL 38–40)
Ep.	*Epistulae* (CSEL 34, 44, 57)
Jo. ev. tr.	*In Johannis evangelium tractatus* (CCL 36)
Serm.	*Sermones* (PL 38–9)
Solil.	*Soliloquia* (CSEL 89)
WSA	*The Works of Saint Augustine: A Translation for the 21st Century* (Hyde Park and Brooklyn, NY: New City Press)
Balthasar, *GL*	Hans Urs von Balthasar, *The Glory of the Lord: A Theological Aesthetics*, 7 vols., trans. E. Leiva-Merikakis,

	A. Louth, B. McNeil et al. (San Francisco: Ignatius Press, 1982–9)
Bernard, *De div.*	Bernard of Clairvaux, *Sermo de diversis*
SSCC	*Sermones super Cantica Canticorum*
Bonaventure, I *Sent.*	*Commentarius in primum librum Sententiarum magistri Petri Lombardi*
II *Sent.*	*Commentarius in secundum librum Sententiarum magistri Petri Lombardi*
III *Sent.*	*Commentarius in tertium librum Sententiarum magistri Petri Lombardi*
Brev.	*Breviloquium*
Comm. in Ioan.	*Commentarius in evangelium Ioannis*
De donis	*Collationes de septem donis Spiritus Sancti*
De red.	*De reductione artium ad theologiam*
De sc. Chr.	*Quaestiones disputatae De scientia Christi*
Hex.	*Collationes in Hexaëmeron*
Itin.	*Itinerarium mentis in Deum*
Sermo 2 in Dom. 12 post Pentec.	*Sermo 2 in Dominicam duodecimam post Pentecosten*
Sermo 6 in Circumc.	*Sermo 6 in Circumcisionem Domini*
Sermo 9 in Epiph.	*Sermo 9 in Epiphaniam*
Sermo 14 in Epiph.	*Sermo 14 in Epiphaniam*
CCL	Corpus christianorum. Series latina (Turnhout and Paris: Brepols)
CSEL	Corpus scriptorum ecclesiasticorum latinorum (Vindobonae, Austria: F. Tempsky, 1800–)
DS	Marcel Viller et al. (eds.), *Dictionnaire de spiritualité: Ascétique et mystique, doctrine et histoire*, 17 vols. (Paris: G. Beauchesne, 1937–95)
FC	Fathers of the Church (Washington, DC: Catholic University of America Press)
GCS	*Die griechischen christlichen Schriftsteller* (Leipzig)

Gregory, *GNO*	Gregory of Nyssa, *Gregorii Nysseni Opera*, ed. Werner Jaeger (Leiden: Brill, 1952–98)
De anima	*De anima et resurrectione*
In Cant.	*In Canticum Canticorum*
Cat. Or.	*Oratio catechetica magna*
Gregory the Great, *Hom. Evang.*	Gregory the Great, *Homiliae in evangelia* (CCL 141)
Hom. Ez.	*Homiliae in Ezechielem* (PL 76)
Mor.	*Moralia in Iob* (CCL 143, 143A, 143B)
PR	*Liber regulae pastoralis* (SC 381–2)
HS	C. E. Hambrick-Stowe, *The Practice of Piety: Puritan Devotional Disciplines in Seventeenth-Century New England* (Chapel Hill: University of North Carolina Press, 1982)
HTR	*Harvard Theological Review* (1908–)
John Locke, *HU*	John Locke, *An Essay Concerning Human Understanding* (New York: Dover, 1959)
John Smith, *SD*	John Smith, *Select Discourses* (New York and London: Garland, 1978)
Jonathan Edwards, *RA*	Jonathan Edwards, *A Treatise Concerning Religious Affections*, ed. J. E. Smith, *Works*, vol. II (New Haven, CT: Yale University Press, 1958)
TV	*The Nature of True Virtue*, ed. P. Ramsey, *Works*, vol. VIII (New Haven, CT: Yale University Press, 1989)
Maximus, *Ad Thal.*	Maximus the Confessor, *Quaestiones ad Thalassium*
Amb.	*Ambigua*
Myst.	*Mystagogia*
Mechthild, *FL*	Mechthild von Magdeburg, *Das fliessende Licht der Gottheit*
Nicholas of Cusa, *ADI*	Nicholas of Cusa, *Apologia doctae ignorantiae*
DB	*De Beryllo*
DC	*De coniecturis*
DI	*De docta ignorantia*

DFD	*De filiatione Dei*
DQD	*De quaerendo Deum*
DVD	*De visione Dei*
DVS	*De venatione sapientiae*
NPNF	Philip Schaff and Henry Wace (eds.), A Select Library of Nicene and Post-Nicene Fathers of the Christian Church (Edinburgh: T. & T. Clark, 1991)
Origen, *Dial. Heraclides*	Origen, *Dialogus cum Heraclide*
In Cant.	*In Canticum Canticorum*
In John	*Commentarii in evangelium Joannis*
In Lament.	*Fragmenta in Lamentationes*
In Psalm	*Fragmenta in Psalmos*
Peter Lombard, *Sent.*	Peter Lombard, *Sententiae in IV libris distinctae*
PG	Jacques-Paul Migne (ed.), Patrologia graeca (Paris: J.-P. Migne, 1857–66)
PL	Jacques-Paul Migne (ed.), Patrologia latina (Paris: J.-P. Migne, 1857–66)
Plato, *Parm.*	Plato, *Parmenides*
Resp.	*Respublica*
Plotinus, *Enn.*	Plotinus, *Enneads*
Pseudo-Dionysius, *CH*	Pseudo-Dionysius the Areopagite, *The Celestial Hierarchy*
DN	*The Divine Names*
EH	*The Ecclesiastical Hierarchy*
Ep.	*Epistles*
MT	*The Mystical Theology*
Rahner, *SW*	Karl Rahner, *Spirit in the World*, trans. William Dych (New York: Herder, 1968)
RAM	*Revue d'ascétique et de mystique*
RSR	*Revue de sciences religieuses*
S	Sermon (for numbered sermons by John Wesley)
SC	Sources chrétiennes (Paris: Éditions du Cerf, 1941–)
Thomas Aquinas, *ST*	Thomas Aquinas, *Summa theologiae*
Catena in Luc.	*Catena aurea, super Lucam*

De ver.	*De veritate*
Ep.	*Epistula*
In Sent.	*Scriptum super libros Sententiarum*
Super I Cor.	*Super primam epistolam ad Corinthios lectura*
Super II Cor.	*Super secundam epistolam ad Corinthios lectura*
Thomas Gallus, *Comm. II*	Thomas Gallus, *Second Commentary on the Canticle of Canticles*
Comm. III	*Third Commentary on the Canticle of Canticles*
Explanatio DN	*Explanatio in librum De divinis nominibus*
Explanatio EH	*Explanatio in librum De ecclesiastica ierarchia*
Glose AH	*Glose super Angelica Ierarchia*
TLG	Thesaurus Linguae Graecae

Introduction

Paul L. Gavrilyuk and Sarah Coakley

> When a man's senses are perfectly united to God, then what God has said is somehow mysteriously clarified. But where there is no union of this kind, then it is extremely difficult to speak about God.[1]

Christian authors of all ages have used sensory language to express human encounters with the divine. In the Old Testament believers are enjoined to 'taste and see that the Lord is good' (Ps 34[33]: 9, 1 Pet 2: 3); the prophets and others 'hear the word of the Lord' (Isa 1: 10; Hos 4: 1); the beatitude promises that 'the pure in heart will see God' (Mt 5: 8); the apostle Paul speaks of receiving the vision of God 'face to face' (1 Cor 13: 12) and beholding 'the glory of the Lord as in a mirror' (2 Cor 2: 18); the faithful are said to inhale the 'sweet aroma of Christ' (2 Cor 2: 15); and the witnesses of the incarnation speak of 'touching with [their] own hands' the Word of Life (1 Jn 1: 1). These biblical passages seem to point to certain features of human cognition that make perception-like contact with God possible. But how precisely should these statements be construed? What implications do these claims have for theological anthropology? Do such statements imply peculiar modes of seeing, hearing, smelling, tasting, and touching divine things?

As might be expected, the claim to have a special form of perception that makes direct human contact with God possible is both epistemologically and metaphysically problematic. While there is a general agreement that humans possess the five physical senses, there is no comparable consensus regarding other modes of perception. Moreover, the claim that God could be perceived by special senses seems to violate notions of divine transcendence and immateriality. After all, when attempting to look at God, one is 'looking at what cannot be seen' (cf. 2 Cor 4: 18, Heb 11: 27). As the creator, God is ontologically different from all ordinary objects of perception.

---

[1] John Climacus, *The Ladder of Divine Ascent*, xxx, trans. C. Luibheid and N. Russell, *John Climacus: The Ladder of Divine Ascent* (New York: Paulist Press, 1982), p. 288.

One may come to terms with these problems in a variety of ways. A sceptical strategy, embraced in most versions of modern rationalism and empiricism, would be altogether to jettison the claims to receive divine revelation or to have religious experience. Another strategy would be to emphasize that God in his self-communication brings it about that humans receive divine revelation without specifying the cognitive equipment enabling such a communication. Throughout history, accounts in which humans have received visions, locutions and other messages from the divine realm have been typically more concerned with conveying the content of such experiences than with analysing the cognitive makeup of human recipients. Theories of divine self-communication tend to focus on the properties of divine action, rather than on the features of human knowers that make the reception of revelation and religious experience possible. Nevertheless, numerous thinkers throughout Christian history have attempted to probe the conditions of the divine–human encounter further. In the process these thinkers have come up with various approaches, some of which could be subsumed under the general idea of spiritual perception, the subject of this volume.

THE VOCABULARY OF SPIRITUAL PERCEPTION

The Christian vocabulary of non-physical perception is extremely fluid, sometimes exasperatingly so. The expression 'spiritual senses' (*sensus spiritales*) is first attested in the Latin translation of the works of Origen of Alexandria (*c.* 185–*c.* 254).[2] It should be noted that patristic authors did not attribute a focal significance to the expression αἴσθησις πνευματική (*sensus spiritalis*) and its equivalents. In contrast, in Western medieval theology the concept of the spiritual sense(s) came to be used more systematically.

For the purpose of this volume, 'spiritual senses' is an umbrella term covering a variety of overlapping, yet distinct, expressions in which 'sense' in general or a particular sensory modality (vision, audition, olfaction, touch or taste) is typically qualified by reference to spirit (e.g. 'eyes of the spirit', 'spiritual touch'), heart (e.g. 'ears of the heart'), soul (e.g. 'eyes of the soul', 'hands of the soul'), mind or intellect (e.g. 'mind's eye', 'intellectual touch'), inner [man] (e.g. 'inner', 'interior' or 'inward' eyes, ears, etc.) or faith (e.g. 'eyes of faith', 'ears of faith'). Taking Origen's idiosyncratic

---

[2] Origen, *Commentarii in Epistulam ad Romanos*, 4. 5 (PG 14. 977D – 978A); *In Cant.* 1. 4 (PG 13. 97B); *Homiliae in Exodum*, 1. 4 (PG 12. 301A). Rufinus of Aquilea (*c.* 345–410), the translator of these and other works of Origen, commonly rendered his original rather freely. As a result, it is by no means certain that αἴσθησις πνευματική (or its equivalent) underlies *sensus spiritalis* in Rufinus's translation.

rendering of Proverbs 2: 5 ('thou shalt acquire a divine sense') as their point of departure, some authors also refer to this perceptual capacity as a 'divine sense' (αἴσθησις θεία) or a 'sense of divinity' (*sensus divinitatis*).[3] The above-mentioned expressions by no means exhaust a rich vocabulary of spiritual perception, but rather serve as points of reference.

At the same time it is not uncommon for Christian authors to use the language of sense-perception to describe divine–human encounter without qualifying the senses as 'spiritual' or correlating them with the soul, mind, heart and so on explicitly. Consider, for instance, the skilful way in which Augustine (354–430) draws on a vast array of sensation imagery in his *Confessions*:

You called and cried out loud and shattered my deafness. You were radiant and resplendent, you put to flight my blindness. You were fragrant, and I drew in my breath and now pant after you. I tasted you, and I feel but hunger and thirst for you. You touched me, and I am set on fire to attain the peace which is yours.[4]

Since by the time he wrote *Confessions*, Augustine shared a common view that God was immaterial, he did not intend to say that God was available to the physical senses in a way similar to material objects.[5] Some other form of direct cognitive contact with God is implied in this passage, perhaps analogous to but not reducible to ordinary sense-perception. Such relatively imprecise use of sensual language – sanctioned by scripture, yet open to the 'Messalian' interpretation that God could be perceived directly by the physical senses – has endured throughout the history of Christian theology. The range of terms describing different properties and modes of non-physical perception has remained fairly broad and fluid to the present day.

By having recourse to the notion of the 'spiritual senses' we thus neither wish to impose an artificial uniformity on diverse materials, nor ignore the acute methodological difficulties that the lack of precise terminology presents in a given author. In particular, our use of the plural form of the expression 'spiritual senses' is not meant to exclude or under-rate a single-mode or unitary conception of spiritual sensation found in some Christian authors. Moreover, the qualifier 'spiritual' before 'senses' is intended to indicate non-physical mode of perception, rather than to prioritize an anthropology in which 'spirit' is consistently differentiated from the other

---

[3] Origen, *In Cant.* I. 4; *Contra Celsum*, I. 48; VII. 34.

[4] Augustine, *Conf.* X. 27. 38, trans. H. Chadwick, *Saint Augustine: Confessions* (Oxford University Press, 1991), p. 201.

[5] As he makes clear in *Conf.* X. 6. 8.

aspects of the self, such as body, soul, intellect or affect.[6] A further variant is that some Christian authors link the language of the spiritual senses explicitly to pneumatology, and thence to their trinitarianism, while others do not, or do so only very implicitly.

A final and additional difficulty is created by the fact that the expression 'spiritual sense(s)' is also applied in classic Christian literature to non-literal modes of interpreting *scripture*. Some, upon hearing about this research project, may therefore surmise that our subject has to do with the history of biblical interpretation. It should however be obvious to the reader by now that in this book we use the expression 'spiritual senses' to designate non-physical human perception, rather than the non-literal interpretations of scripture. While some ancient authorities connect the apprehension of the non-literal meaning of scripture with the exegete's spiritual perception, such a connection is not entailed in our use of the 'spiritual senses' as a general category.

KARL RAHNER'S DEFINITION OF THE 'SPIRITUAL SENSES DOCTRINE': AN EVALUATION

We give preference to the expression 'spiritual senses' in part because it has been adopted in most discussions of related phenomena over the last hundred years. The study of the spiritual senses in the twentieth century received its major impetus from an essay by Karl Rahner (1904–1984), 'Le début d'une doctrine des cinq sens spirituels chez Origène' (1932).[7] In this seminal work Rahner offered the following definition: 'It seems prudent to speak of a doctrine of the spiritual senses only when these partly figurative, partly literal expressions (to touch God, the eyes of the heart, etc.) are found integrated in a complete system of the five instruments of the spiritual perception of suprasensible religious realities.'[8]

Rahner's normative definition of what must count as a proper 'doctrine of the spiritual senses' has the distinctive attraction of clarity. In his article Rahner proposes to understand the spiritual senses on a close analogy with the five physical senses. For lack of a better designation, one could call such an account the 'five senses analogy' of spiritual perception. The physical

---

[6] It should be stressed, however, that there is a strong presumption against reductive materialism in the anthropology that includes the notion of the spiritual senses.

[7] For the discussion of various aspects of this important essay, as well as of Rahner's work in general, see esp. Chapters 1, 2, 9, 12 and 15 in this volume.

[8] K. Rahner, 'Le début d'une doctrine des cinq sens spirituels chez Origène', *RAM*, 13 (1932), 114, my translation.

and spiritual senses could be understood as two different sets of powers or faculties, operating in tandem or separately, or, alternatively, as two states of the same fivefold sensorium directed at different aspects of the same object, or perhaps having different objects altogether. The 'doctrine' of the spiritual senses would then address the nature of the correlation between the physical and the spiritual senses, as well as the integration of the spiritual senses with other aspects of the self.

It should be noted, however, that in our judgement, Rahner's definition of what must count as a proper doctrine of spiritual perception is unduly restrictive. Many ancient authorities had important things to say about spiritual perception, although they had not developed anything amounting to a 'complete system' or a body of 'doctrine' of the five spiritual senses. In fact, most if not all patristic authors, including Origen, to whom Rahner accords the role of the founding father of the spiritual senses 'doctrine', as a rule treat the subject of spiritual perception non-systematically. The accounts of spiritual perception that one finds, for example, in Gregory of Nyssa (*c.* 330–*c.* 395), Augustine (354–430), Pseudo-Dionysius (fl. *c.* 500), Maximus the Confessor (*c.* 580–662) and Gregory the Great (*c.* 540–604) hardly amount to a 'doctrine' in Rahner's sense of the term, although it would be a grave mistake to ignore their insights and influence.

More importantly, many Christian authors treat fewer than *five* 'instruments of spiritual perception' (Rahner's expression): some focus exclusively on a single spiritual sense, such as sight or touch, for example; others variously combine spiritual modalities; still others stress the unification and simplification of the powers of the self as it draws nearer to God. For instance, Alexander of Hales (*c.* 1186–1245), Thomas Gallus (d. 1246) and Bonaventure (*c.* 1217–1274) aligned spiritual sight and hearing with the intellect (*intellectus*), and the remaining three spiritual senses with affectivity (*affectus*). Such a grouping recommends a twofold, rather than a fivefold, division of spiritual perception.

It also should be observed that Rahner himself did not feel constrained by his definition when he included in his survey Diadochus of Photike (mid-fifth century) – an author who emphatically speaks of a single spiritual modality only.[9] Besides, in his later work, particularly in his study of Bonaventure, Rahner was more concerned to emphasize the unitive character of spiritual perception than to justify the fivefold division of the senses, which he had come to consider 'rather forced'.[10]

---

[9] *Ibid.* pp. 141–2. See G. Horn, 'Les sens de l'esprit d'après Diadoque de Photicé', *RAM*, 8 (1927), 402–19.

[10] For a discussion of Rahner's treatment of Bonaventure, see Chapters 9 and 15 in this volume.

PRELIMINARY PHILOSOPHICAL CONSIDERATIONS

In defence of Rahner's normative definition of 'the doctrine of five spiritual senses', it could be observed that if a given author discusses only one
perceptual mode, preferring to speak, for example, of 'intellectual sight',
it is possible that such an author uses sight (or other sense) figuratively
to refer to ordinary mental acts, such as imagination, reflection or understanding, rather than to a special mode of perception. It is true, of course,
that in English and other languages, some verbs drawn from the sphere
of sense-perception have become dead metaphors describing various forms
of thinking. For example, we speak of 'seeing a point', 'having a point of
view', 'viewing a hypothesis', 'envisioning a prospect', 'grasping a concept',
'embracing an idea', 'touching upon a subject', 'hearing what a person
has to say' (in the sense of focusing mental attention), 'smelling trouble' and so on. In everyday discourse 'taste' commonly refers to aesthetic
judgement. There appears to be no need to invoke a special mode of perception to account for these ordinary forms of reflection, imagination and
judgement.

In this regard, it has become common in the twentieth century scholarship on our theme to distinguish between the 'analogical' and 'metaphorical'
functions of the language of spiritual perception. Analogy obtains when the
operation of the spiritual senses is described in terms akin to the operation
of physical sensation. Metaphorical use can be assumed when no close similarity with the functioning of a physical sensorium is intended. Just what
aspect of the self other than physical sensation such metaphors are meant
to portray often has to be further specified. Without such a clarification,
what is meant by 'metaphorical use' remains rather ambiguous, depending
upon, among other things, a given scholar's theoretical assumptions about
metaphorical language in general.[11] Still, in one important limiting case,
the metaphorical use of spiritual perception implies that there is no special
mode or faculty of perception required to account for experience being
ascribed to the relevant senses.

It is by no means obvious, however, that *every* correlation of the senses
with the intellect can be reduced to a metaphor depicting ordinary mental
activity, such as imagination or understanding. It seems that the intellect

<hr />

[11] Those who have wielded this distinction usually have Thomas Aquinas's treatment of the matter in
ST I, q. 13 at least in the back of their minds: analogical statements are literally (*proprie*) true, while
metaphorical statements are not. But we should note that many of the authors in the spiritual senses
tradition precede Thomas and are not familiar with his particular way of making this distinction;
indeed, they may not be operating with a clear demarcation between analogy and metaphor at all.

operates in a non-ordinary, indeed unique, way when God becomes the object of its vision. When Plato spoke of the contemplation of the Forms with 'the eyes of the soul' (ψυχῆς ὄμματα) and the 'sight of the mind' (διανοίας ὄψις) he did not mean ordinary acts of imagining or reasoning. Rather Plato intended to describe a direct, perception-like apprehension of the intelligibles, including the good.[12]

Drawing on Platonic sources, Philo of Alexandria (*c.* 20 BCE–*c.* CE 50) also referred to the faculty responsible for the vision of God as 'the eyes of the soul' (ὄμματα/ὀφθαλμοί ψυχῆς), 'the eyes of the mind' (νοῦ ὄμματα or ὀφθαλμοί) and the 'eyes of understanding' (διανοίας ὄμματα or ὀφθαλμοί).[13] From the second century on this philosophical terminology found its way into the Christian vocabulary of spiritual perception to become towards the fourth century something of a commonplace. Intellectual vision or intellectual intuition, most especially in its application to the divine things, is both a mental act and a unique form of perception. Intellectual vision is a non-discursive mental act involving a direct cognitive contact with the object of contemplation. As the Cambridge Platonist John Smith (1618–1652) put it, 'When reason once is raised by the mighty force of the Divine Spirit into a converse with God, it is turned into sense.'[14]

As a mental act, intellectual vision is less overtly tied to the body. The non-Christian Platonists as a rule treated embodiment as hindering, if not altogether blocking, the vision of the divine. Christian theologians 'baptized' the 'Platonic' version of intellectual vision with different results, tending to maintain an ambivalent attitude towards the role of the body in the contemplation of God. This ambivalence is already evident in Origen, who in some cases views embodiment as an impediment, and in other cases construes it as instrumental to the contemplation of God. For Pseudo-Dionysius, the height of mystical contemplation presupposes the rising above all cognitive powers in the ultimate unification and

---

[12] Plato, *Resp.* VII, 519B, 533D; *Symposium*, 219A; *Sophist*, 254A–B: 'for the eyes of the soul (ψυχῆς ὄμματα) of the multitude are not strong enough to endure the sight of the divine', trans. H. N. Fowler, *Plato*, Loeb Classical Library, 123 (Cambridge, MA: Harvard University Press, and London: W. Heinemann, 1977), p. 403. Cf. Aristotle, *NE* VI. 12, 1144a 30.

[13] Philo, *De confusione linguarum*, 21, 92; *De sacrificiis Abelis et Caini*, 36, 69, 78; *Quod deterius potiori insidiari soleat*, 22; *De Abrahamo*, 58; *De mutatione nominum*, 3, 5, 37, 203; *De ebrietate*, 82; *De plantatione*, 22; *De virtutibus*, 11; *De specialibus legibus*, I. 49, III. 2, 4, 6, IV. 140, V. 12, 16; *De praemiis et poenis*, 37; *Quod omnis probus liber sit*, 5; *De Providentia*, II. 9; *De posteritate Caini*, 8, 18, 118, 167; *De somniis*, I. 199; *De opificio mundi*, 71; *Legatio ad Gaium*, 2; *Questiones et solutiones in Genesim*, II. 34; *Questiones et solutiones in Exodum*, II. 51; IV. 8, 129. Cicero mentions in passing the expressions *oculi mentis* in *De natura deorum*, II. 45, and *oculus animis* at II. 161.

[14] For a discussion of this passage in J. Smith, see Chapter 13 in this volume.

simplification of the self. By comparison, Maximus's incarnational vision is more comprehensive, with the body being more consistently integral to contemplation.

In the West, the fivefold division of the senses originates with Aristotle.[15] The Stagirite considered sight to be the 'chief sense'.[16] He also held that 'indirectly hearing makes the largest contribution to wisdom', since it serves as means of verbal communication.[17] Touch and taste he regarded as the senses that were essential to all animals.[18] Smell, taste and touch were judged to be more implicated in animal desires and passions than the remaining two senses.[19] Aristotle, who himself was not explicit or consistent on this matter,[20] was commonly understood to have sanctioned the following hierarchy of the senses, from the highest to the lowest: sight, hearing, smell, taste and touch.[21]

The Christian spiritual senses tradition variously engages the 'Aristotelian' sensual hierarchy. Some Christian theologians show little awareness of, or interest in, a systematic ordering of the senses, whether physical or spiritual. When sight is assumed to be the highest spiritual sense, it is not always obvious whether this assumption is made for philosophical reasons or on scriptural grounds, or both. It is telling, however, that the eschatological culmination of the encounter with God came to be expressed predominantly in terms of the beatific *vision*, rather than, say, 'beatific olfaction' or 'beatific audition'. Aquinas summed up this tradition with a characteristic economy of words: 'the highest and perfect felicity of intellectual nature consists in the vision of God'.[22]

---

[15] C. Classen, *Worlds of Sense: Exploring the Senses in History and Across Cultures* (London and New York: Routledge, 1993). Cultural anthropologists have recently argued that both the 'Aristotelian' fivefold division of the sense-modalities and the predominance of the language of vision to describe mental activity are culture-bound; see D. Howes (ed.), *The Varieties of Sensory Experience: A Sourcebook in the Anthropology of the Senses* (University of Toronto Press, 1991). While this may be true in some respects, the conclusions of the present study are not affected by this observation, since we limit ourselves to the thinkers who within the Western Christian tradition shared the presupposition of the fivefold division of the physical senses.

[16] *De an.* III. 3, 429a.   [17] *De sensu*, I, 437a 11–12.

[18] Taste for Aristotle was ultimately reducible to touch: see *De an.* III. 12, 434b.

[19] Aristotle, *NE* x. 5, 1176a: 'Sight differs from touch in purity, as do hearing and smell from taste', trans. R. Crisp, *Aristotle: Nicomachean Ethics* (Cambridge University Press, 2000), pp. 191–2.

[20] For example, in *De sensu*, I, 441a he speaks of the sense of smell as being inferior to the rest of the senses. See S. Rosen, *The Quarrel between Philosophy and Poetry* (New York: Routledge, 1988), pp. 119–26.

[21] For a survey of a Christian appropriation of the 'Aristotelian' hierarchy, see R. Jütte, *A History of the Senses: From Antiquity to Cyberspace* (Cambridge, MA: Polity Press, 2005), pp. 61–71.

[22] *Summa contra Gentiles*, III. 1. 60. 2, trans. V. J. Bourke, *St Thomas Aquinas: On the Truth of the Catholic Faith* (Garden City, NY: Image Books, 1956), p. 199.

Those Christian writers who took the Song of Songs as a point of departure for their account of the comparative value of the spiritual senses were however less constrained by the 'Aristotelian' ranking of the senses. Gregory of Nyssa, Alexander of Hales, Bonaventure, Bernard of Clairvaux and other mystical theologians at times freely reversed the 'Aristotelian' order of the senses by positing that in the mystical ascent spiritual hearing and sight were toppled by spiritual touch as the mode of perception implying a closer contact with its subject.[23] Augustine's dictum 'touch is the end of knowing' aligns itself with this insight of mystical theology.[24]

The operation of spiritual taste was often treated within the framework of Eucharistic practices.[25] In the Latin sources wisdom (*sapientia*) was commonly taken to connote 'tasted knowledge' owing to its presumed etymological connection with taste (*sapor*).[26] In patristic and later sources spiritual smell was sometimes associated with spiritual discernment and discrimination, and taken as a paradigm of the 'senses that are trained to discern good and evil' (Heb 5: 14).[27]

With the Protestant Reformation's emphasis on preaching as the main vehicle of communicating Christian teachings, the apostle Paul's words that 'faith comes from hearing' (Rom 10: 17) were freshly appreciated. The iconoclastic impulses of the Reformation further led to increased reliance on audition, often at the expense of vision as well as other sensory modes of receiving the divine. To conclude, the 'Aristotelian' hierarchy of the senses, while undoubtedly influential, was deployed by Christian authors with considerable freedom and historical variation.

Another important item of Aristotelian psychology that Christian authors took on board was the notion of the 'inner senses'. In the *De anima*, as well as in the corpus of writings commonly grouped under the Latin title *Parva naturalia*, Aristotle discusses the powers of the soul that convey the sensory input collected by the five physical senses to the mind. The medieval lists of the 'interior' or 'inner senses', based on Aristotle, count from four to seven such powers, including imagination, memory, estimation and 'common sense' (also called the 'master sense', which had

---

[23] Cf. Aristotle, *De an.* III. I, 424b.

[24] Augustine, *De trin.* I. 9. 18; cf. Plotinus, *Enn.* VI. 7. 34. 8–21; VI. 9. 10. 12–16.

[25] See B. T. Coolman, *Knowing God by Experience: The Spiritual Senses in the Theology of William of Auxerre* (Washington, DC: Catholic University of America Press, 2004), chap. 10; C. W. Bynum, *Holy Feast and Holy Fast: The Religious Significance of Food to Medieval Women* (Berkeley, CA: University of California Press, 1987); G. Frank, '"Taste and See": The Eucharist and the Eyes of Faith in the Fourth Century', *Church History*, 70 (2001), 619–43.

[26] Jütte, *A History of the Senses*, p. 69.

[27] For a discussion of spiritual smell, see S. A. Harvey, *Scenting Salvation: Ancient Christianity and the Olfactory Imagination* (Berkeley, CA: University of California Press, 2006), pp. 169–80.

the function of integrating and creating awareness of the input of each external sense).[28] A special complication was created by the fact that, beginning with Origen, the spiritual senses were associated with the Pauline concept of the 'inner person' (ὁ ἔσω ἄνθρωπος)[29] and commonly called the 'inner' or 'interior' senses, whereas the physical senses were associated with the 'outer person' and called the 'external senses'. Most medieval authors were aware of the difference between the homonymous notions of Aristotelian and 'Origenist' inner senses.[30] Other authors, for example, Nicholas of Cusa (1401–1464), attempted to integrate the two types of senses.

REPRESENTATIVE BIBLICAL LOCI OF THE
SPIRITUAL SENSES TRADITION

The theme of the spiritual senses has been on the radar of Christian theologians since the second century. Much of the reflection on our subject occurs in the context of pondering scripture. What a given author does with the biblical material depends upon such factors as her cultural and ecclesiastical milieu, the range of religious practice and experience that she draws upon and her philosophical views (whether tacit or explicit), as well as the sensory vocabulary current in her time.

Since Philo, the story of Exodus came to be allegorically interpreted as the soul's spiritual ascent to God. Philo's Moses climbs Mount Sinai to receive a vision reminiscent of the illumination afforded to the philosopher of the *Republic*'s cave. Philo's reading of Exodus came to inspire directly, or through shared exegetical *paideia*, such patristic authors as Clement of Alexandria, Origen, Gregory of Nyssa and Pseudo-Dionysius, among others.

Following in the footsteps of Philo, patristic authors – beginning with Theophilus of Antioch and Irenaeus of Lyons – would struggle with the already mentioned problem of how the invisible God, whose theophany was potentially lethal to human beings (e.g. Exod 33: 20; Gen 32: 30), could manifest Godself in a visible form. The Johannine emphasis that it was the incarnate Word who had made the knowledge of the Father possible

---

[28] S. Everson, *Aristotle on Perception* (Oxford: Clarendon Press, 1997). For other bibliographic references to the treatment of Aristotle's theory of interior senses, see Chapter 12 below, nn. 5–7. For Augustine's account of the Aristotelian inner senses, see Chapter 3 in this volume.

[29] Rom 7: 22 and 2 Cor 4: 16. Cf. Eph 3: 16 and the 'hidden man of the heart' of 1 Pet 3: 4.

[30] For example, Roger Bacon (*c.* 1220–1292) treats the 'Aristotelian' inner senses of imagination and common sense separately from the notion of the spiritual vision; see *Opus majus*, II. 5. I. 2 and II. 5. 3. 1–2 respectively. On Bacon, see R. Carton, *L'expérience mystique de l'illumination intérieure chez Roger Bacon* (Paris: J. Vrin, 1924).

provided a crucial epistemic clue for dealing with this problem. Paul's words about the transformative, eschatological vision in 1 Corinthians 13: 12 ('For now we see in a mirror, dimly, but then we will see face to face') and 2 Corinthians 3: 18 ('And all of us, with unveiled faces, seeing the glory of the Lord as though reflected in a mirror, are being transformed into the same image from one degree of glory to another'), as well as his tantalizing remark about his own auditory experience in 2 Corinthians 12: 2–4, also offered a fertile ground for reflection on the beatific vision.[31]

Another foundational text in the history of the spiritual senses was the Song of Songs, which from the time of Hippolytus and Origen elicited meditations on the soul's spiritual union with Christ. While the biblical passages mentioned in the previous paragraph tended to draw spiritual sight into the focus of the exegete's attention, the richly sensuous imagery of the Song – longings, kisses, embraces, scents and so on – prompted a further elaboration of tactile, gustatory and olfactory imagery.

One could add to this admittedly incomplete list of biblical inspirations countless passages in which the listeners hear and obey, or fail to heed, the prophetic message.[32] Either on their own, or combined with the gospel miracles of the healing of sight and hearing,[33] such texts were also drawn into the orbit of the spiritual senses tradition. Beginning with Origen, the authors attuned to our theme saw in the parable of the ten virgins a framework for talking about the five physical senses represented by the foolish virgins, and the five spiritual senses represented by the wise ones. The five yoke of oxen mentioned in the parable of the great dinner (Lk 14: 15–24), as well as the five husbands of the Samaritan woman (Jn 4: 16–18), prompted Augustine to ponder the self's attachment to the five physical senses.[34] Even more suggestive were the post-resurrection recognition scenes, such as the *Noli me tangere* (Jn 20: 17) or the opening of the disciple's eyes during the supper at Emmaus (Lk 24: 30–1).

Origen's discussion of the sacrifice of the paschal lamb in Exodus 12 offers a rich blend of different biblical allusions to the senses, and may serve as an illustration:

For since there are five senses in the human being, unless Christ comes to each of them, He cannot be sacrificed and, after being roasted, be eaten. For it is when he made clay with his spittle and anointed our eyes (John 9: 6–7) and made us see clearly (Mark 8: 25), when he opened the ears (cf. Mark 7: 33–35) of our heart so

---

[31] On this point, see esp. Chapter 12 in this volume.
[32] For example, Isa 6: 9, 42: 18, 43: 8; Ezek 12: 2; Mk 8: 18; Mt 11: 15, 13: 14; Jn 12: 40; Acts 28: 26; Rom 11: 8; Rev 2: 7.
[33] Mt 11: 15, 13: 19; Jn 9: 6–7.   [34] For a discussion, see Chapter 3 in this volume.

that having ears we can hear (cf. Mt 11: 15, 13: 19), when we smell his good odor (2 Cor 1: 15; Eph 5: 2), recognizing that his name is a perfume poured out (Song 1: 3), and if, having tasted, we see how good the Lord is (Ps 34 [33]: 8, 1 Pet 2: 3), and if we touch him with the touch of which John speaks: That which was from the beginning, which we have heard, which we have seen with our eyes and touched with our hands, concerning the word of life (1 Jn 1: 1), then it is that we will be able to sacrifice the lamb and eat it and thus come out of Egypt.[35]

Despite this wealth of material gleaned from scripture, it should be emphasized that the Bible as such offers no 'doctrine of the spiritual senses'. Most patristic authors attuned to our theme commonly offer their insights about spiritual perception when prompted by their favorite biblical passages. But for some early Christian theologians – and Origen is perhaps the first of them – the spiritual senses came to occupy a distinct place in their theological anthropology. This being the systematic focus of our volume, our collection necessarily starts with Origen and seeks to clarify the exact epistemological import of his treatment of the spiritual senses.

BOOK OVERVIEW

Origen, discussed by Mark McInroy in Chapter 1, both drew upon the 'Platonic' intellectual vision and developed the analogy of the five physical senses with considerable sophistication. In tracing out the distinctiveness of Origen's founding Christian account of the spiritual senses, McInroy also clarifies how the twentieth-century attention to Origen on this theme, from Rahner onwards, has tended to distort, as well as illuminate, Origen's particular contribution. There is a deepening exploration of the idea that the physical senses themselves may undergo transformation in developing intimacy with God. This is, to be sure, not a *consistent* position in Origen's writing; but when the theme does appear it gives the lie to the suggestion that Origen's view of the body and sensuality was unduly negative and 'Platonic', and the spiritual senses were understood only disjunctively in relation to the physical. In highlighting the development of Origen's thought on this matter over time, and the remaining tensions and inconsistencies, McInroy is able to correct a number of modern misapprehensions and exegetical distortions.

When one comes from Origen to Gregory of Nyssa (the next great spiritual senses exegete in the patristic Greek tradition), one can find both

---

[35] *Peri Pascha*, 18, trans. R. J. Daly, *Origen: Treatise on the Passover* (New York: Paulist Press, 1992), p. 37.

direct dependence on Origen and important original developments. Sarah Coakley's treatment of Nyssen in Chapter 2 starts, like McInroy's account of Origen, by peeling back behind an influential modern treatment (that of Jean Daniélou), which has tended to mesmerize subsequent commentators. But Daniélou's account was unduly affected by his own theological concerns; and in any case it concentrated almost exclusively on Gregory's last works. The originality of Nyssen's contribution to theological anthropology, it is argued here, can be appreciated only by looking at the full span of his treatments of spiritual senses language, which undergoes crucial changes in his lifetime, and involves an increasing integration of his epistemology with his scriptural account of human assimilation to the Logos. This can only occur over a lifetime of maturation – just as Nyssen's own thoughts on the matter emerge only gradually. As in Origen, then, spiritual senses language is about a *diachronic* spectrum of possibilities in human responses to God; and this is doubtless one of the reasons why it has been so hard for the modern philosophical mind either to comprehend or to approve it. Here is no flat, universalistic account of human reason and affect, but rather an invitation to ongoing epistemic and spiritual transformation, in which some are necessarily more advanced than others. It was the much later secular philosophy of the Enlightenment that was to prise epistemology and spirituality apart; but in their spiritual senses language, Origen and Gregory founded distinctive mystical traditions in which the two undertakings were intrinsically united.

For Pseudo-Dionysius, discussed by Paul Gavrilyuk in Chapter 5, the 'Platonic' intellectual vision is a latent capacity that is specifically activated in believers at baptism. Fourth-century Fathers such as Cyril of Jerusalem, John Chrysostom and Ambrose of Milan had already connected the activation of the spiritual sense to baptismal initiation and participation in the sacramental life of the church. But in Pseudo-Dionysius this line of thinking receives new attention, and is aligned with his particular account of the knowing subject, strongly influenced by neo-Platonism. Intellectual vision is for him a higher-order non-discursive mental apprehension of reality. According to the Areopagite, eros is the energy that summons and directs all cognitive capacities to contemplation and union with God. Pseudo-Dionysius describes the highest point of the mystical ascent as the state of unknowing, wherein all cognitive powers are simplified, unified and ultimately transcended in the hyper-noetic union. The medieval theologians discussed in this volume, among them Thomas Gallus, Alexander of Hales, and Bonaventure, will capture different dimensions of Pseudo-Dionysius's thought, developing their distinct accounts of the operation of 'affective cognition' at various stages of mystical ascent.

As Frederick Aquino points out in Chapter 6, Maximus the Confessor emphasizes that the training of spiritual perception is bound up with growth in virtue and ascetic struggle with vice, and is a part of the process of deification. For Maximus, the goal of deification is to reintegrate the rational, volitional, affective and sensate functions of the self and thereby attain participatory knowledge of God. One can see here a clear continuation of the approach of Gregory of Nyssa, though with the particular influences of Pseudo-Dionysius now assimilated in a new mode.

In the West, Augustine, who more than any other early Latin patristic author stresses the eternal vision of God as the goal of human existence, had earlier also employed the other four senses to describe the apprehension of the divine reality. Matthew Lootens explores in Chapter 3 the often allusive treatment of spiritual sensation throughout the Augustinian corpus and shows how Augustine provides for moments of eschatological perception in the present life if the spiritual senses remain free from the effects and limitations of sin. For Augustine, however, the darknesses (*tenebrae*) of this life are always to be contrasted with the eschatological vision to come; darkness is not, as in Pseudo-Dionysius, accorded a positive mystical stance as a sign of noetic transcendence.

Early medieval monastic writing in the West, following Augustine, deploys the language of spiritual sensation frequently, unselfconsciously and spontaneously to describe divine–human encounter. Consistent with patristic tradition, this language often emerges in the context of scriptural exegesis. Gregory the Great, treated by George Demacopoulos in Chapter 4, ties the cultivation of the spiritual senses to spiritual direction, and more specifically to discernment.

Early scholastic theological discourse (twelfth and thirteenth centuries) continues to use such language, but also begins to give systematic, self-conscious reflection to our theme. An attempt is made to locate this teaching within the larger framework of Christian thought, in relation to broader epistemological issues and in the context of more elaborate theological anthropologies. There is also an emerging separation from the locus of scriptural exegesis, but at the same time, other loci come into a sharper focus, for example, the relation of the spiritual senses to the Eucharist, the ecclesial 'mystical body of Christ' and the beatific vision. It could be said that a conscious 'doctrine' of the spiritual senses emerges during this period for the first time. However, this was not a *topos* taken up by all medieval theologians.

As Boyd Taylor Coolman suggests in Chapters 7 and 8, there seems to be a stronger proclivity towards the doctrine of the spiritual senses within Franciscan theological traditions than elsewhere,[36] as the writings of Alexander of Hales, Thomas Gallus and Bonaventure attest, wherein a strong link to the thought of Augustine is cultivated, and which have a consistent 'voluntarist' orientation. These medieval theologians gave a new expression to the Dionysian account of how eros-driven intellect surpasses and folds its own powers in the supra-intellectual union with God. According to these theologians, at the highest stages of the mystical ascent, *affectus* and the associated spiritual senses of touch and taste supersede and in some ways subsume *intellectus* and the associated spiritual sense of sight, thus suggesting the notion of affective cognition.

As Gregory LaNave shows in Chapter 9, for Bonaventure the spiritual senses are the name of a distinctive kind of experiential knowledge of God, namely, a fivefold way that he can be experienced as present. This is possible only because God expresses himself in the Word – uncreated, incarnate, crucified and inspired. The spiritual senses are seen in one who, like Francis of Assisi, received the signs of Christ's passion.

Earlier we noted some obvious cases when sensation terms are contextually assumed to be dead metaphors referring to ordinary mental acts. As Richard Cross argues in Chapter 10, this is how Thomas Aquinas used the language of spiritual sensation in his cognitive theory. That is, Aquinas did not have to postulate a *special* cognitive faculty to account for the intellect's contemplation of God: his epistemology already catered for that *ab initio*. However, this does not mean that Thomas was uninterested in how the Holy Spirit transformatively engages the human person; and Aquinas deals with this matter richly in his pneumatology in the third part of the *Summa theologiae*. However, it is striking that, in contrast to Franciscan and mystical theologians writing at more or less the same time, Thomas eschews a doctrine of the spiritual senses, as such.

Some of those medieval mystics, whose works are analysed by Bernard McGinn in Chapter 11, spoke of the ways believers might come to a fuller sense of God's presence both through the 'inner senses', as well as in the corporeo-spiritual totality of the human person. Bernard of Clairvaux (1090–1153) and William of Saint-Thierry (*c.* 1085–1148) were pioneers in this latter form of discourse, which was developed by a number of late medieval mystics, such as Hadewijch of Antwerp (fl. mid thirteenth

---

[36] There were exceptions, however. For example, the Spiritual Franciscan Peter John Olivi (*c.* 1248–1298) does not appear to have had much use for the notion of the spiritual senses in his writings.

century), Mechthild of Magdeburg (*c.* 1210–*c.* 1280) and Richard Rolle (*c.* 1300–1349).

In Chapter 12, Garth Green presents the basic features of the Aristotelian doctrine of the 'inner senses' (*sensus interiores*) over against the rather different features of the Origenist account of the spiritual senses (*sensus spirituales*). He does so in order to identify their incongruence, and to propose that the aesthetics of Nicholas of Cusa is determined by his attempt to synthesize these two inherited aesthetic doctrines. He argues that Cusa superposes an Origenist theological aesthetic over an Aristotelian theory of cognition, and that neither escapes in its original form. This synthesis represents an interesting moment of transition, since Cusa stands on the cusp of early modernity, when the spiritual senses tradition was to undergo a certain eclipse.

The theme however does not disappear altogether from the radar of Christian thinkers in the modern period. Most Enlightenment epistemologies tended to cultivate agnosticism vis-à-vis the mind's ability to have cognitive access to the transcendent, or at least to eschew elitist epistemologies which could not be accorded universal application. However, despite considerable sceptical and critical pressure, the spiritual senses tradition did not disappear completely at the Enlightenment. While it is certainly true that the theme is overlooked in most intellectual histories of early and high modernity, one should not fall into the trap of taking such secularizing narratives for granted. In the works of the Cambridge Platonists, as well as of Pietist and Puritan divines, one finds cognitive theories that do not fit well with the standard Enlightenment narrative and can be seen as late extensions of the patristic and medieval traditions of the spiritual senses. As William Wainwright shows in Chapter 13, both the analogy of the five senses and the account of spiritual perception as affect-laden intellectual vision were live options for Jonathan Edwards (1703–1758) and his Puritan predecessors.

Spiritual sensation is also a central category in the theology of John Wesley (1703–1791), by which he defines his doctrines of faith, new birth and the witness of the Spirit. He develops an account of spiritual sensation as an *elenchos*, which he understands as 'the supernatural evidence of things unseen' (Heb 11: 1). In Chapter 14, Mark Mealey argues that Wesley sharply distinguishes between natural sensation and the capacity for spiritual sensation. Spiritual sensation is a direct, immediate knowledge of God as love, impossible in natural capacities. In the fall, humans lost union with God; in conversion, humans recover union with God through the recovery of the spiritual senses. Mealey suggests that although this theological realism is pre-critical, as an epistemology, it represents a response to Enlightenment scepticism.

On the Catholic side, interest in our theme was kept alive (though now largely divorced from philosophy) in treatises on spiritual direction, in such authors as Giovanni Battista Scaramelli (1687–1752) and Augustin-François Poulain (1836–1919). As Sarah Coakley points out in Chapter 2 of the present volume, Karl Rahner's early interest in the spiritual senses tradition received a major impetus from reading these Jesuit spiritual writers, and was perhaps a reaction to the disregard for our topic in neoscholasticism.

According to Mark McInroy, Karl Rahner's treatment of the spiritual senses in Bonaventure had an influence on the reworked version of the *Vorgriff auf esse* ('the pre-apprehension of being') that appears in Rahner's late writings. Specifically, Rahner advances an idiosyncratic reading of Bonaventure's notion of spiritual touch as an immediate 'contact' with God at a level deeper than the intellect. This formulation bears intriguing, highly suggestive, parallels with Rahner's idea of a pre-conceptual awareness of the presence of the absolute as it is rearticulated in his later theological works. As McInroy shows in Chapter 15, Hans Urs von Balthasar also places the spiritual senses at the very heart of the anthropological dimension to his theological aesthetics, since it is precisely through the spiritual senses that one performs the epistemologically central task of 'seeing the form'. According to Balthasar, then, if the glory of God is to be recognized and received by the human being, this mediation of revelation must occur through the spiritual senses.

Drawing upon the work of Robert Campbell Moberly (1845–1903), William J. Abraham shows in Chapter 16 that the accounts of human cognition that took seriously the mind's ability to perceive divine things were not uncommon in Anglican theology as late as the turn into the twentieth century. While such theories fell into disuse during the heydays of Logical Positivism, there are signs that the topic of spiritual perception is regaining attention in contemporary analytic philosophy of religion. Richard Swinburne and Caroline Franks Davis have argued for epistemic parity between ordinary sense-experience and religious experience (though without explicit appeal to the 'spiritual senses' tradition as such). William Alston (1921–2009) has defended Christian Mystical Perception as a socially established system of doxastic practices that are fundamentally reliable, unless shown to be otherwise. The position of Alvin Plantinga is also in the vicinity of the spiritual senses tradition, inasmuch as it is a species of illumination theory, which draws upon Calvin's notion of the *sensus divinitatis*. All these developments are in some way associated with the turn against so-called 'classical foundationalism' in contemporary philosophy of religion. In our view the topic of spiritual perception is therefore likely to generate even greater interest in the years ahead.

To sum up this overview of the book's contents and the themes adumbrated here: it will be clear that what came in the West to be called 'the doctrine of the spiritual senses' had diverse beginnings in the Christian tradition (although always inspired by biblical prototype and suggestion), a hybrid history of marriages of convenience – or natural *attrait* – with classical philosophies and a capacity to produce a range of Christian epistemologies characterized by their subtle attention to the gradations of human intimacy with God. At the heart of this set of traditions, then, is the attempt to do full epistemological justice to the radical implications of the incarnation: that is what unites the various strands. But, as will already have become clear from this brief overview, we look in vain for any systematic, or ordered, development of these traditions; we should speak rather of a series of overlapping 'family resemblances' between them, which require close exegetical attention to avoid over-reading or conflation of them. Moreover, as we have acknowledged, there have been leading thinkers within Christianity (and not only in the modern period) who have resisted these traditions altogether, whether because they have suggested an unnecessarily literal reading of poetic licence, or an offensively elitist grading of human noetic capacity, or a redundant epistemological addendum to an already-assumed theory of the intellect. Hence, the matter remains controversial; but precisely therein lies something of its interest and attractiveness in a post-modern era.

CONCLUSION

Our project, then, is open-ended. The contemporary monographs that have been published on our topic to date have tended to focus on one Christian author, or on a specific period. In this regard we should mention B. Fraigneau-Julien's *Les sens spirituels et la vision de Dieu selon Syméon le Nouveau Théologien* (1985), Fabio Massimo Tedoldi's *La dottrina dei cinque sensi spirituali in San Bonaventura* (1999), Gordon Rudy's *Mystical Language of Sensation in the Later Middle Ages* (2002) and Boyd Taylor Coolman's *Knowing God by Experience: The Spiritual Senses in the Theology of William of Auxerre* (2004). The last author has also contributed two chapters to the present volume, and his monograph *Knowledge, Love, and Ecstasy in Thomas Gallus* is in preparation.

While the present volume surpasses in scope any study of the subject that has to date appeared in English, limitations of space have made it impossible to include all important voices. Syriac patristic writers and Byzantine theologians and a number of further Western medieval authors, as well as the Cambridge Platonists, German Pietists, German and English Romantics, twentieth-century French phenomenologists and present-day charismatics, to name only the most important omissions, would warrant a discussion that has not been allotted to them in this book. Depending upon how widely one wishes to cast one's net, one may also find the motif of the spiritual senses in the spiritual direction of St John of the Cross, in the theosophical musings of Rudolph Steiner, in the concept of metaphysical intuition of Henry Bergson, in the phenomenology of Max Scheler and in the poetry of Paul Claudel. Outside Christianity, related ideas, worthy of comparative analysis, could be found in ancient Greek religion, Judaism, Hinduism, Taoism, Islam (especially Sufism) and other religions.

The contributors hope that this volume will serve as a stepping stone to future research. Interdisciplinary study of the spiritual senses could further benefit from engaging a growing body of work on perception in analytic philosophy,[37] a 'theological turn' in continental phenomenology[38] and what has been described as a 'sensual revolution' in cultural anthropology.[39] Perhaps capable graduate students and established scholars will be inspired to take our research further, to the fields of knowledge that we have only gestured at in this book, including cognitive science, comparative religion, systematic theology, spirituality, cultural anthropology and philosophy of religion.

[37] See the works of W. Alston, B. Brewer, J. Dancy, F. Dretske, J. Foster, T. S. Gendler and J. Hawthorne, A. Goldman, J. Greco, A. Haddock and F. Macpherson, P. Moser, A. Plantinga and A. D. Smith in the Bibliography.
[38] For a discussion of the works of J.-L. Chrétien, J.-F. Courtine, M. Henry, E. Levinas, J.-L. Marion, J.-L. Nancy and P. Ricœur, see D. Janicaud, *Phenomenology and the Theological Turn: The French Debate* (New York: Fordham University Press, 2000).
[39] See the works of M. Bull and L. Back, C. Classen, J. Drobnick, E. Edwards and K. Bhaumik, D. Howes, and C. Korsmeyer in the Bibliography.

CHAPTER I

Origen of Alexandria

Mark J. McInroy

In this chapter I argue for a reassessment of current academic opinion regarding the theme of the spiritual senses in the writings of Origen of Alexandria (*c.* 185–*c.* 254). Specifically, John Dillon has claimed that it is exclusively in Origen's late works that one finds a 'proper' doctrine of the spiritual senses (the crucial features of which will be discussed below).[1] Dillon argues that Origen's early works, by contrast, evince only a metaphorical use of the language of sensation.[2] The early Origen, according to this reading, is not actually describing the perception of spiritual realities, as is typically thought. Instead, in his early writings Origen uses terms such as 'seeing' and 'hearing' in a figurative manner to describe 'understanding', placing no particular value on the sensory dimension to the terms.

In contrast to this assessment, however, I argue here that unexamined aspects of Origen's early writings in fact demonstrate noteworthy continuities between his early and late uses of sensory language. In particular, portions of Origen's early scriptural commentaries and *De principiis* show that his 'doctrine of the spiritual senses' emerges much earlier than has been recently supposed. At a more fundamental level, however, I argue for a revision of the very interpretive apparatus that has been used to classify Origen's uses of sensory language in the modern period, and I suggest that

---

[1] J. M. Dillon, 'Aisthêsis Noêtê: A Doctrine of the Spiritual Senses in Origen and in Plotinus', in A. Caquot, M. Hadas-Lebel and J. Riaud (eds.), *Hellenica et Judaica: Hommage à Valentin Nikiprowetzky* (Leuven and Paris: Peeters, 1986), pp. 443–55. Dillon's thesis has gained noteworthy traction in the contemporary setting: G. Rudy, for one, endorses this distinction between 'early' and 'late' uses of sensory language in Origen's thought in his *Mystical Language of Sensation in the Later Middle Ages* (New York and London: Routledge, 2002), pp. 17–35.

[2] Scholarship on the spiritual senses routinely employs the term 'metaphor' in a manner that some might find reductive. A 'metaphorical' use of sensory language, on these accounts, simply indicates a use of sensory language that does not actually retain any sensory or perceptual dimension. For example, in the colloquial expression 'I see what you mean', the verb 'to see' is used in a metaphorical sense. For purposes of this examination, I use the term in the manner in which it has been used in scholarship on the spiritual senses, the various shortcomings of such a limited concept of metaphor notwithstanding.

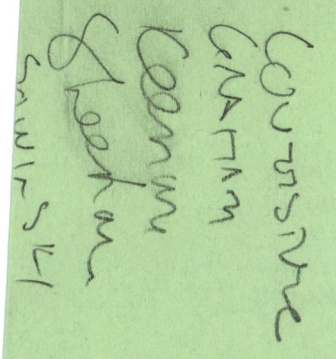

[...]ols developed in the interest of providing conceptual
[...]er sharpened for the profitable examination of Origen's

CATEGORIZATION OF ORIGEN'S USE OF THE LANGUAGE OF SENSATION

[...]terpretive challenges Origen presents his readers, one
[...]ear: he employs an enormous range of sensory terms
[...]ings to describe the relationship between the human
[...] habitually calls on his reader to reconceptualize the
[...] the Bible and place it in a 'spiritual' register. Origen
[...] with 'eyes of the mind' (διανοίας ὀφθαλμοί),[3] hearing
with 'spiritual ears' (ὦτα πνευματικά),[4] speaking to God with a 'bodiless
voice' (φωνὴ μὴ σώματι)[5] and 'breathing Christ in everything' (διὰ παντὸς τὸν Χριστὸν ἀναπνέουσι).[6] He describes a 'sense of touch' (ἀφῆς)
for handling the 'Word of life' (λόγος τῆς ζωῆς), 'smelling... with no
sensible organs of perception' (ὀσφραινομένης... αἰσθήσει οὐκ αἰσθητῇ)
and 'taste that feeds on living bread that has come down from heaven' (γεύ-
σις χρωμένης ἄρτῳ ζῶντι καὶ ἐξ οὐρανοῦ καταβεβηκότι).[7] Drawing on
Romans 7: 22 and 2 Corinthians 4: 16, Origen discusses 'the divine senses
of the inner man'.[8] In fact, he holds that 'every member of the external
human being is also called the same thing in the inner human being' (πᾶν
μέλος τοῦ ἔξω ἀνθρώπου ὀνομάζεται καὶ κατὰ τὸν ἔσω ἄνθρωπον).[9]
He speaks of 'the eyes of the inner human being' (οἱ ὀφθαλμοὶ τοῦ ἔσω
ἀνθρώπου)[10] and 'internal ears which are purified' (τὰς ἔνδον ἀκοὰς

---

[3] *In Lament.* CXVI, trans. J. Trigg, *Origen* (New York: Routledge, 1998), p. 84. For the original Greek text, see P. Koetschau (ed.), *GCS*, vol. III, p. 276. Cf. *In John*, I. II (PG 14. 40D). The term 'eyes of the soul' (ὀφθαλμοὶ τῆς ψυχῆς) is also common in Origen's writings. See *Contra Celsum*, VII. 39 (PG II. 1476C), trans. H. Chadwick, *Contra Celsum* (New York: Cambridge University Press, 1985), p. 427.

[4] *De oratione*, 13. 4 (PG II. 457). Cf. 'Ears of a diviner kind' (θειοτερά ὦτα), *Contra Celsum*, VII. 34 (PG II. 1468D–1469AB).

[5] *In Psalm*, 4. 4 (PG 12. 1142 BC).   [6] *In Lament.* CXVI (*GCS*, vol. VI, p. 276).

[7] *Contra Celsum*, I. 48 (PG II. 749B), trans. H. Chadwick, *Contra Celsum* (New York: Cambridge University Press, 1965), p. 44.

[8] *Unde et in his positi locis, deprecamur auditores horum, ut mortificent carnales sensus, ne quid ex iis quae dicuntur secundum corporis motus excipiant, sed illos diviniores interioris hominis ad haec capienda sensus exhibeant. In Cant.* I. 4 (PG 13. 96A).

[9] *Dial. Heraclides*, 16. For the original Greek text, see J. Scherer (ed.), *Entretien d'Origène avec Héraclide et les évêques ses collègues sur le Père, le Fils, et l'âme*, Textes et Documents, 9 (Cairo: Publications de la Société Fouad I de Papyrologie, 1949), p. 154; trans. R. J. Daly, *Treatise on the Passover; and Dialogue of Origen with Heraclides and his Fellow Bishops on the Father, the Son, and the Soul* (New York: Paulist Press, 1992), p. 70.

[10] *Dial. Heraclides*, 16, ed. Scherer, p. 156; trans. Daly, p. 70.

κεκαθαρμένας).[11] He also claims that 'the inner human being has other nostrils with which to perceive the good odor of righteousness and the bad odor of sins' (ὁ ἔσω ἄνθρωπος ἀντιλαμβάνεται εὐωδίας δικαιοσύνης καὶ δυσωδίας ἁμαρτημάτων ἄλλοις μυκτηρσίν).[12] Most famously for the spiritual senses tradition, he quotes a non-Septuagint Greek version of Proverbs 2: 5 for scriptural evidence of a 'divine sense' (αἴσθησις θεία).[13]

Origen's use of sensory language has unparalleled significance for the spiritual senses tradition that follows in his wake, but it is not until the modern period that classifying his different uses of such terms becomes a particularly urgent scholarly preoccupation. In an influential 1932 article on the subject, Karl Rahner writes that one may speak 'properly' of a 'doctrine of the spiritual senses' when one finds (1) a non-metaphorical use of sensory language in which (2) all five senses are used in 'the spiritual perception of immaterial realities'.[14] In using these two criteria to examine Origen's texts, Rahner is adopting the methodological tools of Augustin-François Poulain. Poulain's classic 1901 treatment of the spiritual senses (which does not examine Origen) insists that the tradition does indeed describe five discrete spiritual senses, and that they bear an analogical relation to their corporeal counterparts.[15] By this key term, Poulain means that 'The words to see God, to hear and to touch Him are not mere metaphors. They express something more: some close analogy . . . We intend to indicate that there is a strong resemblance.'[16]

A simple question, then, lies behind the discussion of analogical and metaphorical uses of the language of sensation in Origen's texts: just how seriously should we take Origen's talk of 'perceiving' God? In particular, if God is understood as immaterial, and perception occurs on the material

---

[11] *Dial. Heraclides*, 17, ed. Scherer, p. 156; trans. Daly, p. 71.

[12] *Dial. Heraclides*, 18, ed. Scherer, p. 158; trans. Daly, p. 71.

[13] *Contra Celsum*, I. 48 (PG 11. 749B); VII. 34 (PG 11. 1469B). Also *sensum divinum* in *De principiis*, I. 1. 9 (PG 11. 129C); IV. 4. 10 (PG 11. 414A). For an extensive list of citations, see M. Harl, 'La "bouche" et le "cœur" de l'Apôtre: Deux images bibliques du "sens divin" de l'homme ("Proverbes" 2, 5) chez Origène', in *Forma futuri: Studi in onore del Cardinale Michele Pellegrino* (Turin: Bottega d'Erasmo, 1975), pp. 2–42; and H. U. von Balthasar (ed.), *Origen: Spirit and Fire: A Thematic Anthology of his Writings*, trans. R. J. Daly (Washington, DC: Catholic University of America Press, 1984), pp. 218–57.

[14] K. Rahner, 'Le début d'une doctrine des cinq sens spirituels chez Origène', p. 114.

[15] A. Poulain, *Des grâces d'oraison*, 10th edn (Paris: G. Beauchesne, 1922), English trans. L. L. Yorke Smith from the 6th edn as *The Graces of Interior Prayer*, and corrected to accord with the 10th French edn (London: Kegan Paul, Trench, Trübner & Co., 1950).

[16] Poulain, *Des grâces d'oraison*, pp. 95–6, trans. Smith, p. 90. Poulain himself indicates a debt to Giovanni Battista Scaramelli (1687–1752), *Il direttorio mistico, indirizzato a' direttori di quelle anime, che iddio conduce per la via della contemplazione* (Venice: S. Occhi, 1754), p. 183; English trans., significantly abridged, by D. H. S. Nicholson, *A Handbook of Mystical Theology: Being an Abridgment of* Il direttorio mistico (London: John M. Watkins, 1913).

plane, then what could 'perceiving God' even mean? The difficulty of the problem tempts one to interpret Origen's language of sensation as metaphor. He may speak of 'seeing' God with the 'eye of the mind', this reader says, but he cannot really mean such a thing; he must be speaking of thinking about God. And yet, if Origen is not speaking in a figurative fashion, but instead holds that the human being can indeed perceive God through some set of spiritual powers then he is saying something theologically significant, even if hermeneutically challenging. Quite a bit depends on this distinction between analogy and metaphor, and it is largely in the interest of guarding against the understandable temptation to reduce Origen's use of sensory language to metaphor that Rahner adopts Poulain's criteria.

With these tools, then, Rahner is able to throw certain features of Origen's thought into high relief, and in many instances their application is appropriate. Origen frequently uses sensory language in a way that is clearly metaphorical or figurative. In *De principiis*, for example, he writes, 'the names of the organs of sense are often applied to the soul, so that we speak of seeing (*videre*) with the eyes of the heart (*oculis cordis*), that is, of drawing some intellectual conclusion (*intellectuale conjicere*) by means of the faculty of intelligence.'[17] 'Seeing' in this passage is equated with 'drawing some intellectual conclusion'. Origen is not talking about 'perception' here, but rather 'understanding'.

In other instances, however, Origen employs sensory language in a manner clearly distinct from this metaphorical use. The following from Origen's exchange with Celsus is a frequently cited text in scholarship on the spiritual senses, and it illustrates our point well:

There is, as the scripture calls it, a certain generic divine sense (θείας τινὸς γενικῆς αἰσθήσεως) which only the man who is blessed finds on this earth. Thus Solomon says (Prov. 2: 5): 'Thou shalt find a divine sense' (ὅτι αἴσθησιν θείαν εὑρήσεις). There are many forms of this sense: a sight (ὁράσεως) which can see things superior to corporeal beings, the cherubim or seraphim being obvious instances, and a hearing (ἀκοῆς) which can receive impressions of sounds that have no objective existence in the air, and a taste (γεύσεως) which feeds on living bread that has come down from heaven and gives life to the world (John 6: 33). So also there is a sense of smell (ὀσφρήσεως) which smells spiritual things, as Paul speaks of 'a sweet savour of Christ unto God' (2 Cor. 2: 15) and a sense of touch (ἀφῆς) in accordance with which John says that he has handled with his hands 'of the Word of life' (1 John 1: 1).[18]

---

[17] *De principiis*, I. I. 9 (PG II. 129C), trans. G. W. Butterworth (Gloucester, MA: Peter Smith, 1973), p. 14.

[18] *Contra Celsum*, I. 48 (PG II. 749AB), trans. Chadwick, p. 44.

In this passage we have forms of sight, hearing, taste, smell, and touch that perceive 'spiritual things', and in so doing closely resemble their corporeal analogues. This use of the language of sensation clearly differs from the metaphorical use above, and drawing a distinction between these two ways of employing such terms is an appropriate way to gain greater clarity in reading Origen's texts. The fact that he is not using such language metaphorically is noteworthy, and highlighting this fact aids the reader in grasping Origen's meaning.

Regarding the particular number of spiritual senses in question, Rahner's 'fivefold criterion' may strike one as an overly narrow definition, but it also serves an important function. Specifically, the distinction can be valuable in that it offers a means by which to differentiate the richly multifaceted perception of God described by Origen and others from an understanding of the relationship with God that involves only a single mode of engagement, for example, only 'sight' in the beatific vision. Of what these different modes consist is, of course, a complex interpretive matter, but it does indeed seem that, when an author speaks of five distinct ways of perceiving God, he or she is advancing an idea importantly different from a model that entails only one dimension to that experience.[19]

In one sense, then, the methodological criteria Rahner adopts from Poulain serve a positive function in that they help one to gain conceptual precision in examining Origen's texts. In another sense, however, Rahner's hermeneutical tools impose an interpretive grid onto Origen's texts that is foreign to the concerns of the author. Origen writes no 'treatise on the spiritual senses' in which a definition of the doctrine might be articulated, nor does he even refer to his use of sensory language as 'the *doctrine* of the spiritual senses'. In fact, he rarely uses the term 'spiritual sense(s)' (αἴσθησις πνευματική; *sensus spiritales*) at all in describing the experience of God.[20] Most importantly for our examination, Origen does not cleanly

---

[19] It is clearly important to Rahner to highlight this distinction. He writes, 'Did Origen really conceive of five distinct organs operating in religious knowledge? Or were spiritual sight, hearing, etc. not rather for him different imaginative expressions for the "spirit", the real organ of perception? The first alternative seems more probable.' Rahner, 'Le début d'une doctrine des cinq sens spirituels chez Origène', p. 124, trans. David Morland, 'The "Spiritual Senses" According to Origen', in *Theological Investigations*, vol. XVI (New York: Seabury Press, 1979), p. 89. Generally speaking, too, one observes a correlation between the extent to which an author speaks of five spiritual senses and the extent to which that individual speaks of seeing, hearing, etc. in more than a metaphorical sense. Put simply, if one goes to the trouble to articulate five distinct forms of perception of God, it is unlikely that one ultimately means only 'coming to understand' by using such language.

[20] Origen does, of course, use the term to describe the spiritual sense of scripture, but use of the phrase 'spiritual sense(s)' to denote a set of perceptual faculties is very rare. For the few cases when Origen does use the term, see *In Cant.* 1. 4 (PG 13. 97B); *Homiliae in Exodum*, 1 .4 (PG 12. 301A); *Commentarii in epistulam ad Romanos*, 4. 5 (PG 14. 977D–978A).

divide his use of sensory language into 'analogical' and 'metaphorical' moments, nor does talk of a one-dimensional perceptual faculty preclude description of five different modes of perception of the divine. Instead, as will be shown below, Origen moves with remarkable fluidity from sensory language that could be deemed analogical to a use of such language that is clearly metaphorical or figurative. Origen also mentions 'one divine sense' in one moment, and the 'many forms of that sense' in the next, as earlier we saw in the passage from *Contra Celsum*, I. 48.

The idea of 'sensing' or 'perceiving' the divine may pervade Origen's texts, then, but he himself offers no sustained definition of what such an idea entails, and his use of sensory language is frustratingly multivalent. Rahner's treatment thus systematizes Origen's remarks and puts them into a structure more rigorously delimited than the author himself finds it necessary to do. Crucially for our investigation, too, unreflective adoption of these criteria can force Origen into artificially forced choices that are ill suited to his texts. I suggest, therefore, that the first methodological step forward in exegeting Origen's works involves recognizing the wide range of often juxtaposed uses of sensory terms and exercising caution in excluding one interpretive option from the other.

Given these remarks, it may seem that the last thing we need is yet another criterion to impose on Origen's different uses of the language of sensation. I propose, however, that sharpening the distinction between analogy and metaphor is necessary for the profitable examination of Origen's thought on this topic. An enormous part of the problem in the interpretation of Origen's doctrine of the spiritual senses has been that the dividing line between metaphorical and analogical uses of sensory language has become blurred. The distinction is crucial (if we have only metaphor, we have no understanding of the spiritual senses as perceptual faculties), but the distinction itself lacks precision in its present articulation. The question at hand is: of what, exactly, does this 'analogical', 'close resemblance' between the corporeal and spiritual senses consist?

In this connection, Poulain offers a helpful measure by which such judgements can be made – interestingly, a feature of his thought not overtly picked up by Rahner – and I propose that resuscitating this standard can advance the examination of the spiritual senses in the texts of Origen and others in the tradition. Poulain outlines the conditions for a 'close resemblance' between the spiritual and corporeal senses as follows: 'Does the soul possess intellectual spiritual senses, having some resemblance to the bodily senses, so that, in an analogous manner and in diverse ways, she is able to perceive the *presence* of pure spirits (*la présence des purs esprits*), and the presence of God in particular?'[21] According to Poulain, then, the key criterion by which one distinguishes an analogical use of the language of sensation from a metaphorical use of such terms involves the idea of presence. The spiritual senses resemble their corporeal counterparts in that they discern a presence, be it of God or other 'spiritual' realities. It is, therefore, precisely when an author speaks of detecting an immaterial presence that he or she is using sensory language in a 'non-metaphorical' manner. This understanding of presence is a necessary – even if not sufficient – condition for spiritual perception. Significantly, too, this criterion can be used to distinguish the spiritual senses from the intellect, broadly understood, which could be said to 'imitate and recall to our minds colors, sounds, etc.' *without* their actual presence, as Poulain puts it.[22] I therefore suggest that it is precisely when Origen uses sensory terms to speak of discerning the *presence* of God that a close resemblance to corporeal perception has been achieved.[23]

EARLY AND LATE USES OF SENSORY LANGUAGE IN ORIGEN

With our interpretive tools thus sharpened, we are now better equipped to examine Origen's early texts to see if we find there the essential features of this 'close resemblance' between spiritual and corporeal perception. If we can find an analogical relationship between spiritual and corporeal sensation, then Dillon's thesis will need to be reconsidered. Dillon agrees with Rahner that Origen articulates a fivefold, analogical doctrine of the spiritual senses in *Contra Celsum* (*c.* 244–9) and other late works. However, Dillon postulates that Origen's thought on this topic may have evolved significantly, and on this point he sees himself as breaking with Rahner.[24] Specifically, Dillon claims that a close examination of Origen's early works yields a model of the spiritual senses that is distinct from that observed in

---

[21] Poulain, *Des grâces d'oraison*, p. 93, trans. Smith, p. 88, italics altered.

[22] Poulain, *Des grâces d'oraison*, p. 93, trans. Smith, p. 88.

[23] For a more thorough account of integrating the idea of 'presence' into the necessary conditions for the perception of God, see W. Alston's reading of Poulain and the spiritual senses tradition in his *Perceiving God: The Epistemology of Religious Experience* (Ithaca, NY: Cornell University Press, 1991), esp. pp. 51–4. For a broader treatment of the significance of presence in the Christian mystical tradition, see B. McGinn, *The Foundations of Mysticism: Origins to the Fifth Century* (New York: Crossroad, 1991), pp. xviii–xx, 278–9.

[24] Dillon writes, 'Rahner . . . sees no development in Origen's thought in this matter, and he may be right. I am prepared to argue for some development, however.' Dillon, 'Aisthêsis Noêtê', p. 443. It should be said here that Rahner does not actually claim there is *no* development in Origen's thought on this topic. Instead, he acknowledges, 'The polemic against Celsus' Ἀληθὴς Λόγος persuaded Origen to develop his doctrine.' Rahner, 'Le début d'une doctrine des cinq sens spirituels chez Origène', p. 117, my translation.

his late writings. He uses the following passage from *De principiis* (229–30) to make his argument:

But if the question is put to us why it was said 'Blessed are the pure in heart, for they shall see God in their heart' (Matt. 5: 8), I answer that in my opinion our argument will be much more firmly established by this passage. For what else is 'to see God in the heart' but to understand and know him with the mind (*mente*), just as we have explained above? For the names of the organs of sense are often applied to the soul, so that we speak of seeing with the eyes of the heart (*oculis cordis*), that is, of drawing some intellectual conclusion by means of the faculty of intelligence. So too we speak of hearing with the ears when we discern the deeper meaning of some statement. So too we speak of the soul as being able to use teeth, when it eats and consumes the bread of life who comes down from heaven. In a similar way we speak of it as using all other bodily organs, which are transferred from their corporeal significance and applied to the faculties of the soul; as Solomon says, 'You will find a divine sense' ('*Sensum divinum invenies*', Prov. 2: 5). For he knew that there were in us two kinds of senses, the one being mortal, corruptible and human, and the other immortal and intellectual, which he here calls 'divine'. By this divine sense, therefore, not of the eyes but of a pure heart, that is, the mind, God can be seen by those who are worthy. That 'heart' is used for mind, that is, for the intellectual faculty (*intellectuali virtute*), you will certainly find over and over again in all the scripture, both the New and Old.[25]

At this point in Origen's career, Dillon claims, talk of the perception of God by sense organs is merely metaphorical. He writes, 'What Origen is saying is that many expressions which appear to refer to activities of our sense-organs really refer to operations of the mind or soul; that is to say, they are metaphors.'[26] Origen makes this clear when he writes, 'What else is "to see God in the heart" but to understand and know him with the mind?' One finds in this portion of Origen's writings, then, an explanation of his use of the term 'seeing' such that it should simply be equated with 'understanding'. 'Hearing' should additionally be understood to mean 'discerning deeper meaning'. This passage would not seem to give us evidence of spiritual organs of perception, and in fact it explicitly tells us to read the language of sensation metaphorically.

Proverbs 2: 5 – which might appear to be a reference to the spiritual senses – should not in this case be understood as positing an actual perceptual faculty, on Dillon's revised understanding of Origen. Instead, 'Prov. 2: 5 is seen as referring to an "immortal and intellectual" sense, which is simply the faculty of intellect (*mens*)'.[27] According to Dillon, then,

---

[25] *De principiis*, I. 1. 9 (PG II. 129B–130A), trans. Butterworth, p. 14.
[26] Dillon, 'Aisthêsis Noêtê', p. 447.   [27] *Ibid.* p. 446.

this passage (which is Origen's favourite proof text for the existence of the spiritual senses) does not mean here what it comes to mean later in Origen's career. Dillon similarly cautions against seeing a doctrine of the spiritual senses in Origen's use of the term 'faculties of the soul' (*virtutes animae*). Dillon writes,

> Certainly, the reference to 'faculties of the soul' (*virtutes animae*) could be taken, in the light of what we know to be his doctrine later, to refer to spiritual sense-organs, but I submit that, in default of other *contemporary* evidence, there is nothing in this phrase, or in this passage, that would lead us to assume such a doctrine of the spiritual senses.[28]

One might be tempted to read the early Origen through the late Origen, then, but Dillon claims that if we take Origen's early texts on their own terms we find a different use of the language of sensation. He concludes, 'It seems to me preferable to assume that, at the time he wrote the *De principiis*, Origen had not yet fully developed a theory of "spiritual" senses.'[29] On the basis of this passage, Dillon charts a trajectory in Origen's thought whereby his early writings articulate an understanding of one divine sense that bears a metaphorical relationship to the corporeal senses, in contrast to his late writings, in which one sees a fivefold doctrine of the spiritual senses closely analogous to their bodily counterparts.

REASSESSING ORIGEN'S TEXTS

One would be hard pressed to deny that *De principiis*, I. I. 9 uses sensory language in a metaphorical way. Origen clearly states that when he says 'seeing', he means 'understanding', and when he says 'hearing', he means 'discerning deeper meaning'. However, I do not think that this fact leads us to the conclusion Dillon draws. I base my comments here on the following three aspects of Origen's writings. (1) Origen's late works (written in his undisputedly 'analogical' period) also evince similarly explicit instructions for the metaphorical understanding of the language of sensation. (2) Further evidence from *De principiis* itself – some of which can be found within the very passages Dillon quotes – points to a more robustly articulated understanding of the idea of the spiritual senses than indicated in Dillon's analysis. (3) Other portions of Origen's early writings contain highly suggestive remarks about spiritual perception that do not readily

---

[28] *Ibid.* pp. 446–7.   [29] *Ibid.* p. 447.

lend themselves to a 'metaphorical' interpretation, especially when our newly honed criteria are brought to bear on those texts.

First, then, one of the pillars in Dillon's argument against an early, analogical understanding of the spiritual senses is that Origen uses sensory language metaphorically in his early works. However, if explicitly stated claims for the metaphorical understanding of sensory language served to falsify any seemingly analogical use of such terms, then Origen's late writings would fall under similar suspicion. For example, in a passage from *Contra Celsum* in which the 'unspeakability' of God is discussed, Origen writes of the metaphorical sense in which the idea of 'hearing' should be regarded. With words that could have been lifted straight from the portion of *De principiis* cited above, he writes, 'when [Paul] says that he "heard unspeakable words which it is not lawful for a man to utter" (2 Cor. 12: 4) . . . he is using the word "heard" in the sense of "understood" as in the phrase "He who hath ears to hear, let him hear" (Matt. 13: 9)'.[30] The biblical passages used here are Origen's most frequently cited scriptural warrants for spiritual hearing. And yet here in this late text we do not find a 'spiritual sense' of hearing at all. Instead, hearing and understanding are equated with each other, just as they are in portions of Origen's early works.

It is surprising, furthermore, that these instructions for metaphorical interpretation closely follow one of Origen's most undisputedly 'analogical' passages in his description of the spiritual senses. Only a few chapters earlier, Origen writes:

We know that the holy Scriptures make mention of eyes, of ears, and of hands, which have nothing but the name in common with the bodily organs; and what is more wonderful, they speak of a diviner sense (αἴσθησιν θειοτέραν), which is very different from the senses as commonly spoken of. For when the prophet says, 'Open thou mine eyes, that I may behold wondrous things out of thy law' (Ps. 119:18) or, 'the commandment of the Lord is pure, enlightening the eyes', (Ps. 19:8) or, 'Lighten mine eyes, lest I sleep the sleep of death', (Ps. 13:3) no one is so foolish as to suppose that the eyes of the body behold the wonders of the divine law, or that the law of the Lord gives light to the bodily eyes, or that the sleep of death falls on the eyes of the body. When our Savior says, 'He that hath ears to hear, let him hear' (Matt. 13:9), anyone will understand that the ears spoken of are of a diviner kind (θειοτέρων ὤτων). When it is said that the word of the Lord was 'in the hand' of Jeremiah or of some other prophet; or when the expression is used, 'the law by the hand of Moses', or, 'I sought the Lord with my hands,

---

[30] *Contra Celsum*, VII. 43 (PG II. 1484A), trans. Chadwick, p. 431.

and was not deceived' (Ps. 77:2 [LXX]), – no one is so foolish as not to see that the word 'hands' is taken figuratively (τροπιῶς), as when John says, 'Our hands have handled the Word of life' (1 John 1:1). And if you wish further to learn from the sacred writings that there is a diviner sense (κρείττονος αἰσθήσεως) than the senses of the body, you have only to hear what Solomon says, 'Thou shalt find a divine sense' (Prov. 2:5 [αἴσθησιν θείαν εὑρήσεις]).[31]

Here Origen uses the very same verse from Matthew regarding hearing, but whereas hearing is equated with understanding in *Contra Celsum*, VII. 43, cited earlier, here, in VII. 34, Origen mentions 'ears of a diviner kind'. What we have, then, is an explicitly metaphorical statement in close proximity to an explicitly analogical one.[32] He develops a notion of 'spiritual hearing' in one moment, and then explicitly equates hearing with understanding in the next. These passages demonstrate an intermingling of analogy and metaphor that suggests Origen does not necessarily intend to exclude one interpretive possibility by advocating the other.

Second, turning to Origen's early works, it should be noted that his curious rendering of Proverbs 2: 5 in the passage from *De principiis*, I. 1. 9 above indicates a clear commitment to the 'sensory' character of knowledge of God. We unfortunately possess only Rufinus's Latin of this portion of the text, but it is instructive that the passage reads, 'You will find a divine *sense* (*sensum divinum invenies*)'.[33] The Septuagint version of Proverbs 2: 5 reads, 'You will find the *knowledge* of God (καὶ ἐπίγνωσιν θεοῦ εὑρήσεις)'.[34] Origen here either misquotes the Septuagint or chooses another translation available to him, and in so doing he adds a sensory dimension to the passage not evidenced in the original text. If Origen simply means that sensory language applied to the perception of God is reducible to 'knowledge', why would he go to the trouble of avoiding the more straightforward term,

---

[31] *Contra Celsum*, VII. 34 (PG 11. 1468D–1469AB). I here prefer F. Crombie's translation, in *Ante-Nicene Fathers*, ed. A. Roberts and J. Donaldson, vol. IV (Grand Rapids, MI: Eerdmans, 1972), p. 624.

[32] Origen also says that the word 'hands' should be taken 'figuratively' (τροπικῶς) – seeming to place a metaphorical use of sensory language in the very midst of analogical uses of such terms. His use of the term 'figuratively' here is ambiguous, however, as it seems actually to admit of an analogical interpretation.

[33] *De principiis*, I. 1. 9 (PG 11. 129C), trans. Butterworth, p. 14, my italics. Although we cannot be completely certain, the Greek underlying this translation is most likely ὅτι αἴσθησιν θείαν εὑρήσεις, as this is Origen's rendering of Prov 2: 5 in his surviving Greek works. See *Contra Celsum*, I. 48; cf. VII. 34.

[34] This translation, according to Dillon, is in line with the original Hebrew, *d'at' 'elohîm timşā'*, and *elohim* is an objective, not subjective genitive. Dillon, 'Aisthēsis Noētê', p. 444.

ἐπίγνωσις, by misquoting the passage in question so as to highlight its sensory character?[35]

Dillon uses one other passage from *De principiis* in his analysis, but here we see that Origen actually brings into even sharper focus the claim that we perceive 'intelligible things'. He writes:

> It is possible that a rational mind . . . by advancing from a knowledge of small to a knowledge of greater things and from things visible to things invisible, may attain to an increasingly perfect understanding. For it is placed in the body, and advances from things of sense, which are bodily, to sense objects (*sensibilia*) which are incorporeal and intellectual. But in case it should appear mistaken to say as we have done that intellectual things are objects of sense (*sensibilia*),[36] we will quote as an illustration the saying of Solomon: 'You will find also a divine sense'. By this he shows that those things which are intellectual are to be investigated not by bodily sense but by some other which he calls divine.[37]

In this remarkable passage, then, we see that intellectual things can in fact be examined via another form of sense perception in the human being. Platonist epistemology involves a similar notion of perception, but the noteworthy point is that here in this early work Origen uses the language of sensation in a manner that does not seem to be metaphorical.

Elsewhere in *De principiis* we find further evidence that points to a more robustly developed understanding of 'sensing' the divine than is indicated in Dillon's investigation. For example, Origen seems to presuppose a spiritual sense of smell in a passage about anointing Christ with the 'oil of gladness', and those who 'run in the odor of his ointments'.[38] Origen then writes, 'They who are his [Christ's] fellows will be partakers and receivers of his odor, in proportion to their nearness to the vessel.'[39] He elsewhere speaks of one who 'will feel his mind and his senses touched by a divine breath',[40]

---

[35] Origen is not the first to render Prov 2: 5 in such a manner. We find in Clement of Alexandria the same mistranslation: ὅτι αἴσθησιν θείαν εὑρήσεις (*Stromata*, I. 4. 27. 2). Origen, then, follows Clement, but it is highly unlikely that he did not have access to the Septuagint version of the passage.

[36] I here emend Butterworth's translation in line with Dillon's modifications. He holds that the manuscript's *insensibilia* 'so spoils the sense as to almost certainly [be] the work of an inept scribe', and instead holds *sensibilia* to convey the meaning of the passage. Dillon, 'Aisthēsis Noētē', p. 447.

[37] *Potest tamen etiam rationabilis mens proficiens a parvis ad maiora et a 'visibilibus' ad 'invisibilia' pervenire ad intellectum perfectiorem. Est enim in corpore posita, et necessario a sensibilibus, quae sunt corporea, ad sensibilia, quae sunt incorporea et intellectualia, proficit. Verum ne cui indecenter dictum videatur sensibilia esse quae intellectualia sunt, utemur exemplo sententiae Salomonis dicentis 'Sensum quoque divinum invenies'. In quo ostendit non corporali sensu, sed alio quodam, quem divinum nominat, ea quae intellectualia sunt, requirenda. De principiis,* IV. 4. 10 (*GCS*, vol. v, p. 364).

[38] *De principiis*, II. 6. 6 (PG II. 214C), trans. Butterworth, p. 113, emended.

[39] *Participes vero ejus quam proximi fuerint vasculo, tam odoris erunt participes et capaces, De principiis,* II. 6. 6 (PG II. 214C), trans. Butterworth, pp. 113–14, altered.

[40] *De principiis*, IV. I. 6, trans. Butterworth, p. 265, emended.

and of 'the only begotten Son of God [who] . . . pouring (*infundens*) himself by his graces into our senses (*sensibus*), may deign to illuminate what is dark, to lay open what is concealed, and to reveal what is secret'.[41] Taken in conjunction with the following passages from Origen's early scriptural commentaries (and assessed with Poulain's criterion of presence), these portions of *De principiis* make a collective case for an early, non-metaphorical use of sensory language.

Third, only a few of Origen's works precede *De principiis*, yet in those early writings we observe a number of passages that are not easily regarded as metaphorical in their use of the language of sensation. For example, if we follow Pierre Nautin in dating Origen's *Commentary on Lamentations* between 222 and 225 (at least four years before *De principiis* and among Origen's earliest works), some important findings emerge.[42] In that text Origen writes, 'Those who are "beholding with unveiled face the glory of the Lord as in a mirror" (2 Cor. 3: 18) . . . are those for whom the Lord is always present to the eyes of the mind (διανοίας ὀφθαλμῶν).'[43] In the same portion of the commentary he also makes a synaesthetic observation that 'those who are beloved of God are breathing Christ in everything, because they have him before their eyes' (οἱ γὰρ θεοφιλεῖς διὰ παντὸς τὸν Χριστὸν ἀναπνέουσι, πρὸ ὀφθαλμῶν αὐτὸν ἔχοντες).[44]

In Origen's *Commentary on the Psalms*, also dated between 222 and 225,[45] one finds more passages that do not use sensory language metaphorically. Origen writes, 'For one must be aware that human beings have in the depth of their heart a bodiless voice (φωνὴ μὴ σώματι) which they, after recollecting themselves and after entering their chamber and closing the door of their senses, and being wholly outside the body, send up to him who alone can hear such a voice.'[46] The Alexandrian theologian continues:

Just as with physical light which enables those with healthy eyes to see both the light itself and other sensible objects, so too does God come with a certain power to the mind of each one. As long as those to whom he comes are not all closed off and their ability to see clearly not impeded by their passions, God makes himself known and leads those illumined by him to a knowledge of other spiritual things.[47]

---

[41] *De principiis*, II. 9. 4 (PG II. 228C), trans. Butterworth, p. 132, emended. See also *De principiis*, III. 1. 17 (PG II. 288A), trans. Butterworth, p. 195.

[42] P. Nautin, *Origène: Sa vie et son œuvre* (Paris: Beauchesne, 1977), pp. 366–71, 410.

[43] *GCS*, vol. III, p. 276, trans. Trigg, p. 84.   [44] *GCS*, vol. III, p. 276, trans. Trigg, p. 84.

[45] Nautin, *Origène*, pp. 366–71, 410.

[46] *In Psalm*, 4. 4 (PG 12. 1142BC), trans. H. U. von Balthasar (ed.), *Origen, Spirit and Fire: A Thematic Anthology of his Writings*, trans. R. J. Daly (Washington, DC: Catholic University of America Press, 1984), p. 232.

[47] *In Psalm*, 4. 7 (PG 12. 1165D–1168A), trans. Daly, pp. 230–1.

Here we observe that the individual must cultivate the proper emotional dispositions before divine grace bestows spiritual perception. Most importantly for purposes of this essay, the language of sensation is used in a non-metaphorical manner.

Most interestingly, perhaps, in the first book of Origen's *Commentary on John* (231), written roughly contemporaneously with *De principiis*, he provides a description of those who see Wisdom, 'delighting in her highly variegated intelligible beauty, seen by intelligible eyes alone, provoking him to love who discerns her divine and heavenly charm (ἐνευφραινόμενος τῷ πολυποικίλῳ νοητῷ κάλλει αὐτῆς, ὑπὸ νοητῶν ὀφθαλμῶν μόνων βλεπομένῳ)'.[48] In that same text, Origen also writes, 'The Savior shines (ἐλλάμπων) on creatures that have intellect and sovereign reason, that their minds may see (βλέπη) their proper objects of vision (ὁρατά), and so he is the light of the intellectual world.'[49] Here it is Origen's talk of 'objects of vision' and 'highly variegated intelligible beauty' that dissuades one from dismissing his use of sensory language as metaphorical.[50] Furthermore, these passages likely betray Origen's debt to a Platonic model of 'intellectual vision' that is distinct from a metaphorical use of the language of sensation.

Looking at these passages from Origen's early writings as a whole, then, we observe talk of seeing, hearing, smelling, eating, touching, breathing and speaking to God or Christ. Drawing on Poulain's notion of presence, we can say that the common feature of these uses of sensory language is that they involve perceiving the presence of the divine. The passages examined above describe those who have Christ before their eyes, those who speak to God with a bodiless voice, and those who delight in variegated intelligible beauty. They describe seeing and hearing the mysteries of divine power, receiving the odour of Christ, being touched by a divine breath and Christ pouring himself into our senses. I propose that God is described as being present to the human being in these passages, and it is because the human being is able to discern that presence that we are justified in speaking of something resembling perception. One could certainly ask for greater

---

[48] *In John*, I. 11 (PG 14. 40D), trans. Menzies, *Ante-Nicene Fathers*, vol. IX (Grand Rapids, MI: Eerdmans, 1951), p. 303.

[49] *In John*, I. 24 (PG 14. 68B), trans. Menzies, p. 312, emended.

[50] Origen also writes in the same commentary, 'Christ, again, the light of the world, is the true light as distinguished from the light of sense; nothing that is sensible is true. Yet though the sensible is other than the true, it does not follow that the sensible is false, for the sensible may have an analogy (ἀνάλογον) with the intellectual.' *In John*, I. 24 (PG 14. 68B), trans. Menzies, p. 312. Although Origen leaves the details unclear, it seems that in this last passage he is drawing some sort of 'analogical' relationship between the light of Christ and the light of sense. The term, of course, does not necessarily have the precise meaning here that is attributed to it by Poulain, but it is striking that divine light seems to bear some similarity to sensible light.

explicitness from Origen about all this, and the many ambiguities that remain beg for a more thorough treatment of these phenomena from a systematic perspective. The important point, however, is that here in these early texts we observe a description of the relationship between the human being and God that is not easily reduced to metaphorical speech, and that in fact bears considerable similarities to the notion of spiritual perception that Origen espouses in later works.

Where does this examination of Origen's writings leave us in our assessment of his 'doctrine of the spiritual senses'? At the most obvious level, the portions of Origen's early works cited above suggest that Origen did in fact articulate a robust model of spiritual perception significantly earlier in his career than has been postulated by Dillon. In this connection, I would contend that Poulain's understanding of presence as a measure for spiritual perception performs an indispensable hermeneutical function. That is, Poulain's notion of presence has aided our examination of Origen's early texts in developing a defence for calling his early use of sensory language 'analogical'. It has also assisted us in articulating the reasons why Origen's model of the spiritual senses – both early and late – can appropriately be viewed as distinct from his model of the intellect. One question posed at the outset of this chapter was: just how seriously should we take Origen's talk of 'perception' as it pertains to God? On the basis of this analysis of Origen's thought, I suggest that Origen has in mind – from an early date in his career – something closely analogous to corporeal perception in his account of the spiritual senses, and that the temptation to dismiss this feature of his thought as metaphorical expression should continue to be resisted.

At a more fundamental level, however, the textual evidence from Origen's early and late writings exposes a certain methodological rigidity in twentieth-century examinations of the spiritual senses that is in need of revision. Modern scholarship on Origen betrays an impulse to codify his use of sensory language as a 'doctrine of the spiritual senses', and in so doing such academic treatments suggest a greater degree of systematicity and consistency on Origen's part than can actually be located in Origen's texts themselves. As we saw above, Origen uses language that is clearly metaphorical in one moment, then language that could be regarded as analogical in the next moment. Instead of an early, metaphorical period that is followed by a late, analogical portion of Origen's career, then, we find in

Origen's works an intermingled use of metaphor and analogy throughout his writings, both early and late. Whereas modern scholarship has excluded one interpretive option by reference to its counterpart, Origen himself does not regard such possibilities as mutually exclusive, and our contemporary tools should be modified so as to accommodate this fact.

This is not to say, however, that such modern hermeneutical methods categorically distort the meaning of Origen's texts, or that the 'doctrine of the spiritual senses' is purely a construction of twentieth-century scholarship. To the contrary, in many cases the application of these tools illuminates the content of Origen's writings. This is particularly helpful for discussions of the spiritual senses, in which one may be lured into dismissing Origen's talk of perceiving the divine as purely figurative description. When appropriately applied to Origen's writings, then, these carefully developed criteria bring key features of Origen's thought to light, and in so doing provide a helpful service to the reader. What the foregoing analysis does indicate, however, is that any narrow delimitation of what counts as Origen's 'doctrine of the spiritual senses' arises as a product of modern scholars, not Origen. Such a definition must be recognized as necessarily provisional, and, as such, it should always remain open to revision based on the evidence from Origen's texts themselves.

CHAPTER 2

Gregory of Nyssa

Sarah Coakley

The purpose of this chapter is to suggest a reconsideration of the so-called 'doctrine of the spiritual senses' in Gregory of Nyssa, and that at two levels.

The first level, with which I shall frame the discussion in my opening section, is that of the modern history of the reception of Nyssen on the spiritual senses; for it is hard to get at the distinctiveness of what Gregory was about in his treatment of this theme without peeling back the particular concerns of modern theological re-interpretation. Here I shall briefly investigate the context, both historical and theological, in which the great French patristic scholar Jean Daniélou drew fresh and important attention to this facet of Gregory's thought in his famous wartime monograph on Nyssen, *Platonisme et théologie mystique*.[1] I shall argue that we must be cautious about a false modern separation between 'spirituality' and epistemology that seemingly infects Daniélou's treatment, for all its richness and importance, and also about an over-concentration here on Gregory's late work *The Commentary on the Song of Songs*.

Secondly, I shall go back to Gregory himself, and, by a focus primarily on his formative dialogue, the *De anima et resurrectione*, suggest that here – in the artfully constructed banter between Gregory and his sister Macrina that constitutes this dialogue – we find already adumbrated a distinctive approach to the spiritual senses which is both progressive and unitive, starting from philosophical questions about ordinary sensation and cognition, and then drawing ethics, ascetics and spiritual practice inexorably into

I would like to express my gratitude to Mark McInroy and James Blackstone for invaluable research assistance in the development of this chapter; and to my co-editor Paul Gavrilyuk for his insightful criticisms which have helped me to refine it. Previous versions of this essay were presented at the Oxford Patristics conference, August 2007, and at a special symposium on Gregory's *De anima et resurrectione* in Lund, April 2009 (at the kind invitation of Samuel Rubenson). I gratefully learned from the comments and questions raised in both contexts.

[1] J. Daniélou, *Platonisme et théologie mystique: Essai sur la doctrine spirituelle de saint Grégoire de Nysse* (Paris: Aubier, 1944; 2nd edn 1953). Note that I use the pagination from the first edition in what follows; the second edition, although not significantly different in substance, is typeset in a slightly more condensed form, resulting in different pagination.

their train as the full significance of the meaning of the resurrection body is considered. In short (and here is the nub of my thesis): it is a *modern* reading which has rent philosophy (in this case, epistemology) and 'spirituality' apart in Gregory, by a one-sided emphasis on what Daniélou calls 'the spiritual life' ('la vie spirituelle') and 'mystical experience' ('l'expérience mystique'), and this leads to a partial and misleading reading of Gregory on the theme of spiritual sensation. A closer look at the way Gregory utilizes the key terminology of the spiritual senses in his oeuvre as a whole reveals a more integrative and multifaceted dimension to his epistemic vision, one which jousts seductively with almost every available pagan epistemology of the time, yet ultimately trumps them all with a characteristically biblical correction and an appeal to the epistemic uniqueness of the special physicality of the resurrection body.

It then falls to me in a final section of the chapter briefly to position the particular significance of the developments found in *De anima et resurrectione* in relation to Gregory's treatment of the spiritual senses theme at other moments in his career. This will allow me to hypothesize a development in Gregory's thought on this topic over his life-work, one in which the explorations of the *De anima* form a crucial moment of transition, but not a stopping point. Ironically, Daniélou's own work on the chronology of Gregory's oeuvre proves particularly useful here, and especially his supposition that Gregory's theological career can be seen as moving in roughly three stages of intellectual development.[2] If we apply this insight to the specific topic of the spiritual senses, we are able to get a truer, and less distorted, understanding of the significance of the climax of these developments in his last works than Daniélou's more partial treatment could afford.

But let us turn first to Daniélou's important wartime reception of Nyssen.

THE 'DOCTRINE' OF THE SPIRITUAL SENSES
ACCORDING TO DANIÉLOU

The importance and subsequent influence of Daniélou's *Platonisme et théologie mystique* for the way contemporary scholars now think about

---

[2] J. Daniélou, 'La chronologie des œuvres de Grégoire de Nysse', *Studia patristica*, 7 (1966), 159–69. Daniélou's reconstruction of the order of Gregory's writings is necessarily somewhat speculative, given our lack of precise knowledge of the original context and date of many of the texts; and his proposals have not gone uncontested. However, one of the criteria revealingly used by Daniélou for placing texts in different periods of Gregory's career is the changing attitude to the body in evidence, and particularly the relation of the soul to the body of the resurrection life.

Nyssen's theology can scarcely be overestimated. Naturally this influence is felt markedly in France among Daniélou's pupils and successors; but it does not stop there. Although the monograph has never been translated into English, many of its central themes are enunciated in Herbert Musurillo's *From Glory to Glory* (to which Daniélou contributed the long introduction);[3] and subsequent writers on Gregory in English, such as Andrew Louth in his important and influential *Origins of the Christian Mystical Tradition*, have relied heavily on Daniélou's analysis of the spiritual senses, taking Daniélou's categories of analysis for granted.[4] But it is as well to remind ourselves about some of the concerns Daniélou *brought* to the text of Gregory, as well as what he educed from it. A number of points can be made here, and succinctly.

First, the very idea that Gregory has a 'doctrine' (*sic*) of the spiritual senses was entirely Daniélou's, and he devotes more than thirty important pages to the subject in his monograph.[5] Although he rightly draws careful attention here to the range of family-resemblance terms that Gregory uses when talking about 'sensing' the divine (τὰ αἰσθητήρια τῆς ψυχῆς; ὁ ὀφθαλμὸς τῆς ψυχῆς; ἡ ὄψις τῆς ψυχῆς; ἡ ἀκοη τῆς καρδίας),[6] he is not as open as he might be in admitting that to call this cluster of terms a 'doctrine' is a bit of a sleight of hand: it suggests a systematicity and consistency which I would argue Gregory neither intends nor delivers. In my view, Gregory no more has a 'doctrine' of the spiritual senses (a term incidentally he never actually uses) than he has a 'doctrine' of ἐπέκτασις (another theme Daniélou is famous for highlighting, with reference to Gregory's exegesis of Philippians 3: 13).[7] This may appear a niggling semantic point, but I think it is nonetheless important, as we shall shortly disclose.

Second, if we attend to the footnotes in this important section of Daniélou's monograph, we get clearer about what is driving his interest at the time in his enunciation of the theme of spiritual senses. The influence of Karl Rahner's first published article – precisely devoted to the spiritual

---

[3] J. Daniélou and H. Musurillo (eds.), *From Glory to Glory: Texts from Gregory of Nyssa's Mystical Writings* (New York: Scribner, 1961), Introduction, pp. 3–78.

[4] A. Louth, *Origins of the Christian Mystical Tradition from Plato to Denys* (Oxford University Press, 2007). See pp. 91–4 for the discussion of the spiritual senses in Gregory, in which Louth acknowledges his close reliance on Daniélou's treatment.

[5] See Daniélou, *Platonisme et théologie mystique*, pp. 235–66, within chap. 2. Admittedly, in using the language of a 'doctrine', Daniélou is probably following Rahner on Origen: see n. 8 below.

[6] Daniélou, *Platonisme et théologie mystique*, pp. 240–1. These Greek terms may be translated: 'the senses of the soul'/'spiritual senses'; 'the eye of the soul'; 'the sight of the soul'; and 'the hearing of the heart'. There are a few other related phrases and themes which Gregory also utilizes, as I shall discuss in the last section of this chapter, below.

[7] See *ibid.* pp. 309–26.

senses – is writ large;[8] and since that article (in both its original longer French version and its later German translation[9]) gives ample coverage to Origen, and then breaks off rather oddly after a mere mention of Gregory ('Further evidence is here unnecessary', writes Rahner),[10] we may take it that Daniélou is taking up the baton to extend Rahner's analysis more satisfactorily where Gregory is concerned, and that he does so through the comparative lens of Origen. Indeed Daniélou avers that Gregory does not significantly advance on the position of Origen,[11] despite a few character-istic phrases in his *Commentary on the Song of Songs* which are novel and distinctive.[12] We shall have reason to return critically to this point.

Third, there was a particular reason that spiritual senses were suddenly voguish again in the 1930s and 1940s in any case, after long neglect except in textbooks of spiritual direction. We cannot divorce this new interest, I would suggest, from the burgeoning Catholic *ressourcement* movement of the time, which came to be dubbed *la nouvelle théologie*;[13] for it was precisely motivated by an urgent quest for a new religious epistemology, founded in the Fathers, which would break down the seemingly rigid disjunctions between nature and grace that had characterized the neo-scholasticisms of the late nineteenth and early twentieth centuries, following the promul-gation of the magisterial document *Aeterni Patris* (1879). In this context Nyssen's vision of a participation in God fuelled 'from below' by endless 'desire' had obvious attractions, even as Aquinas's thought was simultane-ously being re-read to stress a 'natural desire for God'. Further rummaging

---

[8] K. Rahner, 'Le début d'une doctrine des cinq sens spirituels chez Origène', *RAM*, 13 (1932), 113–45.

[9] The German version that appeared later was newly edited and somewhat shortened: 'Die "geistlichen Sinne" nach Origenes', in *Schriften zur Theologie*, vol. XII: *Theologie aus Erfahrung des Geistes*, ed. K. Neufeld, SJ (Zürich: Benziger Verlag, 1975), pp. 111–36. The English translation of the German by Dom David Morland, OSB ('The "Spiritual Senses" According to Origen', in *Theological Investigations*, vol. XVI: *Experience of the Spirit: Source of Theology* (New York: Seabury Press, 1979), pp. 81–103), reads mellifluously but is somewhat loose. On any point of exegetical significance it is therefore wise to consult the original French and compare it with the German.

[10] Rahner, 'Le début d'une doctrine des cinq sens spirituels chez Origène', p. 144.

[11] Daniélou, *Platonisme et théologie mystique*, pp. 238–41. It is one of the goals of this chapter to reassess this claim with some care and nuance. Daniélou does announce (*ibid.* p. 240) that he is looking for ways in which Gregory may have gone beyond mere 'dependence' on Origen, but he concentrates here mainly on the distinctive theme of purificatory *darkness* in Gregory (see *ibid.* p. 245).

[12] *Ibid.* pp. 238, 240.

[13] For recent accounts of this movement and its exponents (all key anticipators of Vatican II the-ology), see: Stephen Duffy, *The Graced Horizon: Nature and Grace in Modern Catholic Thought* (Collegeville, MN: Liturgical Press, 1992); Hans Boersma, *Nouvelle Théologie and Sacramental Ontol-ogy: A Return to Mystery* (Oxford University Press, 2009); and Jürgen Mettepenningen, *Nouvelle Théologie – New Theology: Inheritor of Modernism, Precursor of Vatican II* (New York: T. & T. Clark, 2010). For a useful introduction to Daniélou's part in the *ressourcement* dimension of the movement, see Brian Daley, 'The *Nouvelle Théologie* and the Patristic Revival: Sources, Symbols and the Science of Theology', *International Journal of Systematic Theology*, 7 (2005), 362–82.

in Daniélou's footnotes, indeed, reveals acknowledged debts to de Lubac
and Maréchal, precisely in the same crucial section on the spiritual senses;
and Balthasar is fleetingly mentioned too, even though his first volume
of *Herrlichkeit* (which was to contain another treatment of the spiritual
senses, under the rubric of 'The Experience of Faith') was published only
considerably later (in 1961).[14]

But fourth, for all the theological voguishness involved just under the
surface, Daniélou's treatment of the 'spiritual senses doctrine' is in any
case, I would suggest, discernibly and datably *modern* in a number of
important respects. It is modern because of its 'turn to the subject', in
the sense of a validating appeal to a 'spiritual sense' which has all the
frisson of so-called 'mystical experience' ('L'éxperience mystique' is the title
of chapter 2), ostensibly thereby escaping, in something like a Jamesian
mode, the Kantian blockage to speculative theological metaphysics; and
it is modern in its remaining separation – despite the attempt to slide
over this very gulf for obvious apologetic reasons – of 'la vie spirituelle'
('spirituality') on the one hand and 'philosophy' on the other.

Finally, and fifthly, there is, I detect, an important tradition of post-
Enlightenment Jesuit spiritual direction that also lies behind Daniélou's
account of Gregory on the spiritual senses, and itself helps to contextualize
the immediate background of Rahner's first essay as well. Fr. Augustin
Poulain's celebrated volume *Des grâces d'oraison*,[15] which eventually went
through ten editions and numerous translations into different languages,
presented a controversial reading of the Carmelite doctrine of mystical
ascent from a Jesuit perspective, and not without a significant excursus
(chapter 6) on the spiritual senses. Daniélou repeatedly cites Poulain in his
section on Gregory on the spiritual senses; but reaching behind him he also
cites an influential eighteenth-century Jesuit, Giovanni Battista Scaramelli,
whom Poulain too had relied upon for his view that the spiritual senses
are a 'purely intellectual imitation' of the bodily senses specially capable
of 'perceiving the presence of God'.[16] In other words, there is seemingly
a distinctively modern tradition of interpreting the spiritual senses in this
'purely intellectual way' that had been kept alive in Jesuit circles of spiritual
direction between the eighteenth and early twentieth centuries, and was

[14] H. U. von Balthasar, *Herrlichkeit: Eine theologische Ästhetik*, 3 vols. (Einsiedeln: Johannes Verlag, 1961–9), published in English as *GL*.
[15] A. Poulain, *Des grâces d'oraison*, 10th edn (Paris: G. Beauchesne, 1922), published in English as *The Graces of Interior Prayer*, trans. L. L. Yorke Smith from the 6th edn and corrected to accord with the 10th French edn (London: Kegan Paul, Trench, Trübner & Co., 1950).
[16] Poulain, *Des grâces d'oraison*, p. 124.

now being brought to bear in the new revival of interest in spiritual senses at this time. It cannot be a coincidence that all the major players in the revival were themselves Jesuits (Poulain, Rahner, Daniélou, Balthasar); and one may trace a line of influence back to the age of Enlightenment in the person of Fr. Scaramelli, to an age when spiritual direction (for which a personal vocation and *attrait* was obviously necessary) and 'epistemology' (a branch of philosophy now supposedly universal) had fatally floated apart.[17]

Why then do I say that Daniélou himself failed to hold philosophy and spirituality together in his account of Gregory's 'doctrine' of the spiritual senses? Should he not precisely have been motivated to knit them together, given his own apologetic need, already mentioned, to indicate some kind of *intrinsic* propulsion towards the divine in any account of the human he might want to recommend? The problem, as I see it, is that although the section on 'Les sens spirituels' starts most promisingly, with a special underscoring of the point that, in Gregory, the 'doctrine' must not be read as merely about a 'psychological experience' (though it is that too, says Daniélou),[18] but just as much as about a whole 'anthropology', the discussion rapidly progresses to the distinctive account of divine darkness in Gregory's late work, and especially to an analysis of the transformed workings of touch, taste and smell in the *Commentary on the Song of Songs*. Here, Daniélou is right to insist that Gregory is describing 'advanced' states at the level of 'contemplation' (θεωρία), beyond the preparatory stages, in the three-tiered ascent, of 'ethics' and 'physics' (ἐθική and φυσική);[19] but what he does not adequately explain is *how* the 'purgation' (or – less misleadingly in English – 'purification') of external sense and ordinary cognition can occur so that the original image of God in the human can begin to be refurbished.[20] And despite citing passages in which Gregory[21] continues to follow passages in Origen which set up a profound rhetorical *disjunction*

---

[17] For insights into Scaramelli's influence as a spiritual director, see G. B. Scaramelli, *Il direttorio mistico, indirizzato a' direttori di quelle anime, che iddio conduce per la via della contemplazione* (Venice: S. Occhi, 1754), available in English as *A Handbook of Mystical Theology: Being an Abridgment of* Il direttorio mistico, trans. D. H. S. Nicholson (London: John M. Watkins, 1913).

[18] Daniélou, *Platonisme et théologie mystique*, p. 235.

[19] Gregory follows Origen in positing a three-stage ascent to intimacy with Christ: first the 'ethical', then the stage which allows a proper purview of the 'physical' world, and finally the 'contemplative'. For a useful introductory discussion, see Louth's treatment of this theme in Origen and Gregory in *Origins of the Christian Mystical Tradition*, pp. 56–72 and 78–94 respectively.

[20] Daniélou, *Platonisme et théologie mystique*, p. 242. Daniélou goes on here to trace the passage of the soul through the 'darkness' of Moses' ascent in Gregory's *Life of Moses*; but he makes no connection here to Gregory's *philosophical* discussions on the nature of the soul and its relation to the body, despite having essayed some discussion of their (adjusted) 'Platonism' in an earlier section (pp. 223–35).

[21] Uncharacteristically, in my view, at this late stage of his career: see further below.

between 'inner' and 'outer' sense,[22] Daniélou fails to trace the path that
Gregory elsewhere adumbrates in the Song of Songs (especially in Homily
10), in which the working *with* outer sense is precisely the means of its transformation and purification.[23] To be sure, Daniélou is anxious to insist –
in line with his own theological predilections – that the development of the
spiritual senses is part of the 'normal' effects of sanctifying grace: 'le fruit
normal du progrès de la vie de la grâce en nous'.[24] But he does not spell out
how sensation (αἴσθησις) in the ordinary, physiological sense can *become*
'spiritual sensation'. Implicitly, it seems, he has left that topic of ordinary
physiological sensation or perception to some sort of *philosophical* analysis
in Gregory, whereas what he is discussing under the rubric of 'the spiritual
senses' is what he calls 'la vie spirituelle'. But is this disjunction true to
Gregory himself? It is an odd hiatus in Daniélou for a scholar who rightly (in
chapter 1 of his study) makes the drama of death and resurrection the con-
taining issue for his whole account of Gregory's theology. To this reconsideration of how to read Gregory himself on the spiritual senses we now turn.

THE SPIRITUAL SENSES IN GREGORY'S *DE ANIMA ET RESURRECTIONE*

I have already remarked that the relation between Origen's and Gregory's
treatment of the spiritual senses theme is more complicated than Daniélou
allows. Whereas Daniélou sees Gregory as largely – sometimes slavishly –
reliant on Origen on this theme (despite introducing his own distinctive
understanding of noetic divine darkness), I propose in contrast that Gregory's works, from the time of his *De anima* on, go well beyond Origen's
approach; for they set out a developing and systematic account of how
ordinary perception and the gross physical senses are capable of a progressive transformation in this life into spiritual senses via a purgative process
of 'death' and regeneration. It is true that something like this transformative and purgative approach is occasionally anticipated at some points

---

[22] Daniélou, *Platonisme et théologie mystique*, pp. 238–9, citing (p. 239) PG 44. 780C. For the modern
Greek edition, see *GNO*, vol. VI, pp. 34–5: 'Perception within us is twofold – bodily and divine . . . the
scent of the divine perfumes is not perceived by the nose, but by a certain spiritual and immaterial
power'. Trans. C. McCambley, *Commentary on the Song of Songs* (Brookline, MA: Hellenic College
Press, 1987), p. 52.

[23] *In Cant.* X (*GNO*, vol. VI, pp. 298–314), trans. McCambley, pp. 188–95; see esp. *GNO*, vol. VI,
p. 298, trans. McCambley, pp. 188–9.

[24] Daniélou, *Platonisme et théologie mystique*, p. 266. In this passage Daniélou is evidently seeking to
find in Gregory the thesis of a 'normal' or 'natural desire' for God, as was central to the exponents
of the 'new theology' (and their controversial reading of Thomas Aquinas on this point).

in Origen's writings as well.[25] But the rhetorically disjunctive approach to flesh and spirit is for him much the more common *topos*, and is particularly marked when he suspects that his listeners may not be spiritually mature enough to understand the dangers of reading The Song physically and sexually (rather than allegorically and 'mystically').[26] As I shall argue in detail below, in contrast to this ongoing ambivalence in Origen about how to use the language of spiritual sensation, Gregory's work moves over time from a predominant emphasis on the more 'Platonic' disjunctive approach in his earlier work to a more consistently purgative and transformative approach in his later work. However, even then he fairly obviously works (out of *pietas*?) with Origen's *Commentary on the Song of Songs* closely in mind,[27] and sometimes 'adds' to Origen's approach, as he puts it, while at other times reverting to Origen's more disjunctive rhetoric to make a special point of ethical caution. But when Gregory deliberately changes Origen's drift or tone on a passage in the Song, we should certainly presume that he means to make a special point of his own.

Mariette Canévet, in her article 'Sens spirituels' in the *Dictionnaire de spiritualité*, rightly draws attention to this same ambiguity in the Christian spiritual senses tradition between those who posit a 'discontinuité' between corporeal and interior senses and those who urge the possibility of a 'transfiguration' of the 'sens corporels'.[28] By the time Gregory is discoursing on the spiritual senses in the individual homilies of the *Commentary on the Song of Songs*, some such transfiguration has clearly already occurred,[29]

---

[25] This occurs most memorably at certain moments in Origen's own Song commentary, his *Dialogue with Heraclides* and his *Homilies on Luke*: see, e.g., *In Cant.* III. 12 (PG 13. 172D), trans. R. P. Lawson, *The Song of Songs, Commentary and Homilies* (New York: Newman Press, 1956), p. 218; *Dial. Heraclides*, 8. 10–17, 16. 20 – 24. 23 (SC 67, pp. 72, 90–102), trans. R. Daly, *Treatise on the Passover* and *Dialogue with Heraclides* (New York: Paulist Press, 1992), pp. 63, 70–6; *Homilies on Luke*, 15 (*GCS*, vol. IX, pp. 92–4), trans. J. T. Lienhard, *Homilies on Luke* (Washington, DC: Catholic University Press, 1996), 62–4.

[26] See esp. *In Cant.* Prol., 2 (PG 13. 65A–67A), trans. Lawson, pp. 23–9; and *Contra Celsum*, VII. 39 (PG 11. 1476B), trans. H. Chadwick, *Contra Celsum* (New York: Cambridge University Press, 1965), p. 427. As Mark J. McInroy convincingly shows in Chapter 1 above, a recent attempt by John Dillon to find in Origen a *shift* from 'metaphorical' to 'analogical' enunciations of the spiritual senses in the course of his career is not supported by the textual evidence: Origen displays both approaches in all phases of his career, and seemingly applies one or the other depending on context. Overall, however, he exercises much more explicit caution about utilizing physical and erotic metaphors for the soul's relation to Christ (even though these metaphors are in one sense indispensable) than does Gregory: it is hard to imagine Origen saying straight out, as does Gregory, that 'The most acute physical pleasure ... is used as a symbol in the exposition of this doctrine of love' (*In Cant.* I, *GNO*, vol. VI, p. 27, trans. McCambley, p. 49).

[27] See *GNO*, vol. VI, p. 13, trans. McCambley, p. 39.

[28] Mariette Canévet, 'Sens spirituels', in *DS*, vol. XIV (1990), pp. 599–617, at p. 600.

[29] See, e.g, the opening remarks of the Prologue (*GNO*, vol. VI, pp. 3–4, trans. McCambley, p. 35: on which see further comment, below); and *GNO*, vol. VI, pp. 6–7, trans. McCambley, p. 36, where

and only very occasionally does he still utilize the rhetorical disjunction
between bodily and divine sense with which he would have been familiar from the dominant strands in Origen's treatment. One such example
does come in the first homily, as we noted above, when Gregory, following Origen, is exegeting Proverbs 2: 5[30] and remarks, apparently to make
a deliberate disjunction: 'perception within us is twofold – bodily and
divine'. But even then, and in contrast to Origen, Gregory immediately
stresses the 'analogy' between the two forms of perception.[31] So the intriguing exegetical question for our purposes is this: *how* does the transfiguration
of the bodily sense occur, according to Gregory? In an early and revealing
moment in the Prologue to the *Commentary on the Song of Songs*, Gregory –
significantly again striking a different tone from the Origenistic prototype
he has inherited at this point[32] – announces that he is actually writing
'*for* the fleshly minded' (τοῖς σαρκωδεστέροις), in order to invite them
with him into the purified world of the Song.[33] So how are we to explicate the continuum in Gregory between fallen sensuality and redeemed
sensuality?

It is here that Gregory's *De anima et resurrectione*, written at a crucial
transition juncture for him just after the successive deaths of his older
siblings Basil (in 379) and Macrina (in 380), is so important a testimony,
but it is curiously neglected by Daniélou in the 'spiritual senses' section

---

Gregory writes of the 'shift from the corporeal to the spiritual' and of 'the merely human element'
being 'changed'.

[30] 'Then you will understand the fear of the Lord and find the knowledge (ἐπίγνωσιν) of God'. See
Chapter 1 above for McInroy's discussion of the importance of this passage for Origen's founding
discussion of the spiritual senses.

[31] *In Cant.* 1 (*GNO*, vol. vi, p. 34), trans. McCambley, p. 52. An even more obviously rhetorical
disjunction between the 'old man' and the new is made at the very start of the first homily (*GNO*,
vol. vi, pp. 14–15, trans. McCambley, p. 43). But again, Gregory immediately insists that the
example of the Mount of Transfiguration shows that we are capable of 'being *transformed* with [Christ] into
a state which is free from passion' (*ibid.*, my italics).

[32] Origen writes, in contrast: 'I advise and counsel everyone who is not yet rid of the vexations of
flesh and blood and has not ceased to feel the passion of his bodily nature, to refrain completely
from reading this little book.' *In Cant.* Prol. 1 (PG 13. 63CD), trans. Lawson, p. 23.
   Two final points of caution perhaps need to be added about attempting to make a tidy comparison
of Origen and Gregory on their respective treatment of the spiritual senses. First, we have only
Rufinus's translation and excerption of Origen's Song commentary, and we know from the few
fragments remaining in Greek that Rufinus translated freely and according to his own theological
interests. The same problems apply of course to the *De principiis* and other relevant texts. Second,
the rather artificial and distracting debate in modern scholarship (animated by an anachronistic
Thomist distinction) about whether Origen has a 'metaphorical' or 'analogical' rendition of the
spiritual senses (see, again, Chapter 1 above) is not quite the same issue as the one I am crucially
interested in in this Chapter, *viz.* the possibility, or otherwise, of the spiritual senses being *continuous*
with the life of the gross physical senses, as opposed to being a *parallel* realm of spiritual sensation
(as is more commonly suggested by Origen).

[33] *In Cant.* Prol. (*GNO*, vol. vi, p. 4), trans. McCambley, p. 35.

of his monograph.[34] Yet once we remember that Gregory does not have a consciously enunciated 'spiritual senses *doctrine*' as such, but rather certain key phrases which signal his wrestling with the manifold epistemological issues of sensuality and its relation to the mind (νοῦς) and soul (ψυχή), we are freed up to consider what he is about in this dialogue in a way not constrained by the modern boxed-up categories of 'philosophy' versus 'spirituality' or 'mystical experience'. Terms related to 'spiritual sensing' (the main ones being 'senses of the soul', 'eye of the soul', 'sense of the mind', 'divine sense' and the Pauline 'inner man') are in fact scattered all through his corpus, as a search with the aid of the TLG[35] readily discloses; but they undergo a notable change (including the introduction of the new language of the 'senses of the heart' (αἰσθητήρια τῆς καρδίας)) in the late commentary work. However, it is misleading and circular to set one's compass on the issue only by these late and distinctive developments.

It is precisely in *De anima et resurrectione*, as I want to argue, that we begin to get the emerging sense of an epistemological continuum between ordinary sensation and perception (which is subject to the effects of the fall) and 'spiritual sensation' as it leads us into the transformed life of resurrection. For the sake of our discussion I want to draw attention only to a number of selected features of this intriguing and complicated dialogue. But if I am right, what we witness here is the moment at which Gregory – largely through Macrina's voice – starts to develop his own distinctive views on spiritual sensation. They are views which may well have been activated by the crisis of the deaths of his siblings; they are also views which appear at odds with at least some dimensions of the spiritual sensation tradition that Gregory had inherited from Origen, and which until then he had fairly unthinkingly replicated in his own writings.

First, it is surprising how many recent commentators on the *De anima et resurrectione* omit to read to the end of the text, or even note the importance of the reference to biblical material right at the beginning of the piece as well. Yet the whole dialogue is constructed around a Pauline frame, with a primary focus on 1 Corinthians 15. When Gregory goes into his fit of grief over Basil's death at the outset, Macrina immediately chides him for grieving 'for them that sleep', appealing directly to the authority

---

[34] Daniélou mentions the dialogue only a couple of times, and that fleetingly: *Platonisme et théologie mystique*, pp. 224, 236.

[35] The Thesaurus Linguae Graecae (a research centre based at the University of California, Irvine) provides a searchable database of over 10,000 Greek works from Homer to the fall of Byzantium in 1453. For the purposes of this essay, Nyssen's corpus was searched for terms associated with the spiritual senses tradition. See also αἴσθησις and related entries in Friedhelm Mann, *Lexicon Gregorianum: Wörterbuch zu den Schriften Gregors von Nyssa*, vol. 1 (Leiden: Brill, 1998), pp. 104–15.

of 'the Apostle'. It is Gregory's expostulations against the impossibility of repressing grief, and his resistance, in his unreasoning state, to accepting mere 'biblical commands' as conversation-stoppers, that fuel the entire philosophical discussion that follows, in which Gregory first doggedly plays the sceptical Epicurean, and then the Stoic, for as long as it takes to persuade Macrina that some sort of *integration* of passion with intellect is a positive good. But when that lengthy process of debate has finally come to a more-or-less satisfactory end, Gregory returns to the biblical doctrine with which Macrina started, reminding her that 'The argument has not yet touched the most vital of all the questions relating to our Faith' (οὔπω, φημὶ, τοῦ κυριωτάτου τῶν κατὰ δόγμα ζητουμένων ὁ λόγος ἥψατο).[36] It is at this point that the view is proposed that at the end time all the atoms 'belonging to each soul' will be reassembled and reintegrated 'in the same order as before' in a 'reconstitution of human life' at the general resurrection;[37] and Macrina makes the wry comment that the resurrection is the one, crowning, point of discussion which has so far been left 'unnoticed in what has been said . . . ' Yet 'Much', she says, 'in our long and detailed discussion' has already pointed precisely to it.[38] The dialogue ends with a sustained meditation on the restoration of the *imago Dei* in the human implied by the 'perfection of bodies' to which we are all ultimately destined. We shall all pass through the 'Fire', but be 'born again in our original splendour'.[39] In other words, once we set Gregory's language of 'senses of the soul' in this biblical (and specifically Pauline) frame, it is hard to see how Gregory can ultimately sustain a dualism between different *sorts* of 'sensing' which have, at best, only metaphorical relation.

Secondly, a close reading of *De anima et resurrectione* surely makes it futile to attempt to box either Macrina or Gregory up into any one of the pagan philosophical epistemologies with which they are undeniably progressively playing throughout their dialogue. As various commentators have recently shown, there are brilliantly devised allusions as we move along to Plato's *Phaedrus*, to Aristotle's *De anima*, to Epicurus, Galen, Posidonius and Lucretius.[40] We do, of course – as in Plato – have the

---

[36] *De anima et resurrectione* (PG 46. 129A), trans. W. Moore and H. A. Wilson, *On the Soul and the Resurrection*, in NPNF, series 2, vol. v (Grand Rapids, MI: Eerdmans, 1979), pp. 430–68, at p. 459.

[37] *De anima* (PG 46. 129B), trans. Moore and Wilson, p. 460.

[38] *De anima* (PG 46. 129B), trans. Moore and Wilson, p. 460.

[39] *De anima* (PG 46. 157B, 160C), trans. Moore and Wilson, pp. 467–8.

[40] For analyses of these philosophical allusions, see esp. R. Williams, 'Macrina's Deathbed Revisited: Gregory of Nyssa on Mind and Passion', in *Christian Faith and Greek Philosophy in Late Antiquity: Essays in Tribute to George Christopher Stead . . . in Celebration of his Eightieth Birthday*, Vigiliae Christianae, 19 (1993), 227–46 (which contains useful bibliography of earlier studies); Michel R. Barnes,

problem of discerning which voice is ventriloquizing the final view of Gregory himself, since Gregory plays the stooge for much of the action; yet he does not leave his 'master' (διδάσκαλος) Macrina without a few dents in her own edifice too by the end. She is forced to modify her initially rather rigid and biblicist resistance to the *Phaedrus*, and he his initial (and presumably feigned) Epicurean epistemological scepticism at the very existence of a soul; but it would be wholly false to follow Christopher Stead in his assessment that the result is merely 'Aristotle's mistake of regarding man simply as an animal with reason added on as an extra capacity'.[41] Stead here is another commentator who has seemingly not read to the end of the dialogue. No, the effect of the philosophic banter *within* the frame of the biblical doctrine of resurrection is precisely a final judging of philosophic pretension, yet with a deep accompanying respect for philosophic acuity and distinction-making. As so often in Gregory – and he enunciates this principle most memorably in his exegesis of *The Life of Moses* – philosophy is ultimately declared to be 'always in labour but never giving birth'.[42] But philosophy is not set aside until it has been allowed to be brought into searching and illuminating critical interaction with the biblical text itself.

How do these two initial points help us with our reconsideration of the spiritual senses in the *De anima et resurrectione*? It is, I submit, because they provide the biblically inflected context within which Gregory can express a fascinating view (given largely through the mouth of Macrina) about the possibility of a human continuum of epistemic transformation; and this dimension of the spiritual senses theme is completely neglected by Daniélou. The main relevant passage is worth citing in detail, and comes quite close to the start of the dialogue when Macrina is responding explicitly to both Epicurean and Stoic scepticism about the immaterial soul, forcefully expounded here by Gregory. He has just thrown down his sceptical gauntlet: 'if a thing can be found nowhere, plainly it has no existence', he says of the soul. At this the διδάσκαλος 'groaned softly' and said:

'The Polemical Context and Content of Gregory of Nyssa's Psychology', *Medieval Philosophy and Theology*, 4 (1994), 1–24; and J. Warren Smith, 'Macrina, Tamer of Horses and Healer of Souls: Grief and the Therapy of Hope in Gregory of Nyssa's *De anima et resurrectione*', *Journal of Theological Studies*, 52 (2000), 37–60. My former Harvard pupil Ashley S. Evans, in her 'The Mind Sees: Spiritual Senses in Gregory of Nyssa's *De anima et resurrectione*', undergraduate dissertation, Harvard College, Cambridge, MA, March 2002, also provides an incisive and painstaking account of the shifts in philosophical allusion in the opening sections of the *De anima*.

[41] G. C. Stead, 'The Concept of Mind and the Concept of God in the Christian Fathers', in B. Hebblethwaite and S. Sutherland (eds.), *The Philosophical Frontiers of Christian Theology: Essays Presented to Donald MacKinnon* (Cambridge University Press, 1982), pp. 39–54, at p. 48.

[42] *De vita Moysis*, II. II (*GNO*, vol. VII/1, p. 36), trans. E. Ferguson and A. J. Malherbe, *The Life of Moses* (New York: Paulist Press, 1978), p. 57.

The Stoics and Epicureans might have brought forward these words, and others like them, when they met the apostle Paul in Athens. For indeed I hear that Epicurus especially was led in this direction by his assumptions. He conceived the nature of beings to be fortuitous and automatic because he believed that there was no providence pervading events. In consequence, therefore, he thought that human life was also like a bubble, inflated by some kind of breath from our body, as long as the breath is held in by its container; but when the swollen bubble bursts, then the contents are extinguished along with it. For him appearance was what defined the nature of beings, and he made perception (αἴσθησις) the standard by which all things are comprehended. *He completely closed the senses of the soul* [τῆς ψυχῆς αἰσθητήρια: this is the term Daniélou will elsewhere translate as 'spiritual senses'], and was unable to look at any of the bodiless things which are known by the intellect, just as someone who is shut up in a little hut remains unaware of the heavenly marvels which he is prevented by the walls and roof from seeing what is outside. All perceptible things which are seen in the universe are simply a sort of earthly walls [*sic*] which shut off *small-souled people* (Ἀτεχνῶς γὰρ γήϊνοί τινές εἰσι τοῖχοι τὰ αἰσθητὰ πάντα, ὅσα ἐν τῷ παντὶ καθορᾶται, πρὸς τὴν τῶν νοητῶν θεωρίαν δι' ἑαυτῶν τοὺς μικροψυχοτέρους διατειχίζοντες).[43]

Now what this passage suggests to me is a capacity for the sense organs to develop from 'small-souled' to 'large-souled' apprehensions; yet what is also given is the simultaneous temptation 'completely to close' down the spiritual senses (αἰσθητήρια τῆς ψυχῆς). If this is right, then the view being proposed is that our perceptual capacities have labile and transformative possibilities, but ones that not all activate – whether through sin, laziness, blindness or philosophical obtuseness.

But how do we know whether Macrina here intends the αἰσθητήρια τῆς ψυχῆς to refer to the transfigured workings of ordinary perception, not rather as Origen would – at least in some moods – have had it,[44] as utterly separate sets of cognitive faculties parallel to, and infinitely better than, the bodily ones? The key clue here, I think, comes a little later when Macrina appeals again to the 'thinking eyes of the soul', and insists that '*by the very operation of our senses* we are led to conceive of that reality and intelligence which surpasses the senses' (δι' αὐτῆς τῆς κατὰ τὴν αἴσθησιν ἡμῶν ἐνεργείας εἰς τὴν τοῦ ὑπὲρ αἴσθησιν πράγματος καὶ νοήματος ἔννοιαν ὁδηγούμεθα).[45] Moreover, and conversely, at the end of the long discussion that follows about the value or otherwise of the passions, Macrina can insist that 'according to our previous reasoning, the

---

[43] *De anima* (PG 46. 21B–24A), trans. C. Roth, *On the Soul and the Resurrection* (Crestwood, NY: St Vladimir's Seminary Press, 2002), p. 31, my italics. I use Roth's translation from here on, as it best captures the points in the Greek to which I want to draw special attention.

[44] See again Origen, *In Cant.* Prol. 2 (PG 13. 66CD), trans. Lawson, p. 28.

[45] *De anima* (PG 46. 28C), trans. Roth, p. 34, my italics.

rational power cannot enter into the bodily life *otherwise than by entering through perception*' (κατὰ τὸν ἤδη προαποδοθέντα λόγον, οὐκ ἔστιν ἄλλως τὴν λογικὴν δύναμιν ἐγγενέσθαι τῇ σωματικῇ ζωῇ, μὴ διὰ τῶν αἰσθήσεων ἐγγινομένην).[46] In other words, perception is the precious and indispensable *bridge* between soul and body; the soul cannot do what it has to do without ordinary perception, and bodily perceptions cannot do without the soul if they are to undergo transformation into αἰσθητήρια τῆς ψυχῆς.

Such, at any rate, is my proposed reading of this admittedly elusive thread of thought in the dialogue. It is certainly not a reading which has previously been canvassed; but if it is persuasive as a proposal, it raises further interesting questions about the *development* of Gregory's thought about spiritual sensation in the course of a long career as a theologian. If something novel and suggestive is emerging in this dialogue for the first time, as appears to be the case, what is the relation of this position to Gregory's views both earlier and later? We recall that Daniélou's account does not hypothesize such a development in the so-called 'doctrine' of the spiritual senses, and scarcely treats of *De anima et resurrectione* at all. While it does briefly cite passages from some earlier works of Gregory (including Gregory's very first treatise, the *De virginitate*), the overriding emphasis is on the last works, especially the *Commentary on the Song of Songs*, and there is no suggestion of changes of mind or varieties of perspective on the topic. A systematic gathering of all the examples of spiritual senses language in Gregory's oeuvre, however, such as I have recently attempted, reveals certain important shifts and developments in his usage and application of this language over time. In the last section of this chapter I shall thus essay a brief overview of what this TLG search has revealed. It may be pedagogically most revealing here to work backwards from Gregory's last works, since this is where Daniélou's analysis lays most of the emphasis, and where certain new developments undeniably occur. From here we shall be able to work counter-clockwise and see how the transition effected in the *De anima et resurrectione* provides a significant bridge between earlier and later treatments of the theme.

THREE PHASES OF DEVELOPMENT IN NYSSEN'S TREATMENT: THE SPIRITUAL SENSES, LATE, MIDDLE AND EARLY

What, then, does my new proposal for how to read the *De anima et resurrectione* mean for Gregory's later expansion and deepening of his views

---

[46] *De anima* (PG 46. 60CD), trans. Roth, p. 56, my italics.

of the αἰσθητήρια τῆς ψυχῆς in the *Commentary on the Song of Songs*?
I do not here intend, I must stress, to detract in any way from the great
illumination Daniélou throws on the *Commentary on the Song of Songs* by
reading it together with *The Life of Moses*, especially when he charts the
theme of necessary darkness that emerges in these late works – for he too
recognizes the theme of necessary 'purgation' in that process. That is,
the 'senses of the soul', once awakened and developed through ascetical
training, still have to pass through a further and final passage in the elevated
stage of θεωρία; and this is where the mind in its 'seeing' capacity (as
we know from the entry of Moses into the dark cloud in *The Life of
Moses*[47]) is completely darkened in the intimacy of divine closeness. Thus,
to judge from selected passages from the *Commentary on the Song of Songs*
which Daniélou treats revealingly, the supposedly 'lower' senses, in their
transformed and purged condition, seem to topple the higher ones at last.[48]

As Gregory also puts it in an important passage in Homily 3 which
underscores this progression and development in specifically christological
terms:

> The child Jesus born within us advances by *different* ways in those who receive him
> in wisdom, in age, and in grace. He is not the same in every person, but is present
> according to the measure of the person receiving him . . . Christ is never seen with
> the same form upon the vine, but he changes his form with time – now budding,
> now blossoming, now mature, now ripe and finally as wine. Thus the vine holds
> out a promise with its fruit. It is not yet ripe for wine, but it awaits maturity.
> Meanwhile it does not lack any delight, for it gladdens our sense of smell before
> our taste with its expectation of the future; by its fragrance of hope it sweetens the
> soul's senses.[49]

So, in the *Commentary on the Song of Songs*, smell, taste and touch finally
come into their own in purged activation. And it is only in the *Commentary
on the Song of Songs*, as Daniélou rightly points out, that Gregory once uses
the phrase 'sense of the heart', in the context of a discussion of how even the
'belly' can be a positive symbol of the transformed self wrought into the
bodily life of Christ by the power of the Spirit.[50] But all this is possible only,
one should stress, because the 'soul's eye' (such as appealed to in the *De
anima et resurrectione* and is often still mentioned in the *Commentary on the
Song of Songs*) has already been worked upon and purged from improper
passions. As Gregory puts it in the very first passage of the Prologue to

---

[47] *De vita Moysis*, II. 162–9 (*GNO*, vol. VII/I, pp. 86–9), trans. Ferguson and Malherbe, pp. 94–7.
[48] See Daniélou, *Platonisme et théologie mystique*, pp. 242–52.
[49] *In Cant.* III (*GNO*, vol. VI, pp. 95–7), trans. McCambley, pp. 86–7, slightly adjusted.
[50] *In Cant.* XIV (*GNO*, vol. VI, p. 414), trans. McCambley, p. 251.

the *Commentary on the Song of Songs*, addressing Olympias, the woman to whom he had dedicated the work: 'I do not offer you anything that would benefit your conduct, for I am persuaded that your soul's eye is [already] pure from every passionate, unclean thought, and that it looks without hindrance at God's grace by means of these divine words of the *Song*.'[51]

Now Macrina, it must be said, does not anticipate any of these developments in what she says in *De anima et resurrectione*. Indeed, and on the contrary, she still seems to assume at this stage (and presumably Gregory with her) the complete hegemony of sight amid the senses, and the necessary *unification* of the senses of the soul in the νοῦς: we do not hear at this stage of *five* spiritual senses operating distinctively. This position thus contrasts somewhat forcibly with what emerges in Gregory's late commentary work, when sight is toppled from its leadership by noetic darkness, and the five senses are no longer gathered into the mind but find their true, and distinctive, operations in darkness. They no longer eschew the body, but rejoice in its transformed anticipation of the resurrection. The gesturing forward to the elusive implications of the resurrection body found in the *De anima et resurrectione* have thus only now come to complete fulfilment.[52]

On the strength of these evidences, we must hypothesize, moving beyond Daniélou's flatter analysis, that Gregory's views on this important matter of spiritual sense developed through time, presumably as he himself matured and changed his mind about the ways in which bodily transformation could be possible – through the power of the Spirit and in union with Christ. And as mentioned at the outset of this chapter, it is somewhat ironic that Daniélou's own work on the successive dating of Gregory's texts,[53] albeit remaining hypothetical in parts, can help give us the key to how Gregory's mind may have changed on the matter of the 'senses of the soul', through three discernible stages of his career.

As Daniélou himself rightly highlights, the earlier works of Gregory (up to the crucial transition at the deaths of his two elder siblings in 379–80) are much more consistently 'Platonist' in their representation of the body

---

[51] *In Cant.* Prol. (*GNO*, vol. VI, p. 4), trans. McCambley, p. 35.
[52] The christological transformation involved in such absorption into the life of the resurrection, according to Gregory, is spelled out in Brian E. Daley, '"The Human Form Divine": Christ's Risen Body and Ours According to Gregory of Nyssa', *Studia patristica*, 41 (2006), 301–18. For an account of Gregory's contentious use of 'mingling' language in relation to Christ's natures, and particularly for how this relates to themes in the Song commentary, see my '"Mingling" in Gregory of Nyssa's Christology: A Reconsideration', in Andreas Schuele and Günter Thomas (eds.), *Who is Jesus Christ for Us Today: Pathways to Contemporary Christology* [Festschrift for Michael Welker] (Louisville, KY: Westminster John Knox Press, 2009), pp. 72–84.
[53] Daniélou, 'La chronologie des œuvres de Grégoire de Nysse'.

as disjunct from the mind;[54] and they tend to represent this earthly life as a cave-like existence in exile from the realm of the forms. The crisis of Gregory's siblings' demise, however, and especially his witness to Macrina's passing as described in the *Life of Macrina*,[55] seem to have caused him to reconsider the whole matter of the resurrection and its implications for transformed physical life even in this life, in the era of the church. The third and last phase of Gregory's career – as we have just explored – sees yet a further development of this theme, as Gregory considers his own mortality, the frailty of the mind and yet also the capacity for 'erotic' intimacy with Christ, via the spiritual senses, in this life.

What my own exploration of the uses of the characteristic phrases 'the sense of the soul', 'the eye of the soul', 'the inner man' and 'the sight of the soul' throughout the gamut of Gregory's corpus have shown to me, through a consistent TLG search, is that this threefold developmental pattern is well confirmed by the textual evidence. As long as we do not make a false disjunction between modern categories at the outset ('epistemology' and 'spirituality'), what we see is an emerging and developing sense of the significance of bodily life for 'spiritual sensation', as 'Platonic' presumptions about the body become increasingly critiqued and queried. To be fair, Daniélou also points out this withdrawal from 'Platonic' categories in his own treatment of the spiritual senses; but what he seemingly does not grasp is that the whole range of development on this theme in Gregory's thinking brings *ordinary* cognition, ethics and ascetics all together in its train.

---

[54] I place 'Platonic' in inverted commas here to indicate that the Platonic dialogues themselves evidence, in a complex way worthy of discussion, more than one view of the material world and the body. It is therefore something of a caricature to represent Plato's view as wholly 'negative' towards the material and bodily world. For one sophisticated treatment of this problematic and its reception in ancient philosophy more widely, see Lloyd P. Gerson, *Aristotle and Other Platonists* (Ithaca, NY: Cornell University Press, 2005), chap. 1, esp. pp. 34–7.

[55] The narrative structure of the *Life of Macrina* may even reflect this transition: immediately preceding Macrina's death, Gregory dwells at length on the notion that her soul seems unrestrained by the fetters of her body. 'It was as if an angel had providentially assumed human form, an angel in whom there was no affinity for, nor attachment to, the life of the flesh . . . the flesh did not drag it down to its own passions.' *Vitae Sanctae Macrinae* (*GNO*, vol. VIII/1, p. 396), trans. K. Corrigan, *The Life of Saint Macrina* (Toronto: Peregrina, 2001), p. 40. After Macrina's death, however, Gregory is considerably more occupied with her body as reflective of the grace she exemplified in life: 'Her eyes needed no arranging, since they were covered gracefully . . . and her lips were firmly closed and her hands rested naturally on her breast, and the whole position of her body was so spontaneously and beautifully harmonised that any hand to compose the features was superfluous.' *Vitae Sanctae Macrinae* (*GNO*, vol. VIII/1, p. 399), trans. Corrigan, p. 43. He also buries Macrina next to their mother so 'that after death their bodies should be reunited and that the partnership which they enjoyed while they lived should not be dissolved even in death'. *Vitae Sanctae Macrinae* (*GNO*, vol. VIII/1, pp. 409–10), trans. Corrigan, p. 51. For a brief, but perceptive, treatment of the theme of the body of Macrina as anticipated 'relic', see Caroline Walker Bynum, *The Resurrection of the Body* (New York: Columbia University Press, 1995), pp. 81–6.

And the early treatment, although tainted by 'Platonism' in Daniélou's perspective, is already in my reading showing certain intimations of later developments. Thus, in the texts that many scholars, following Daniélou's lead, tend to class as 'early' (such as the *De virginitate*, the *De mortuis* and the commentaries on the Psalms, and the Beatitudes), it is always the 'eye of the soul' that is in discussion, and this is invariably represented as an 'inner' realm disjunct from the body and greatly in danger of being dragged down by the realm of the passions.[56] Yet even in this first stage of Gregory's career, there is already at least one hint, in the *Sixth Homily on the Beatitudes*, that there might be a progression from this dualistic condition to a state in which the 'eye of the soul' may enjoy more undisturbed contemplation – not via an 'instant vision', as in the *Symposium*, but more through a certain 'purification of the heart' and of the passions.[57] From this perspective, the dialogue with Macrina in the *De anima et resurrectione* still represents a crucial philosophical transition, bringing – as we have seen – classic pagan debates about the soul, its perception and knowledge, into close relation to a transformed understanding of the body in the light of 1 Corinthians 15. But the discussion of 'seeing God' in the *Homilies on the Beatitudes* in one sense already prepares for this development. The anti-Eunomian writings are strikingly consistent in their representation of the spiritual senses as easily besmirched by a corporeality weighed too heavily against the spirit,[58]

[56] See, e.g., *De virginitate*, XI. 20–5 (*GNO*, vol. VIII/1, p. 292), trans. W. Moore and H. A. Wilson, *On Virginity*, in NPNF, series 2, vol. V, pp. 343–71, at pp. 355–6. Cf. *De mortuis non esse dolendum* (*GNO*, vol. IX, pp. 47–8); *In inscriptiones Psalmorum*, 6. 45; 8. 76 (*GNO*, vol. V, p. 41; vol. V, p. 52), trans. R. E. Heine, *Treatise on the Inscriptions of the Psalms* (Oxford University Press, 1995), pp. 99, 109; *De beatitudinibus*, II. 5 (*GNO*, vol. VII/2, p. 98), trans. S. G. Hall, *On the Beatitudes* (Leiden: Brill, 2000), pp. 37–8.

[57] 'He [Christ] does not seem to me to be offering God as an instant vision to the one whose spiritual eye is purified, but what the grandeur of the text proposes to us is that which the Word sets out more directly to others, when he says that the kingdom of God is within us (Lk 17, 21), so that we might learn that the person who has purged his own heart of every tendency to passion perceives in his own beauty the reflexion of the divine nature . . . When the mind in you is unmixed with any evil, free from passion, and far away from any stain, you are blessed for your sharpsightedness, for by becoming pure you have perceived what is invisible to those not purified, and, with the materialistic fog removed from the eye of the soul, in the pure shining of the heart you see clearly the blessed sight'. *De beatitudinibus*, VI. 4 (*GNO*, vol. VII/2, p. 141), trans. Hall, pp. 70–1.

[58] 'Over the perceptive powers of the souls (τῶν τῆς ψυχῆς αἰσθητηρίων) of men who handle what is written in too corporeal a manner, the veil is cast; but for those who turn their contemplation to that which is the object of their intelligence, there is revealed, bared, as it were, a mask, the glory that underlies the letter.' *Contra Eunomium*, III, 5, 11 (*GNO*, vol. II, p. 164), trans. W. Moore and H. A. Wilson, *Against Eunomius*, in NPNF, series 2, vol. V, pp. 33–248, at p. 192. Note here that in the anti-Eunomian writings, in the context of bitter doctrinal dispute, there is a notable stress on the darkening of the spiritual senses through sin; this gives way in the later Song commentary to more exaltative positive enjoyment of the spiritual senses (cf. *Contra Eunomium*, I, 1, 411 (*GNO*, vol. I, p. 233), trans. Moore and Wilson, p. 73; II, 1, 22 (*GNO*, vol. I, p. 233), trans. Moore and Wilson, p. 252;

whereas the *De opificio hominis*[59] and *The Catechetical Oration*[60] witness
to the gradual enrichment of Gregory's perception of bodily capabilities,
stressing increasingly the transformation effected by the incarnation, the
resurrection and the Spirit: *The Catechetical Oration*, chapter 8, in particular, includes an explicit discussion of the progression of sensuality from
baseness to Christlikeness.[61] In all these texts the language of 'spiritual
sensation' is repetitively present, although never lifted up to the status of
an explicit 'doctrine'. It is, one might say, the doctrine of *Christ* that is
increasingly at stake, whereas the spiritual senses are the epistemological
means of progressively internalizing that doctrine.

Finally, the late writings, as we have seen (and *On Infants' Early Deaths*
is a poignant and revealing text to lay here alongside *The Life of Moses* and
the *Commentary on the Song of Songs*[62]), stress further the difference made
in older age to the body which has successfully fought its battles with the
passions, so that now even the 'lower' senses can come into their own at last
in a profound intimacy with the bridegroom, Christ. The last phase, then,
becomes the more explicitly christological as the hegemony of the mind
wanes, and a concomitant celebration of sensual *wisdom* waxes accordingly.

CONCLUSIONS

To conclude: my purpose in this short study has been to lay bare, first, some
of the concerns that may have been in play in Daniélou's initial theory of

---

III, 2, 28 (*GNO*, vol. II, p. 61), trans. Moore and Wilson, p. 155; III, 2, 80 (*GNO*, vol. II, p. 78),
trans. Moore and Wilson, p. 161; III, 8, 4 (*GNO*, vol. II, p. 240), trans. Moore and Wilson, p. 220).

[59] '[T]he whole body is made like some musical instrument . . . the mind, passing over the whole
instrument, and touching each of the parts in a mode corresponding to its intellectual activities,
according to its nature, produces its proper effect on those parts which are in a natural condition,
but remains inoperative and ineffective upon those which are unable to admit the movement of its
art; for the mind is somehow naturally adapted to be in close relation with that which is in a natural
condition, but to be alien from that which is removed from nature.' *De opificio hominis*, XII, 8 (PG
44. 161CD), trans. W. Moore and H. A. Wilson, *On the Making of Man*, in NPNF, series 2, vol. V,
pp. 387–427, at p. 398. See also *De opificio hominis*, XII, 4 (PG 44. 157D–160A), trans. Moore and
Wilson, p. 397.

[60] *Cat. Or.* (*GNO*, vol. III/4), trans. W. Moore and H. A. Wilson, *The Great Catechism*, in NPNF,
series 2, vol. V, pp. 473–509.

[61] '[T]he maker of our vessel, now that wickedness has intermingled with our sentient part, I mean that
connected with the body, will dissolve the material which has received the evil, and, remoulding
it again by the Resurrection without any admixture of the contrary matter, will recombine the
elements into the vessel in its original beauty'. *Cat. Or.* VIII (*GNO*, vol. III/4, p. 31), trans. Moore
and Wilson, p. 483.

[62] In *On Infants' Early Deaths*, Gregory, himself now old, likens himself to a retired racehorse, yet
points out to his addressee, Hierius, that even in the decaying body, the spiritual eyes may be at
their strongest. *De infantibus praemature abraeptis* (*GNO*, vol. III/2, pp. 68–9), trans. W. Moore
and H. A. Wilson, *On Infants' Early Deaths*, in NPNF, series 2, vol. V, pp. 372–81, at p. 372.

a so-called 'doctrine' of spiritual senses in Gregory of Nyssa. His work was not only pioneering, but enormously important and influential, and we have seen towards the end of this chapter how many of his insights still need to be preserved. Yet his selective approach in *Platonisme et théologie mystique* to the spiritual senses as such seems to have mesmerized people into a certain uncritical slumber about the precise range of texts and terms that need to be considered to gain a full picture of what Gregory intended in speaking of 'spiritual sense', and how he may have changed his mind over time. The recovery of such an approach today, in a post-modern context of philosophy in which the Enlightenment propulsion to universality in epistemology has been brought so radically into question, raises new questions about Gregory's possible applicability to the contemporary philosophical scene. That our very acts of visual perceiving and sensual response might be affected by our moral fibre, our spiritual maturity or our depths of scriptural engagement now seems – dare I say it – not an impossible line of new philosophical investigation. As ever, Gregory's sometimes infuriating inconsistency and philosophical elusiveness never cease to allure and engage. The reconsideration of such a teaching on the spiritual senses, not only in Gregory himself, but as a live philosophical and theological option for today, seems to me already overdue.[63]

---

[63] I plan to take this constructive contemporary task forward in the second volume of my systematic theology, prospectively entitled *Seeing Darkly: An Essay 'On the Contemplative Life'* (Cambridge University Press). The preliminary essays in which I have already started to develop such a project philosophically are 'The Resurrection: The Grammar of "Raised"', in D. Z. Phillips and Mario von der Ruhr, eds., *Biblical Concepts and Our World* (Basingstoke: Palgrave, 2004), pp. 169–89; and 'On the Identity of the Risen Jesus: Finding Jesus Christ in the Poor', in Beverly Roberts Gaventa and Richard B. Hays, eds., *Seeking the Identity of Jesus: A Pilgrimage* (Grand Rapids, MI: Eerdmans, 2008), pp. 301–19. However, it should be noted that my account of the relation and difference of Origen's and Gregory's accounts of the spiritual senses has here been significantly modified and changed since I wrote these earlier essays.

CHAPTER 3

Augustine

Matthew R. Lootens

That human happiness consists in the perpetual vision of God is one of the hallmarks of Augustine's thought and the tradition that he left to the Western theological world. However, Augustine also employs the language of sound, smell, taste and touch – collectively or individually – to describe the Christian's relationship with and experience of God. In order to participate in this sensory life, Augustine suggests that in addition to the bodily senses the human being possesses the spiritual senses, capable of perceiving God and God's activity in the world. Both sets of senses are an integral part of an embodied human existence in this life and the next.

Since the publication of Karl Rahner's influential essay on Origen and the spiritual senses in 1932, a limited but important body of scholarship has sought to explore Augustine's treatment of the spiritual senses.[1] Many of these studies have concentrated on spiritual vision (an emphasis reflected in the Augustinian corpus), have been restricted to specific texts or have appeared in larger discussions of Augustine's epistemology and mysticism.[2] Despite these studies, no exhaustive examination of spiritual sensation has yet appeared.[3] Space limitations rule out the possibility of producing such a study here, but this chapter will provide a survey of Augustine's

I would like to thank Profs. Boyd Taylor Coolman, Brian Daley and Paul Gavrilyuk for their feedback on earlier versions of this chapter.

[1] Karl Rahner, 'Le début d'une doctrine des cinq sens spirituels chez Origène'. For a general overview of the idea in the Christian tradition, see Mariette Canévet, 'Sens spirituel', *DS*, vol. xiv (1990), pp. 598–617.

[2] See the works of E. Vance, M. Sastri, J. Pépin, C. Harrison, D. Chidester, M. Miles and P. L. Landsberg in the Bibliography. Bernard McGinn's chapter on Augustine in *The Foundations of Mysticism*, vol. i of *The Presence of God: A History of Western Christian Mysticism* (New York: Crossroad, 1991), pp. 228–62, offers a helpful survey of many of the related themes discussed in this chapter.

[3] Augustine's sources for his understanding of spiritual sensation also need further exploration. Rahner tentatively suggests Origen as Augustine's source ('Le début d'une doctrine des cinq sens spirituels chez Origène', p. 144, n. 238), though Pépin notes that Rufinus's translations of Origen were made too late to account for Augustine's early treatment of the topic especially in the *Conf.* ('Augustin et Origène', p. 23). Martin Sastri, 'The Influence of Plotinian Metaphysics', has convincingly argued

understanding of the spiritual senses by first discussing their corporeal counterpart before proceeding to follow the spiritual senses in three thematic areas: the goal of human perceptual life in the beatific vision, the current dysfunction of these senses due to sin and finally their conversion and restoration by grace. By exploring this topic in such a way, this chapter will show that, according to Augustine, the spiritual senses allow embodied humans to know God and God's immaterial and ineffable presence in the world in an immediate and intimate way.

In the *Retractationes* Augustine remarks that he had been carelessly ambiguous when discussing the senses in several of his early writings by failing to distinguish between *sensus mortalis corporis* and *sensus mentis*.[4] The distinction between the senses of the body and the senses of the mind (or, as will be seen, also the senses of the *cor*, *anima/animus* and *homo interior*) remains fundamental throughout his writings, and both perceptual capacities are frequently discussed. Among early Latin Christian authors, Augustine has perhaps the most developed physiological and psychological theory of corporeal sensation and draws on a variety of ancient philosophical and medical theories.[5] Although his discussion of the spiritual senses is less structured and detailed, it too receives sustained treatment throughout his writings. In order to help explain the operation and role of the spiritual senses in his thought, a brief discussion of corporeal sensation will first be offered.

CORPOREAL SENSATION

Augustine's account of corporeal sensation seeks to maintain the soul's activity in sensation. His discussions often focus on the eye and sight, and

for the Plotinian basis of this theory. While there are significant overlaps with Plotinian theory of cognition, perhaps the most immediate source is Ambrose, whom Augustine cites in support of the eyes of the heart as the locus of the *visio Dei* (see *Ep.* 147 and 148). On Ambrose's understanding of the spiritual senses, see, for example, *Hexaëmeron*, v. 24. 86 and *Explanatio Psalmorum XII*, 40. 39 and 48. 4. At *De Gn. litt.* x. 25. 41, Augustine also quotes Tertullian's *De anima*, 9. 8, in which Tertullian describes the process by which the soul, which he believed to be corporeal, receives its form by being moulded into the body. As such, the soul is described as a literal *homo interior* possessing all the parts of the outer human, including inner eyes and ears capable of perceiving God.

4 *Retractationes*, I. 1. 2, I. 3. 2, I. 4. 2.

5 Gerard O'Daly offers a good overview of both aspects of corporeal sensation in his *Augustine's Philosophy of Mind* (Berkeley: University of California Press, 1987), pp. 80–105. On Augustine's indebtedness to Stoicism, see Marcia L. Colish, *The Stoic Tradition from Antiquity to the Early Middle Ages*, 2 vols., 2nd corrected printing (Leiden: Brill, 1990), vol. II, pp. 169–77. Some of the more detailed passages in Augustine's works include *De musica*, VI. 5. 8–15; *De q. an.* XXIII. 41 – XXIX. 61; *De lib. arbit.* II. 3. 8 – 8. 24; *De Gn. litt.* VII. 13. 20 – 18. 24 and book XII; and *De trin.* XI.

he holds an extramission theory of vision.[6] Every act of vision comprises three things: the object seen (*ipsa res quam uidemus*), vision itself (*uisio*) and the will to hold the eye in contact with the object (*animi intentio*).[7] The *intentio* is an intentional activity of the soul that initiates sense perception and maintains the connection between eye and object.[8] The eye in turn emits a ray (*radius*) by which the eye can 'touch' the object and receive an image of the object.[9] Only by such a visual touching, Augustine suggests, can the eye (and thus the soul) perceive an object that is spatially distant. The production of this image in the eye is a transformation from *sensus* – a latent capacity for sensation which the healthy eye possesses even in the dark – to *sensus informatus*, an informing of the eye by the object.[10] Just as a solid object leaves its form in water only as long as the object remains on the surface, so too this bodily image produced in the eye remains only as long as the sense and object maintain their physical connection.[11] The mind is able to judge the image produced in the eye or store it in memory by the immediate production of a second, spiritual image. Through a similar process, the mind is able to visualize these stored images of sense objects in the imagination.[12] This spiritual image and its recollection in the imagination should not be confused with spiritual sensation. In this case, the spiritual image refers to any immaterial image perceived in the *spiritus* or *mens*, most often an image recollected from memory of a previously sensed object.

Several important aspects emerge from Augustine's understanding of corporeal sensation that shape his discussion of the spiritual senses. First, sensation is an intentional process; the soul is not merely a passive recipient of objects bombarding the sense organs in continual acts of sensation.[13]

---

[6] Of course, he also recognizes that passive reception also takes place in the body and the sense organs. Both aspects of sensation, extramission and intromission, are acknowledged in the early *De q. an.*, where he famously defines *sensus* as *passio corporis per seipsam non latens animam. De q. an.* xxv. 48 (CSEL 89. 193). In another early work, he discusses the role of sounds, odours and flavours in audition, olfaction and taste. *De musica*, vi. 5. 10–12.

[7] *De trin.* xi. 2. 2 (CCL 50. 334).

[8] This *intentio* is also called a *uoluntas animi* (*De trin.* xi. 2. 5 (CCL 50. 338)).

[9] On the *radius* and its function in the process of vision, see also *De trin.* ix. 3. 3; *Conf.* x. 6. 9; *Ep.* 147. 17. 41 (here *acies* is used); and *Serm.* 277. 10. *De q. an.* xxiii. 43 suggests that it is a material 'rod' (*virga*) sent forth from the eye to touch the object. It is the *intentio* that begins the physiological process of moving a rarified substance (*subtilius corpus*) from the brain to the sense organs, where it is then sent out to the object (*De Gn. litt.* iii. 5. 7 and vii. 13. 20 – 18. 24).

[10] *De trin.* xi. 2. 3 (CCL 50. 336).   [11] *De trin.* xi. 2. 3 (CCL 50. 336).

[12] On memory, see *Conf.* x. 8. 13–15 and *De trin.* xi. 3. 6. The distinction between the first 'bodily' image in the sense organ and the second 'spiritual' image is developed in *De Gn. litt.* xii. 6. 15 – 10. 21.

[13] This theory of active sensation was common in the ancient world. On the Stoic theory, see Colish, *The Stoic Tradition*, pp. 170–1, and for Plotinus, see Michael F. Wagner, 'Sense Experience and

While these objects do bring about a *sensus informatus*, Augustine consistently maintains that the soul itself remains the active agent by which all corporeal sensation originates and is able to take place. Second, the bodily senses serve as mediators between the external world and the soul, and function both as the 'doors' by which the soul activates the desire to sense and as the 'messengers' that the soul uses to learn about the physical world.[14] They carry out these functions by following a natural order and logic; each sense organ operates individually and has its own proper object, so that only the eye sees and the nose smells. Each must also remain healthy to be able to function properly. Finally, there are long-term effects of corporeal sensation even after the absence of the sense object by means of the spiritual images that are stored in the memory and sensed again in the act of imagination.

THE INNER SENSES AND THE MIND

It is by means of these bodily senses that the soul is able to come to knowledge about the physical world. However, as Augustine's famous prayer from the *Soliloquia* indicates, the main objects of his account of cognition are self and God: *Deus semper idem, noverim me, noverim te. Oratum est.*[15] Knowledge of the world (*scientia*) remains entirely secondary to wisdom (*sapientia*), a wisdom that cannot be found in the material world of mutability and change but only in God. The human journey to God is a *via interior* to the depths of the self and the image of God found there. Augustine identifies this inner self using a variety of terms including *anima/animus, cor, mens* and *homo interior*, and suggests that it is this inner self that alone is able to know God.[16] Like the *homo exterior* that uses the corporeal senses for knowing the material world, Augustine maintains, the *homo interior* is also equipped with a sense capacity that is able to perceive God and God's presence in the world. However, whereas his explicit

---

the Active Soul: Some Plotinian and Augustinian Themes', *The Journal of Neoplatonic Studies*, 1.2 (1993), 37–62, and Mary Ann Ida Gannon, 'The Active Theory of Sensation in St. Augustine', *The New Scholasticism*, 30 (1956), 154–80.

[14] *foris* (*De Gn. litt.* XII. 20. 42 (CSEL 28.1. 410)) and *nuntio* (XII. 24. 51 (CSEL 28.1. 416)).

[15] *Solil.* II. 1. 1 (CCSL 89. 45).

[16] Augustine's focus on interiority is well studied; see, for example, Charles Taylor, *Sources of the Self: The Making of the Modern Identity* (Cambridge, MA: Harvard University Press, 1989), pp. 127–42, and Phillip Cary, *Augustine's Invention of the Inner Self: The Legacy of a Christian Platonist* (New York: Oxford University Press, 2000). A historical overview of the concept of the *homo interior* in ancient and early Christian sources can be found in Christoph Markschies, 'Innerer Mensch', in Ernst Dassmann et al. (eds.), *Reallexikon für Antike und Christentum* (Stuttgart: Anton Hiersemann, 1998), vol. XVIII, pp. 266–312.

and detailed treatment of corporeal sensation remains relatively consistent
throughout his life, spiritual sensation is much harder to pin down and
lacks any systematic framework. At times, Augustine seems to use language
of inner sensation merely in a metaphorical way to describe any ordinary
act of understanding, whereas at other times he seems to posit a set of
discrete inner senses for spiritual sensation – and sometimes, it is simply
not clear what he means by such language. Adding further complexity
is Augustine's illumination theory, which, however understood or interpreted, also draws on the language of corporeal vision to describe acts of
human intellection.[17] These three broad modes of perceptual language –
metaphorical usage, spiritual sensation and divine illumination – are not
always easily distinguished in Augustine's writings.

Throughout Augustine's early writings the inner sensory life is dominated by language of vision (*oculus/oculi*, *aspectus* and *visio* are frequently
used), and knowing God or anything true in the world is described as a
visionary experience of the soul. The visual language in these texts has generally been interpreted as an early articulation of his illumination theory
and intellectual vision, but it is also at the same time suggestive of acts
of spiritual perception. In *Soliloquia*, 1. 6. 12 – 7. 13, a personified reason
suggests that God will be seen by the mind just as the sun is seen by
pure and healthy eyes. Reason is here understood as the *aspectus animae*,
or the desiring gaze of the soul or mind. When God is presented to the
gazing mind, a vision occurs that results in the conjunction of the soul
with God in an analogous way to the conjunction of eye and object in
corporeal vision.[18] The emphasis in this passage on the conjunction of the
soul and God in this act of divine illumination tends towards the intimacy and immediacy of spiritual sensation in later writings. In other early
works, it is the mind's eyes that are able to perceive order in the world
by overcoming the restricted view of the corporeal senses, which narrowly
focus on individual objects: 'If he raises the eyes of the mind (*mentis oculos*)
and broadens his field of vision and surveys all things as a whole, then he
will find nothing unarranged, unclassed, or unassigned to its own place.'[19]

---

[17] For a concise overview of the main interpretations of Augustine's illumination theory and relevant
    bibliography, see Ronald H. Nash, 'Illumination, Divine', in Allan D. Fitzgerald (ed.), *Augustine
    through the Ages: An Encyclopedia* (Grand Rapids, MI: Eerdmans, 1999), pp. 438–40.

[18] *Iam aspectum sequitur ipsa visio dei, qui est finis aspectus, non quod iam non sit, sed quod nihil amplius
    habeat, quo se intendat. Et haec est vere perfecta virtus, ratio perveniens ad finem suum, quam beata
    vita consequitur. Ipsa autem visio intellectus est ille, qui in anima est, qui conficitur ex intellegente et eo
    quod intellegitur, ut in oculis videre quod dicitur, ex ipso sensu constat atque sensibili, quorum detracto
    quolibet videri nihil potest* (*Solil.* 1. 6. 13 (CSEL 89. 21–2)). On reason as the *mentis aspectus* and
    knowledge as a form of vision in the early writings, see also *De q. an.* XIV. 24 and XXVII. 53.

[19] *De ordine*, II. 4. 11 (CCL 29. 113), trans. R. P. Russell, FC 5 (1948), p. 287.

Despite their capacity for such vision, these eyes need health and above all divine illumination for any vision to occur. If the soul's eyes remain in the shadows bereft of this light, the soul too easily mistakes creation for creator and remains in the darkness of ignorance.[20] Furthermore, this light of divine illumination is not only that which renders things intelligible but also becomes the object of vision itself:

This hidden sun pours into our innermost eyes (*interioribus luminibus nostris*) that beaming light. His is all the truth that we speak, even though, in our anxiety, we hesitate to turn with courage toward this light and to behold it in its entirety, because our eyes, recently opened, are not yet strong enough. This light appears to be nothing other than God.[21]

Throughout these early works, therefore, the human mind has a sensory capacity for perceiving God and truth but needs to preserve its health and is ultimately dependent on divine illumination.

In his later writings, Augustine develops his language of the inner senses in two principal directions: first, he expands the discussion to include all five senses, and second, he begins to articulate a perceptual model that can more properly be called spiritual sensation, that is, inner senses capable of directly perceiving God and God's presence in the world. Like Origen's and Ambrose's treatment of the spiritual senses, it is his encounter with biblical texts describing a sensory experience of God that provides Augustine with the occasion to articulate a more robust account of spiritual sensation.[22] As a result, it is primarily in his many sermons and exegetical writings that he develops his understanding of spiritual sensation. His language continues to be flexible and unsystematic, but the focus still remains on the interiority of these senses: *oculi interiores*,[23] *aures cordis*,[24] *olfactum cordis*,[25] *palatum cordis*[26] and *tactum interius*.[27] Similar to his earlier works, these exegetical writings also develop the language of intellectual vision and illumination.

---

[20] *De lib. arbit.* II. 16. 43 (CCL 29. 266–7).

[21] *De beata vita*, IV. 35 (CCL 29. 84), trans. L. Schopp, FC 5 (1948), p. 83.

[22] His homilies on the Psalms and John are especially rich with language of the spiritual senses. The *Jo. ev. tr.* were preached *c.* 406–22; the *En. Ps.* were given over a much longer span from *c.* 391 to 422 (McGinn, *Foundations*, p. 229).

[23] *En. Ps.* XXVI. 2. 15 (CCL 38. 162), and also *Serm.* 159. 4 (*oculi interiores*) and *Jo. ev. tr.* XVIII. 6 (*oculum cordis*). Occasionally Augustine also speaks of the *oculi fidei* (*En Ps.* CXXXIV. 24).

[24] *En. Ps.* XLI. 9 (CCL 38. 467), and also *Serm.* 159. 4 (*aures interiores*) and *Jo. ev. tr.* XVIII. 10 (*aures in corde*).

[25] *Serm.* 180. 7. 8 (PL 38. 976), and also *Serm.* 23B (= Dolbeau 6), 5 (*olfactum hominis interioris*); *Serm.* 159. 4 (*olfactum interius*); and *En. Ps.* CXXXIV. 24 (*nares*).

[26] *En. Ps.* XXX. S3. 6 (CCL 38. 217), and also *Serm.* 159. 4 (*gustatum interius*); *Serm.* 28. 2 (*fauces interioris hominis*); and *Serm.* 23B (= Dolbeau 6), 5 (*os hominis interioris*).

[27] *Serm.* 159. 4 (PL 38. 869). Cf. the *manus cordis* (*Conf.* X. 8. 12).

SPIRITUAL SENSATION

In addition to illustrations of intellectual vision, Augustine provides his congregation with practical examples of how spiritual sensation occurs in this life. In *Sermones*, 159, for example, he suggests that Christians now live as sojourners in exile from their homeland and must live by faith in this world until they come to the promised final vision (*speciem*), a theme frequently encountered throughout Augustine's discussion of the spiritual senses.[28] The return from this temporary exile is quickened by preferring justice to physical pleasures, but justice is perceptible only to the five interior senses (*sensus interiores*), by which one can see the light of justice, hear its voice and smell its odour.[29] In an illustration of how these spiritual senses operate, Augustine provides his congregation the example of two slaves, one who is beautiful but a liar, and one who is ugly but trustworthy. In choosing which to love more, one has recourse to two sets of eyes; the corporeal eyes are delighted by physical beauty, but the eyes of the heart delight in the beauty of the trustworthy slave.

You see, you have ignored the eyes in your head, and raised the eyes in your heart [*Contempsisti enim oculos carnis, et erexisti oculos cordis*]. You questioned the eyes in your head, and what information did they give you? This one's beautiful, that one's ugly. You rejected them, turned down their evidence [*testimonium*]; you raised the eyes in your heart to the faithful slave and the faithless slave; you found the first to have an ugly body, the other a beautiful one; but you gave judgement and said, 'What can be more beautiful than fidelity, what more misshapen than faithlessness?'[30]

Both sets of eyes are able to look at the two slaves, but only the eyes of the heart can perceive the qualities of justice and beauty. Here moral judgement is treated as a sense of the heart. By using the inner eyes and rejecting the suggestions of the corporeal senses, one is able to train the inner senses and proleptically experience the kind of sensory life that is promised in the future life.

The use of the spiritual senses is even more necessary when one seeks to know God, who by nature remains entirely beyond apprehension by the corporeal senses. The knowledge of the material world provided by

---

[28] *Serm.* 159. 1 (PL 38. 867–8). This sermon is a *locus classicus* for Augustine's account of spiritual sensation and is dated to 417. The theme of exile is common throughout his exegetical writings and his discussions of spiritual sensation.

[29] *Serm.* 159. 4 (PL 38. 869). Justice is a common object of the inner senses; it can be 'eaten' (*Jo. ev. tr.* XIII. 5) and is perceived only by the *interioris hominis sensum* (*Civ. Dei*, XI. 27 (CCL 48. 347)).

[30] *Serm.* 159. 3 (PL 38. 869); trans. Edmund Hill, *Sermons, WSA*, part III, vols. I–XI (1990–7), vol. V, p. 123. The same example is used at *De trin.* XIII. 6. 9.

the bodily senses can lead to the recognition of God's creative activity in the world, but such a recognition falls short of truly understanding God; rather, God is known in this life by the experience of charity. The greater the experience of charity, the more one realizes the limitations of words: 'Before you became so vividly aware of him you thought yourself qualified to speak about God; but now you begin to feel what he is, and you realize that what you perceive is something that cannot be spoken.'[31] Like knowing justice and beauty in the world, the soul's quest for God is mediated neither by the bodily senses nor through language but is accessible to the spiritual senses. In more direct experiences of God, Augustine develops in greater detail what he means by sensing God and makes God the object of all five of the spiritual senses of the *homo interior*. Unlike the objects of corporeal sensation, however, God is an entirely different kind of sensory object:

Neither is God bread nor is God water, nor is God this light, nor is God clothing, nor is God a house. For all these are visible things and are individual [*Omnia enim haec uisibilia sunt, et singula sunt*] . . . God is everything for you. If you are hungry, he is bread for you; if you are thirsty, he is water for you. If you are darkness, he is light for you because he remains incorruptible. If you are naked he is the clothing of immortality for you, when this corruptible body puts on incorruption and this mortal body puts on immortality.[32]

Unlike the fragmented experience of corporeal sensation, the experience of God is characterized by the unity of the senses as God becomes a polymorphous sensory object that fulfils everything that the soul needs and desires. At the same time, God suffers neither division, nor change nor diminishment, unlike physical food that is consumed and destroyed by tasting and eating it. Only such a rich sensory experience can truly satisfy the spiritual senses, and it is precisely such an experience that these senses desire.

VISIO BEATIFICA

Augustine thus suggests that humans have corporeal senses by which they can apprehend the physical world, as well as senses of the heart or the *homo interior* by which God, justice and beauty alone can be perceived. While

---

[31] *En. Ps.* XCIX. 6: *Ante enim quam sentires, dicere te putabas Deum: incipis sentire, et ibi sentis dici non posse quod sentis* (CCL 39: 1396), trans. Maria Boulding, *Expositions of the Psalms, WSA*, part III, vols. XV–XX (2000–4), vol. XIX, p. 18.

[32] *Jo. ev. tr.* XIII. 5 (CCL 36. 133), trans. J. W. Rettig, FC 79 (1988), p. 49. A similar description is found in *Conf.* X. 27. 38, which is discussed below. On the lack of diminishment and change in God when perceived by the spiritual senses, see also *Serm.* 28.

the tension between these is found throughout his writings, as Augustine considers the goal of human existence in the beatific vision, he offers the fullest discussion of the inadequacy of corporeal sensation and the necessity of this inner sensory life that extends to the resurrected spiritual body.[33] His views on the eschatological vision are first detailed in response to a group of Italians who claimed that the bodily eyes would be able to see God in the resurrection. In customary fashion, Augustine dispatched letters stating his opinion on the matter and attempted to gain further information about his opponents; he continued to reflect on the matter throughout the remainder of his life.[34]

All of the letters develop a similar argument that draws upon the logic of corporeal vision: since the bodily eyes function by establishing rays between organ and object, the bodily eyes by nature can perceive only things that exist in space. God is wholly incorporeal, and therefore cannot be seen by corporeal eyes. Any claim that these eyes can see God would jeopardize this attribute of God, and Augustine vigorously argues that God will not be seen by the bodily eyes even of the spiritual body.[35] If the spiritual body were able to see God, its nature would have to change to such a degree that it would entirely cease to be like the current body.[36] The issue becomes further complicated by a mixed biblical record on the vision of God, and much of this correspondence attempts to reconcile these conflicting scriptural authorities by distinguishing between corporeal and spiritual sensation in an effort to preserve both God's immateriality and the truth of the biblical statements.[37] In *Epistolae*, 147 and 148 he turns to earlier authorities, especially Ambrose, to argue that the vision of God

[33] Augustine's view of the spiritual body is based on Paul's discussion in 1 Cor 15: 35–58.

[34] On this group see *Ep.* 92. 4 and 92A (these are the two initial letters, which were both written prior to 408). *Ep.* 147, 148 and 162 (written between 413 and 415) cover the same topic, though they do not seem to be directly occasioned by the controversy. Other major discussions are found in *Civ. Dei*, XXII. 29, *De trin.* XIV. 16. 22 – 19. 26, *Serm.* 277 and *De Gn. litt.* XII. 35. 68 – 36. 69. *Ep.* 147 (a 'letter treatise' also called *De videndo Deo*) is the longest and most detailed explication of the eschatological vision. For a discussion of the letters, see Erich Naab, *Augustinus: Über Schau und Gegenwart des unsichtbaren Gottes* (Stuttgart and Bad Cannstaat: Frommann-Holzboog, 1998), pp. 1–62.

[35] God's immateriality and omnipresence are, of course, fundamental to his conversion (*Conf.* VII. 1. 1 – 1. 2), and he remains preoccupied with safeguarding these attributes throughout his career.

[36] For this argument, see *Ep.* 148. 1. 3. In *Civ. Dei*, XXII. 29, however, Augustine suggests that 'it is entirely possible and likely' (*potest ualdeque credibile*; CCL 48. 861) that the eyes of the spiritual body will be able to see God. He is clearly speculating on these matters and offers no firm conclusions; he seems willing to hold open this possibility so long as one does not think that God will be seen as a body.

[37] Exod 33: 20, Jn 1: 18 and 1 Tim 6: 16 suggest that vision of God is impossible, while 1 Jn 3: 2 and Mt 5: 8 suggest the opposite.

promised in the Bible, as Matthew 5: 8 states, occurs only in the pure heart (*mundum cor*).[38]

In discussing how the vision of the pure heart will take place, Augustine argues that the eschatological vision will not be like those of the prophets because the prophetic visions occurred by means of bodily eyes. In these visions, God appeared 'as he willed to be seen' (*sicut uult uideri*) in bodily form and accessible to the bodily eyes, but the final vision will be a vision 'as he is' (*sicuti est*).[39] The precise mode of this vision will be that of the incorporeal angels, who see God directly without bodily eyes: 'Hence, when the Only-Begotten, who is in the bosom of the Father, makes him known by an ineffable revelation, the pure and holy rational creature is filled with an ineffable vision of God, which we shall attain when we shall have been made equal to the angels.'[40] Like the angelic vision, the *visio beatifica* will be a perpetual vision. Drawing on the Pauline distinction of 1 Corinthians 13: 12, he stresses that this vision will be 'face to face' and characterized by utter intimacy, clarity and immediacy, as opposed to looking 'through a mirror in an enigma', which remains only an adumbration of the fullness of the future vision.[41]

Moving ever closer to the 'face to face' vision, one in turn draws closer to God and becomes more like God. As 1 John 3: 2 suggests, the very possibility of any vision of God is grounded in a likeness to God, a likeness that is not based in the body – as God is entirely without body – but in the soul and the *homo interior*. Throughout this life this likeness continues to grow, but only in the resurrection will it be complete enough to see God. By stressing the necessity of an ever-growing likeness to God and the process of the purification of the heart, Augustine rules out the participation of the devil and the wicked in this vision, while at the same time allowing for a limited vision in this life as the heart becomes increasingly cleansed.[42]

---

[38] In *Ep.* 147. 6. 18, Augustine quotes and then comments on a lengthy passage from Ambrose's commentary on Luke. On this citation see Basil Studer, *Zur Theophanie-Exegese Augustins: Untersuchung zu einem Ambrosius-Zitat in der Schrift De videndo Deo* (Rome: Herder, 1971).

[39] The distinction between vision *sicut uult* and *sicuti est* is fundamental to his entire argument; see *Ep.* 147. 15. 37 (CSEL 44. 310–12). The two exceptions are Moses and Paul, who saw God *sicuti est* (*Ep.* 147. 13. 31–2).

[40] *Ep.* 147. 9. 22; trans. Roland Teske, *Letters, WSA*, part II, vols. I–IV (2001–5), vol. II, pp. 330–1. On the angelic mode of this vision, see also *Ep.* 147. 15. 37 and *En. Ps.* XXXVI. S2. 8. Augustine suggests that, like humans, the angels also possess a sensory life that includes not only vision but also tasting and eating (see *Jo. ev. tr.* XIII. 5, where angels are described as eating God).

[41] *hoc autem utrumque interioris hominis munus est, siue cum in ista peregrinatione adhuc per fidem ambulatur, in qua utitur speculo et aenigmate, siue in illa patria, cum per speciem contemplabitur, pro qua uisione positum est 'facie ad faciem'* (*Ep.* 92. 4 (CSEL 34. 441)).

[42] *Ep.* 147. 11. 25.

SENSORY DYSFUNCTION AND EXILE

If it is the case that God cannot be perceived by everyone, and that it is only a pure heart that will experience the eschatological vision of God, this seems to imply a moral dimension which impinges on the proper functioning of the spiritual senses. Augustine holds that sin, like all other aspects of human life, has rendered human sensation disorganized and dysfunctional, and that as a result humanity remains in a state of sensory exile while waiting for the clarity of the 'face to face' vision. While the fullness of the perpetual vision of God will occur only in the eschaton, this present life is characterized by the activation, development and refinement of the spiritual eyes and other senses. As with Augustine's general account of spiritual sensation, the exact causes of this dysfunction and its effects on the use of the spiritual senses are portrayed in various ways, but the loss of the proper use of these senses is entirely unnatural and ultimately leads to discontent.

Humanity's sensory dysfunction extends to corporeal sensation as well, a situation that only exacerbates the difficulty of the proper use of the spiritual senses. Though humans share corporeal sensation with animals, humans are distinct not only by the presence of reason and mind but also by the organization of their bodies. Humans were created walking upright with their head directed upwards to look towards heaven and God; as such, the body is naturally configured to allow for the proper use of the bodily senses.[43] However, because of sin and the misuse of these senses, the head and the senses located there are now directed down to the ground. In a sermon on the parable of the great dinner (Lk 14: 15–24), Augustine interprets the man's excuse for missing the dinner on account of his five yoke of oxen as revealing a deep attachment to the bodily senses.[44] For those who have these senses yoked together like oxen and directed to the ground, the sum of their knowledge and experience is simply what they perceive in the material world; as a result, they are unable to participate in the delights of God's table.

This reconfiguration of the senses of the body results in their habitual misuse to such a degree that 'from the habit of living in the flesh, a crowd of phantasms surges into even those interior eyes in the likenesses of bodies'.[45] The images left in the memory from corporeal sensation spread unnoticed

[43] The bent-over body is a common metaphor for the misuse of the bodily senses; see *En. Ps.* XXVI. 2. 8, *Ep.* 147. 17. 42 and *Civ. Dei*, XXII. 24.
[44] *Serm.* 112. 3.
[45] *Ep.* 147. 17. 42 (CSEL 44. 316, trans. Teske, p. 341): *inruit enim de consuetudine carnalis uitae in ipsos quoque interiores oculos turba phantasmatum in similitudinibus corporum.*

into the inner senses and dominate them. As a result, these senses remain in a state of confusion and are unable to distinguish between material images and God. The strong force of habit renders this form of sensation into something all too familiar, and this familiarity causes the soul to forget about the very existence and use of the inner senses. Like the five husbands of the Samaritan woman, the soul is successively married to each of the five senses and is thus caught in an adulterous affair by forgetting about her true husband, the *mens* or *intellectus*.[46] Caught up in such a state, the soul is no longer the active agent in sensation but is compelled to sense by lust (*libido*).[47]

The inability to perceive God is in no way the result of God's absence, but remains fundamentally a problem of either the sensing agent or the sense itself. Just as blind men cannot blame their blindness on the lack of things to look at, so too those spiritually blind simply are unable to sense anything because they choose not to use the inner senses – a kind of self-imposed spiritual blindness – or because the disease of sin has deadened them. Not only have such people forgotten about the spiritual senses, but it is as though these senses no longer exist: 'How can I demonstrate this immense sweetness to you, who have lost your faculty of taste in the fever of sin (*qui palatum de febre iniquitatis perdidisti*)? ... You have no palate in your heart (*palatum cordis*) capable of tasting the good things I am telling you about.'[48] However, for those who still possess some use of their spiritual senses moments of the perception of God are possible in this life. In *Enarrationes in Psalmos*, 41, Augustine describes an everlasting eschatological party, the music of which can reach the ears of the heart even in the present life so long as the world does not drown it out. This momentary awareness quickly recedes as one slides back into the habits of ordinary sensation:

Our corruptible body weighs down the soul, and this earthly dwelling oppresses a mind that considers many things. At times we may in some measure scatter the clouds as our yearning draws us on, and even come within earshot of that melody (*ad hunc sonum peruenerimus interdum*), so that by pressing forward we may conceive something of the house of God. Yet under the weight of our weakness we fall back into familiar things, and slide down again into our ordinary way of life (*onere tamen quodam infirmitatis nostrae ad consueta recidimus, et ad solita ista dilabimur*).[49]

---

[46] *Jo. ev. tr.* xv. 19–22 (CCL 36. 157–9). See *De diversis quaestionibus* LXXXIII, 64. 7 for a similar interpretation of Jn 4: 16–18.

[47] *Contra Iulianum*, IV. 14. 65. In *De trin.* XI. 2. 6 (CCL 50. 339), it is *turpis cupiditas* that leads to the soul's attachment to these senses.

[48] *En. Ps.* xxx. S3. 6 (CCL 38. 217), trans. Boulding, vol. xv, p. 351.

[49] *En. Ps.* XLI. 10 (CCL 38. 467), trans. Boulding, vol. xvi, p. 248.

A CONVERSION OF THE SENSES

This momentary glimpse of the eschatological sensory life echoes Augustine's well-known accounts of the visions at Milan and Ostia in the *Confessions*. All three of these instances focus on the sensory aspects of the experience as well as on their brevity, owing to human weakness and frailty pulling the soul back to ordinary ways of perceiving.[50] While these visions remain among the most famous sections of the *Confessions*, language of the spiritual senses is encountered already in one of the prayers that open the book: 'Speak to me so that I may hear. See the ears of my heart (*aures cordis*) are before you, Lord. Open them and "say to my soul, I am your salvation."'[51] The soul's quest for God is again described as a desire of the inner senses. These inner ears are not satisfied by hearing the words of the Psalmist proclaimed by a human mouth, but only when God speaks these words is the heart's desire fulfilled.

In the tenth book of the *Confessions* the five senses are used collectively to describe Augustine's conversion and experience of divine grace.[52] He begins this book, which offers a discussion of memory, by contrasting the confidence with which he knows his love of God and the difficulty of understanding his own memory. The assurance that he loves God is based in a 'certain awareness' (*certa conscientia*) when loving God;[53] this is neither an abstract or general feeling nor is it rooted in the material world, but it is a kind of concrete, immediate and personal sensory experience of the *homo interior*:

Yet there is a light I love, and a food, and a kind of embrace when I love my God – a light, voice, odour, food, embrace of my inner man, where my soul is floodlit by light which space cannot contain, where there is sound that time cannot seize, where there is a perfume which no breeze disperses, where there is a taste for food no amount of eating can lessen, and where there is a bond of union that no satiety can part (*et ubi haeret, quod non diuellit satietas*). That is what I love when I love my God.[54]

---

[50] *Conf.* VII. 10. 16 – 17. 23 (the Milan vision) and IX. 10. 23–6 (the Ostia vision). Like *En. Ps.* XLI. 10, the vision at Milan ends with a return to the ordinary (*repercussa infirmitate redditus solitis* (*Conf.* VII. 17. 23; CCL 27: 107)). McGinn notes that especially in the 'vision' at Ostia, the focus is more on hearing and touching than on seeing (McGinn, *Foundations*, pp. 234–5).

[51] *Conf.* I. 5. 5 (CCL 27. 3), trans. H. Chadwick, *Saint Augustine: Confessions* (Oxford University Press, 1991), p. 5, which cites Ps 35 [34]: 3.

[52] The focus on visual and aural language has been noted by David Chidester, who suggests that the narrative of the *Conf.* is structured 'between the exclusively verbal orientation of rhetoric and the exclusively visual orientation of Manicheism that both dominated Augustine's life before his conversion'. *Word and Light*, p. 76.

[53] *Conf.* X. 6. 8 (CCL 27. 158).

[54] *Conf.* X. 6. 8 (CCL 27. 159), trans. Chadwick, p. 183. See also *Jo. ev. tr.* XIII. 5, discussed above.

Here again God becomes the object of all of the spiritual senses while never diminishing and always remaining whole, stable and immediately available to the *homo interior*. Such an experience is exactly the opposite of Augustine's pre-conversion life, in which he was frantically running around infatuated and enslaved to the bodily senses and pleasures they aroused in him.[55] Because he failed to take the *via interior*, his spiritual senses became enervated. Memory and the lingering images of corporeal sensations stored there continued their pernicious effects even after the sense objects left.

As a result, his conversion is retold in this book as the move from the outer, fragmented perception of the world to an inner, stable perception of God. In moving inwards, the bodily senses are not rejected but placed under the subordinating control of reason and judgement, so that created things are no longer confused with their creator.[56] This return inwards to the senses of the *homo interior* offers a new perceptual model that reveals and proclaims God as creator of all and offers the fullness of perceptual experience. It is only God, however, who can ultimately bring about this new sensory life, as Augustine makes clear in the dramatic retelling of his conversion:

You called and cried out loud and shattered my deafness. You were radiant and resplendent, you put to flight my blindness. You were fragrant, and I drew in my breath and now pant after you. I tasted you, and I feel but hunger and thirst for you. You touched me, and I am set on fire to attain the peace which is yours.[57]

The moment of conversion and the advent of grace is a kind of sensory overload that heals the dysfunction of the inner senses and redirects sensory desire completely to God. The newness of his Christian life is described as the awakening to the inner sensory life of the *homo interior*, a life characterized by directing the desire, will and *intentio* not to the bodily senses or their vestigial images in memory but to the use of the spiritual senses that have their proper object solely in God. Language suggestive of the role of human effort must therefore be tempered by Augustine's insistence on the need for grace in the conversion of the spiritual senses and their proper functioning.[58]

[55] Augustine details his disordered attachment to each of the five senses in *Conf.* x. 30. 41 – 34. 53 by reversing the Aristotelian order of the senses: sight, sound, smell, taste and touch. On the classical background and Augustine's use of this ordering in structuring this section of the *Conf.*, see James O'Donnell, *Augustine: Confessions*, 3 vols. (Oxford: Clarendon Press, 1992), vol. iii, pp. 167–8.
[56] *Conf.* x. 6. 10.
[57] *Conf.* x. 27. 38 (CCL 27. 175), trans. Chadwick, p. 201.
[58] Often, human effort and divine grace seem to cooperate in Augustine's treatment of the spiritual senses (e.g., 'Purify your heart so that he may himself enlighten you, and he whom you invoke

CONCLUSION

Our treatment of the spiritual senses has come full circle. The human being, endowed with both corporeal and spiritual senses, finds true happiness and fulfilment in the use of the spiritual senses completely directed to God, something that will fully occur only in the resurrection. In the present life these senses can be activated and used to varying degrees – especially for discerning justice, beauty and truth – but it is only the grace and activity of God that can adequately heal these senses and overcome their dysfunction due to sin. Although Augustine consistently emphasizes spiritual perception over corporeal – as does any thinker so indebted to the Platonic tradition – the bodily senses are neither rejected nor valorized. Instead, the focus remains on the resurrected life, which will continue to involve both modes of perception. As such, all human perception in this life – whether bodily or spiritual – is a dim reflection of this future life. Bodily and spiritual perception in the resurrected body will no longer offer a fragmented and limited experience but one of immediacy, clarity and fulfilment, in which 'God will be known to us and visible to us in the sense that he will be spiritually perceived (*Deus nobis erit notus atque conspicuus, ut uideatur spiritu*) by each one of us in each one of us, perceived in one another, perceived by each in himself.'[59] Spiritual sensation in Augustine's thought – albeit allusively and unsystematically presented – thus develops out of a cluster of interrelated ideas and issues. It is articulated in its most mature fashion only in later works, written after he had turned to careful reading and studying of the biblical texts, but throughout his corpus many of the basic themes are present. Above all, his treatment of the spiritual senses seeks to preserve God's immateriality, while at the same time guaranteeing that the perceptual life remains an essential aspect of human existence both in this life and the next.

may enter it' (*En. Ps.* 30. S3. 8, CCL 38. 218, trans. Boulding, vol. xv, p. 353)); however, Augustine consistently maintains the necessity of grace, illumination or healing. On the general need of grace in spiritual sensation, see *En. Ps.* xxvi. 2. 17 and 99. 6, and on God as the physician of the inner senses, see *En. Ps.* xxxvi. S2. 8. The combination of human effort and divine grace in spiritual vision has also been noted by Margaret Miles, 'Vision: The Eye of the Body and the Eye of the Mind in St. Augustine's *De trinitate* and *Confessions*', *The Journal of Religion*, 63 (1983), pp. 138–9.
[59] *Civ. Dei*, xxii. 29 (CCL 48. 861–2), trans. Henry Bettenson (London: Penguin, 1972), p. 1087.

CHAPTER 4

Gregory the Great

George E. Demacopoulos

When attempting to extract a precise theological position from Gregory the Great, bishop of Rome from 590 to 604, one is often confounded by his lack of systematic categories and his frequent variations in terminology.[1] It is not surprising, therefore, that Gregory never articulated a comprehensive epistemological method nor did he conceptualize the spiritual senses in a philosophical fashion. This is not to say, however, that he lacked a cognitive theory or that he did not employ various applications of the spiritual senses. Indeed, a careful reading of the pontiff's corpus demonstrates that a theory of spiritual perception provides the foundation for his more explicit ascetic and pastoral theologies. By foregrounding the ascetic and pastoral dimensions of Gregory's thought, therefore, we can glimpse the principal elements of Gregory's understanding of spiritual perception – that the spiritual senses were diminished by the fall, that their recovery is, in large part, a consequence of ascetic progress and that God grants the greatest spiritual insights to those who are willing and able to share what they learn with others.

The following chapter is in two parts. The first part attempts to weave together Gregory's fragmented statements about true knowledge, concluding that a limited knowledge of God can be ascertained (primarily through the scriptures), so long as the aspirant is in good moral standing and is willing to share his or her insights with others. The second part argues that Gregory's application of the collective spiritual senses and his frequent use

---

In addition to the other contributors to this volume, and especially its co-editor, Paul Gavrilyuk, I would like to thank Perry Hamalis and Aristotle Papanikolaou, who offered many helpful comments on an earlier draft of this chapter.

[1] One need look no further than to his influential treatise on the priesthood, *Liber regulae pastoralis*, wherein Gregory displays a remarkable unwillingness to offer a consistent name or title to the subject under investigation: the person in charge of a religious community is intermittently identified as *sacerdos, rector, praedicator* and *pastor* (interestingly, he is never identified as *episcopus*). See G. E. Demacopoulos, 'Introduction', in *St Gregory the Great: Book of Pastoral Rule*, ed. and trans. G. E. Demacopoulos (Crestwood, NY: St Vladimir's Seminary Press, 2007), p. 14.

of expressions connoting individual senses, such as the 'eyes of the mind', were almost exclusively employed in a figurative manner to explain the cognition of spiritual concepts within the mind or soul. By exploring these two elements distinctly, we gain a better understanding of the extent to which Gregory's more explicit theological concerns were supported by a multifaceted theory of spiritual perception.

KNOWLEDGE OF GOD

Although Gregory never offered a comprehensive epistemology, we might characterize his cognitive theory as comprising six general principles that were common among patristic authors: (1) true knowledge is knowledge of God; (2) in the post-lapsarian condition, knowledge of God is limited but not entirely remote; (3) what can be known about God derives primarily from a study of the scriptures; (4) a correct understanding of the scriptures depends upon ascetic purity and an active mental reflection upon the text; (5) both the method and practice are, at least in part, contingent upon grace; and, finally, (6) Christians acquire a fuller understanding of God and truth only after they have submitted themselves to a spiritual guide who has the ability both to open the scriptures for them and to oversee the cultivation of their spiritual purity.[2]

Like most Christian authors of late antiquity, Gregory believed that true knowledge was knowledge of God but that the possibility for humans to know God during this lifetime had been limited by Adam's fall.[3] Although Gregory was familiar with Augustine's views on the post-lapsarian human condition, he did not fully share his predecessor's pessimism and, as a consequence, was more inclined to believe that some knowledge of God could be ascertained in this world through a combination of human initiative and divine grace.[4] Indeed, although Gregory argued that God's teachings remained shrouded in mystery[5] and that God himself 'lamented' the fact

---

[2] See C. Beeley, *Gregory of Nazianzus on the Trinity and the Knowledge of God: In Your Light We shall See Light* (New York: Oxford University Press, 2008).

[3] In the *Moralia*, Gregory argued that at the moment of death the body–soul dichotomy reaches a more complete or appropriate balance, wherein the soul (*animus*) is awakened and sees with its eyes with a 'true recognition' (*vera cognitione*) all of those things that it refused to see during life. Gregory, *Mor.* XVIII. 18. 29.

[4] For a summary of Gregory's anthropological perspective in the post-lapsarian world, see G. E. Demacopoulos, 'The Soteriology of Pope Gregory I: A Case against the Augustinian Interpretation', *American Benedictine Review*, 54 (2003), 312–27.

[5] Gregory, *Hom. Ez.* I. 8. 17. Even the prophets and apostles did not understand all of God's mysteries or even the full meaning of the scriptures.

that he was not known,[6] God's obscurity also provided an opportunity for Christians to pursue the divine by exerting their senses to the point of fatigue.[7]

According to Gregory, the most direct way for a Christian to ascertain knowledge of God is through a study of the sacred scriptures. The scriptures contain 'divine speech' (*eloquiorum Dei*)[8] and provide 'food and drink' for the soul.[9] Not only are they the foundation of Christian beliefs, but they serve as the inspiration for a life in Christ.[10] Although some of the truths contained in the scriptures are beyond human comprehension,[11] all Christians who strive for knowledge of God are able to gain something from the Bible. For Gregory, Christians who achieve exceptional degrees of ascetic progress and/or humility are more equipped than others to discern the 'mysteries' of the sacred texts. Establishing these points in his commentary on the prophet Ezekiel, Gregory noted: 'many things were written simplistically so that the youthful might be nourished, whereas other things surely were concealed in obscure notions (*obscurioribus sententiis*) that occupy [the minds of] the strong because things that are comprehended after great effort are the more gratifying'.[12]

According to Gregory, the more difficult passages of scripture require the interpretive lens of allegory but, for the spiritually advanced, they contain discernible divine truths. Earlier in the same commentary, Gregory had argued that the reason why 'holy preachers' (one of his more frequent phrases for qualified spiritual leaders) were able to comprehend the scriptures more effectively than others was that they were able to discern when a passage should be interpreted 'historically' versus when a passage should be read as a 'spiritual allegory' (*spiritalem allegoriam*).[13] Sometimes, he argues, the scriptures require a historical reading; sometimes only an allegorical reading is appropriate; occasionally, both will prove fruitful. Through the

---

[6] *PR* I. I.

[7] *Magnae vero utilitatis est ipsa obscuritas eloquiorum Dei, quia exercet sensum ut fatigatione dilatetur.* Gregory, *Hom. Ez.* I. 6. I.

[8] *Hom. Ez.* I. 6. I.

[9] *Hom. Ez.* I. 10. 1–3. The drink symbolizes that which is the easiest for humans to understand; food is a metaphor for that which is the more obscure.

[10] In his *PR* II. II, Gregory argued that a pastor must continuously return to the scriptures in private meditation whenever he feels that his secular responsibilities have diluted his focus. Only this can protect him and re-invigorate him for his work in the secular world.

[11] In *Hom. Ez.* I. 8. 33, Gregory argues that the scriptures are 'veiled in mysteries' (*obvolutum mysteriis*). In *Hom. Ez.* II. 5. 3, he notes that although 'the whole of scripture was indeed written for us', it cannot be fully 'understood (*intelligitur*) by us'.

[12] *Hom. Ez.* II. 5. 4. Gregory seems to share Origen's position, which introduced three levels of interpretation (for beginners, intermediates and experts) in his *De principiis*, IV. II.

[13] *Hom. Ez.* I. 3. 4.

scriptures, the holy preacher who possesses the proper hermeneutical discernment is able to gain true knowledge of God.[14]

Despite his promotion of a balanced reading, Gregory's biblical commentaries are primarily a display of various allegorical and moral interpretations of the biblical narrative.[15] The pontiff repeatedly speaks of the
'hidden' message of scripture that can only be ascertained through an
allegorical or spiritual reading.[16] More often than not, these interpretive
readings originate from a metaphorical play on the biblical text. When,
for example, the text of Ezekiel mentions simply that 'the sole of their foot
was like the foot of a calf' (Ezek 1: 7), Gregory interprets the foot of a calf,
which is, of course, cloven, as a metaphor for the split nature of a spiritual
director who must discern when to speak boldly and when to speak with
subtlety.[17]

Here we see a fluidity in Gregory's language. Not only is discernment
(*discretio*) the cognitive act by which a spiritual leader chooses his words
when speaking in public, as it is in this particular case, but it is described
in other settings as a mystical insight that God provides to a pastor who
counsels a penitent.[18] It is also the term that Gregory frequently associates
with the proper interpretation of scripture. In each of these forms, however, the acquisition of *discretio* remains elusive. Following the lead of John
Cassian and other ascetic authors, Gregory held that *discretio* was bestowed
by God primarily upon those spiritual leaders who had successfully combined ascetic experience with humility.[19] In other words, Gregory viewed
ascetic achievement as a precondition for the grace that made both exegetical and pastoral discernment possible, because the two were intimately
linked. A *pastor* could not offer sound spiritual advice if he did not understand the scriptures, and he could not understand the scriptures if he had
not purged himself of worldly attachments. Discernment, however, was
a gift of grace and could not be merited. Thus, only those ascetics who

---

[14] *Hom. Ez.* 1. 12. 20–1.
[15] For a concise statement of his threefold interpretative method, see the introduction to his volumi-
nous commentary on the book of Job (*Mor.* Pref.), wherein he argues that the scriptures contain
a historical, allegorical and moral sense. This threefold interpretive method became the defining
approach to scriptural exegesis in the medieval West.
[16] For example, *Hom. Ez.* 1. 9. 30.
[17] *Hom. Ez.* 1. 3. 4. As we will see in the next section, Gregory's penchant for allegory carries through
to his appropriation and application of the various spiritual senses. In other words, whereas the
spiritual senses may have served Origen and others in additional interpretative ways, for Gregory,
the spiritual senses remained primarily an exercise in allegorical reading.
[18] *PR* II. 9–10.
[19] See G. E. Demacopoulos, *Five Models of Spiritual Direction in the Early Church* (University of Notre
Dame Press, 2007), pp. 112–13 and 131–7.

retained humility were worthy of the gift of discernment and the spiritual benefits that it entailed.[20]

For Gregory, the connection between *discretio* and spiritual perception lies in the belief that this insight is a basic requirement for the accurate interpretation of scripture, which is, in turn, the primary conduit for knowledge of God. Making this precise point in his homilies on Ezekiel, Gregory argues that *discretio* is vital to acquiring knowledge from scripture because it guarantees a proper interpretation; if left to our own interpretive abilities, we will believe that we are reading scripture spiritually when, in fact, we are being deceived by our carnal impulses, which lead to a false reading.[21] Elsewhere, Gregory warns that a carnal life prevents, even blinds, the reader of scripture from accessing its divine truths.[22]

Gregory does occasionally describe additional media, often in combination with the reading of scripture, which provide knowledge of the divine. For example, in the first of his homilies on the prophet Ezekiel, the pontiff suggests that the singing of religious hymns can prompt God to grant the gift of grace, which enflames the heart.[23] Later, in the same passage, he adds that worship, the 'sacrifice of praise' (*in sacrificio igitur laudis*), leads to the gift of revelation.[24] At the beginning of another homily on Ezekiel, he expresses confidence that God will grant him the ability to interpret the prophetic book correctly because the prayers of his disciples will enlist the action of the Holy Spirit.[25] Not surprisingly, Gregory also frequently describes both grace and virtue as prerequisites for the acquisition of knowledge.[26]

Perhaps the greatest challenge in explaining Gregory's cognitive theory lies in understanding his view of the role of the human mental faculties in the acquisition of knowledge. Not only does his corpus lack an extended

---

[20] *Ibid.* See also Gregory, *Hom. Ez.* II. 5. 19, wherein he argues that we should not presuppose that we possess this 'gift' of discernment because of our own virtue, but that it is a gift of God.

[21] *Hom. Ez.* I. 5. 3.

[22] See, for example, his allegorical interpretation of Lev 21, which removed the 'bleary-eyed' from ancient Jewish priesthood. Gregory understands the bleary-eyed to symbolize those who 'naturally spring toward knowledge of the truth (*ingenium ad cognitionem veritatis emicat*)' but whose carnal deeds obscure that truth. *PR* I. 11.

[23] *Hom. Ez.* I. 1. 15. 'When we sing to him, we make it possible for him to come to our hearts and enflame us with the grace of his love' (*Cui dum cantamus, iter facimus, ut ad nostrum cor veniat, et sui nos amoris gratia accendat*).

[24] *Hom. Ez.* I. 1. 15.

[25] *Hom. Ez.* II. 2. 1. This communal dimension of Gregory's cognitive theory shows a great distance between the pontiff and the individualistic epistemologies that dominate many subsequent Western philosophers.

[26] For example, in *Hom. Ez.* I. 5. 1, Gregory argues that grace 'allows us to penetrate the secrets' (*libet ejus intima, gratia duce, penetrare*) of scripture. See also *Hom. Ez.* I. 9. 4, I. 10. 4 and II. 5. 8.

discussion of the matter, but those excerpts that do exist rarely examine the mind's or the soul's capabilities in isolation from the knowledge ascertained from scripture or through divine fiat. To be sure, Gregory offers numerous positive statements about the ability, even the necessity, of the mind's activity in the acquisition of knowledge. For example, he argues in his commentary on the prophet Job that humanity's greatest attribute is its rational soul (*anima rationalis*), which allows holy men and women, like Job, to resist evil by the power of their reasoning faculties.[27] Later in the same text, he argues that we are able to employ the mind to comprehend spiritual things that we are unable to apprehend through our physical senses, especially our sight.[28] Similarly, in his commentary on Ezekiel, Gregory describes the saints as being able to ponder the ineffable wisdom of God, without the clamour of words (*sine strepitu verborum*).[29]

Such affirmations of our mental capacity, however, are rarely isolated in Gregory's corpus from a discussion of the knowledge that is mediated through scripture. Moreover, by describing cognition as something contingent upon both humility and grace, Gregory's characterization of the mind's acquisition of knowledge simply mirrors his treatment of discernment, which is, in itself, a kind of discussion about mental activity. For example, in his *Book of Pastoral Rule*, the pontiff argues that one either knows or does not know who he is through humility. The person who lacks humility will 'forget' who he is; the person who possesses humility will learn through no other effort who he is.[30] Although Gregory does not say so directly, he seems to suggest that true knowledge of self is the reward for (or, at the very least, the consequence of) the acquisition of humility. Always looking to strike a balance between human initiative and grace, however, he argues later in the same work that 'God perfects, to a great extent, the mind of spiritual directors' so that they may achieve their pastoral responsibilities among the laity.[31] A statement near the end of the *Moralia* echoes this balance by asserting that the mind, left to its own devices in a fallen world, slumbers and grows cold, unless it is revived by the 'breath of divine grace' (*divinae gratiae aspiratione*), which restores internal thoughts to a spiritual sensibility (*ad spiritalia sensificetur*), thus making possible knowledge of divine things.[32]

Underpinning these statements is Gregory's conviction that the acquisition of knowledge, whatever the source, is to some extent preconditioned

---

[27] *Mor.* XIV. 15. 17. Of course, for the soul to operate successfully in this regard, it must be fed by 'interior food' (*interni cibi*).

[28] *Mor.* XXIII. 19. 35.   [29] *Hom. Ez.* I. 8. 17.   [30] *PR* I. 3.

[31] *PR* IV. 1.   [32] *Mor.* XVII. 16. 32.

by an ascetic life that is both active (including physical ascetic acts) and contemplative (including the adoption of an ascetic theology, which would include an asceticizing hermeneutic).[33] Once that knowledge is obtained, a similar active–contemplative balance conditions the retention and dissemination of knowledge. In other words, what is attained through contemplation or through a study of scriptures is not pursued for its own sake, nor is it to be kept to one's self. Rather, Gregory believes that the spiritual director receives knowledge of God for the benefit of others. Properly balancing the two (i.e. self and neighbour) allows the spiritual direction to fulfil the commandment to love both God (contemplative) and neighbour (active).[34]

Drawing upon the classical tradition, which understood philosophy to be a way of life (not just an exercise in mental abstraction), many influential authors within the early Christian community understood Christianity to demand orthodox thought and action.[35] Origen, for example, believed that a sinful life prevented the proper reception of divine knowledge, literally blocking, or obscuring, mental receptors from acquiring spiritual truth. Conversely, he held that one could prepare the soul for spiritual knowledge through ascetic virtue.[36] Gregory Nazianzen, a more direct source for Pope Gregory's thought, also consistently described the precondition of ascetic accomplishment to the acquisition of divine knowledge.[37] It was for this reason that Pope Gregory so strongly argued that the clergy needed to be drawn from the ranks of experienced ascetics and that the Christian community should turn to these ascetic priests for knowledge of the spiritual life.[38]

For Gregory, the experienced ascetic who embraces pastoral responsibility (whether in a monastic setting or within the institutional church) is the one who is the most likely to possess true knowledge of God. Not only is this a consequence of the elder's own enlightenment, but it is part of God's grand design to disseminate spiritual knowledge through the teacher–disciple relationship – the very premise of Gregory's *Book of Pastoral Rule*. Indeed, for Gregory, the spiritual director is the mediator between God

---

[33] *Hom. Ez.* ii. 6. 2–4.   [34] Cf. 1 Jn 4: 8, 20–1.

[35] Aristotle, for example, argues in the *Politics*, 7. 3 that virtue in itself is not enough, and that the philosopher must transform his insights into action. See, of course, the collective works of P. Hadot, but esp. his *Philosophy as a Way of Life*, ed. A. Davidson, trans. M. Chase (Oxford: Blackwell, 1995).

[36] See K. Rahner's ground-breaking essay 'Le début d'une doctrine des cinq sens spirituels chez Origène'.

[37] See G. E. Demacopoulos, 'Leadership in the Post-Constantinian Church According to St. Gregory Nazianzen', *Louvain Studies*, 30 (2005), 223–39.

[38] See Demacopoulos, *Five Models*, pp. 131–9.

and the Christian community.[39] In the commentary on Ezekiel, Gregory notes, 'the word of the preacher is the seed in the heart of the hearer'.[40] This is because 'the obscurity of the Holy Scriptures is revealed openly to preachers'[41] and because they are able to impart knowledge of 'that light which cannot be put into words' (*illius luminis quod voce exprimi non potest*).[42] Echoing Hebrews 5: 12–13, Gregory notes that an enlightened director must have the discernment to know what he may share with his disciples and what must remain unsaid.[43] It is vital, however, that those who are blessed with spiritual insight suspend their own contemplation in order to share their knowledge with others.[44]

According to Gregory, the Holy Spirit grants the gift of eloquent speech to the enlightened preacher, so that he may share his knowledge of the divine with others.[45] Indeed, there is an important connection in Gregory's writings between divine speech (*divina vox*), which is recorded in the scriptures, and the pastor's responsibility to proclaim this truth through the public homily. The pastor does not simply repeat the words of scripture for his flock, but rather, enlightened by the grace of his position and through the gift of discernment, the pastor interprets the words of scripture in such a way as to provide in a single exhortation a multitude of messages that can be received by a community with distinctive spiritual needs.[46] In short, it is through the cleric's public interpretation of scripture that much of the Christian community obtains its knowledge of the divine. And so the communal dimension of Gregory's cognitive theory is shown to have come full circle. Not only is the pastor's knowledge of God increased by the prayers of his disciples, but he is able to disseminate what he learns to his community through the grace of the Holy Spirit in the form of the public homily.

THE SPIRITUAL SENSES

In one of his later homilies in the commentary on the prophet Ezekiel, the pontiff describes a three-stage process by which a Christian can prepare his or her soul to contemplate God.[47] The first stage, he argues, is to compose

---

[39] *Hom. Ez.* I. 3. 5; *PR* I. 5.   [40] *Hom. Ez.* I. 3. 6.   [41] *Hom. Ez.* I. 9. 29.
[42] *Hom. Ez.* II. 6. I.   [43] *Hom. Ez.* I. 3. 5; *PR* II. 4; III. I.
[44] Gregory argues that God is more willing to impart knowledge to those who are willing and able to pass it on than to those who have obtained the state of contemplation but remain selfish in their service of others. Gregory, *Hom. Ez.* I. 9. 4; *PR* I. 5–6. Here Gregory follows John Cassian and Gregory Nazianzen, who had argued that St Paul, for the sake of others, willingly suspended his personal contemplation of the divine for the sake of others. See Cassian, *Conferences*, XXIV. 8. 3; Gregory Nazianzen, *Orationes*, II. 34.
[45] *PR* II. 4.   [46] *PR* II. 4; III. 36.   [47] *Hom. Ez.* II. 5. 9.

oneself in such a way as to gain control of the images that pass before the mind's eye. To do so, the Christian must cast out the stimulation of the physical senses that distract the soul from spiritual contemplation.[48] The second stage requires the aspirant to visualize the soul as distinct from the body, putting the body entirely into the service of the soul. By employing discernment, he argues, one understands the body–soul dichotomy and acknowledges that the soul is superior to the body but inferior to God. In the third stage, the Christian rises above the needs of the body by directing the soul to pursue only those things that are spiritual.[49]

In describing this three-stage process, Gregory draws a comparison between the individual organs, which are responsible for different forms of sense perception (the eyes offer sight, the ears hear, etc.) but affect just one body, and the distinct members and senses of the soul, which must be directed towards a single spiritual goal.[50] The example provides a rare direct comparison between the physical senses and the spiritual senses as collective units. The passage is all the more unique in Gregory's corpus because it employs the concept of the spiritual senses in a broader discussion of the appropriation of true knowledge. Although Gregory often utilized the spiritual senses (both collectively and individually), he rarely applied them directly to epistemological concerns.

Perhaps the most unique example of Gregory's comparison of the physical and spiritual senses derives from an earlier homily in his commentary on Ezekiel.[51] Here the pope argues that the prophets are distinguished from others in that their senses have a heightened spiritual dimension, which gives them a different form of knowledge: 'We must consider that just as we behold things corporeally, the senses of the prophet are able to behold things spiritually, which, due to our ignorance, appear absent to us.'[52] He then continues: 'Thus, it happens that in the mind of the prophets the internal things are joined to the external, such that they see both at the same time and simultaneously hear the word of God internally and speak it externally.'[53] It would seem that Gregory ascribes to the prophets a special capacity to discern the will of God. As in the case of spiritual directors, this special knowledge is provided to the prophets for the specific purpose that they share what they have learned with others. Also of note is Gregory's

---

[48] *Hom. Ez.* II. 5. 9. Similarly, in *Mor.* XIV. 15. 18, Gregory argues that the senses of the soul (*sensus animi*) are invaded when the mind cannot control its thoughts and therefore concerns itself with the external rather than the internal.

[49] Although Gregory's language is not especially consistent, there are some obvious similarities here between Gregory's view and the Platonic idea of the three parts of the soul, which function properly only when the *nous*, or rational faculty of the soul, controls the appetitive and irascible components.

[50] There is no explanation of what these individual members or senses are.

[51] *Hom. Ez.* I. 2.   [52] *Hom. Ez.* I. 2. 2.   [53] *Hom. Ez.* I. 2. 2.

suggestion that the prophet hears the locutions of God without the use of external or physical sounds.

Perhaps the longest examination of the spiritual senses in Gregory's corpus is found in his eighth homily on Ezekiel. Exploring the meaning of Ezekiel 1: 25 ('For, when a voice came from above the firmament . . .'), Gregory begins by comparing the 'voice' that we perceive with our physical sense of hearing to the 'voice of the soul' (*vox animus*) and the voice that comes from above the firmament.[54] He implies that any of these distinct 'voices' can be the source of our mental activity. These voices can be motivated by carnal desires (originating with the body), they can be motivated by the goodness in our souls, or they can be motivated by external inspiration (both good or evil). Often, Gregory argues, the images of the mind are inspired by carnal things (either the desire to do evil to one who has wronged us or the distraction of mental memories that impose themselves on our mind and thereby disturb our prayers).[55] But, if we are able to subdue these carnal images, he argues, 'we find a certain intellectual spirit (*quemdam intellectualem spiritum*) living through the power of the Creator, giving life to the body that sustains it, but nevertheless hidden in oblivion and subject to change' (*sed tamen oblivioni subditum, mutabilitati subjectum*).[56] He then adds, 'this very intellect is the voice of the soul (*Ipse itaque intellectus animae vox ejus est*) because it speaks what is, which is, however, still a voice below the firmament'.[57]

Pushing this examination in a different direction, Gregory then adds, 'God can be perceived by the senses, yet cannot be seen' (*sentiri potest, et videri non potest*).[58] He then continues: 'when the soul moved by these things considers the power of this nature (*Hujus naturae potentiam cum strictus in ea cogitat animus*) the voice comes from above the firmament, because the soul receives an understanding (*intellectum concipit*), which in its incomprehensibility transcends even the perception (*sensum*) of the angels'.[59] In other words, knowledge is granted by God, is conditional upon spiritual preparation, is comprehended by a set of mental receptors that correspond, in some vague way, to the physical senses and is at its most advanced stage when the knowledge that it imparts is even greater than what is possessed by the angels.

Lacking a separate vocabulary to describe this spiritual perception, Gregory enlists the language of the physical senses. Such a figurative use of the senses, however, promotes a paradoxical reality. God is both seen and

---

[54] *Hom. Ez.* 1. 8. 12.   [55] *Hom. Ez.* 1. 8. 13.   [56] *Hom. Ez.* 1. 8. 13.
[57] *Hom. Ez.* 1. 8. 13.   [58] *Hom. Ez.* 1. 8. 16.   [59] *Hom. Ez.* 1. 8. 16.

unseen, heard and unheard. He is seen and heard within the soul, but invisible and inaccessible to the physical senses.

Elsewhere, Gregory holds that the spiritual senses are not accessible to everyone. 'Truly the eyes and ears of the heart (*oculi vero atque aures cordis*) are only possessed by the spiritual who see the invisible through the understanding and hear the praise of God without sound.'[60] Not surprisingly, sin prevents the proper function of the spiritual senses. Just as knowledge of God is obscured by a lack of virtue, so too the spiritual senses are rendered inoperative in those individuals who wallow in sin and remain tied to carnal endeavours. In the *Book of Pastoral Rule*, Gregory notes that the spiritual senses of the pastor are weakened by ties to the carnal world.[61] Later in the same text, he extends the metaphor a step further when he argues that 'the laity are not able to apprehend the light of truth (*subjecti veritatis lumen apprehendere nequeunt*) because, while the shepherd's mind is occupied by worldly matters, dust, driven by temptation, blinds the eyes of the Church (*Ecclesiae oculos pulvis caeca*)'.[62] There may be no stronger statement of the communal dimension of the spiritual senses in Gregory's corpus. Not only does God reveal something of himself to the prophets and spiritual directors for the benefit of the community, but the spiritual director, who befouls his ability to comprehend the divine, places the entire community in jeopardy.

Scriptural interpretation provides an additional context for Gregory to employ the language of the spiritual senses as a collective unit. In his commentary on the prophet Ezekiel, for example, he argues that allegory offers us the opportunity to feed upon 'the food of truth in many spiritual senses of which we are already aware'.[63] Commenting on Ezekiel 3: 2 ('And I opened my mouth and he caused me to eat that book'), Gregory notes, 'we open our mouth when we prepare the senses for the understanding of the sacred word'.[64] He then adds:

Almighty God, as it were, as often as He offers his hand to the mouth of our hearts, so often opens our understanding (*intellectum*) and instills the food of Holy Scripture into our senses (*nostris sensibus*). Therefore, He feeds us with the book when by imparting He opens our senses to Holy Scripture and fills our thoughts (*nostras cogitationes*) to overflowing with its sweetness.[65]

As elsewhere, Gregory's discussion of the spiritual senses in the context of allegorical interpretation illustrates an advancement in a spiritualized type

---

[60] *Hom. Ez.* II. 2. 2.   [61] *PR* I. 11.   [62] *PR* II. 7.

[63] *et in multis spiritalibus sensibus, quos jam cognovimus, veritatis pabulo pascimur. Hom. Ez.* I. 9. 30.

[64] *Os ergo aperimus, quando sensum ad intelligentiam sacri verbi praeparamus. Hom. Ez.* I. 10. 5.

[65] *Hom. Ez.* I. 10. 5.

of mental cognition. Here, the spiritual senses are presented as a collective unit that does not require elucidation or analysis. Gregory simply presumes that his reader can understand his meaning.

Discussions of individual spiritual senses (e.g. hearing, seeing, etc.) appear far more frequently in Gregory's corpus than discussions of the collective senses. For example, in the *Book of Pastoral Rule*, the pontiff argues that the nose represents the gift of spiritual discernment – a man who had a small nose was prevented from obtaining the priesthood because he lacked the ability to discern a sweet smell from a stench (i.e. he could not discern between virtue and vice).[66] Gregory similarly employs the sense of hearing, arguing that a proper application of the 'ear of the heart' (*auris cordis*) prevents an unworthy candidate from pursuing pastoral leadership[67] and, conversely, allows the true pastor to harness the spiritual speech that comes from God.[68] In his commentary on Job, Gregory differentiates between the sinner who spoke and/or listened through a carnal sense (*sensu carnis*) and Job, who spoke spiritually (*spiritaliter*) because he listened to the Lord through a spiritual sense (*sensum spiritus audio*).[69]

Perhaps the most striking example of the spiritual hearing, however, derives from his fifteenth homily on the gospels.[70] Therein, Gregory describes an illiterate beggar who often had people read the scriptures and sing church hymns for him. As the man was dying, however, the beggar asked those present to stop singing because their hymns were preventing him from hearing the 'praises in heaven'. In other words, Gregory casts the man's spiritual and physical senses as disjunctive faculties, in active competition with one another. According to Gregory, the holy beggar then 'directed the ears of his heart to the praises he heard inwardly and at that time his soul was freed from his body'.[71]

It was the sense of sight, however, that provided Gregory with the greatest interpretive flexibility and served as the most frequent example of his use of an individual spiritual sense. Indeed, through the language of sight, Gregory explored various aspects of mental cognition, divine illumination and, conversely, spiritual blindness. Gregory's favourite phrase to convey spiritual perception was the 'eye of the mind' (*oculus mentis*), which he occasionally modified as the 'eye of the heart' (*oculus cordis*). For

---

[66] *PR* I. II. *Hom. Ez.* I. II. 7 similarly employs the nose as a metaphor for a pastor needing to differentiate between good and evil.
[67] *PR* I. 2.   [68] *Hom. Ez.* I. II. 8.
[69] *Mor.* XII. 32. 44. Similarly, in the *Book of Pastoral Rule*, Gregory argues that excessive speech can prohibit divine illumination because it distracts the mind. *PR* III. 14.
[70] *Hom. Evang.* XV. 5.   [71] *Hom. Evang.* XV. 5.

Gregory, everyone possesses an eye of the mind but not everyone employs it properly.[72] In the commentary on the book of Job, he explains that there is a difference between those who are open to wise counsel and those who are not. 'For these persons never raise the eyes of their mind to the light of truth, which they were created for, they never bend their desires to the contemplation of the eternal country.'[73] Conversely, he describes the virtuous as those who 'open the eyes of their mind to the beams of true light' (*ad ueri luminis radios, oculos mentis aperimus*).[74] Likely drawing on the Platonic concept of the *nous*, which is the rational faculty within the soul, Gregory often speaks of the mind's eye as the locus of rational control that, when operating properly, makes sound decisions and receives, through grace, the insights of divine knowledge.[75]

For example, in his commentary on the book of Job, Gregory holds that we must 'open the eyes of the mind to the more perfect perception of the light of righteousness' (*ad perspiciendam lucem iustitiae subtilius oculos mentis aperimus*) in order to discern what we need to do to make good decisions.[76] At times, Gregory connects this application of the mind's eye to the idea of memory. Thus, in book III of his commentary on Job, the pontiff uncharacteristically slips into the first person, when he mentions that thinking about the virtue of Job led him suddenly to call back the eye of his mind to the story of John the Baptist.[77] In his *Book of Pastoral Rule*, the pontiff employs the concept of sight to express a form of advanced knowledge of self that indicates spiritual enlightenment. In one example, he describes an illness of the body as a blessing because it brings a memory of our sins before our eyes, thus 'enlightening our eyes to our past evil actions'.[78] Later in the same text he argues that sinners must 'recall their sins before their eyes constantly, and, in this way, view the actions of their life'.[79]

In addition to describing the cognitive activity that takes place within the mind, Gregory employs the language of sight and light to describe the reception of divine illumination, which is obtained from an external source. For example, in the *Book of Pastoral Rule*, Gregory writes of the 'illumination of divine inspiration', which is brought to the mind by the Holy Spirit and 'shows the mind to itself by enlightening it' (*cum in mentem*

---

[72] Here Gregory suggests that not everyone employs their spiritual senses properly. In *Hom. Ez.* II. 2. 2, he is more critical, implying that not everyone has spiritual perception.
[73] *Mor.* I. 25. 34.　[74] *Mor.* I. 35. 48.　[75] *PR* I. 9.　[76] *Mor.* II. 51. 81.
[77] *Mor.* III. 7. 10–11. Similarly, in his commentary on Ezekiel, he contends that we 'must keep before the mind's eye both the virtues and the tears of the perfect'. *Hom. Ez.* I. 7. 24.
[78] *PR* III. 12.　[79] *PR* III. 29.

hominis venerit, eam sibimetipsi illuminans ostendit).[80] In the commentary
on Ezekiel, Gregory interprets Ecclesiastes 2: 14 ('the eyes of a wise man are
in his head') to mean that 'we have eyes in our head when we perceive the
life of our redeemer in silent contemplation, when all of our attention rises
in imitation of Him, so long as the eye of the mind is not prevented from
beholding the ways of light, whence it would immediately be enclosed in
the darkness of error and fall'.[81] Indeed, for Gregory, the acquisition of the
divine light is preconditioned by a pure heart and remains operative only
if the recipient maintains humility and understands this illumination to be
the gift of God.[82] In the *Moralia*, he notes that this illumination remains
incomplete until death, when the body–soul dichotomy reaches its true
balance, allowing the soul to see with a 'true recognition' (*vera cognitione*)
all of those things that it refused to see during life.[83]

As noted, both Gregory's cognitive theory and his application of the
spiritual senses are in the service of his more explicit pastoral and ascetic
concerns. Note, for example, his statement in the commentary on Ezekiel
that teachers have the ability to impart knowledge of 'that light which
cannot be put into words' (*illius luminis quod voce exprimi non potest*).[84]
It was with these same concerns in mind that he employed the inverse
metaphors of blindness and darkness. For example, in the *Book of Pastoral
Rule*, Gregory interprets the proscription against blind priests (cf. Lev 21)
to suggest that blindness refers to the 'ignorance of the light of supernal
contemplation',[85] and he also interprets the ailment of being 'bleary-eyed'
as meaning that although some might have a natural gift for a 'knowledge
of the truth', their carnal deeds obscure that truth because their spiritual
vision has been tainted by bad habits.[86] Indeed, the idea that carnality or
concern for the temporal world obscured divine sight is a frequent refrain
in Gregory's corpus.[87] Pride, of course, serves as yet another source of
spiritual blindness.[88]

In short, Gregory frequently employs the spiritual senses, both collectively and individually, because they offer an effective mechanism to
relate his pastoral and ascetic concerns to his audience. Addressing clerical
and ascetic leaders, he utilizes the spiritual senses to differentiate between
effective and ineffective strategies for spiritual direction and to encourage

[80] *PR* III. 12.   [81] *Hom. Ez.* I. 2. 19.   [82] *Hom. Ez.* II. 5. 18.   [83] *Mor.* XVIII. 18. 29.
[84] *Hom. Ez.* II. 6. 1.   [85] *PR* I. 11.   [86] *PR* I. 11.
[87] See, for example, *Mor.* III. 7. 10–11: 'Because the soul is inflated by the circumstances that surround
the body, and by the way that men behave toward us, the frailty of the body is removed from before
the eyes of the heart (*ab oculis cordis amovetur*) . . .' See, also, *Mor.* XI. 33. 45, which speaks of the
interior senses (*interni sensus*) being clouded by the actions of the body.
[88] See, e.g., *Hom. Ez.* II. 1. 18.

the type of ascetic behaviour that he believed to be necessary for quality spiritual leadership. For more general audiences, Gregory employed the spiritual senses to communicate basic theological principles and codes for moral behaviour (both of which he derived from scripture). Although he did not present the spiritual senses within an explicitly self-conscious or philosophical framework, his repeated use of them reflects his belief in the interconnection between spiritual discernment, moral purification and spiritual perception.

A careful examination of Gregory's corpus reveals that the pontiff frequently interchanged terms key to his understanding of spiritual perception (e.g. *mens, animus* and *cor*).[89] The dominance of ascetic and pastoral considerations in Gregory's thought may well have subordinated concerns for the type of philosophical or linguistic precision that we find in the works of Augustine and the later medieval thinkers, but those same considerations should not be misinterpreted to betray a lack of theological sophistication. Gregory was not the only patristic authority to interchange his terminology when speaking of spiritual perception. The linguistic fluidity shown by Gregory should not be read as intellectual weakness but as an indicator of other theological preoccupations. In Gregory's case, however, the charge of philosophical recklessness is especially acute because there have been a handful of modern commentators who have suggested that the Gregory of the *Dialogues* lacks the intellectual rigour of previous Christian authors and thus well characterizes the decline in Western thought at the beginning of the Middle Ages.[90] That assessment, in my judgement, is deeply flawed. The brilliance of Gregory's thought is to be found in his unique blending of ascetic and pastoral concerns, which brought a fresh reading to the biblical record and recast the Christian heroes of the past in a way that brought a knowledge of God to all.

[89] For example, see *Mor.* III. 7. 10–11 and XXVI. 13. 20.
[90] See F. Clark, *The Pseudo-Gregorian Dialogues* (Leiden: Brill, 1987).

CHAPTER 5

Pseudo-Dionysius the Areopagite

Paul L. Gavrilyuk

Despite a considerable amount of scholarly attention that Dionysian mystical theology garnered in the last century, relatively little had been written about the Areopagite's account of non-physical perception. For example, Karl Rahner's and Hans Urs von Balthasar's historically structured accounts of the doctrine of the spiritual senses treat the works of Origen, Gregory of Nyssa, Evagrius of Pontus, Pseudo-Macarius, Augustine, Diadochus of Photice and Maximus the Confessor, but pass over the Areopagite's contribution in silence.[1] In the second volume of his theological aesthetics Balthasar considers Pseudo-Dionysius's aesthetics at length and briefly mentions the Areopagite's concept of spiritual vision, but does not connect this concept to his earlier extensive discussion of the spiritual senses.[2]

In his lectures read at the Sorbonne in 1945–6, Vladimir Lossky credits Dionysius's[3] mysticism with being a 'synthesis of all that we have encountered so far in the Fathers of the first five centuries on the subject of the vision of God'.[4] Lossky observes that Dionysius has 'the doctrine of the spiritual senses', but says surprisingly little about the content of this

---

The author wishes to thank all of the volume's contributors, but especially Frederick Aquino, Sarah Coakley, Boyd Taylor Coolman, Richard Cross and Mark McInroy for their invaluable critical comments on earlier versions of this chapter.

[1] K. Rahner, 'Le début d'une doctrine des cinq sens spirituels chez Origène'; Balthasar, *GL* vol. I, pp. 365–425. Balthasar mentions in passing Dionysian influences upon William of Saint-Thierry and Bonaventure, *GL*, vol. I, pp. 371, 373.

[2] Balthasar, *GL*, vol. II, pp. 144–210; Balthasar (ed.), *Origen: Spirit and Fire: A Thematic Anthology of his Writings*, trans. R. J. Daly (Washington, DC: Catholic University of America Press, 2001), pp. 218–57.

[3] In the discussion that follows I will drop 'Pseudo' from the name 'Pseudo-Dionysius' for the sake of brevity, with the understanding that the author who wrote under the pseudonym of Paul's convert in Athens (Acts 17: 34) flourished in Byzantium *c.* 500. I have recently argued that certain peculiar features of the baptismal rite described by the author of the *Corpus Dionysiacum* point to Constantinople as the author's possible location. See P. Gavrilyuk, 'Did Pseudo-Dionysius the Areopagite Live in Constantinople?', *Vigiliae Christianae*, 62 (2008), 505–14.

[4] V. Lossky, *The Vision of God* (Leighton Buzzard: Faith Press, 1973), p. 103.

doctrine in his lectures or elsewhere. Other scholars likewise acknowledge the presence of the spiritual perception motif in the *Corpus Dionysiacum*, but do not dwell upon Dionysius's peculiar reworking of this theme at length.[5] The present chapter aims at filling this lacuna.

One possible reason for such a guarded attitude is the suggestive, yet elusive character of Dionysius's treatment of spiritual perception. In the *Corpus Dionysiacum* the most common descriptors of spiritual perception are 'the eyes of the mind' (νοεροί or νοὸς ὀφθαλμοί,[6] νοερὸν ὄμμα[7]), 'noetic vision' (νοερὰ ὄψις)[8] and 'divine vision' (θεοπτία)[9]. Discussing the state of the mystical union, which surpasses ordinary sensation and reasoning, Gregory Palamas (1296–1359) maintained that the concept of αἴσθησις πνευματική was introduced by Dionysius: 'This is why the Fathers, following the great Denys, have called this state "spiritual perception" (αἴσθησιν πνευματικὴν), a phrase appropriate to, and somehow expressive of, that mystical and ineffable contemplation.'[10] However, contrary to Palamas's observation, in his extant writings Dionysius does not use such expressions as 'spiritual perception' (αἴσθησις πνευματική), 'the eyes of the heart' or 'the eyes of faith', previously deployed by Origen, Pseudo-Macarius, Ephrem the Syrian and other patristic authors. Dionysius draws most of the terms that qualify non-physical perception from the sphere of intellection.

Apart from these terminological peculiarities, it is of central importance to this study to analyse what functions Dionysius accords to spiritual perception in the mystical ascent towards God. The Areopagite repeatedly insists that the mystical union (μυστικὴ ἕνωσις)[11] with God is beyond knowledge:

> But when our soul is moved by intelligent energies in the direction of the intelligible things then our senses (αἰσθήσεις) and all that go with them are no longer needed. And the same happens with our intelligent powers (νοεραὶ δυνάμεις)

---

[5] See, e.g., Y. de Andia, *Denys l'Aréopagite: Tradition et metamorphoses* (Paris: J. Vrin, 2006), p. 70; Rudy, *Mystical Language of Sensation in the Later Middle Ages*, pp. 42–3.

[6] *CH* I. 2, 121B 4; III. 3, 165D 12; *EH* III. 12, 441D 9; IV. 6, 480D 9; *DN* IV. 5, 700D 14. Cf. Philo, *De posteritate Caini*, 167.

[7] *CH* XV. 1, 328A 13.

[8] *EH* I. 2, 428C 12; II. 3, 397D 14; II. 3, 400A 1; *CH* IX. 3, 260D 6.

[9] *CH* VII. 1, 205C 3; VIII. 2, 240C 7; XIII. 3, 301A 24; XV. 3, 332B 24; *EH* IV. 9, 481C 6; V. 4, 504D 6; V. 5, 505A 13; VI. 6, 537C 10; *DN* I. 8, 597A 11 (θεία φάσμα).

[10] *Triads*, I. 3. 21, trans. N. Gendle, *Gregory Palamas: The Triads* (Mahwah, NJ: Paulist Press, 1983), pp. 37–48.

[11] *DN* II. 9, 648B 3. In this context μυστικὴ may be rendered not only as a technical term 'mystical', but as 'mysterious' or 'mystery-filled', consistent with its meaning in, e.g., *DN* I. 6, 596A 4 and I. 8, 597B 2.

which, when the soul becomes deiform (θεοειδὴς), concentrate sightlessly (ἀνομ-μάτοις) and through an unknowing union (δι' ἑνώσεως ἀγνώστου) on the rays of 'unapproachable light'.[12]

According to Dionysius, the dynamic of divine ascent is as follows: one first relinquishes the physical senses, then the intellect and, ultimately (one might not unreasonably suppose), all cognitive powers, including even non-physical perception. However, when Dionysius attempts to describe the indescribable mystical union, which is beyond knowledge, the use of perceptual analogies, especially those related to vision, becomes nearly inescapable. The language of spiritual perception, as the statement from Gregory Palamas quoted earlier implies, is crucial for verbalizing this experience. Two related questions arise. Does spiritual perception operate at any level of ascent towards God? Does the highest level of ascent – μυστικὴ ἕνωσις – require some form of non-physical perception?

My chapter will address these difficulties by first providing the framework of what could be regarded as a version of divine illumination theory in the *Corpus Dionysiacum*. I will then consider the function that Dionysius ascribes to the sacraments in activating and sustaining spiritual perception. I will subsequently show that for Dionysius the main modality of spiritual perception is noetic vision. I will also explore the connections that Dionysius makes between non-physical perception on the one hand and the operations of desire and intellectual purification of the knower on the other hand. Throughout this discussion, I will attend to Dionysius's terminological preferences in describing the phenomenon of spiritual perception. When appropriate, I will also register the extent to which Dionysius is indebted to Christian and pagan forms of later Platonism (although the tracking of all such parallels is beyond the scope of this study). Finally, I will return to the problem mentioned earlier, namely, what role precisely do the spiritual senses play at various stages of the mystical union with God?

DIVINE ILLUMINATION THEORY

Broadly speaking, Dionysius's mode of theologizing belongs to the philosophical trajectory of later Platonism. Dionysius endorses the essentials

---

[12] *DN* IV. 11, 708D 15–19, trans. C. Luibheid, *Pseudo-Dionysius: The Complete Works* (New York: Paulist Press, 1987), p. 80, altered. Cf. *DN* I. 1, 585B; I. 1, 588B; II. 7, 645A; V. 3, 817B; *MT* IV, 1040D; *Ep.* I, 1065A.

of Plato's division between the sensible and the intelligible realms.[13] The Areopagite is aware of the problem of the fallibility of beliefs based upon the perceptual flux. Like other Platonists he equivocates between the understanding of sensation as pre-cognitive (sensory output as such has yet to acquire propositional content and therefore cannot be true or false) and the error theory of perception, which presupposes that the output of the senses has some cognitive content, which may cause the subject to be deceived by the senses.[14] Dionysius also endorses Plato's position that the intelligibles can be known by mind directly, independently of the senses. As I will demonstrate in this chapter, for Dionysius the spiritual senses are not equally prone to the cognitive malfunctions associated with the physical senses and discursive reasoning.

Still there are some methodological differences between Dionysius and his Platonist predecessors. Although Dionysius is aware of the Platonic distinction between opinion and knowledge, he is not as keenly interested as Plato was in resolving the problem of how true opinion becomes knowledge.[15] Dionysius's epistemological emphasis lies elsewhere, namely, in a version of divine illumination theory.[16]

The luminosity of consciousness – the observation that light provides a suitable conceptual paradigm for the workings of the mind – is a trans-cultural and trans-religious insight, common to many ancient thinkers. The analogy of light is central to Plato's metaphysics and psychology.[17] Aristotle, likewise, draws upon it in his discussion of the activity of self-reflective rationality.[18] In the Judaeo-Christian tradition, such influential thinkers as Philo, Origen, Gregory of Nyssa and Augustine have explored the biblical imagery of light with much philosophical ingenuity.[19] Following

---

[13] At *EH* I. 2, 373C 18 and II. 2, 397C 8, Dionysius mentions what is probably a fictitious treatise of his, *On the Sensible and the Intelligible*. At *CH* II. 4, 144C he speaks of 'the great divide between the intelligible and the sensible'.

[14] *DN* IV. 11, 708C–709A.

[15] *DN* IX. 5, 913A. Cf. Plato, *Meno*, 97C–100B; *Thaetetus*, 187A–210D.

[16] For a survey of various pre-modern theories of the divine illumination, see R. Pasnau, 'Divine Illumination', *Stanford Encyclopedia of Philosophy*, at http://plato.stanford.edu/entries/illumination/ (accessed 28 April 2011); and Pasnau, 'Henry of Ghent and the Twilight of Divine Illumination', *The Review of Metaphysics*, 49 (1995), 49–75.

[17] Plato, *Resp.* IV, 435A; *Phaedrus*, 250C; Plato (?), *Epistle* VII.   [18] Aristotle, *De an.* III. 5, 430a.

[19] Philo observes in *De plantatione*, 24, that 'mind is intrinsically light' and in *De specialibus legibus*, I. 42, that 'light is not known by the agency of anything else'. See also Philo, *De praemiis et poenis*, 45; *De migratione Abraham*, 39–40; *Quis rerum divinarum heres*, 263; Origen, *Commentary on the Psalms*, IV. 7; *In Cant.* II. 3; Plotinus, *Enn.* VI. 4. 7–8; Gregory of Nyssa, *Vita Moysis*, II. 19–22, 162; Damascius, *De principiis rerum dubia et solutiones*, I. 305. 9. For the patristic use of the image of light, see J. Pelikan, *The Light of the World: A Basic Image in Early Christian Thought* (New York: Harper, 1962).

this tradition, Dionysius conceives of the workings of consciousness, of the structure of being and of divine agency in terms of the controlling analogy of illumination.[20]

Dionysius's vocabulary of light-related terms is exceedingly rich. The English term 'illumination' is rendered in the *Corpus Dionysiacum* by at least four different nouns: ἔλλαμψις, φωτισμός, φώτισμα and φωταγωγία. In addition, the author is fond of an extremely rare compound, 'manifestation of light' (φωτοφάνεια), for which we have only one precedent in all extant Greek writings prior to the *Corpus Dionysiacum*.[21] He also uses twice an equally arcane word, 'light-stream' (φωτοχυσία).[22] With characteristic philological ingenuity, he has coined three additional compounds: 'source of light' (φωτογονία), 'light-making' (φωτουργός) and an almost untranslatable pair, 'name of light' or 'light-namedly' (φωτωνυμία or φωτωνυμικῶς).[23] The breadth of Dionysius's light-related imagery shows him to be no slave of the illumination conceptuality of earlier thinkers, especially that of the non-Christian philosophers.

Divine illumination has multiple functions: (1) it sustains all things in being; (2) it gives to all rational creatures the ability to cognize; (3) it imparts to all intelligible entities the property of being intelligible; (4) it makes dark and obscure things luminously clear; (5) it purifies the eyes of the mind and rectifies errors; (6) it enables the knowers to approach everything in creation as a symbol and a manifestation of the energies of God; (7) it increases the rational creature's ability to know God according to each creature's capacity and desire to receive knowledge. In addition, the notion of illumination features prominently in two other related contexts: (8) it is the second term in the triad of purification, illumination and

---

[20] Dionysius repeatedly points out that he is talking about transcendent (ὑπερούσιον) and noetic (νοητὸν), not physical, light: *CH* II. 5, 144C 10 – D 13; *EH* IV. 2, 476B 13; *DN* I. 4, 592C 1; IV. 5, 700D 9 – 701A 11; IV. 6 701B 9; *Ep.* IX. 2, 1108C 14. For a similar distinction between noetic and physical light, see Philo, *De opificio mundi*, 31, 55; *De vita Mosis*, II. 271. It should be noted that Dionysius also uses other analogies drawn, for example, from the sphere of olfaction. For example, at *EH* IV. 5, 480B the discussion of the consecration of the chrism makes him turn to the analogy of 'a great flood of fragrant odours', which streams from God and is inhaled by the highest angels and those below them. Shortly afterwards, however, he switches back to the analogy of light and vision. Cf. a similar pattern in *CH* I. 3, 121D. See S. Gersh, *From Iamblichus to Eriugena: An Investigation of the Prehistory and Evolution of the Pseudo-Dionysian Tradition* (Leiden: Brill, 1978), pp. 23–6.

[21] *DN* I. 3, 589B 11; *CH* I. 1, 120B 5; IV. 4, 181C 10. Prior to Dionysius, this term is used only once, by Cyril of Alexandria in *De exitu animi* (PG 77. 1081B), according to a TLG search for φωτοφάν-.

[22] *DN* IV. 6, 701A 2; *Ep.* V, 1073A 5, is a *hapax legomenon* found in the second-century apocryphon *Apocalypse of John*, 2. 6.

[23] These terms are *hapax legomena* in the *Corpus Dionysiacum*: φωτογονία in *Ep.* IX. 1, 1105A 1; φωτουργός in *CH* VIII. 2, 240C 10; φωτωνυμία in *DN* IV. 5, 700D 10; and φωτωνυμικῶς in *DN* IV. 4, 697C 3. These findings are based on the TLG searches for φωτογον-, φωτουργ- and φωτωνυμ-.

perfection, embraced and developed by later mystics; (9) finally, illumination is a concept traditionally referring to Christian initiation. It should be noted that the first five functions of illumination allow for both general and strictly theological applications, whereas the remaining four functions pertain exclusively to the process of coming to know divine things. Since my primary concern is Dionysius's account of spiritual perception, not the general contours of his illumination theory, I will assume the framework of all nine aspects of illumination, focusing in what follows more closely on the ninth, sacramental aspect.

THE BAPTISMAL ACTIVATION OF SPIRITUAL VISION

In the *Ecclesiastical Hierarchy*, Dionysius provides an anagogical commentary on the sacraments. Each chapter is dedicated to one of the sacraments and is divided into three sections: a brief introduction, a section describing the associated ritual actions and a theological 'reflection' (θεωρία) on the spiritual significance of the ritual. Following the tradition of *disciplina arcani*, Dionysius repeatedly warns his readers that sacramental theology must not be disclosed to the uninitiated.[24] He is driven both by the mystagogical concern to preclude the profanation of the sacred things and by the philosophical conviction that the uninitiated are not yet cognitively equipped to experience God.[25] Those who despise Christian mysteries and deride baptism are characterized as 'stone deaf' and having 'no eye for the imagery'.[26] In other words, the uninitiated lack both the spiritual hearing and the spiritual sight. They need to undergo a suitable purification and illumination in the sacrament of initiation. Those who lead unrepentant lives are similarly compared to the blind, whose eyes are torn out and whose noetic vision is 'closed off'.[27]

During the pre-baptismal catechesis the candidates' minds receive preliminary purification, when the scriptural teaching is imparted to them.[28]

---

[24] *EH* I. 1, 372A 9–10; I. 5, 377A 12–B 21; *MT* I. 2, 1000A 15–16; *CH* II. 5, 145C. Cf. Philo, *De cherubim*, 42; *De fuga et inventione*, 85.

[25] Cf. Plato, *Soph.* 254A–B: 'the eyes of the soul of the multitude (τῆς τῶν πολλῶν ψυχῆς ὄμματα) are not strong enough to endure the sight of the divine (τὸ θεῖον)'. Trans. H. Fowler, *Plato: Theaetetus, Sophist* (Cambridge, MA: Harvard University Press, 2006), p. 403.

[26] *EH* III. 6, 432C. John Meyendorff advanced a plausible hypothesis that the target of Dionysius's criticism was neo-Platonic intelligentsia, to which Dionysius himself used to belong. See *Christ in Eastern Christian Thought* (Crestwood, NY: St Vladimir's Seminary Press, 1975), p. 100.

[27] *EH* II, 392C; II. 3, 397D; v. 2, 501C; VII. 6, 561A. Cf. 3 Jn 11; Philo, *De mutatione nominum*, 203; Theophilus of Antioch, *Ad Autolycum*, 2.

[28] *EH* 477A. Somewhat surprisingly, Dionysius passes over other means of preparation, such as fasting, prayer and exorcisms before baptism.

Dionysius introduces a compound noun, θεογενεσία ('divine birth'), in order to emphasize that baptism marks the beginning of the process of illumination and the activation of the spiritual senses.[29] In an uncharacteristically autobiographic passage, Dionysius writes:

> The sacrament of divine birth (θεογενεσία) first introduces light and is the beginning of all divine illumination (ἀρχὴ τῶν θείων φωταγωγιῶν). And because this is so we praise it, giving the designation of what it achieves, that is, illumination (φωτίσματος). It is true of course that all the hierarchic operations have this in common, to pass the light of God on to the initiates, but nevertheless it was this one [baptism] which first gave me the gift of sight (ἰδεῖν ἐδωρήσατό). The light coming first from this led me towards the vision of the other sacred things (ἱερῶν ἐποψίαν φωταγωγοῦμαι).[30]

As I stated earlier, for Dionysius illumination has a plethora of functions and provides a paradigm for all divine acts vis-à-vis creation. Nonetheless he singles out baptism in particular as the beginning and source (ἀρχὴ) of all subsequent forms of illumination. He states that in the sacrament of baptism a gift of vision (ἐποψία), or a new capacity to see (ἰδεῖν) the divine things, is granted to those initiated. Shifting his emphasis from the faculty of sight to that of hearing, Dionysius notes that one of the purposes of baptism is 'to dispose our souls to hear the sacred words as receptively as possible'.[31] Drawing attention to this material, Alexander Golitzin observes that we have here 'at least implicit doctrine of the "spiritual senses"'.[32]

While Dionysius's sacramental theology is thoroughly steeped in the conceptuality of later Platonism, this theory also taps into the rich resources of the preceding pagan and Christian mystagogy. The idea that participation in the mysteries grants a vision of the divine is present, for example, in the hermetic corpus.[33] From the time of Justin, the terms φώτισμα and φωτισμός became virtually synonymous with baptism.[34] The candidates preparing for baptism in the East were called φωτιζόμενοι or φωτισθησόμενοι ('those preparing to receive illumination').[35] Some Latin-speaking

---

[29] The Johannine imagery of baptism as 'birth from above' (Jn 3: 3, 7) is behind this neologism. See P. Gavrilyuk, 'Baptism in Pseudo-Dionysius's *Ecclesiastical Hierarchy*', *Studia liturgica*, 39.1 (2009), 1–14.

[30] *EH* III, 425A 23–B 4, trans. Luibheid, p. 210, slightly modified.

[31] *EH* II, 392A, trans. Luibheid, p. 200.

[32] A. Golitzin, 'Dionysius Areopagites: A Christian Mysticism?', in B. Lourié and A. Orlov (eds.), *The Theophaneia School: Jewish Roots of Eastern Christian Mysticism* (St Petersburg: Vizantinorossika, 2007), p. 135.

[33] This point is noted by N. Russell, *The Doctrine of Deification in the Greek Patristic Literature* (Oxford University Press, 2004), pp. 45–50.

[34] Justin, *1 Apology*, 61. 12: 'This washing is called illumination (φωτισμός), since the understanding (διάνοιαν) of the candidates is being illumined.'

[35] Surprisingly, Dionysius does not apply the terms φωτιζόμενοι or φωτισθησόμενοι to the catechumens. Possibly, this is because the process of baptismal initiation in his time did not include a clear

churches also followed this terminology and called them *illuminandi.* The catechetical sermons of Cyril of Jerusalem, Ambrose of Milan, Augustine, John Chrysostom and Theodore of Mopsuestia are filled with allusions to spiritual perception.[36]

Although Dionysius does not refer overtly to the patristic authorities just mentioned in order to avoid compromising his 'apostolic' credentials, he clearly draws upon this tradition in various subtle ways. For him, as for the earlier Christian mystagogues, the transformation that occurs in baptism involves both the moral and existential reorientation of life, as well as new cognitive gifts. The baptizand is granted a new capacity to discern the divine light and the whole world as a symbolic manifestation of the energies of God. This is an especially telling example of how Dionysius succeeds in baptizing, both literally and metaphorically, the Platonic epistemology of noetic vision. For Dionysius spiritual perception is activated not by studying geometry or mastering the art of dialectic, as it was for some Platonists, but by means of dying and rising with Christ in baptism.[37] Baptismal illumination is a prelude to 'not only learning, but suffering divine things'.[38]

Given this starting point of Dionysius's phenomenology of spiritual perception, there is some plausibility to Alexander Golitzin's hypothesis that Dionysius was concerned to address Messalian sensibilities in ascetic circles.[39] For the purpose of this chapter, I take Messalianism to include a view that God can be perceived by the physical senses and that the sacraments and liturgical experience in general ought to be subordinated, and even in principle could be replaced with the experience of God attained through training (ἄσκησις). Dionysius, in contrast, repeatedly emphasizes that God cannot be perceived by the bodily senses.[40] He also singles out baptismal initiation as a crucial beginning point of mystical ascent, a move that a Messalian ascetic would have been reticent to make. For Dionysius, spiritual perception is cultivated in the context of the

distinction between the catechumens of the remote stage and those who made the decision to be baptized some time soon.

[36] See G. Frank, '"Taste and See": The Eucharist and the Eyes of Faith in the Fourth Century', *Church History*, 70 (2001), 619–43. One should also point to such New Testament precedents as, for example, the opening of the eyes of the disciples who encountered the resurrected Christ on the road to Emmaus and recognized him in the context of a meal with strong Eucharistic overtones (Lk 24: 16, 30–2). In Acts 9: 18, blindness-stricken Paul receives his physical sight back in the context of baptism. The anagogical implications of this story were explored by later mystagogues.

[37] *EH* II. 6, 404A.

[38] *DN* II. 9, 648B 1–2. For a commentary on this phrase, see de Andia, *Denys l'Aréopagite*, pp. 17–36.

[39] Golitzin, 'Dionysius Areopagites', pp. 145, 151, 162.

[40] '[God] is neither perceived nor is perceptible'. *MT* v, 1048B; cf. *DN* I. 5, 593B 4.

communal liturgical life. He mentions with approval a priest who experienced 'propitious visions' (εὐμεναί ὁράσεις) during the prayers before the liturgy.[41] Anecdotal reports about visionary experiences accompanying liturgical action were popular in the West Syrian churches of Dionysius's time.[42] As the Areopagite notes, it is the responsibility of the clergy 'to guide the initiates to the divine visions of the sacraments' (τὰς θείας τῶν τελετῶν ἐποψίας),[43] an unusual expression indicating an anagogical function of the ritual. To conclude, for Dionysius, the sacraments are the fountainhead of mystical contemplation.

THE VARIETIES OF SPIRITUAL PERCEPTION

Thus far we have largely focused on noetic vision as the primary modality of spiritual perception. The privileging of this perceptual mode as a key descriptor of a higher mode of cognition is typical of Platonism, but by no means peculiar to this philosophical tradition alone.[44] On a phenomenological level, we have direct cognitive access to all five physical modes of perception in the sense that sight, for example, is not mediated by touch or any other sense. Since the time of Plato it has become commonplace in philosophy to use sensation (αἴσθησις) language to describe mental activity (νόησις).[45]

Plato himself appears to have equivocated between two possibilities. On the one hand, he may be interpreted as postulating a disjunction between the sensibles, perceived by the bodily senses, and the intelligibles, cognized by the rational souls, preferably freed from the limitations of embodiment.[46] This would seem to indicate that νόησις should be sharply distinguished from αἴσθησις. On the other hand, for Plato the sensibles function as the images triggering the recollection of the intelligibles. The sensibles are also said to participate in the reality of the intelligibles. Given

---

[41] *Ep.* VIII. 6, 1097C 12–13. It is unclear what specific part of the worship service Dionysius has in mind. This may be a reference to the rite of the preparation of the Eucharistic gifts, or the morning service preceding the Eucharist.

[42] See R. F. Hathaway, *Hierarchy and the Definition of Order in the Letters of Pseudo-Dionysius* (The Hague: Nijhoff, 1970), pp. 92–8.

[43] *EH* v. 6, 505D.

[44] Philo, for example, speaks of sight as the 'queen of the senses' in *De Abrahamo*, 150 and 164; cf. *De confusione linguarum*, 141. Plotinus, *Enn.* III. 8, goes so far as to advance a paradoxical claim that 'nature is contemplation', that is, that everything in the cosmos is reducible to a form of mental agency. See J. N. Deck, *Nature, Contemplation, and the One: The Study in the Philosophy of Plotinus* (University of Toronto Press, 1967).

[45] For example, Plato, *Resp.* VI, 508; Plotinus, *Enn.* V. 3.   [46] *Timaeus*, 28A.

these metaphysical and epistemological assumptions, the analogical under-standing of νόησις in terms of αἴσθησις becomes natural.

In *De anima*, III, Aristotle considers a possibility that 'intellection is like perception' (τό νοεῖν ὥσπερ τό αἰσθάνεσθαι) and speculates that 'as the objects of perception are to perception, so must the objects of thought be to the mind' (ὥσπερ τό αἰσθητικὸν πρὸς τὰ αἰσθητά, οὕτω τὸν νοῦν πρὸς τὰ νοητά).[47] However, the Stagirite is equally if not even more concerned to emphasize the disanalogies between the thinking (ἥ νοητική) and the perceiving (αἴσθητικη) powers of the soul.[48]

Since the Greek language from the time of Plato and Aristotle became increasingly well equipped to convey various modalities of mental activ-ity by means of analogies drawn from sense-perception, the terminology at Dionysius's disposal was well suited to convey the slightest nuances of his thought. However, precisely because of the wealth of plausible con-notations, this terminology at times presents staggering interpretative dif-ficulties. For example, how should one translate θεωρία in the *Corpus Dionysiacum*, given its rich philosophical history and equally sophisticated Christian appropriations? Should one translate θεωρία as 'contemplation', 'meditation' and 'spiritual vision', or instead should one de-emphasize the term's technical meaning by rendering it as 'reflection', 'observation', 'per-ception', 'sight' and so on?[49] What is of critical importance for this study is the differentiation of contexts in which θεωρία refers to a form of per-ception, and those cases when the term describes cognitive activities quite different from perception, such as reflective thinking.

A similar problem arises in ascertaining the meaning of 'the eyes of the mind' in Dionysius. The problem is certainly not peculiar to the *Corpus Dionysiacum*, since the expression in question has been commonly used as a metaphor of thought, imagination, deliberation and related mental activity.[50] It should be conceded that some Dionysian references to the

[47] Aristotle, *De an.* III. 4, 13–14, 17–18. See S. Rappe, *Reading Neoplatonism: Non-Discursive Thinking in the Texts of Plotinus, Proclus, and Damascius* (Cambridge University Press, 2000), p. 218.

[48] For Aristotle, sensation is largely passive and inextricably tied to the body. Reflective thinking, in contrast, has both passive and active aspects, and is in principle separable from the body. *De an.* III. 5, 430a.

[49] G. W. H. Lampe, *A Patristic Greek Lexicon* (Oxford: Clarendon Press, 1968), pp. 648–9, lists the following meanings of θεωρία: seeing, beholding, sense of sight, sight, spectacle, consideration, investigation, study, intellectual apprehension, supervision, theory, speculation, science, philosoph-ical contemplation and, finally, spiritual contemplation.

[50] For a discussion of the problem of distinguishing between the metaphorical and analogical uses of the terminology of spiritual perception, see Chapter 1 in this volume as well as J. M. Dillon, 'Aisthêsis Noêtê: A Doctrine of Spiritual Senses in Origen and in Plotinus', in A. Caquot, M. Hadas-Lebel and J. Riaud (eds.), *Hellenica et Judaica: Hommage à Valentin Nikiprowetzky* (Leuven and Paris: Peeters, 1986), pp. 443–55.

'eyes of the mind' may indeed be read as dead metaphors of ordinary discursive reasoning,[51] but the author's emphasis lies elsewhere. In the previous section we saw that in baptism the initiated were granted a special ability to see. To identify this ability with the physical sight or discursive reasoning makes no sense, since the candidates obviously possess these faculties prior to baptism. Dionysius does not elaborate, however, whether the gift of spiritual sight involves a new power or faculty, analogous to the existing cognitive faculties.

As a Platonist, Dionysius holds that apart from physical sensation and discursive reasoning, rational creatures are capable of a higher-order, non-discursive mental apprehension of reality (νόησις).[52] God's non-discursive, non-propositional and non-temporal knowledge of himself – if one can speak of God's self-reflective knowledge at all – is the highest form of this unifying cognitive act.[53] The angels follow next on the scale of cognitive capacities. The Areopagite explains that the angelic minds surpass human minds because:

They do not draw together their knowledge of God from fragments (ἐν μεριστοῖς) nor from bouts of perception (ἀπὸ μεριστῶν ἢ αἰσθήσεων) or discursive reasoning (λόγων διεξοδικῶν). And at the same time they are not limited to perception and reason. Being free from all burden of matter and multiplicity, they think the thoughts of the divine realm intelligently, immaterially, and in a single act.[54]

Dionysius speculates that different orders of angels possess this capacity in different degrees. The first triad of cherubim, seraphim and thrones is capable of contemplating God most directly by virtue of its proximity to him. Other angelic orders receive divine illumination, according to their

---

[51] As, perhaps, in *CH* xv. 1, 328A.

[52] The term νόησις is sometimes rendered in English as 'intuition' or 'intellection'. Cf. Alcinous, *Didaskalikos*, iv. 6, 7: 'Intellection (νόησις) is the activity of the intellect as it contemplates the primary objects of intellection . . . The primary intelligibles are judged by intellection not without the aid of scientific reason, by means of a kind of comprehension, not discursive reasoning'. Trans. J. Dillon, *Alcinous: The Handbook of Platonism* (Oxford: Clarendon Press, 1993), p. 7. Plotinus, who frequently speaks of non-discursive intellection, calls it ὑπερνόησις (*Enn.* vi. 8. 16), the term that Dionysius does not deploy.

[53] God's knowledge is 'a single embracing causality which knows and contains all things'. *DN* vii. 2, 869B, cf. *DN* i. 7, 596D. God is also 'mindless mind' (νοῦς ἀνόητος, *DN* i. 1, 588B 14, cf. *MT* i. 3, 1000C) in the sense that the causal non-propositional knowledge that he possesses cannot violate his oneness. See also Plotinus, *Enn.* i. 8. 2; Gregory of Nyssa, *De vita Moysis*, ii. 24, 163–4.

[54] *DN* vii. 2, 868B 4–7, cf. *DN* v. 3, 817B. As Thomas Aquinas comments: 'According to Dionysius between man and angel there is this difference, that an angel perceives the truth by simple apprehension, whereas man arrives at the perception of a simple truth by a process from several premises.' *ST* ii-ii. 180. 3, trans. Fathers of English Dominican Province, at www.catholicbook.com/AgendaCD/Summa/SecundaSecundae179-4.htm (accessed 7 March 2009).

capacity, in the form mediated by the higher angels.[55] For human beings, the exercise of this non-discursive power requires considerable cognitive stretching.[56] Nevertheless, such self-transcendence is possible, and indeed it is a part of human cognitive endowment: 'The human mind (νοῦς) has a cognitive capacity (εἰς τὸ νοεῖν), through which it sees (βλέπει) the intelligibles, and a unity which transcends the nature of the mind, through which it is joined to things beyond itself.'[57] Following his Platonist predecessors, Dionysius describes this higher-level cognitive capacity in terms of the perceptual modality of vision.[58] In this context, to reduce vision-related terminology to mere metaphors of reflective thinking is to miss the point that noetic vision indicates an openness of the mind to the transcendent in the way not available to ordinary thinking about God.

Dionysius also introduces his own expressions, such as, for example, the 'supercosmic eyes' (ὑπερκοσμίοι ὀφθαλμοί), which may have been inspired by Philo.[59] The multi-eyed cherubim, who alone are capable of looking at God directly, possess this form of vision. If acquired by the humans in the process of contemplative stretching, 'the eyes that look beyond the world', as Colm Luibheid aptly translates the expression ὑπερκοσμίοι ὀφθαλμοί, are capable of discerning God in all things.[60]

We should note that Dionysius prefers the spatial descriptors of below and above to those of exterior and interior. There are no allusions to the Pauline distinction between 'inner' and 'outer' person anywhere in the *Corpus Dionysiacum*.[61] Unlike Origen, Plotinus, Gregory of Nyssa, Augustine and the medieval mystics, the Areopagite does not express the soul's progress towards God in terms of increasing interiority. Dionysius also does not correlate the process of coming to know God with self-knowledge as closely as do other Platonists.[62] For Dionysius, the movement

---

[55] *CH* VIII. 2, 240D; *Ep.* VIII. 2, 1029B.

[56] *DN* III. 1, 680C 13, trans. Luibheid, p. 68: 'So let us stretch (ἀνατείνωμεν) ourselves prayerfully upward to the most lofty elevation of the kindly Rays of God.'

[57] *DN* VII. 1, 865C, trans. mine.

[58] For the comparison between Gregory of Nyssa and Dionysius, see A. Meredith, *Gregory of Nyssa* (London: Routledge, 1999), p. 101.

[59] *CH* IV. 1, 177C 5; VIII. 1, 237B 14; *EH* IV. 12, 484D 8; *DN* V. 7, 821B 17. The compound adjective ὑπερκόσμιος is relatively rare; the expression 'supercosmic eyes' is not found in the Greek authors prior to Dionysius at all. Philo in *De plantatione*, 21–2 takes the capacity of physical eyes to raise their sight to heaven to be symbolic of the 'eyes of the soul' (ψυχῆς ὄμματα), which 'overpass the very bounds of the entire universe and speed away toward the Uncreate'. Trans. F. H. Colson, *Philo* (Cambridge, MA: Harvard University Press, 1968), vol. III, pp. 223–5. Cf. Philo, *De opificio mundi*, 31.

[60] *DN* V. 7. 821B 17, trans. Luibheid, p. 100.   [61] Rom 7: 22; 2 Cor 4: 16; Col 3: 9–10; Eph 3: 16.

[62] For a hint at such a correlation, see *DN* IV. 9, but compare Dionysius's allusive references to the accounts in, e.g., Philo, *Quis rerum divinarum heres*, 69; Plotinus, *Enn.* IV. 8. 1; and Evagrius of

from the symbol to the archetypal reality revealed by the symbol is always an ascent from the lower to the higher, not a progress from the outer to the inner. Dionysius prefers to speak of 'lifting up', 'climbing' and 'striving upward (coming down)', rather than of 'looking within (outside)'.[63] The dialectic of external appearance or internal meaning is integral to the mystagogical interpretation of the sacraments, but Dionysius as a rule expresses himself anagogically, in terms of the mind's being raised from the lower things to the higher. While he does not ignore introspection altogether, he subordinates self-knowledge to self-transcendence, that is, to the ecstatic lifting up of the mind to the contemplation of God.[64] Hence, his terminological choice of the 'supercosmic eyes', rather than the 'inner eyes' that gaze into the depth of one's self.

In the *Celestial Hierarchy* Dionysius has recourse to all five modalities of perception as figures of the higher-order cognitive powers possessed by the angels:

I also think that each of the many parts of the human body can provide us with images (εἰκόνας) which are quite appropriate to the powers of heaven. One could say that the powers of sight suggest their ability to gaze up toward the lights of God and, at the same time, to receive softly, clearly, without resistance but flexibly, purely, openly, yet impassibly, the enlightenments coming from the Deity. The powers to discern smells indicate their capacity to welcome fully those fragrances which elude the understanding and to discern with understanding those opposites which must be utterly avoided. The powers of hearing signify the ability to have a knowing share of divine inspiration. Taste has to do with the fill of conceptual nourishment and their receptiveness to the divine and nourishing streams. Touch is understanding how to distinguish the profitable from the harmful.[65]

The author continues his parallels by considering the symbolic significance of eyelids, eyebrows, teeth, shoulders, arms, breast, back, feet, heart and so on. The spiritual capacities of angels, described in this passage, may by extension be applied to human beings *coram Deo*. The cognitive equipment that is necessary for the divine ascent includes the power of discrimination, symbolized by the senses of smell and touch.[66] One also needs

---

Pontus, *Maxims*, 2. 2. In *CH* x. 3, 273C and *Ep.* VIII. 3, 1093A there is a hint that the ontological subordination of the lower order of being to the higher must correspond to the interior order of intelligent beings. This hint was seized upon by the medieval Western mystics. See, e.g., Thomas Gallus, *Commentary on the Song of Songs*, 5–11.

[63] *DN* I. 4, 592C; II. 2, 640A; XIII. 3, 981B; *MT* 997B; 1000A; 1001A; *CH* XV. 1, 328A.

[64] *EH* II. 4, 400C.

[65] *CH* XV. 3, 332A 12 – B 24, p. 185, trans. Luibheid, p. 185, slightly altered. Cf. Origen, *In Cant.* Prol. 2.10; *Dial. Heraclides*, 15–24.

[66] Cf. *EH* IV. 3. 4, 477D. Cf. Aristotle, *De sensu*, I, 436b 16–17. Aristotle regarded smell as inferior to all the other senses. *De sensu*, IV, 441a.

to acquire the receptivity towards the divine, symbolized by taste. Hearing serves as a figure of the capacity to comprehend the inspired teachings. Elsewhere he mentions that 'our hearing is made holy as we listen to the explication of the divine names', that is, to the anagogical commentary on scripture.[67] Dionysius also draws upon the analogy of hearing to illustrate how the good is shared 'indivisibly by all in the same way that one and the same sound is perceived by numerous ears'.[68] He likens divine energies to potent sounds that can penetrate even a deafened ear.[69]

While Dionysius does not overlook entirely the spiritual significance of other perceptual modalities, as was noted earlier, he gives the pride of place to noetic vision. According to Dionysius, sight indicates the capacity of the highest rank of angels to have the most immediate (ἄμεσος) access to God.[70] This capacity is not granted to the lower angels and humans, who contemplate God indirectly as mediated by higher angels, as well as through God's energies in creation, in perceptual and mental symbols, in the sacramental signs and in visions.[71]

The passage just quoted is illustrative of Dionysius's overall approach to what he calls 'symbolic theology'.[72] Unlike Origen, Dionysius does not develop a sustained account of the five spiritual senses. The fact that the mystical ascent is described as progressive unification and simplification speaks against the idea of the division of non-physical perception into the five distinct modalities, analogous to the five physical senses. As was noted repeatedly, for Dionysius, noetic vision is the main modality of spiritual perception. The core insight of Dionysius's mystical theology consists in the bold claim that illuminated by the divine light, the mind is potentially capable of infinitely extending itself in order to achieve increasingly immediate, perception-like contact with God.

NOETIC VISION AND EROS

For Dionysius the field of spiritual perception is a graded continuum. Spiritual perception is a continuum, as opposed to a set of discrete faculties distinct from physical perception, because one's cognitive capacities are 'stretched' and transformed as one draws closer and closer to God. One

---

[67] *DN* I. 8, 597B; cf. XIII. 4, 984A.   [68] *DN* V. 9, 825A.   [69] *DN* VIII. 2, 892A.
[70] *CH* VI. 2, 200D–201A; VII. 2, 208D; VII. 3, 209C; VII. 4, 212A; VIII. 2, 240C; X. 1, 272D; *EH* VI. 6, 537C.
[71] *CH* II. 2, 140A 13; IV. 3, 180C; VI. 2, 201A; VII. 1, 205B; VIII. 2, 240C; XIII. 3, 301C and 304D; *EH* IV. 2, 476B; VI. 6, 537C.
[72] At *DN* I. 8, 597B; IX. 5, 913B; *CH* XV, 336A; and *MT* III, 1033A, Dionysius mentions a separate treatise with this title, but we know nothing more about it beyond these four references.

symbolic way of grading this continuum is by means of the nine ranks of angels. The higher the rank of the angelic power, the more unified, continuous and immediate is its capacity to perceive God. Dionysius links this capacity to the erotic longing of all rational creatures for God. The Areopagite is quite aware of the fact that eros has objectionable pagan pedigree in the eyes of his Christian contemporaries. Still, he proceeds to baptize the term by alluding to a few Old Testament precedents and, more importantly, breaking down a sharp contrast between eros (thus baptized) and agape.[73] Later Byzantine theologians, such as Maximus the Confessor and Symeon the New Theologian, have readily embraced Dionysius's Christianization of eros.

For Dionysius, eros is first of all a capacity to affect the union with God.[74] As such, eros is at the core of all beings, since everything was produced by the love of God.[75] As John Rist aptly put it, 'true Eros needs nothing and indeed is perpetually overflowing in goodness to the entire universe'.[76] All things long for God, each according to its capacity.[77] The angels possess divine eros to the degree proportionate to their illumination.[78] The highest angelic powers are endowed with perfect and unfailing longing for God. Divine eros is poured upon all creation and is reciprocated by the rational creature's yearning for the union with God.

Understood as a force that draws towards God, eros brings about detachment from sinful thoughts and passions. In *Epistle* x. 1, Dionysius connects the erotic thrust towards God with ἀπάθεια, the state of freedom from evil imaginations and desires.[79] Erotic longing for God brings about purification and permanently establishes the soul in God's goodness.[80] Hence, eros is inseparable from the practice of virtues, although Dionysius does not develop this point with the specificity characteristic of the ascetic literature of his time.

Furthermore, eros is the energy of self-transcendence, of ecstasy which makes possible the extension of one's perceptual faculties. Eros is the driving force of spiritual perception. The noetic vision that is unerotic, devoid of longing for God, is an impossibility for Dionysius, as it was for most Christian Platonists. There are some intriguing parallels between Dionysius's

---

[73] *DN* iv. 11–12, 708B–709B.   [74] *DN* iv. 11, 708C–D.

[75] *DN* iv. 7, 704A. While Dionysius rarely speaks of divine grace, arguably such notions as divine energies and divine eros fill this lacuna in his theology.

[76] J. Rist, 'A Note on Eros and Agape in Pseudo-Dionysius', *Vigiliae Christianae*, 20 (1966), 243.

[77] *DN* i. 5, 593D; iv. 10, 708A.   [78] *DN* i. 2, 589A.

[79] Cf. *CH* vii. 1, 205D; *EH* ii. 8, 404C. On this paradoxical connection of eros and impassibility see de Andia, *Denys l'Aréopagite*, pp. 26–30.

[80] *EH* ii, 401C.

'erotic epistemology'[81] and twentieth-century phenomenology, Gestalt psychology and more recent accounts of perception by analytic philosophers, emphasizing the role of intention, will, desire, emotions and background experience in the formation of perceptual beliefs.[82] For Dionysius, eros is the energy that summons and directs all cognitive capacities to the contemplation and delight in God. The elevation of the νοῦς is inconceivable without eros. Deified νοῦς is erotic, or eros-driven, and eros, in turn, is noetic, energizing the mind to acquire the unitive knowledge of God.

THE ROLE OF NOETIC VISION IN THE MYSTICAL UNION

Spiritual perception is activated in baptism, purified by participating in the sacramental life of the church and energized by eros to achieve contact with God. We now turn to the last question raised in the introductory section: what role does spiritual perception play at the pinnacle of the divine ascent, in the mystical union with God? There are strong reasons for believing that in the mystical union envisioned by Dionysius, all cognitive powers, including non-physical perception, are folded. The union is described as a silent state of 'unknowing' (ἀγνωσία), correlated with the concept of divine 'dark' (γνόφος) in Dionysius's illuminationist epistemology.[83] What Dionysius seeks to capture by the notion of 'unknowing union' can be interpreted in at least three ways.[84] First, this notion draws upon the assumption, going back to Parmenides, that the realm of everything knowable is coextensive with the realm of being. Dionysius maintains that as the cause of all things, God is 'beyond being' (ὑπερούσιος, ὑπὲρ οὐσίαν).[85] Therefore, on the Parmenidean assumption, God surpasses everything knowable.[86]

---

[81] The expression of Sergius Bulgakov in *Svet Nevechernii* (Moscow: Respublika, 1994), p. 108.

[82] M. R. Wynn, *Emotional Experience and Religious Understanding: Integrating Perception, Conception and Feeling* (Cambridge University Press, 2005); J. Cottingham, *The Spiritual Dimension* (Cambridge University Press, 2005).

[83] *DN* VII. 3, 872A; *MT* III, 1001A. Dionysius built on the interpretation of Exod 20: 21 by Philo, *De mutatione nominum*, 7–9, and Gregory of Nyssa, *Vita Moysis*, II. 152, 162–5, 169, 229, 315.

[84] For a different approach to the function of unknowing, see R. T. Wallis, 'The Spiritual Importance of Not Knowing', in A. H. Armstrong (ed.), *Classical Mediterranean Spirituality* (New York: Crossroad, 1986), pp. 460–80.

[85] *DN* I. 1, 588A; I. 3, 589A–B; *MT* IV, 1040D. He also describes the cause of being as ὑπέρθεος or ὑπερθεότης. There seems to be a bifurcation of the Platonic tradition, with some Platonists preferring to speak of the cause of all things as 'the [truly] existing One' (ὁ [ὄντως] ὤν, following LXX translation of Exod 3: 14), as do Philo, *De mutatione nominum*, 11 ('it is [God's] nature to be'); *De posteritate Caini*, 15; *De Decalogo*, 81; *De Abrahamo*, 121, 124, 143; *De vita Mosis*, I. 75; II. 161. Following Plato, *Resp.* VI, 509B and *Parm.* 142A–E, Dionysius prefers the language of 'beyond being' (ὑπερούσιος).

[86] *DN* I. 4, 593A: 'And if all knowledge is of that which is and is limited to the realm of the existent, then whatever transcends being must also transcend knowledge'. Trans. Luibheid, p. 53.

Second, following Plotinus, Dionysius envisions that the subject–object distinction disappears once the union is complete.[87] Since knowledge ordinarily presupposes subject–object distinction, such a union, if achievable, will be beyond knowledge. Third, as Dionysius emphasizes repeatedly, the union is ineffable, imageless and beyond the cognitive grasp of all human faculties:

> Just as the senses can neither grasp nor perceive the things of the mind, just as representation and shape cannot take in the simple and the shapeless, just as corporal form cannot lay hold of the intangible and incorporeal, by the same standard of truth beings are surpassed by the infinity beyond being, intelligences by that oneness which is beyond intelligence. Indeed the inscrutable One is out of the reach of every rational process.[88]

In fact, 'someone beholding God (ἰδὼν θεὸν) and understanding what he saw has not seen God himself (οὐκ αὐτὸν ἑώρακεν) but rather something of his which has being and which is knowable'.[89] As one is progressively more united to God, one's cognitive powers become stretched to their limits, at once undergoing simplification and unification. Since the unitive experience of God himself (as distinct from the experience of divine energies) has no cognitive content, such experience does not seem to require the engagement of the spiritual senses, or of any other faculties, for that matter. Yet, in the sentence just quoted, Dionysius continues to refer to the unitive experience in terms of 'beholding' and being able to 'see' God. Is Dionysius's description of *unio mystica* in terms of *visio Dei* purely figurative, or does the notion of 'vision' still retain any link with a form of perception?

To address this possibly unanswerable question, I would like to revisit my suggestion, made earlier, that for Dionysius spiritual perception is a cognitive continuum, rather than a discrete, unchanging set of faculties. As an imperfect illustration, consider the eyes that become capable of seeing a progressively wider spectrum of light, or the ears that acquire the ability to hear an increasingly broad range of sounds. Similarly, spiritual perception is gradually stretched and extended, as one approaches closer to God (along with one's awareness of the inexhaustible depth of the mystery of God). The ecstatic going out of oneself, what Dionysius calls 'an undivided and absolute abandonment of oneself and everything',[90] is the overcoming of

---

[87] *MT* I. 3, 1001A. Cf. Plotinus, *Enn.* VI. 7. 36. See J. M. Rist, *Eros and Psyche: Studies in Plato, Plotinus, and Origen* (University of Toronto Press, 1964), p. 83.

[88] *DN* I. 1, 588B, trans. Luibheid, pp. 49–50.

[89] *Ep.* I, 1065A; cf. Philo, *De mutatione nominum*, 8–9.   [90] *MT* I. 1, 1000A, trans. Luibheid, p. 135.

the limitations of the self, especially of all cognitive barriers on the road to God. As the self becomes increasingly transparent to the transcendent, all cognitive powers, including spiritual perception, are simplified, unified, extended and ultimately transcended:

The holiest and highest of the visible and intelligible things are but the ratio-nale which presupposes all that lies below the Transcendent One . . . But then he [Moses] breaks free of them, away from what sees and is seen, and he plunges into the truly mysterious darkness of unknowing. Here, renouncing all that the mind may conceive, wrapped entirely in the intangible and the invisible, he belongs completely to him who is beyond everything. Here, being neither oneself nor someone else, one is supremely united by a completely unknowing inactivity of all knowledge, and knows beyond the mind by knowing nothing.[91]

---

[91] *MT* I. 3, 1000D–1001A, trans. Luibheid, p. 137.

CHAPTER 6

Maximus the Confessor

Frederick D. Aquino

Maximus's religious epistemology of perception, and more specifically his account of the spiritual senses, is grounded in the larger projects of ascetic theology and deification.[1] These theological endeavours, as I hope to show, provide the backdrop for understanding why and how he links spiritual perception with the integration of the self. As Polycarp Sherwood rightly points out, deification for Maximus is all about gnomic reform, that is, whether humans will deliberate and move in the direction of realizing fully the capacities of their nature.[2] Accordingly, Maximus's religious epistemology of perception focuses on the interplay of the rational, the volitional and the sensate, fleshing out how the process of deification redirects the self and reaffirms its true nature, dignity and nobility. This involves cultivating a properly disposed mind that moves perceptual and intellectual capacities to 'the place of divine wisdom'.[3]

Redirecting the self to its proper end, however, does not suggest the annulment of the natural faculties; rather the aim is to purge the self of its divisive and destructive tendencies and move towards a more holistic way of existence. According to Maximus, receiving 'the mind of Christ comes along not by any loss of our mental power, nor as a supplementary mind to ours, nor as essentially and personally passing over into our mind, but rather as illuminating the power of our mind with its own quality and bringing the same energy to it'.[4] As a result, Maximus's account of spiritual perception neither pits the intellectual, volitional and the sensate against

[1] See A. Louth, *Maximus the Confessor* (London: Routledge, 1996), pp. 19–47.
[2] *St. Maximus the Confessor: The Ascetic Life, the Four Centuries on Charity*, trans. P. Sherwood (New York: The Newman Press, 1955), p. 235, n. 351. Louth, *Maximus the Confessor*, p. 62, taking a cue from the work of Iris Murdoch, adds that, for Maximus, the deliberative aspect of the gnomic will is 'the experience of accurate vision'. So the issue, as I hope to show, is that virtuous and contemplative practices purge those things that cloud the human agent's vision.
[3] *Amb.* LXXI. 1412A, trans. Louth, *Maximus the Confessor*, p. 165.
[4] *Capita theologica et oeconomica*, II. 83, trans. G. Berthold, *Maximus Confessor: Selected Writings* (Mahwah, NJ: Paulist Press, 1985), 165. The same stress on the continuity of spiritual perception and natural faculties can be seen in *Ad Thal.* LIX. 604D–608C: 'We are not permitted to say that

one another, nor does it demand a radical shutting-down of the natural faculties. Conversely, the goal is to bring together these different facets of human selfhood, and to reflect the unity of all things recapitulated in the incarnation.

In this chapter, I unpack three aspects of spiritual perception in Maximus. First, I locate Maximus within the spiritual senses tradition, uncover some of the terminology and show how he connects spiritual perception with liturgical, interpretive and contemplative practices. Second, I explain the relationship between virtue and perception. In my estimation, this connection has been largely ignored in the scholarly literature. For Maximus, the virtues, along with contemplation, aid the self in perceiving correctly its proper end and instantiating the mind of Christ. Third, I argue that Maximus operates with a twofold understanding of perceptual knowledge, involving training in perception and direct perception of God. The higher end is immediate and direct perceptual knowledge of God by acquaintance, which is set up by virtuous and contemplative practices. I hope to show that, for Maximus, virtuous and contemplative practices are a different kind of perception, though not radically discontinuous with perceptual knowledge of God by acquaintance. Perceptual knowledge of God is not the beginning but the fulfilment of the ascetic struggle.

SPIRITUAL PERCEPTION

Hans Urs von Balthasar notes that Maximus 'speaks positively' of the spiritual senses.[5] Such an impression is confirmed by a close analysis of the corpus of Maximus's writings, though, as I will argue, his use of such terminology fits the larger projects of ascetic theology and deification. Spiritual perception does not imply a secret sense, letting go of the natural

---

grace alone brings about, in the saints, insight into the divine mysteries without any contribution from their natural capacity to receive knowledge . . . The point is that the grace of the Holy Spirit does not bring about wisdom in the saints without the receptivity of their intelligence, does not give knowledge without their ability to grasp the Word, does not give faith without the stability of mind and the confident readiness to face the still-unrevealed future in hope . . . For the grace of Holy Spirit never destroys the capabilities of nature. Just the opposite: it makes nature, which has been weakened by unnatural habit, mature and strong enough once again to function in a natural way and leads it upward toward insight into the divine. For what the Holy Spirit is trying to accomplish in us is a true knowledge of things . . . For as the Logos accomplished divine works in the flesh, but not without the cooperation of a body animated by a rational soul, so the Holy Spirit accomplishes in the Saints the ability to understand mysteries, but not without the exercise of their natural abilities or without their seeking and careful searching for knowledge.' H. U. von Balthasar, *Cosmic Liturgy: The Universe According to Maximus the Confessor*, trans. B. Daley, SJ (San Francisco: Ignatius Press, 2003), pp. 72–3.

[5] Balthasar, *Cosmic Liturgy*, p. 285. See also Chapter 15 in this volume.

faculties or shutting down the physical in order to open the spiritual. Instead, the task at hand, for Maximus, is to perceive correctly how these various aspects of human selfhood function together properly and, more importantly, aid the self in achieving its final end.

The terminology of the spiritual senses can be found in the corpus of Maximus's writings, reflecting, though not uncritically, the antecedent influences of Origen, Evagrius of Pontus, Macarius, Pseudo-Dionysius the Areopagite and Diadochus of Photice. Some of the terms include 'divine perception' (αἴσθησις θεία),[6] 'noetic perception' (αἴσθησις νοερά),[7] 'noetic eyes' (νοερόι ὄμματα),[8] 'the eyes of the mind' (νοὸς ὀφθαλμοί)[9] and 'the eyes of the soul' (τῆς ψυχῆς τὰ ὄμματα).[10] More importantly, Maximus envisions a potential unity in the five bodily senses and the five faculties of the soul:

The sensible world is naturally fitted to provide the five senses with information, since it falls within their scope and draws them to an apprehension of itself. In a similar way, the intellectual world of the virtues falls within the scope of the faculties of the soul and guides them towards the spirit, rendering them uniform through their unvarying movement around the spirit alone and through their apprehension of it. And the bodily senses themselves, in accordance with the more divine inward essences befitting them, may be said to provide the faculties of the soul with information . . . Thus the senses have been called exemplary images of the faculties of the soul, since each sense with its organ, that is, its organ of perception, has naturally been assigned beforehand to each of the soul's faculties in an analogous manner and by a certain hidden principle. It is said that the sense of sight belongs to the intellective faculty (νοερᾶς), that is, to the mind, the sense of hearing to the rational faculty (λογικῆς), that is, to reason, the sense of smell to the incensive faculty (θύμος), the sense of taste to the appetitive faculty (ἐπιθυμῆτικης), and the sense of touch to the vivifying faculty. Or to put it more plainly, the organ of sight, that is, the eye, is simply an image of the mind; the organ of hearing, that is, the ear, is an image of reason; the organ of smell, that is, the nose, is an image of the incensive faculty; taste is an image of the appetitive faculty; and touch an image of life. The soul, then, according to the law of God who has wisely created all things, naturally makes use of these senses through its own faculties, and in various ways reaches out through them to sensible things. If it uses the senses properly, discerning by means of its own faculties the manifold inner essences of created beings, and if it succeeds in wisely transmitting to itself all the visible things in which God is hidden . . . Thus, the soul, moving in a wise manner and operating in accordance

[6] *Myst.* XXIII. 36, trans. Berthold, p. 205.
[7] *Expositio orationis dominicae*, II. 129, trans. G. E. H. Palmer, P. Sherrard and G. Ware, *The Philokalia*, vol. II (London: Faber and Faber, 1981), p. 288.
[8] *Ad Thal.* XVII. 112, trans. P. M. Blowers and R. L. Wilken, *Maximus the Confessor: On the Cosmic Mystery of Jesus Christ* (Crestwood, NY: St Vladimir's Seminary Press, 2003), p. 105.
[9] *Myst.* XXIII. 2, trans. Berthold, p. 204.   [10] *Ad Thal.* XVII. 114, p. 107; *Scholia in Ecclesiasten*, I. 23.

with the divinely perfect principle of its origin and existence, apprehends sensible things in a profitable way through the senses, since it has assimilated the spiritual essences that are in them, and appropriates the senses themselves, now endowed with reason through the abundance of rationality (λόγος) which they contain, using them as intelligent vehicles of its own. It joins these faculties to the virtues, and itself through the virtues to the more divine essences within these virtues. The more divine essences of the virtues are united with the spiritual mind hidden invisibly within them, and the spiritual mind of the more divine essences in the virtues... brings the soul, once it has been rendered simple and whole, as an offering to the whole of God.[11]

Maximus sees a correspondence between the five physical senses and the five faculties of the soul. Unlike Origen and others, he does not speak of the five spiritual senses as analogous to the five physical senses. Instead, Maximus correlates sight with the synthetic function of the mind, hearing with the discursive workings of reason, smell with spirit (θύμος), taste with desire (ἐπιθυμίας), and touch with the vivifying faculty. His mapping of the five physical senses onto the five powers of the soul represents a mature Platonic anthropology, with its more consistent distinction between *nous* and logos. Maximus's account also absorbs the relevant Aristotelian distinctions between the irascible, desiring and vegetative functions of the soul.[12]

Though they have distinctive aims, the intelligible and the sensible are not inherently at odds with each other. Rather, they are 'naturally related to each other through an indissoluble power that binds them together. Manifold is the relation between intellects and what they perceive and between the senses and what they experience.'[13] In this regard, Maximus describes three natural and interrelated movements of the self, highlighting the deep connection between perceptual knowledge and theological anthropology. This noetic arrangement entails three modalities of knowing: according to intellect or mind (νοῦς), according to discursive reason (λόγος) and according to sense-perception (αἴσθησις). Though each one has its own natural motion, the unifying movement of these modalities is the reintegration of the self. Hence, the faculties of sense and reason are correlated and interrelated by the mind, the spiritual subject that has 'the indissoluble power' to unite them.[14]

---

[11] *Amb.* XXI. 1248A–C, trans. P. Nellas, *Deification in Christ* (Crestwood, NY: St Vladimir's Seminary Press, 1987), pp. 216–18.

[12] I am indebted to Paul Gavrilyuk for this point.   [13] *Amb.* x. 1153A, trans. Louth, p. 124.

[14] *Amb.* x. 1153A, trans. Louth, p. 124. In *Amb.* x. 1112C–1113B, Maximus draws from Dionysius's teaching about the three motions of the soul, and argues that the faculties of the mind, reason and sense 'converge into one'. Trans. Louth, pp. 100–1.

The first modality, *nous*, involves a pure encounter with God. It entails knowing God non-inferentially and is therefore not dependent upon any other existent thing or reality. The second modality, logos, corresponds to the activity of deducing theological truths from causes. The third modality, *aisthesis*, 'is composite motion, according to which, affected by things outside as by certain symbols of things seen, the soul gains for itself some impression of the meaning of things'.[15] The key is to discern how each modality converges into a synthetic account of things, thereby reflecting the unity embedded in the intelligible realities. Human agents of deification unearth 'the spiritual reasons of things perceived through the senses, ascend by means of reason up to the mind, and, in a singular way, unite reason, which possesses the meanings of beings, to mind in accordance with one, simple and undivided sagacity'.[16] Another way of putting it is that reason and sense are to fit within the larger call to actualize the potential unity in humans; they are to 'be fully integrated into the unity which the νοῦς represents'.[17]

Ascetic formation of the self, then, calls for a 'higher collaboration of the faculties and, within the same scope, a natural reunion of νοῦς and αἴσθησις'.[18] The natural state of the self, as intended by God, entails continuity, not division, between body and soul. The same unitive reality is expressed in the cosmos. The intelligible and the sensible 'make up one world as body and soul make up one [person]'. Neither of these facets 'joined to the other in unity denies or displaces the other according to the law of the one who has bound them together'.[19] A unitive emphasis of this sort implies that there is a proper function and maturation of 'the good gift of our natural powers'.[20] Conversely, the propensity to act 'contrary to nature' results in abusing 'the natural power of uniting what is divided'.[21] The potential unity envisioned here requires the intersection of the rational, the volitional and the sensate.

Discerning these intersections (e.g. between body and soul, between the intelligible and the sensible) requires training in perception. The *Mystagogia*, for example, contends that perception of this sort enables the deiform person to decipher the intelligible realities embedded in the self, nature, the cosmos and liturgical practices. Maximus writes:

---

[15] *Amb.* x. 1113A, trans. Louth, p. 100.   [16] *Amb.* x. 1113A–B, trans. Louth, p. 100–1.
[17] L. Thunberg, *Microcosm and Mediator: The Theological Anthropology of Maximus the Confessor*, 2nd edn (Chicago: Open Court, 1995), p. 112.
[18] P. M. Blowers, *Exegesis and Spiritual Pedagogy in Maximus the Confessor: An Investigation of the Quaestiones ad Thalassium* (University of Notre Dame Press, 1991), p. 138.
[19] *Myst.* VII. 10–11, trans. Berthold, p. 196.   [20] *Amb.* VII. 1097C, trans. Blowers and Wilken, p. 71.
[21] *Amb.* XLI. 1308C, trans. Louth, p. 158.

For the whole spiritual world seems mystically imprinted on the whole sensible world in symbolic forms, for those who are capable of seeing (φαίνεται) this, and conversely the whole sensible world is spiritually explained in the mind in the principles which it contains . . . Indeed, the symbolic contemplation of intelligible things by means of visible realities is spiritual knowledge and understanding of visible things through the visible. For it is necessary that things which manifest each other bear a mutual reflection in an altogether true and clear manner and keep their relationship intact.[22]

Grasping the intelligible content of such materials (e.g. self-reflection through the practices of the virtues, contemplation of nature) requires a 'divine perception' (αἴσθησιν θείαν) with the 'undaunted eyes of the mind' (νοὸς ὄμματα or νοὸς ὀφθαλμόι).[23] A 'truly wise' person, 'through the abundance of virtue', possesses 'a mind illuminated by divine light' and can thus 'see what others do not see'.[24] As a result, the intelligibility of the mystery is not found in bifurcating reality into two worlds. Conversely, the illumined self recognizes that the worlds of the intelligible and the sensible are 'the same reality viewed in two different ways'.[25] Perception is neither purely spiritual nor is it purely sensual. Though not to be confused with one another, the intellectual and the sensible form a profound symbolic whole.

The same impact of the spiritual senses tradition can be seen in Maximus's interpretation of scripture. The link between spiritual exegesis and ascetic formation shapes the basic project.[26] In *Ad Thalassium*, XVII, for example, Maximus carefully interfuses 'the resolution of the scriptural ἀπορία (viz., the alleviation of the apparent injustice of God toward Moses) with a thoroughgoing exposition of the unceasing progress of the soul toward virtue'.[27] Coupled with the stable path of virtue, the 'eyes of the soul' (τῆς ψυχῆς τὰ ὄμματα) decipher the 'noumenal sense of the text' (τὸ νοούμενον τῆς γραφῆς). The key is to make sure that vices do not impede 'the perfect motion of the mind [τῆς διανοίας κίνησιν] toward divine

---

[22] *Myst.* II. 37–54, trans. Berthold, p. 189.   [23] *Myst.* XXIII. 2, 36–37, trans. Berthold, pp. 204–5.
[24] *Myst.* Proem. 75–80, trans. Berthold, p. 185.
[25] D. Bradshaw, *Aristotle East and West: Metaphysics and the Division of Christendom* (Cambridge University Press, 2004), p. 203. A. Cooper, *Body in St Maximus the Confessor: Holy Flesh, Wholly Deified* (Oxford University Press, 2005), p. 59, rightly points out that 'according to their natural, created state, human faculties in their psycho-somatic totality are receptive to divine revelation since they are naturally ordered to respond to the symbolic revelatory data available to them in the sensible and intelligible world'.
[26] As Blowers, *Exegesis and Spiritual Pedagogy*, p. 16, points out, 'human beings are summoned to undergo both cognitively, through the interchangeable contemplation of creation (φυσικὴ θεωρία) and scripture (γραφικὴ θεωρία), and morally, through the practice (πραξίς) of virtue'.
[27] *Ibid.* p. 65.

things' so that the self can 'consider, with noetic eyes [νοεροῖς ὄμμασιν], the power of the literal meaning in the Spirit, since this power is constantly being realized and abounding into its fullness'.[28]

The logic of διάβασις (spiritual transition) undergirds Maximus's approach to biblical interpretation. The move from sensible to intelligible truths does not relegate the former to an insignificant or irrelevant status. Alternatively, the interpretive process is a deeper perception of the higher meaning in and through the literal. Maximus sees the 'necessity of first passing through or penetrating sensible objects en route to the intelligible or spiritual truth that inheres by grace, in those sensible things'.[29] Accordingly, a properly formed mind pursues and receives divine thoughts:

The mind, who subsisting in that habitude and dwelling in this world, is instructed in true knowledge through the contemplation of created beings, receives a hidden and mystical commission from God invisibly to lead out of the *Egypt* of the heart – that is from the realm of flesh and sense – divine thoughts of created beings (τὰ θεῖα τῶν ὄντων νοήματα) ... Yet the mind who remains faithful in this divine ministry – having Gnostic wisdom (γνῶσιν σοφίας) joined with him like a companion, and having the noble demeanor and reflection that arise therewith – invariably travels in a holy way of life the road of the virtues, a road that in no way admits of any stalling on the part of those who walk on it.[30]

The stable path of spiritual perception, fostered by a robust set of virtuous and contemplative practices, brings about a more felicitous rendering of the text and thereby corrects any misunderstandings.

Maximus makes a similar point in his commentary on the Lord's Prayer. The Eucharist, for example, provides one way for the deiform person to share in the life of God and to be transformed by engaging in such a practice.[31] Through this liturgical practice the Logos empowers human agents of deification 'to participate in the divine life by making himself our food, in a manner understood by himself and by those who have received

---

[28] *Ad Thal.* XVII. 112, trans. Blowers and Wilken, p. 105.

[29] Blowers, *Exegesis and Spiritual Pedagogy*, p. 97. Such a spiritual *diabasis* 'not only involves the intellect but integrates the whole of human nature. The body must by its virtue ascend to and mirror the soul, while sense too, by its very synthetic power to apprehend the sensible symbols of the λόγοι of things, must rise to the service of reason and the mind' (p. 99). Also, 'the natural tension within the macrocosm between the sensible the intelligible reality – that is, between ἐπιφάνεια and λόγος in creation, between γράμμα and πνεῦμα in scripture, and thus too between sense (αἴσθησις) and intellect (νοῦς) in human nature – must be mediated in the human microcosm through the individual's own spiritual vocation of ascetic practice (πρᾶξις) and contemplation (θεωρία)' (p. 131).

[30] *Ad Thal.* XVII. 112–13, trans. Blowers and Wilken, p. 106.

[31] As N. Russell, *The Doctrine of Deification in the Greek Patristic Tradition* (Oxford University Press, 2004), p. 268, points out, the 'Word is received as spiritual food through a "noetic", or intellectual, appropriation of the divine, but the eucharistic allusion is no doubt also intentional'.

from him a noetic perception (αἴσθησις νοερά)'. In 'tasting this food', they come to know the divine virtues, and enhance their noetic vision. The Lord 'transmutes with divinity those who eat it, bringing about their deification, since He is the bread of life and of power in both name and reality'.[32]

However, the ascetic cultivation (maturation) of the self envisioned here is not simply a return to a pre-fallen state of stability, or the restoration of a primordial unity. On this point, Maximus rejects the Origenist claim that originally 'rational beings' enjoyed a state of rest (stability) and unity with God, from which they fell, and as a result, 'God envisaged the creation of this corporeal world to unite them with bodies for their former transgressions'.[33] For Maximus, the order of becoming, movement and rest more adequately captures the human condition than the Origenist order of rest, movement and becoming. The actual state of affairs suggests that becoming precedes movement. Body and soul come together simultaneously 'to form a particular person',[34] and so becoming issues in movement that has rest as its ultimate end.[35] For if God is the only unmoved reality, 'and everything that was brought from non-being to being is moved (because it tends toward some end), then nothing that moves is yet at rest'.[36] Since no 'creature by nature is unmoved', then progress towards a 'proper end is called a natural power, or passion, or movement passing from one thing to another'. Thus, it seems 'impossible to have movement before something has come into being'.[37]

Movement, then, is not the problem, and it does not necessarily imply a divisive status. Positively stated, movement, regulated by the ascetic virtues of the mind, is fundamental to the actualization of the good in human beings. It entails 'a natural beginning in being toward a voluntary end in well-being. For the end of the movement of those who are moved is "eternal well-being" itself, just as its beginning is being itself which is God who is the giver of being as well as of well-being.'[38] In other words, the virtues are crucial for moving humans towards their proper end – likeness to God.

[32] *Expositio orationis dominicae*, II. 129, trans. Palmer, Sherrard and Ware, vol. II, p. 288.
[33] *Amb.* VII. 1069A, trans. Blowers and Wilken, pp. 45–6.
[34] *Amb.* VII. 1101C, trans. Blowers and Wilken, p. 74.
[35] For Maximus, 'stability [rest] is not a potential condition of becoming... but is rather the end-stage of the realization of potency in the development of created things' (*Amb.* XV. 1220C–D, trans. Blowers and Wilken, p. 48, n. 8).
[36] *Amb.* VII. 1069B, trans. Blowers and Wilken, p. 46.
[37] *Amb.* VII. 1072A, trans. Blowers and Wilken, p. 47. Maximus adds that if God is sufficient for human well-being, then a fall from a perfect state of rest, stability and unity presupposes that God is incapable of satisfying human well-being. So what would prevent the same problem from happening again?
[38] *Amb.* VII. 1073C, trans. Blowers and Wilken, p. 50.

The real problem, for Maximus, arises from misunderstanding the actual nature of things. As a result, the self fails to 'cultivate its natural powers'.[39] The mind, reason and the senses are not inherently evil, since they are all derivative works of God. Thus, healing, not annulling, the cognitive and gnomic dimensions of human existence is fundamental to thinking about, desiring and perceiving the things of God. The reconstitution of intellect and will involves drawing out and actualizing the potential to be God-like, thereby redirecting misguided desire and integrating the deiform person into the natural state of affairs. The whole person, 'as the object of divine action, is divinized by being made God by the grace of God who became man. He remains wholly man in soul and body by nature, and becomes wholly God in body and soul by grace and by the unparalleled divine radiance of blessed glory appropriate to him.'[40]

PERCEPTION AND VIRTUE

The intersection of perception and virtue is particularly relevant to the process of cultivating the deiform self. The virtues aid the self in perceiving and taking the proper steps towards actual unity – from potential (image of God) to actual (divine likeness). The distinction between image and likeness pertains to the difference between the logos of nature and the *tropos* of virtue. As Maximus notes, 'Every intelligent nature is in the image of God, but only the good and the wise attain His likeness.'[41] Though movement towards achieving the human end of divine likeness certainly presupposes natural faculties (e.g. perception), training these faculties requires the cultivation of the virtues of Christ.

The ascetic struggle, for Maximus, is a basic component for perceiving divine matters correctly. 'Curb the irascible soul with love, weaken its concupiscible with self-mastery, give flight to its rational element with prayer, and the light of your mind will never be eclipsed.'[42] Perception, refined by virtuous and contemplative practices, moves the intellect towards the ultimate goal of immediate awareness of God (θεολογία). Consequently, Maximus rejects the separation of will and knowledge, at least in terms of the human desire to know God conceptually and experientially. More to the point, perception is a graded reality that gradually integrates and immerses the whole person into the life of God. Roberts and Wood make

---

[39] *Capita de caritate*, III. 4, trans. Palmer, Sherrard and Ware, *The Philokalia*, vol. II, p. 83.
[40] *Amb.* VII. 1088C, trans. Blowers and Wilken, p. 63.
[41] *Capita de caritate*, III. 25, trans. Palmer, Sherrard and Ware, vol. II, p. 87.
[42] *Capita de caritate*, IV. 80, trans. Berthold, *Maximus Confessor*, p. 84.

a contemporary point about such a connection, 'the functioning of the "intellect" is shot through with "will". The life of the intellect is just as much a matter of loves, concerns, desires, emotions, and the like as the other parts of our lives.'[43]

Virtuous practices clear away epistemic and emotional distractions, and thereby enable the person to refocus, perceive and embody the deeper realities in the world, in the self and in liturgical practices. Furthermore, the virtues are not properties of the soul; rather, they are instantiated dispositions, given that their formation reflects the interweaving of 'the faculties of the soul with the corresponding senses and sense organs of the body, and with the operations of the senses by means of which the soul embraces sensible things'.[44] The virtue of moral judgement, for instance, emerges from intertwining 'the contemplative and epistemic activity belonging to the intellective and rational faculty with the senses of seeing and hearing, which are directed toward the sensible objects appropriate to them'.[45] Thus, Maximus sees the unnatural division between mind and body as one example of faulty perception; the antidote is properly aligned perception through virtuous and contemplative practices.

Virtue, then, plays a fundamental role in training perception of the self, the world and the divine.[46] When held together, virtue and knowledge enable the epistemic agent to enter into 'God's light' (ἐν φωτὶ τῷ θεῷ).[47] 'Virtue is the form in which knowledge appears to us, but knowledge is the center that holds virtue together. Through them both, virtue and knowledge, one single wisdom (σοφίαν) comes into being.'[48] Maximus certainly values perceptual knowledge by acquaintance as something better than conceptual depictions of God, as I will show in the last section of this chapter. Yet both the process of and the aim of deification presume the cultivation of ascetic virtues as a precondition to direct perceptual knowledge of God.

An epistemically virtuous way of life forms a deiform self that intensely longs for and ceaselessly pursues God. It also enables the self to view things correctly and according to their true nature: 'A pure intellect sees things

---

[43] R. Roberts and J. Wood, *Intellectual Virtues: An Essay in Regulative Epistemology* (Oxford: Clarendon Press, 2007), p. 40.

[44] Nellas, *Deification in Christ*, p. 55. [45] *Amb.* XXI. 1248A–1249C, trans. Nellas, p. 217.

[46] M. Wynn, *Emotional Experience and Religious Understanding: Integrating Perception, Conception, and Feeling* (Cambridge University Press, 2005), pp. 2, 28, argues that moral perception is a 'habitual kind of seeing', that is, the capacity to take stock of the various elements of the situation at hand with 'due salience'. I hope to show in this section that something similar takes place in terms of Maximus's connection between virtue and perception.

[47] *Ad Thal.* VIII. 285A, trans. Balthasar, p. 332. [48] *Ad Thal.* LXIII. 681A, trans. Balthasar, p. 332.

correctly. A trained intelligence puts them in order. A keen hearing takes in what is said.'[49] A fitting example is love, the reality that solidifies the other virtues and illumines the process of deification.[50] The person 'who is deemed worthy of divine knowledge and who through love has attained its illumination will never be blown about by the spirit of vainglory'.[51] Though the mind is the organ of contemplative activity, its noetic perception is undergirded by love. That is to say, love endows the deiform person with 'a holy state of the soul, disposing it to value knowledge of God above all created things'.[52] Deifying illumination is 'born of love for God'.[53] 'As the memory of fire does not warm the body, so faith without love does not bring about the illumination of knowledge in the soul.'[54]

Love for God, then, fosters the right state of heart. The one 'who loves God values knowledge of God more than anything created by God, and pursues such knowledge ardently and ceaselessly'.[55] The deiform self values p because p precipitates such a value. Other things may have value but they are derivative of this knowledge. So the basis for knowing God is love precipitated by the subject and object of human enquiry – the triune God. The premise is that if God is the origin of all things, then it seems incoherent to place the inferior over the superior. 'Since the light of spiritual knowledge is the intellect's life, and since this light is engendered by love for God, it is rightly said that nothing is greater than divine love.'[56]

Envisioned here is a person who advances in moral understanding by internalizing the virtues of Christ, follows contemplative practices that engender spiritual knowledge, and desires to experience directly the qualities of God. The longing to know and participate in the life of God includes proper motivation and reliable process. One does not perceive divine things simply by following reliable belief-forming processes external to the noetic awareness of the deiform person. Rather, sharpening faculties and redirecting desire enable the human agent of deification to perceive, discriminate and discern. For example, a person can pursue the virtues through proper practices (e.g. fasts and vigils, prayer) but still miss the mark by doing this from an inappropriate motivation (e.g. vainglory). Training in perception

---

[49] *Capita de caritate*, II. 97, trans. Palmer, Sherrard and Ware, vol. II, p. 82.
[50] In *Amb.* XXI, Maximus claims that love more than any of the other virtues 'is productive of deification'. Trans. Nellas, p. 218.
[51] *Capita de caritate*, I. 46, trans. Berthold, p. 39.
[52] *Capita de caritate*, I. 1, trans. Palmer, Sherrard and Ware, vol. II, p. 53.
[53] *Capita de caritate*, I. 9, trans. Berthold, p. 36.
[54] *Capita de caritate*, I. 31–2, trans. Berthold, p. 38.
[55] *Capita de caritate*, I. 4, trans. Palmer, Sherrard and Ware, vol. II, p. 53.
[56] *Capita de caritate*, I. 9, trans. Palmer, Sherrard and Ware, vol. II, p. 54.

about divine matters presupposes intellectual and gnomic maturation. This is precisely the case because 'God searches the intention of everything that we do, whether we do it for him or any other motive'.[57] Virtuous acts stem from praiseworthy dispositions, and therefore, acts of kindness certainly have an objective status but what makes them praiseworthy is not simply the act but the properly formed motivation from which the act is done.[58]

The virtues reorder the passions, and thereby enable the intellect to see properly and move towards divine likeness. To the person who has 'through habit trained the soul's spiritual sense to discern good and evil', Christ 'gives himself as solid nourishment'.[59] When 'sown by God with seeds of virtue', the cultivated self is 'able to bring forth the power to see with knowledge what is in front of it, through a religious attention to contemplation'.[60] This kind of perception enables the self to actualize its gnomic (deliberative) potential towards divine likeness:

> It is evident that every person who participates in virtue as a matter of habit unquestionably participates in God, the substance of virtues . . . To the inherent goodness of the image is added the likeness (cf. Gen. 1: 26) acquired by the practice of virtue and the exercise of the will. The inclination to ascend and to see one's proper beginning was implanted in [humans] by nature.[61]

As we have seen, the virtues are crucial for perceiving correctly and actualizing the self's proper movement from potency to reality. Moreover, Maximus defines the truly satisfactory mode of philosophical reflection as 'true judgment concerning reality and activity, supported by ascetic struggle'.[62] For this reason, ascetic struggle is not merely a preparatory stage in the process of deification; it is an ongoing part of the formation of the deiform person into the likeness of God.

Spiritual perception, then, has a transformative dimension. Now the point is not that one must be epistemically virtuous to perceive basic things (e.g. to perceive that there is a bird in the back yard). However, pursuing God does call for the aligning of knowledge with evaluative qualities precisely because conforming to the goodness of God presupposes maturation of the epistemic agent. More to the point, deifying illumination results from virtuous and contemplative practices. People will perceive

---

[57] *Capita de caritate*, II. 35, trans. Berthold, p. 52.
[58] On the connection between motivation and act, see R. Adams, *A Theory of Virtue* (Oxford University Press, 2006).
[59] *Capita theologica et oeconomica*, I. 100, trans. Berthold, p. 147. This is a common patristic allusion to Heb 5: 14b.
[60] *Amb.* X. 1124D–1125A, trans. Louth, p. 107.
[61] *Amb.* VII. 1081C–1084A, trans. Balthasar, pp. 58–9.   [62] *Amb.* X. 1108A, trans. Louth, p. 97.

divine mysteries 'when they purify themselves by love and self-mastery, and the more intensely they strive the fuller will their vision be'.[63] The path of deification, if properly followed, restores the human 'appetite for what is naturally lovely'.[64]

The basic claim here is that ongoing participation in God's goodness requires the actualization of goodness. Illumination about achieving this proper human end 'is like the light from the stars. The stars do not shine in the day. When the greater and incomparable light of the sun appears, they are hidden and cannot be seen by the [physical] senses.'[65] Thus, when the epistemic agent throws off distractions and cultivates praiseworthy dispositions and virtuous practices, then he or she will perceive 'the clear meaning of truth' and become a recipient of 'genuine knowledge'. In Pauline fashion, the scales that 'cling to the clear-sighted part of the soul' will be gone and therefore they will no longer 'hinder the passage to the pure meaning of truth'.[66] The key, as we have seen, is the cultivation of virtue, which clears the 'soul's sight'.[67]

PERCEPTUAL KNOWLEDGE BY ACQUAINTANCE

Included in Maximus's account of the spiritual senses is a description of how training in perception leads to direct and immediate perception of God. As we have seen, virtuous and contemplative practices aid the self in purging misguided desires, in perceiving correctly the *logoi* in nature and in making progress towards divine likeness. In this sense, human agents of deification are active insofar as they 'have operative, by nature, a rational faculty for performing the virtues, and also a spiritual faculty, unlimited in its potential, capable of receiving all knowledge, capable of transcending the nature of all created beings and known things and even of leaving the "ages" of time behind it'.[68] Though virtue and perception form an integral relationship, direct perceptual knowledge of God seems to play a greater role in his epistemology of deification. It is the end to which the self is directed.

In this regard, Maximus distinguishes rational knowledge from experiential knowledge of God. Such a distinction corresponds to the difference between propositional knowledge (e.g. Elizabeth *knows that*

---

[63] *Capita de caritate*, IV. 70, 72, trans. Berthold, p. 83.   [64] *Amb.* X. 1132B, trans. Louth, p. 111.
[65] *Amb.* VII. 1077A, trans. Blowers and Wilken, p. 53.
[66] *Capita theologica et oeconomica*, II. 75, trans. Berthold, p. 164.
[67] *Amb.* X. 1116C, trans. Louth, p. 102.
[68] *Ad Thal.* XXII. 141–2, trans. Blowers and Wilken, p. 117.

there is an external world) and knowledge by acquaintance (e.g. David *knows* Michelle, not simply something about her) in contemporary epistemology.[69] However, the former has received more attention than the latter.[70]

In *Ad Thalassium*, LX, for example, Maximus distinguishes rational knowledge of God from direct perceptual (αἴσθησις) and experiential (πεῖρα) knowledge of God. The former kind of knowledge is not necessarily grounded in first-hand experience, and so a person may know that (conceptualize about) *p* but not have experiential knowledge of *p*. Since it lacks an experiential base, conceptual knowledge is not fully realized by the human agent of deification. Formally speaking, a *person* may know that *p* (in this case that God exists) but may not have experienced *p* (the triune God). For Maximus, conceptual knowledge is 'rooted only in reason (λόγος) and concepts (νοήμασιν)', and therefore is 'lacking in the kind of experiential perception of what one knows through active engagement; such relative knowledge is what we use to order our affairs in our present life'.[71]

The latter kind of knowledge entails direct, immediate, perceptual experience (πεῖρα) of God. It is acquired 'only by actual experience, [and Maximus adds] apart from reason and ideas, which provides a total perception (ὅλην τὴν αἴσθησιν) of the known object through a participation (μέθεξις) by grace'.[72] The experiential base here implies that knowledge of God is not simply knowing that *p*, though this certainly follows from the natural mode of contemplation (knowing God through inference of the natural world), but more importantly, the cultivation of ascetic virtues of the mind moves the intellect towards *theologia* – immediate awareness of God. Perception in this sense presupposes participation and an actualized experience. 'By this latter knowledge, we attain, in the future state, the supernatural deification (θέωσις) that remains unceasingly in effect.' Conceptual knowledge, however, 'can motivate our desire for the participative knowledge acquired by active engagement'.[73]

---

[69] Epistemologists also include 'how to' knowledge (e.g., Robert *knows how* to wire a house).

[70] The question of whether these two modes of knowledge can be reduced to one mode is for another time. For recent discussion of knowledge by acquaintance, see B. Brewer, *Perception and Reason* (Oxford: Clarendon Press, 1999); R. Fumerton, *Metaepistemology and Skepticism* (Lanham, MD: Rowman & Littlefield, 1995); and Roberts and Wood, *Intellectual Virtues*.

[71] *Ad Thal.* LX. 77, trans. Blowers and Wilken, p. 126.

[72] *Ad Thal.* LX. 77, trans. Blowers and Wilken, p. 126.

[73] *Ad Thal.* LX. 77, trans. Blowers and Wilken, p. 126. Balthasar, *Cosmic Liturgy*, p. 288, perceptively adds that, for Maximus, 'non-experiential knowledge of God – knowledge that contemplates God in the mirror of his creatures – has its overall purpose to awake in us a desire for mystical participation; but it is also designed to purify the soul in a positive way and prepare it for the transcendental experience'.

It seems clear that Maximus distinguishes propositional knowledge from knowledge by acquaintance. The union of the divine and human in Christ can be received intellectually, but more importantly 'the union has been manifested [in Christ] so that they [naturally mobile creatures] might also acquire, by experience, an active knowledge of him in whom they were made worthy to find their stability and to have abiding unchangeably in them the enjoyment of this knowledge'.[74] Knowledge by acquaintance is mystical theology, the third stage of the process of deification. Maximus speaks of this knowledge (θεολογία) as purely passive and graced,[75] but at other times he speaks of honed perception as leading to this higher form of perception. The human agent of deification perceives God immediately, not through deductive, inductive or abductive processes of belief-formation. Such knowledge, for Maximus, applies primarily to a future state. The emphasis here is less on apophatic theology than on the distinction between two modes of knowing, especially since Maximus stresses the importance of antecedent practices (virtue, natural contemplation) and sees *theologia* as direct perception of God and as 'active knowledge'.[76] So the ascent to God in this final sense presupposes the importance of love, the purgation of vices and the cultivation of virtues, and the relevance of contemplative practices. These practices 'are not so much overcome as taken up'.[77]

Perceptual knowledge, then, is a progression, a transition from knowledge that p to direct perceptual knowledge. Various kinds of indirect perception of God in the self, cosmos, scripture and so on are not irrelevant; they simply enable the self to become integrated and to participate, to a greater extent (from one degree to another), in the divine energies. So, *theologia* is the fulfilment and perfection of antecedent modes of knowledge.[78] Training in perception, shaped by virtuous and contemplative practices, fosters a 'firm and stable disposition, a willing surrender, so that from the one from whom we have received being we long to receive being moved as well. It is like the relation between image and its archetype.'[79]

Judgement and perception play a complex role in Maximus's account of spiritual perception. That is to say, virtuous and contemplative practices help the self to see, act and perceive correctly. More specifically, a

[74] *Ad Thal.* LX. 76–7, trans. Blowers and Wilken, pp. 125–6.
[75] See *Ad Thal.* XXII. 141, trans. Blowers and Wilken, pp. 117–18.
[76] *Ad Thal.* LX. 77, trans. Blowers and Wilken, pp. 125–6.
[77] A. Nichols, *Byzantine Gospel: Maximus the Confessor in Modern Scholarship* (Edinburgh: T. & T. Clark, 1993), p. 29. See also Thunberg, *Microcosm and Mediator*, pp. 351–81.
[78] Bradshaw, *Aristotle East and West*, p. 193.
[79] *Amb.* VII. 1076B, trans. Blowers and Wilken, p. 52.

virtue-based account of perceptual knowledge (and in this case the spiritual senses) undergirds Maximus's conception of deification. The intellect is to be changed by the knowledge, understanding and wisdom acquired through the ascetic struggle. The ascetic virtues of the mind are fundamental to reorienting and assisting the intellect in its natural move towards deification. Perceptual knowledge of God by acquaintance presupposes that perceptual capacities are trained through ascetic virtues of the mind, and, as a result, the deiform intellect learns to see self, nature and God clearly. In this sense, the ascetic virtues of the mind regulate how a person ought to pursue the path of deification, though perceiving God, via acquaintance, is a different mode of knowledge.

Perhaps another way of putting it is that, for Maximus, virtue, perception and acquaintance are interconnected. In one sense, it seems that acquaintance depends upon traits of virtue – virtues requisite for seeing things correctly and making progress on the path to deification. The virtues that condition perception are dispassion, discrimination, humility, love, knowledge and wisdom. In another sense, training in perception is not to be confused with perception on another level. Perceptual knowledge of God by acquaintance suggests that the deiform person is 'supernaturally stripped bare of every energy that operates in accordance with sense or reason or mind, and ineffably and unknowably attains the divine delight that is beyond reason and mind, in the form and fashion that God who gives such grace knows and those who are worthy of receiving this from God understand'.[80]

CONCLUDING REMARKS

Spiritual perception involves training perceptual capacities through ascetic virtues of the mind, and learning to see clearly the nature of things through contemplative practices. The ultimate goal is direct perception of divine energies. Experiencing God in this more profound sense would be less abrupt and, in fact, more natural in Maximus's sense of the term. Ascetic virtues clear the mind of distractions, contemplation of nature reorients the self, and *theologia* entails immediate awareness of God. Obviously, the deiform person leans upon antecedent experiences, traditions and exemplars to form his or her theological perceptual capacities. Yet its ultimate goal is to move towards direct perception of God.

---

[80] *Amb.* x. 1153C, trans. Blowers and Wilken, p. 125.

My claim, then, is that spiritual perception, for Maximus, is twofold.[81] It is a matter of progression, from training in perception to direct perception, and is accordingly undergirded by a profound commitment to the integration of the intellectual, volitional and sensate. As a result, the natural state of the intellect is movement towards divine likeness, and such a movement requires the cultivation of the virtues of Christ. In contemporary terms, knowledge by acquaintance presumes participation in the life of God.

---

[81] As A. Millar, 'The Scope of Perceptual Knowledge', *Philosophy*, 75 (2000), 79, points out, 'perceptual knowledge about something is knowledge of that thing from the way it appears relative to some sense'. It can refer to something that is 'phenomenologically immediate, in the sense that is not acquired via inference from prior assumptions' (p. 73). It is also true that 'sometimes we are interested in how things look, for example, relative to the powers of discrimination of *any* perceivers with properly functioning sight. It is clear, however, that an adequate account of worldly appearances must acknowledge appearances which some of those who have the relevant sense in good working order may not be able to discriminate. As a student I received training in discriminating some sixty varieties of potato from the look of their plants. This put me in a position to make discriminations I could not make prior to the training and could not make now. Relative to those who had the training the look of King Edwards was very different from the look of Pentland Crown. Similar points obviously apply to the tastes and smells of wines' (p. 79). However, Millar argues that 'it is important not to confuse the claim that appearances are relative in the way acknowledged here with the claim that the notion of the appearance of a thing is to be explained in terms of a prior notion of a thing's appearing some way to some individual' (p. 79, n. 12).

CHAPTER 7

Alexander of Hales

Boyd Taylor Coolman

'Do not touch me.'

Jesus to Mary Magdalene[1]

Touch consummates knowledge.

Augustine[2]

INTRODUCTION

Near the end of *Proslogion*, Anselm of Canterbury invoked the language of spiritual sensation to mourn the absence of the God whose existence, though perhaps proved certain, eluded his experience:

Still you are hidden, O Lord, from my soul . . . For it looks, and does not see your beauty. It listens, and does not hear your harmony. It smells, and does not perceive your fragrance. It tastes, and does not recognize your sweetness. It touches, and does not feel your pleasantness. For you have these attributes in yourself, Lord God, after your ineffable manner, who has given them to objects created by you, after their sensible manner; but the sinful senses of my soul have grown rigid and dull, and have been obstructed by their long listlessness.[3]

As often with Anselm, his remark looks back to his patristic forebears, East and West. Seven centuries earlier, Augustine of Hippo had confessed an opposite experience, though in similar terms:

Yet there is a light I love, and a food, and a kind of embrace when I love my God – a light, voice, odour, food, embrace of my inner man, where my soul is floodlit by light which space cannot contain, where there is sound that time cannot seize, where there is a perfume which no breeze disperses, where there is a taste for food no amount of eating can lessen, and where there is a bond of union that no satiety can part.[4]

---

[1] Jn 20: 17.   [2] *De trin.* I. 9. 18 (PL 42. 833): *Tactus enim tanquam finem facit notionis.*

[3] *Proslogion*, 17, ed. F. S. Schmitt, *S Anselmi Cantuariensis Archiepiscopi: Opera omnia*, vol. I (Stuttgart: Friedrich Frommann, 1984).

[4] *Conf.* x. 6. 8, trans. H. Chadwick, *Saint Augustine: Confessions* (Oxford University Press, 1991), p. 183.

Anselm's reference to the 'senses of the soul' also recalls the doctrine of the spiritual senses of the soul inaugurated in the east by Origen of Alexandria. Commenting on Leviticus 6: 3, conveyed to medievals by the *Glossa ordinaria* (at Lev 7: 5), Origen said:

> The five physical senses are able to be redeemed, as they are converted to good acts, just as are the five interior senses: so that with a pure heart we may see God and hear what he says to us, and smell the good odour of Christ and taste him. Concerning which the Psalm says, *taste and see that the Lord is good* (Ps 34 [33]: 8); and we will touch with Saint John *concerning the word of life* (I Jn 1: 1).[5]

After Origen, this teaching found varied expression in the East with Gregory of Nyssa, Pseudo-Dionysius and Maximus the Confessor.[6]

But Anselm's description looks forward too, offering a point of departure for an investigation of early scholastic teaching on the spiritual senses. After him, the topic received consistent attention from medieval thinkers spanning a wide spectrum of theological styles and milieux: monastics, like William of Saint-Thierry and Bernard of Clairvaux;[7] mystics, such as Hadewijch of Antwerp and Ruusbroec;[8] and, perhaps surprisingly, scholastics like William of Auxerre[9] and Bonaventure,[10] and, investigated below, Alexander of Hales.

Given his reputation as the 'father of scholasticism', Anselm's description rather ironically leaves implicit a conspicuous feature of subsequent scholastic teaching on the subject, namely, its ecclesial dimension. Especially for scholastics of the twelfth and thirteenth centuries, the dominant conception of the church was that of the *corpus mysticum*, the mystical body of Christ, with Christ as head and the faithful corporately and organically linked to him as his body.[11] Here, the explicit condition for the possibility of spiritually sensuous perception of God was participation in this mystical body. Only if 'made sensate by their Head' (*sensificentur a capite*)[12] could members of the *ecclesia* perceive the divine nature.

---

[5]   In Lev 6: 3, Lyranum 1, 223r, ed. K. Froehlich and M. T. Gibson, *Biblia latina cum glossa ordinaria*, 4 vols. (Turnhout: Brepols, 1992).

[6]   See Chapters 2, 5 and 6 in this volume.

[7]   See G. Rudy, *Mystical Language of Sensation in the Later Middle Ages* (New York and London: Routledge, 2002), pp. 45–65; R. Fulton, '"Taste and see that the Lord is sweet" (Ps 33: 9): The Flavor of God in the Monastic West', *Journal of Religion*, 86.2 (2006), 169–204.

[8]   See Rudy, *Mystical Language*, pp. 67–100, 112–19, and Chapter 11 in this volume.

[9]   See B. T. Coolman, *Knowing God by Experience: The Spiritual Senses in the Theology of William of Auxerre* (Washington, DC: Catholic University of America Press, 2004).

[10]   See Chapter 9 in this volume; F. M. Tedoldi, *La dottrina dei cinque sensi spirituali in San Bonaventura* (Rome: Pontificium Athenaeum Antonianum, 1999); and Rudy, *Mystical Language*, pp. 103–9.

[11]   See H. de Lubac, *Corpus Mysticum: The Eucharist and the Church in the Middle Ages* (University of Notre Dame Press, 2007).

[12]   Hugh of St Victor, *De scripturis et scriptoribus* (PL 175. 10A).

FROM AN *INTELLECTUS FIDEI* TO A *SENSUS FIDEI*

For a particular scholastic trajectory – finding a point of departure in Peter Lombard, arcing through such early thirteenth-century masters as William of Auxerre and Alexander of Hales, reaching its zenith in Bonaventure – this ecclesial context seems to account for, or to be at least correlated with, four additional features of scholastic teaching on the matter.

First, Anselm's text reflects the typically analogical conception of the spiritual senses and their objects, as well as a corresponding theological anthropology, in scholastic teaching. Just as the created, physical world has sensible objects that the physical senses can perceive, so the spiritual soul has senses that perceive the uncreated, divine nature. Assumed characteristics of physical sense perception will often justify claims made for the nature of spiritual perception.

Second, Anselm's text suggests that, while in some sense proper to the soul as such, the spiritual senses are also susceptible to decreased capacity or even suppression due to sin and negligence. Conversely, later scholastics assumed that these senses require habilation and activitation through sacramental grace and moral preparation and purification in order to function properly.

Third, Anselm assumes, as will later scholastics, that despite the essential simplicity of the divine nature *in se*, it has diverse and distinguishable attributes that the soul may encounter variously, through its own diversified spiritual sensorium. Later scholastics will consistently orient the spiritual senses towards two transcendental properties of God, in particular: the true (*prima veritas*) and the good (*summum bonum*). These are sensed spiritually as real, objective determinations and genuine self-manifestations of the divine nature, flowing down from the first truth and the highest good. This will give a certain philosophical cast to their teaching on the matter, while also fostering an existential, experiential dimension to speculative enquiry.

Fourth, the spiritual senses played a role in the larger practice of reception of, and formation in, ecclesial faith. From the second quarter of the twelfth century, scholastic theologians pursued an *intellectus fidei* within a self-consciously ecclesial framework. The faith, whose depths they probed, whose coherence they perceived, whose intelligibility they searched out, was that received authoritatively in the church. Their project is aptly summarized as 'the active reception of the Church's understanding of divine revelation as proposed in Scripture and as received by way of the Church's teaching, that is, by way of the Fathers, the Councils, and the liturgy'.[13]

---

[13] R. Hütter, 'Transubstantiation Revisited: *Sacra doctrina*, Dogma, and Metaphysics', in R. Hütter and M. Levering (eds.), *Ressourcement Thomism: Sacred Doctrine, the Sacraments, and the Moral*

Or, as Peter Lombard put it programmatically: 'we have attempted to reveal the hidden depths of theological investigations and to pass on an understanding of the Church's sacraments'.[14]

The goal of this scholastic pursuit of an ecclesial *intellectus fidei* was not merely a deeper speculative understanding of the faith, but also a wisdom, an experiential savouring (suggested by the Latin etymology of *sapientia*) of the God thus revealed and known. More precisely, this *intellectus fidei* culminated in a more mystical *sensus fidei*, an experience of the realities towards which faith pointed, mediated by the spiritual senses of the soul.[15] In this way, the doctrinal principle 'I believe in order to understand' (*credo ut intelligam* – championed by Anselm) found its parallel and its organic consummation in a mystical principle, 'I believe in order to experience' (*credo ut experior* – cultivated typically in monastic contexts),[16] in a self-consciously ecclesial framework, and was given theoretical interpretation in the scholastic doctrine of the spiritual senses of the *corpus mysticum*.

These characteristics of scholastic teaching on the spiritual senses appear in the teaching of Alexander of Hales. Early thirteenth-century scholastic theologian at Paris, high-profile convert to the Franciscan Order and Bonaventure's revered teacher, Alexander was immensely influential on later scholastic theology, especially on the 'Franciscan school'.[17] He was 'the first not only to publicly lecture on the *Sentences* but also to divide the Lombard's text into distinctions, a division retained by Albert, Bonaventure, and Thomas'.[18] Like his older contemporary William of Auxerre, Alexander evinced a robust interest in the soul's spiritual senses.[19] Scattered reflections emerge in his commentary (1223–7) on the *Sentences* of Peter

---

Life: Essays in Honor of Romanus Cesaro, O.P. (Washington, DC: Catholic University of America Press, 2010), pp. 21–79, at p. 24.

[14] Peter Lombard, *The Sentences*, bk. 1: *The Mystery of the Trinity*, trans. Giulio Silano, Mediaeval Sources in Translation, 42 (Toronto: Pontifical Institute of Mediaeval Studies, 2007), Prol. 1, p. 3.

[15] Hütter, 'Transubstantiation Revisited', p. 68.

[16] See B. McGinn's discussion of these two goals of medieval theology in *The Presence of God: A History of Western Mysticism*, vol. II: *The Growth of Mysticism* (New York: Crossroad, 1994), p. 367.

[17] See W. H. Principe, *The Theology of the Hypostatic Union in the Early Thirteenth Century*, vol. IV: *Philip the Chancellor's Theology of the Hypostatic Union* (Toronto: Pontifical Institute of Mediaeval Studies, 1975), pp. 32, 192.

[18] P. Gondreau, *The Passions of Christ's Soul in the Theology of St. Thomas Aquinas*, Beiträge zur Geschichte der Philosophie und Theologie des Mittelalters, new series, 61 (Münster: Aschendorff, 2002), pp. 88–9.

[19] In his magisterial discussion of the spiritual senses in the Christian tradition, K. Rahner gave Alexander relatively little attention ('The Doctrine of the "Spiritual Senses" in the Middle Ages', in *Theological Investigations*, vol. XVI, trans. David Morland (New York: Seabury Press, 1979), p. 108). Rahner appears to have been unaware of Alexander's extensive discussion in his *Quaestiones disputatae* and elsewhere, citing only the *Summa halensis*.

Lombard[20] (*Glossa in quatuor libros Sententiarum*[21]). His *Quaestiones disputatae 'antequam esset frater'* (before 1236),[22] though, contains an entire *quaestio 'De sensu spirituali'* (hereafter, '*Quaestio disputata* 31'), the largest focused treatment of the topic since Origen of Alexandria. Finally, in the next decade (before 1245), some of his earlier teachings were incorporated into the *Summa theologiae* or *Summa fratri Alexandri*[23] (hereafter, *Summa halensis*),[24] while others, intriguingly, were omitted. Along with William, Alexander prepared the way for the more celebrated teaching of Bonaventure. Yet Bonaventure's teacher is of additional interest in that, *pace* recent claims to the contrary, his theorizing on the spiritual senses tended to privilege the senses of taste, and especially touch, over vision and audition in sensing God.[25]

SENTIRE CUM ECCLESIAE: SENSING CHRIST ECCLESIALLY IN THE TWELFTH CENTURY

The above-noted ecclesial context for scholastic discussion of the spiritual senses of the soul is widely apparent in various contexts in the twelfth century. William of Saint-Thierry, whose *On the Nature and Dignity of*

---

[20] See Peter Lombard, *Magistri Lombardi Sententiae in IV libris distinctae*, 2 vols., Spicilegium Bonaventurianum, 4–5 (Grottaferrata: Collegium Sancti Bonaventurae ad Claras Aquas, 1971–81).

[21] Alexander of Hales, *Glossa in quatuor libros Sententiarum Petri Lombardi*, ed. Quaracchi, vols. XII–XV (Florence: Collegium Sancti Bonaventurae, 1951–7).

[22] Alexander of Hales, *Quaestiones disputatae 'antequam esset frater'*, ed. Quaracchi, vols. XIX–XXI (Florence: Collegium Sancti Bonaventurae, 1960).

[23] Alexander of Hales, *Summa theologiae (Summa halensis)*, ed. Quaracchi, vols. I–IV (Florence: Collegium Sancti Bonaventurae, 1924–48).

[24] As W. H. Principe explains, 'an important theological work written after 1240, the so-called *Summa Fratris Alexandri*, was long thought to be Alexander's own work. In recent decades, however, scholarly opinion has concluded that, however great the influence of Alexander on the composition of this *Summa*, his own authentic teaching must be sought in the *Glossa* and in his *Quaestiones* rather than in the *Summa Fratris Alexandri*'. *The Theology of the Hypostatic Union in the Early Thirteenth Century*, vol. II: *Alexander of Hales' Theology of the Hypostatic Union* (Toronto: Pontifical Institute of Mediaeval Studies, 1967), p. 15.

[25] Rudy, *Mystical Language*, pp. 39–43, recently advanced the claim that the dominant strand of thought in the history of Christian teaching on the spiritual senses of the soul has privileged the so-called 'superior' senses, hearing or audition and especially sight or vision, over the inferior (because 'closer to the body') senses of smell, taste and touch. Rudy labels these interpretive traditions as 'dualist' and, in addition to Origen and Augustine, includes the medieval scholastics William of Auxerre, William of Auvergne, Alexander of Hales and Albert the Great among them. Rudy concludes: 'Yet [these scholastic thinkers] still subordinate this knowing [i.e. spiritual taste and touch] to the knowledge by the intellect that "sees"' (p. 43). As will be seen below, Rudy's conclusion is not borne out by careful examination of the writings of Alexander of Hales. Rudy's brief treatment of Alexander considers only the discussion in the *Summa halensis*, a work largely of Alexander's students which lacks the fuller discussion found in his earlier works (pp. 41–2). This narrow purview also causes Rudy to attribute various points of originality to Albert the Great (pp. 42–3) that are in fact already present in Alexander.

Love contains an extensive discussion of the spiritual senses, observes: 'The Body of Christ is the universal Church . . . In the head of this body . . . there are four senses: sight, hearing, smell and touch.'[26] William then singles out the sense of taste for extended treatment. More typical is the description attributed to Hugh of St Victor (d. 1141): 'For this reason Christ is called the head of the church: since just as all the bodily senses are completely in the head of a man, namely, sight, hearing, smelling, tasting and touching; so in Christ is the fullness of all the spiritual senses, namely, the fullness of grace, "from whom we have all received (Jn 1)"'.[27] As head, Christ possesses all the spiritual senses. Joined to Christ as head, the church as body receives from him the capacity for spiritual sensation, as Hugh's contemporary Hildebert explains: 'since Christ is related to the Church as head to body, he provides for the Church and rules it, and in him are all the spiritual senses of the Church, just as all the senses of the body are in the head'.[28] Endowed with these senses, the members of the church are enabled to know and perceive God through the spiritual senses of their head in whom they participate, a point stressed by Herveus, another little-known twelfth-century figure, invoking biblical texts oft-cited in this discussion: 'all the spiritual senses of the church are in Christ, so that in him, the church might see God and hear his word, and "taste how sweet he is" (Ps 33) and draw [to itself] the odour of his knowledge and touch him spiritually, saying: "it is good for me to adhere to God" (Ps 72)'.[29] Here, then, Christ is the head, from whom the spiritual senses flow down into the ecclesial body. In this sense, the traditional phrase *sentire cum ecclesiae* might be invoked, in its more literal denotation of sensing or perceiving, to capture this scholastic approach to the spiritual senses.

This apparently widespread sentiment concerning the ecclesial 'location' of the spiritual senses finds its way into the writings of Peter Lombard at mid-century. In his commentary on the Pauline letter to the Ephesians, the Lombard wrote: 'God gave him to be the head, in whom are all the spiritual senses of the church, namely the gifts of grace.'[30] In his commentary on the letter to the Colossians, moreover, the Lombard repeats nearly verbatim the text of Hildebert quoted above.[31] In his soon-to-be famous and influential *Sentences* (book III, d. 13), though, Peter proffered a controversial opinion

---

[26] *William of St. Thierry: The Nature and Dignity of Love*, trans. T. X. Davis (Kalamazoo, MI: Cistercian Publications, 1981), IV. 29, 88–9.
[27] *In Epistolam ad Ephesios* (PL 175. 570C).
[28] Hildebertus Cenomanensis, *XIII In Epiphania Domini*, Sermo primus (PL 171. 408B–C).
[29] Herveus Burgidolensis, *In Epistolam ad Ephesios* (PL 181. 1219B).
[30] Peter Lombard, *In Epistolam ad Ephesios* (PL 192. 178D).
[31] Peter Lombard, *In Epistolam ad Colossenses* (PL 192. 263D–264A).

on the matter. While concurring with the earlier consensus regarding the presence of all the spiritual senses in Christ the head, he restricted the sense capacity of the ecclesial body to that of touch alone (taking his cue from Augustine and perhaps intentionally disagreeing with the statement of Origen, quoted above):

Augustine said *To Durandus*[32] that Christ was filled with all grace; but grace does not so inhabit the saints: 'Just as in our body there is a sense in the individual members, but not as in the head; for in the head is sight, hearing, smelling, tasting and touch, but in the other members there is only touch.' So in Christ 'all the fullness of divinity dwelled' (Col 2: 9), since he is the head in which are all the senses; but in the saints it is as if there is touch alone, to whom the Spirit was given according to measure, since 'from him they have all received' (Jn 1: 16).[33]

The Lombard's comments stimulated discussion of the topic among later scholastic commentators.[34]

ALEXANDER OF HALES'S TEACHING ON THE SPIRITUAL SENSES

Following the above-noted trajectory, Alexander of Hales locates his teaching squarely within an ecclesial and sacramental context, as is evident already in his commentary on the Lombard's *Sentences*. There, he pursues and extends the ecclesiology of the mystical body, with Christ as head and the members of the church as his ecclesial body. While earlier authors had affirmed that the spiritual senses flowed down into the ecclesial body from Christ their head, for his part Alexander affirms more explicitly the implication that the incarnate Christ himself possessed the spiritual senses: 'Christ possessed these senses, since he was a *comprehensor* in this life.'[35] So endowed, Christ communicates the spiritual senses to the members of his body:

That Christ is the head, take from Eph 1, at the end: 'the church, which is his body', [on which] the *Gloss* [says]: 'Gave him to be the head, in whom are all the spiritual senses of the church (*sensus spirituales Ecclesiae*), namely, the gifts of grace'. Just as the body has life in the head, so the Ecclesia [has] spiritual life [in the head]. Hence, on Col 1: 18: 'He is the head of the body of the Ecclesia', the *Gloss* [says]: 'Just as the soul animates and vivifies our whole body, but in the head it perceives with all the senses, for this reason all [the senses] are subject to the

---

[32] *Ep.* 187. 13. 40 (PL 33. 847; CSEL 57. 117).

[33] Peter Lombard, *Magistri Lombardi Sententiae in IV libris distinctae*, bk. II, d. 132.

[34] It appears that the Lombard is here influenced by Pseudo-Hugh of St Victor, *Quaestiones et decisiones in Epistolas D. Pauli*, 5. *In Epistolam ad Ephesios, quaestio* 10.

[35] *Glossa in III Sent.* d. 13, n. 22 (ed. Quaracchi, pp. 135–6).

head for their operations . . . ' Therefore, he is called head by reason of which flow all the senses from the head to the members of the Ecclesia.[36]

For Alexander, then, Christ is the source of spiritual sensation, first to the church as his body, and then, by extension, to individual members.[37]

Alexander's assumption regarding the ecclesial foundation for the presence and operation of the spiritual senses in members of Christ's body is confirmed in his teaching on the sacraments. In baptism, for example, capacities for spiritual sensation are habilitated in the baptizand through the symbolic actions of the rite. The baptismal action of anointing the mouth, nose and ears is meant 'to open the baptizand to the spiritual senses'. He correlates these three senses with the three theological virtues: 'The habilitation for charity is signified by taste; the habilitation toward the understanding of the faith [is signified] by the opening of the ears; the habilitation toward hope [is signified] in the smell of the nose. For odor is of remote things.'[38] Why only these three? Why are sight and touch excluded? 'In these three senses is noted a threefold habilitation for the purpose of cognition (*cognitio*), namely, for the understanding of the truth through audition, which pertains to remote things; for the tasting of the good through taste; for discerning its opposite, which occurs through the discretion of spiritual smell.'[39] Already apparent here are the basic shape and orientation of Alexander's spiritual sensorium. He arranges them on a continuum of proximity to their object: vision and audition are most remote; smell, taste and touch are respectively closer to their objects. Tellingly, he does not construct a vertical hierarchy here of 'lower' to 'higher' senses. He observes, rather, a progression from faith's vision and audition of divine *veritas*, through hope's olfaction of divine things, to charity's taste and especially touch of divine *bonitas*,[40] a movement from the most distant to the most intimate and certain knowledge of God.[41] Alexander seems to assume here that sacramental grace does not establish the spiritual senses in the soul, but rather activates them; habilitation rather than capacitation.

A similar movement from faith's understanding to charity's adhering is apparent in Alexander's conception of the Eucharistic reception.[42] Here,

---

[36] *Glossa in III Sent.* d. 19, n. 41 (ed. Quaracchi, p. 220).

[37] It is worth noting that Alexander explicitly rejects the notion that the Holy Spirit is the source of spiritual sensation in the members of Christ's body. See *Glossa in III Sent.* d. 19, n. 41 (ed. Quaracchi, p. 220).

[38] *Glossa in IV Sent.* d. 6, n. 15 (ed. Quaracchi, pp. 121–2).

[39] *Glossa in IV Sent.* d. 6, n. 17 (ed. Quaracchi, p. 126).

[40] For a similar notion in William of Auxerre's teaching on the spiritual senses, see Coolman, *Knowing God*, pp. 139–58.

[41] For a discussion of a similar approach in Albert the Great, see Rudy, *Mystical Language*, p. 42.

[42] For William of Auxerre's teaching on the spiritual senses and the Eucharist, see Coolman, *Knowing God*, pp. 218–34.

though, he adds anthropological specification. He interprets Augustine's well-known phrase 'believe and you have eaten' as a reference to 'faith working through love', so-called formed faith, which 'unites us to the head' in two ways. On the one hand, 'faith *per se* unites the *intellect* to Christ the head'; on the other hand, 'faith *with charity* unites the *affect*'.[43] To cinch his point, Alexander pursues an analogy with ordinary eating. For him, there is a direct correlation between the delectation that food generates and its nutritional value. In ordinary eating, delectation via the physical senses is maximal at the point of direct contact. Similarly, '[the Eucharist] is the food of the soul by reason of the spiritual delectation which is in the food', and there is 'maximal delectation through the maximal 'conjunction of the fitting with the fitting'.[44] Such conjunction occurs when both intellect and the affect are united to the Eucharistic Christ. The intellect is united by 'recalling to memory Christ's passion'; the affect is united when the will is 'informed by charity' for Christ. Thus Christ becomes the 'food of the soul, since by that delectation in Christ the soul draws out its nutrients'.[45] For 'the spiritual mouth is the mind (*mens*) in relation to the intellect (*intellectus*); the spiritual stomach is [the mind] with respect to the affect'.[46] Later in his *Quaestiones disputatae*, Alexander will again focus the spiritual senses on the incarnate Christ, though without an explicit Eucharistic framing. Concerning a remark from the twelfth-century *De spiritu et anima* (often attributed to Augustine in the Middle Ages) – that 'the *sensus interior* is restored (*reficitur*) by the contemplation of [Christ's] divinity, the exterior sense is restored by the contemplation of his humanity' – Alexander comments: 'the incarnation would have been useful even if Christ had not suffered'.[47] Here, then, the importance of sensing Christ spiritually becomes a warrant for a signature feature of later Franciscan teaching on the incarnation, namely, that there would have been an incarnation even in the absence of a fall.

THE NATURE OF THE SPIRITUAL SENSES

Alexander's *ex professo* treatment of the spiritual senses (their nature, activity and object) in his *Quaestio disputata* 31 presumes this baptismal activation and Eucharistic exercise within the *corpus mysticum Christi*. Manifold spiritual sensation is made possible by 'the gifts of in-forming grace (*dona*

---

[43] *Glossa in IV Sent.* d. 9, n. 3 (ed. Quaracchi, pp. 148–9).
[44] The phrase is Avicenna's, often cited by the early scholastics in their discussion of spiritual delectation. See Coolman, *Knowing God*, p. 30, for a discussion in William of Auxerre.
[45] *Glossa in IV Sent.* d. 10, n. 7 (ed. Quaracchi, pp. 161–2).
[46] *Glossa in IV Sent.* d. 9, n. 1 (ed. Quaracchi, p. 147).
[47] *Qu. disp.* q. 15, n. 46 (ed. Quaracchi, p. 208).

gratiarum informantium)'[48] and the 'grace that makes us graced' (*gratiam gratum facientem*).[49]

To begin, his teaching on the matter presumes a particular conception of the human person. Though his terminology shifts over time, as he more fully appropriates Aristotelian sense-psychology, the basic shape of Alexander's anthropology remains intact. Early on, he employs the tripartite, Pauline conception of the person as composed of body (*corpus*), soul (*anima*) and spirit (*spiritus*) (1 Thess 5: 23). For Hales, the latter terms subdivide the soul into an inferior and a superior part: the soul 'is called spirit in relation to the superior part; [it is called] soul in relation to the inferior part'.[50] Later, he will re-label these in Aristotelian terms as the inferior, sensible part and the superior, rational or intelligible part of the soul.[51] Within this framework he locates different forms of sensation. Up front, he clearly distinguishes the physical senses, whose proper objects are bodily, from the spiritual senses, whose proper objects are intelligible: 'however much the corporal sense is changed for the better, it cannot arrive at the point where it senses *intelligibles* themselves (*secundum se*), that is, thoughts (*cogitationes*).[52] By contrast, the spiritual sense 'is established (*fundatur*) in the spiritual nature', in the soul as *spiritus*[53] or 'in relation to the spiritual man (*hominem spiritualem*)'.[54] Thus, the spiritual senses 'are understood in relation to the intellect (*secundum intellectum*)'[55] for 'cogitations themselves are perceived by the eye of the mind (*oculis mentis*)'.[56] The spiritual senses then are not transformed physical senses, but altogether different capacities for sensing non-physical realities.[57]

Distinguished in this way from their physical counterparts, the spiritual senses for Alexander stand in the superior, rational part of the Aristotelian soul identified with the Pauline spirit. Though it is not perfectly clear, he seems to imply that the spiritual senses of the soul are, at least to some degree, part of its natural, created endowment: the spiritual sense (singular) 'is not [founded] in the spiritual nature through grace (*per gratiam*) or glory (*per gloriam*) . . . rather, as it says in Rom 12: 2: *be renewed in the spirit*

---

[48] *Qu. disp.* q. 31, mem. 6, n. 33 (ed. Quaracchi, p. 551).
[49] *Qu. disp.* q. 31, mem. 8, n. 39 (ed. Quaracchi, p. 553).
[50] *Qu. disp.* q. 31, mem. 4, n. 24 (ed. Quaracchi, p. 545).
[51] See *Summa halensis*, Inq. IV, tract. I, sect. II, quaest. III, tit. I, chaps. i–vi.
[52] *Qu. disp.* q. 31, mem. I, n. 9 (ed. Quaracchi, p. 537).
[53] *Qu. disp.* q. 31, mem. I, n. 8 (ed. Quaracchi, p. 537).
[54] *Qu. disp.* q. 31, mem. 8, n. 38 (ed. Quaracchi, p. 553).
[55] *Glossa in III Sent.* d. 13, n. 22 (ed. Quaracchi, pp. 135–6).
[56] *Qu. disp.* q. 31, mem. I, n. 9 (ed. Quaracchi, p. 537).
[57] 'Nor am I speaking of spiritual sense as corporal senses that will become spiritual in the future.'
      Qu. disp. q. 31, mem. I, n. 8 (ed. Quaracchi, p. 537).

of your mind (renovamini spiritu . . .)'.[58] At the same time, they require the above-noted habilitation or activation by sacramental grace:

We speak of formed senses, and I say that they are formed by the character of the forms and also by grace . . . Hence, they are called gifts, because they are formed by gifts, not because they are gifts in themselves. The gifts therefore are like forms informing the senses. What is able to be informed, though, are the different senses and they [are informed] according to their diverse modes of perceiving.[59]

In short, the spiritual senses for Alexander are collectively a distinct capacity of the spiritual nature for sensing God, running parallel to, as it were, the capacity of body and soul for physical sensation. Alexander explicitly acknowledges the parallel: The spiritual sense is defined 'with a certain similitude to bodily sense' since 'the intellect is called "sense", by a metaphor drawn from bodily sense'.[60] Yet he also pinpoints the limitations of the comparison. To be sure, there is a plurality of senses in both spheres, but for different reasons: 'the [spiritual] senses are multiplied otherwise than [according to] sensible things'.[61] For him, there is a greater unity in the acts of the intellect than in the physical senses, which are discrete acts of distinct powers. The plurality of the spiritual senses is not then a function of 'multiple objects or because of several powers, but by reason of the mode of perceiving'.[62] In light of this 'unity of powers and objects, to see is the same as to hear'. But 'in relation to the mode of perceiving, these are not the same'.[63] Alexander does not elaborate on what precisely these diverse 'modes of perceiving' are, but by it he seems to find a middle way between affirming five discrete spiritual senses on the one hand and removing all diversity of spiritual sensation on the other.

THE OBJECT OF THE SPIRITUAL SENSES: DIVINE
VERITAS AND *BONITAS*

With the anthropological subject of spiritual senses, along with their modal diversity, now in view, the issue of their objects presents itself. What do these spiritual senses perceive and in what manner? Like that of William

---

[58] *Qu. disp.* q. 31, mem. 1, n. 8 (ed. Quaracchi, p. 537).
[59] *Qu. disp.* q. 31, mem. 6, n. 34 (ed. Quaracchi, p. 551): *Loquimur de sensibus formatis, et dico quod ratione formarum formantur et a gratia; secundum vero ipsas potentias sumuntur iuxta actum. Unde dicuntur dona quia ex donis formantur, non quod sint dona in se. Dona ergo sunt sicut formae formantes sensus; formabilia vero sunt diversi sensus secundum diversos modos comprehendendi.*
[60] *Qu. disp.* q. 31, mem. 1, n. 10 (ed. Quaracchi, p. 538).
[61] *Qu. disp.* q. 31, mem. 4, n. 26 (ed. Quaracchi, pp. 546–7).
[62] *Qu. disp.* q. 31, mem. 2, n. 16 (ed. Quaracchi, p. 540).
[63] *Qu. disp.* q. 31, mem. 2, n. 18 (ed. Quaracchi, p. 541).

of Auxerre, Alexander's fundamental conception of the divine nature lends
itself in a particular way to human capacities for spiritual sensation. Here
too, Alexander's thinking betrays a certain development. Early, in the
Glossa, he rather vaguely allows that 'in so far as God sounds (*sonat*) in
the ears of the perfect, God is audible (*auditus*); in so far as God [is] in
the mouth of the perfect, God is tasted (*gustus*), and so forth . . .'[64] In the
same discussion, though, a more specific description appears: 'Vision is of
truth, audition is of jubilation, smell is of the desire for continuation in
eternity, taste is of satiety, touch is of goodness through charity.'[65] Each
sense is here given a distinguishable object, two of which are identified
with what scholastics will soon call the transcendentals, namely, truth and
goodness, which are aligned respectively with the sensory extremes of sight
and touch. This adumbrates the logic that Alexander exploits more fully in
Quaestio disputata 31, where he allows the intervening senses to be 'drawn
into orbit' with one or other of these transcendental manifestations of the
divine nature: 'The spirit has five senses in relation to God: two related to
the true (*ad verum*), three related to the good (*ad bonum*)'[66] or 'five modes
of perceiving', two directed to 'the highest truth' (*summa veritas*), three to
'the highest goodness' (*summa bonitas*).[67] Specifically, he links sight and
hearing with *veritas*, and smell, taste and touch with *bonitas*.

Divine truth engages spiritual hearing (*auditus*) 'in a sign' (*in signo*)
and 'through inspiration' (*inspirationem*), and this inspired audition 'is
converted to a word'; divine truth engages spiritual sight (*visus*), not in a
sign, but in truth's 'own species'. More precisely, the soul sees 'the highest
truth' either 'in its uncreated species, as in the future' or 'in its created
[species], as now by faith' and 'as in a mirror' (1 Cor 13: 12). Here, then,
Alexander associates the theological virtue of faith with the spiritual senses
of vision and audition, and then orients both towards divine truth as their
object. When these senses are related thus to truth, he avers, the result
is 'cognition' (*cognitio*) of God. Intriguingly, he also affirms a formabil-
ity in these senses. Spiritual sight and hearing are 'disciplinable' (*disci-
plinales*), which implies that they can learn and develop in their relation to
truth.[68]

In relation to the *summum bonum*, there are three modes of perceiving,
namely, touch (*tactus*), taste (*gustus*) and smell (*olfactus*). Smell perceives the

[64] *Glossa in III Sent.* d. 13, n. 22 (ed. Quaracchi, pp. 135–6).
[65] *Glossa in III Sent.* d. 13, n. 22 (ed. Quaracchi, pp. 135–6).
[66] *Qu. disp.* q. 31, mem. 4, n. 25 (ed. Quaracchi, p. 546).
[67] *Qu. disp.* q. 31, mem. 3, n. 20 (ed. Quaracchi, pp. 542–3).
[68] *Qu. disp.* q. 31, mem. 3, n. 20 (ed. Quaracchi, pp. 542–3).

good through actual grace, gifts given freely (*dona gratis data*), by which 'we sense' (*sentimus*) a kind of fleeting aroma of divine goodness, more remotely than touch or taste. Taste perceives the good 'through gifts of the grace' (*donis gratuitis*) that 'make the soul graced' (*facientia gratum*), so-called habitual grace. Alexander associates this with wisdom (*sapientia*), which 'possesses a kind of taste of eternal goodness'. Touch is an act of adhering (*adhaerentiam*), following 1 Corinthians 6: 17: 'whoever adheres (*adhaeret*) to God [is one spirit with him]'. Touch occurs 'when one perceives (*percipit*) through experience (*per experientiam*) that one is *one spirit with God*'.[69]

In sum, Alexander concludes that there are 'five senses in relation to the goodness and truth of God'. While in the divine simplicity, *veritas* and *bonitas* are not ultimately distinct, are 'the same thing in reality (*in re*)', they are yet distinguishable manifestations of the divine nature, which are 'perceived in diverse modes'.[70]

'TOUCH CONSUMMATES KNOWLEDGE'

The ecclesiology of the *corpus mysticum* and the analogy between physical and spiritual senses raise the question, posed influentially by Peter Lombard, of whether only the spiritual sense of touch was present in the ecclesial body, while Christ as head alone possessed all the senses. In the *Glossa*, Alexander seems content with this position, but he changes his mind later on.[71] This reversal is apparent throughout *Quaestio disputata* 31, as he posits all the spiritual senses in the ecclesial body. Yet the spiritual sense of touch retains, it seems, a prominent place. Addressing the question of the order of the spiritual senses and which is 'the more principal', he sides with touch, traditionally the 'lowest' of the senses. In relation to God, 'the nearest and principal sense is touch'.[72] Nodding at Origen on Leviticus and citing Augustine's *De trinitate* (1. 9. 18) that 'touch is the end of knowledge (*finis notionis*)', Alexander argues that 'touch is the most complete knowledge (*completissima notio*)' and 'the most complete sense' (*sensus completissimus*) in relation to God. The other senses are ordered to this end. Jesus' words to Mary Magdalene, 'do not touch me' (Jn 20), were tantamount to saying: 'you have perceived me with your other senses, but

[69] *Qu. disp.* q. 31, mem. 3, n. 20 (ed. Quaracchi, pp. 542–3).
[70] *Qu. disp.* q. 31, mem. 3, n. 20 (ed. Quaracchi, pp. 542–3).
[71] *Glossa in III Sent.* d. 13, n. 22 (ed. Quaracchi, pp. 135–6): 'It should be seen what those five spiritual senses are and how touch alone is in us.'
[72] *Qu. disp.* q. 31, mem. 7, n. 37 (ed. Quaracchi, p. 552).

you are not yet able to touch (*potes tangere*)'.[73] To touch God, then, for Alexander is the goal and fulfilment of all spiritually sensuous knowledge.

The implied ordering of the other senses seems to follow the order already intimated above in relation to the true and the good. The movement seems to be from sight and hearing to smell, taste and finally touch. It is a movement from remote to intimate knowledge of God, as Alexander observes in his discussion of baptism: 'vision' is a form of 'distinct cognition', but the sense of touch 'is the most certain cognition'.[74] This order seems also to be aligned with a progression among the theological virtues, from faith to charity. Early, in the *Glossa*, he says simply that 'faith pertains to sight (*visum*), wisdom to taste (*gustum*), charity to touch (*tactus*)'.[75] In *Quaestio disputata* 31, he explains that 'touch is said to belong to charity (*penes charitatem*), which . . . is the principal virtue; therefore touch is the more principal sense'.[76]

It is this ordered progression from faith's vision and audition of truth to charity's olfaction, degustation and finally adhesion to goodness that allows Alexander to link this spiritually sensuous cognition of God with the soul's affection for God. For him, the spiritual senses are acts of the cognitive or knowing power of the soul, not of its affective or moving power. Strictly speaking, they do not 'have something of affection', but pertain 'only to the conjunction with the cognizable'. Nevertheless, he argues (again citing Augustine): 'it is impossible to be moved into God by whatever sense, without the delectation that attends to the good; and this is on account of the inseparability of the affective part from the cognitive part'.[77] That is, affection necessarily follows on that cognition associated with the spiritual senses (not from the spiritual sense-knowledge itself), because there is always 'a certain movement' of the affection towards the good thus perceived. 'For when the highest cognizable thing is loved (*quia summum amatum cognitum*), it also draws the moving [part] along with the cognitive [part].'[78] Ultimately, this is due to the nature of the object thus perceived: 'For the spiritual [sense object] has such power (*potestatem*) over the cognitive part, that it simultaneously draws the affection; hence it draws both the motive power and the cognitive power.'[79]

---

[73] *Qu. disp.* q. 31, mem. 7, n. 37 (ed. Quaracchi, p. 552). From another perspective, Alexander finds a way to make sight the principal sense, but in a qualified way, not *simpliciter* as with touch.
[74] *Glossa in IV Sent.* d. 6, n. 17 (ed. Quaracchi, p. 126).
[75] *Glossa in III Sent.* d. 13, n. 22 (ed. Quaracchi, pp. 135–6).
[76] *Qu. disp.* q. 31, mem. 7, n. 35 (ed. Quaracchi, pp. 551–2).
[77] *Qu. disp.* q. 31, mem. 5, n. 31 (ed. Quaracchi, p. 550).
[78] *Qu. disp.* q. 31, mem. 5, n. 31 (ed. Quaracchi, p. 550).
[79] *Qu. disp.* q. 31, mem. 5, n. 32 (ed. Quaracchi, pp. 550–1).

TOWARDS AN ESCHATOLOGICAL *SENSUS DEI*

For Hales, as for William of Auxerre, the present activity of the spiritual senses finds its consummation in the next life. *In patria*, there is an eschatological perfection of the *sensus Dei* begun *in via*. The spiritual senses 'will exist in a more perfect mode in the next life'. Yet the framework noted above seems to remain intact. *In patria*, 'the highest truth' will be known 'as vision (*ut species*) and as word (*ut verbum*)'.[80] The 'highest good' will 'flow into' (*influet*) the spiritual sense of smell, and, turned thereby towards it, the sense of taste will then 'adhere' (*adhaerens*) and the sense of touch will 'unite' (*uniens*) to the good.[81] Elsewhere, Alexander directs this beatific sensation to the Christological focus noted above with respect to the Eucharist, with the oft-quoted text from *De spiritu et anima* (attributed to Augustine). In the next life, the '*sensus interior* is restored (*reficitur*) by the contemplation of [Christ's] divinity, the exterior senses are restored by the contemplation of [Christ's] humanity'.[82]

To sum up: in his undisputed writings, Alexander of Hales posits within members of Christ's ecclesial body the presence of the spiritual senses of the soul, which are sacramentally habilitated and Christologically oriented. Activated thus, they are various modalities of spiritual perception by which the transcendental divine attributes, *veritas* and *bonitas*, are known and experienced by the intellectual power of the soul. Significantly, these are not haphazard modes of spiritual perception, but are rather arranged in a dynamic sequence. Beginning with faith's hearing and seeing, there is a movement that gradually narrows the distance between sensor and sensed, as spiritual smell leads to taste and finally to the union of touch. In this way, the experience of spiritual touch, as the most intimate sense delivering the most certain knowledge, is the term and goal not just of spiritual perception, but of the entire ecclesial activity of theology, of faith seeking both *intellectus* and *sensus Dei*. In short, for Alexander, touch brings all knowledge of God to its consummation. When such spiritually sensuous cognition occurs, moreover, the *affectus* is inexorably drawn in and engaged. Ultimately, one might speak of both an intellectual understanding and an experiential perception of the faith (a *sensus fidei*) on the part of the faithful (a *sensus fidelis*); an ecclesial seeing and hearing that culminates in mystical tasting and touching.

---

[80] *Qu. disp.* q. 31, mem. 8, n. 40 (ed. Quaracchi, p. 554).
[81] *Qu. disp.* q. 31, mem. 8, n. 40 (ed. Quaracchi, p. 554).
[82] *Qu. disp.* q. 66, n. 33 (ed. Quaracchi, p. 1327).

CONCLUSION: TOWARDS THE ECLIPSE OF THE SCHOLASTIC
SPIRITUAL SENSES TRADITION?

The early thirteenth-century was a time of oft-noted rapid and profound change in the intellectual climate of the nascent universities, such as Paris and Oxford, as thinkers increasingly assimilated the fuller corpus of Aristotle's philosophy, especially his teaching on physics and metaphysics, as well as the *logica nova*. Of particular interest, Aristotle's theory of knowledge, and its attendant psychology of sense perception (mediated by the Arabic commentator Avicenna), offered a new conception of both the nature of the human soul and its acts of cognition and sensation. While the issues are complex and difficult to assess with certainty, the gradual adoption of Aristotelian sense-psychology by scholastic thinkers, in particular its conception of the 'interior senses' (*sensus interior*) of the soul, appears correlated with an eclipse of the traditional doctrine of the spiritual senses (*sensus spirituales*) of the soul. This appears to be the case with Alexander. A brief comparison of the teaching found in the *Glossa* and *Quaestio disputata* 31, discussed above, with that found in the *Summa halensis*, purportedly his students' posthumous compilation of Alexander's teaching, illustrates the point.[83]

The theme of spiritual sensation figures prominently in two places in the *Summa halensis*: in the Prologue to the entire work and, later, in the discussion of human nature. For a reader familiar with *Quaestio disputata* 31, the *Summa*'s discussion of the spiritual senses in the treatise, *de homine*, is jejune. Gone is the label of the 'spiritual senses', to be replaced by the more general 'interior senses', which seems vaguely to comprehend the older, mystico-biblical and newer, natural-Aristotelian paradigms. While borrowing some material verbatim from *Quaestio disputata* 31, the treatise is primarily concerned to 'locate' the spiritual senses within an Aristotelian anthropological framework. Overlaying the above-noted Pauline distinction between soul (*anima*) and spirit (*spiritus*) with the Aristotelian distinction between the sensible soul or inferior part of reason and rational soul or superior part of reason, the *Summa halensis* associates the 'interior senses' with the former and the 'spiritual senses' with the latter. The *Summa* thus quite explicitly distinguishes the Aristotelian interior senses (*sensus communis, vi imaginativa, aestimativa* and *cognitiva*), which are part of a complex of powers oriented towards physical sense perception (*sensibilia*), from the traditional spiritual senses, which pertain to the

---

[83] See explanatory n. 24 above.

superior, rational part of the soul and are oriented towards intelligible things (*intelligibilia*).[84] Absent, however, is any discussion of the activity of the spiritual senses, individually or as a whole, their interrelation, their proper objects or their place in the larger theological or spiritual endeavour, all of which had figured prominently in *Quaestio disputata* 31. The not easily avoided impression is that of a dutiful attempt to incorporate material for which there is little intrinsic interest.

The methodological discussion of the nature of theology in the Prologue of the *Summa halensis* also contains a telling treatment of spiritual sensation, but for different reasons. Present here is the now familiar starting point of the ecclesial character of theology: 'the subject matter of divine Scripture', and therefore of all theology, is 'the whole Christ, head and body, Christ and the church'.[85] Within this context, *theologia* is the *scientia Dei*; yet it is more properly deemed *sapientia*, on two counts. First, God is truly the 'cause of causes', and Aristotle claimed that the knowledge of this cause (i.e. 'first philosophy' or metaphysics) is for its own sake and ought to be called wisdom. This 'knowledge of the first causes' is wisdom, but in a scientific mode, 'as a science'. Its object is truth and it 'perfects knowledge in relation to truth'. 'Alexander' evokes this modality with the language of vision – it is knowledge 'according to sight'. Hence, though a kind of wisdom, it is more properly called 'an absolute science'.[86] It is *sapientia ut scientia*. The implication is that such *scientia Dei* is somehow detached, possessed indifferently, as if from a distance. By contrast, there is a *scientia Dei* that 'moves the affection to goodness'. This 'perfects the soul according to the affection', by 'moving it to the good' through 'fear and love'. The operative sensation here is not vision, but taste. This is termed 'wisdom' from 'the savour of the affection'.[87] This *scientia Dei*, then, is 'sapientia ut sapientia', wisdom as 'tasted knowledge'. The appeal to diverse sense modalities fosters further differentiation. Engaging 'the sense of taste', wisdom-as-wisdom is more certain than the philosophical knowledge that comes 'through reason, through the testimony of created beings', and thus 'through the sense of sight'.[88] Tasted knowledge, 'born of experience', is more certain than the

---

[84] See *Summa halensis*, Inq. IV, tract. I, sect. II, quaest. III, tit. I, chaps. iii–vi.

[85] *Summa halensis*, Intro., q. I, ch. 3, obj. 6 and ad 6 (ed. Quaracchi, vol. I, pp. 6–7). Replying to objections, the *Summa* distinguishes between the *de Deo* subject, God, from the *circa quam* subject, Christ and the church.

[86] *Summa halensis*, Intro., q. I, ch. I, *solutio* (ed. Quaracchi, vol. I, p. 2).

[87] *Summa halensis*, Intro., q. I, ch. I, *solutio* (ed. Quaracchi, vol. I, p. 2).

[88] *Summa halensis*, Intro., q. I, ch. 4, a. 2, *sed contra* (ed. Quaracchi, vol. I, p. 8), trans. A. J. Minnis and A. B. Scott, *Medieval Literary Theory and Criticism, c. 1100–1375: The Commentary Tradition* (Oxford: Clarendon Press, 1988), p. 216.

merely seen knowledge 'born of speculation'. The former is the certainty of the *affectus*; the latter, of the *intellectus*. The former is the certainty of Paul's 'spiritual man', who discerns all things; the latter is the certainty of Paul's 'carnal man', who does not perceive the things of the Spirit (cf. 1 Cor 2: 14).[89]

The Prologue elaborates on the genesis of this uniquely sapiential divine science. First, its point of departure is faith (*fides*), from which comes understanding (*intellectus*). Citing the older version of Isaiah 7: 9 – 'unless you believe, you will not understand' – the *Summa* specifies the process: 'this science first generates faith, and afterwards, when the heart is made clean through faith working through love, it generates understanding'.[90] Such faith, moreover, is 'inspired to assent to the first truth or to the first being for its own sake'.[91] This inspired character of theology is accented: 'the theological discipline is not acquired, but is inspired by the Holy Spirit (citing 2 Tim 3: 16).[92] But *intellectus* is not the final goal of wisdom. Theology's inspired character has implications for the manner in which its object, God, is encountered. Because this *sapientia ut sapientia* comes from the Holy Spirit, to whom goodness is appropriated, the truth of revelation is revealed under the aspect or formality of the good: its object is the 'truth *as good*' (*verum ut bonum*), while philosophy merely speculates regarding the 'true as true' (*verum ut verum*) or the 'good as true' (*bonum ut verum*). By contrast, theology is 'an assimilation to the Holy Spirit, who is goodness'. Revealed as the good by the Holy Spirit, theology is about God (*de Deo*), not as the 'cause of causes', but as the triune God who is both Creator and Saviour, and it leads into God (*in Deum*) as the loved good,[93] and as what in the next life 'will be enjoyed, the Father and the Son and the Holy Spirit, unchangeable good'.[94] In short, theology as true wisdom leads to contact.

In the *Summa*'s Prologue, then, is visible a fundamental dynamic at the heart of Alexander's theology, adumbrated earlier in *Quaestio disputata* 31: from faith's vision of divine *veritas* to love's taste of divine *bonitas* (here intriguingly given a pneumatological shading). But beyond these similarities, important differences emerge. Though the language of spiritual sensation is invoked, it is a weaker, more metaphorical allusion. Gone

---

[89] *Summa halensis*, Intro., q. 1, ch. 4, a. 2, *respondeo* (ed. Quaracchi, vol. 1, p. 8), trans. Minnis and Scott, p. 216.

[90] *Summa halensis*, Intro., q. 1, ch. 1, ad 3–4 (ed. Quaracchi, vol. 1, p. 3).

[91] *Summa halensis*, Intro., q. 1, ch. 1, ad 4 (ed. Quaracchi, vol. 1, p. 3).

[92] *Summa halensis*, Intro., q. 1, ch. 2, *sed contra* (ed. Quaracchi, vol. 1, pp. 4–5).

[93] *Summa halensis*, Intro., q. 1, ch. 2, ad 1–4 (ed. Quaracchi, vol. 1, p. 5).

[94] *Summa halensis*, Intro., q. 1, ch. 3, ad 5 (ed. Quaracchi, vol. 1, p. 7).

is the robust activity of the whole spiritual sensorium; gone too is the tactile consummation, perhaps assimilated to taste because of the more prominent category of wisdom, whose etymology centres on a gustatory idea. Moreover, contrary to the teaching in *Quaestio disputata* 31, where all the spiritual senses are associated with the intellect, here only *visus* is, while *gustus* has migrated to the *affectus*. In some sense, the spiritual senses of the soul have begun to be a means of post-cognitional affective experience, rather than a means of 'affective cognition'.

CHAPTER 8

Thomas Gallus

Boyd Taylor Coolman

While in respect of all the other senses we fall below many species of animals, in respect of touch we far excel all other species in exactness of discrimination. That is why man is the most intelligent of all animals. This is confirmed by the fact that it is to differences in the organ of touch and to nothing else that the differences between man and man in respect of natural endowment are due; men whose flesh is hard are ill-endowed by nature, men whose flesh is soft, well-endowed.

Aristotle[1]

INTRODUCTION

In the unfinished *opus* of Bonaventure's mature career, his *Collationes in Hexaëmeron*, the Franciscan describes the nature of contemplation: 'Just as fruit delights both sight and taste, yet it delights the sense of sight principally by its beauty and loveliness, and [delights] the sense of taste by its sweetness and suavity, so do these *theoriae* nourish the *intellectus* by their loveliness and the *affectus* by their suavity.'[2] That Bonaventure should invoke the language of sensation to characterize contemplative experience is not surprising.[3] Since the work of both Karl Rahner and Hans Urs von Balthasar in the mid-twentieth century, his teaching on the spiritual senses has been well known, if also intensely debated.[4] But two issues are note-worthy here. First, his alignment of sight with *intellectus* and taste with *affectus*, while not original, is an important feature of scholastic theorizing

---

[1] Aristotle, *De an.* II. 9, 421a 25, trans. J. A. Smith (Oxford: Clarendon Press, 1931), p. 57.
[2] *Collationes in Hexaëmeron*, 17. 3, trans. J. de Vinck, *The Works of Bonaventure*, vol. V (New York: St Anthony's Guild Press, 1970), p. 252.
[3] See F. M. Tedoldi, *La dottrina dei cinque sensi spirituali in San Bonaventura* (Roma: Pontificium Athenaeum Antonianum, 1999).
[4] See K. Rahner, 'The Doctrine of the "Spiritual Senses" in the Middle Ages'; H. U. von Balthasar, *GL*, vol. II, pp. 260–362, esp. pp. 309–26.

regarding the spiritual senses.[5] The distinction between *intellectus* and *affectus* and the alignment of each with distinct spiritual senses imply, on the one hand, a specific anthropology with two basic and (perhaps) irreducible modalities in the soul. The fact, on the other hand, that these modalities are nonetheless united within a single, spiritual sensorium prevents too radical a divorce between them and raises the tantalizing question of their precise relationship: how discontinuous are these two 'modes of apprehension'?[6] Second, the object of apprehension for both *intellectus* and *affectus* is *theoriae* – which I intentionally avoid translating for now. What precisely does Bonaventure mean by *theoriae*? Does the apparent assumption that these can be both seen by the *intellectus* and tasted by the *affectus* imply that there is some continuity, overlap or direct interaction between these two modes?

Whatever the case with Bonaventure, his text recalls an earlier thirteenth-century precedent for his approach to this matter, which raises the same set of questions, namely, the writings of the Victorine Thomas Gallus (d. 1246). Though the terminology and the corresponding distinction between *intellectus* and *affectus* precede him, Gallus appears to be the first to formulate the nature of mystical contemplation thus: by aligning *intellectus* and *affectus* with a different pole of the spiritual sensorium, but orienting both towards the *theoriae* as a common object. The burden of what follows, however, is neither to argue for Gallus's originality in this regard nor to claim his direct influence on Bonaventure,[7] but to explicate Gallus's own teaching on the spiritual senses, which teaching is, in fact, 'essential to all that [Gallus] has to say on the knowledge which is unitive contemplation'.[8] Gallus's doctrine on this matter sheds crucial light on the contentious issue of his conception of the highest mode of relation to God available to created minds. That is, Gallus uses the notion of a spiritual sensorium to posit a continuum of created apprehension of God (*cognitio Dei*).

---

[5] See, for example, the approach of Alexander of Hales discussed in Chapter 7 in this volume.

[6] See B. T. Coolman, *Knowing God by Experience: The Spiritual Senses in the Theology of William of Auxerre* (Washington, DC: Catholic University of America Press, 2004), pp. 3–6, which argues that the English term 'apprehension' best captures what William of Auxerre intends by the relationship between the spiritual senses and their respective objects.

[7] See G. Théry, 'Thomas Gallus: Aperçu biographique', *Archives d'histoire doctrinale et littéraire du Moyen Âge*, 12 (1939), 179, n. 1, who notes that the Franciscans moved their *studium generale* from Padua to Vercelli in 1228. On the possible links between Gallus and the Franciscans, especially St Anthony of Padua, see the other articles of G. Théry in the Bibliography.

[8] J. Walsh, *Sapientia Christianorum: The Doctrine of Thomas Gallus Abbot of Vercelli on Contemplation* (Rome: Pontificia Universitas Gregoriana, 1957), p. 93, n. 2.

GALLUS: THE ORIGINATOR OF AN ANTI-INTELLECTUAL
MYSTICAL TRADITION?

Thomas Gallus remains strikingly understudied, and so a brief biographical sketch is in order.[9] Probably born in France in the late twelfth century, he was active on the university scene in Paris in the first two decades of the thirteenth century.[10] An Augustinian canon (canon regular) at the abbey of St Victor in Paris,[11] Thomas became a university master of theology some time between 1210 and 1218.[12] Around 1218–19, Thomas (and two other canons) went to Vercelli in northern Italy to found an abbey and a hospital dedicated to St Andrew.[13] Known in Italy as 'Thomas of Paris' (*Thomas Parisiensis*) or 'Gallus' ('the Frenchman'), he became prior of the new abbey in 1224, and abbot by 1226. After two decades as *abbas Vercellensis*, interrupted only by a year in England in 1238 and a brief period of exile in 1243, Thomas died in 1246.[14]

Twentieth-century scholarship has viewed Gallus as the inaugurator of an anti-intellectual theory of mystical experience and subsequent tradition of such, which includes such authors as Hugh of Balma, Jan Ruysbroeck and the author of *The Cloud of Unknowing*. Much of this claim centers on his appropriation of the Pseudo-Dionysian corpus, and especially of the Dionysian treatise *The Mystical Theology*. Put simply, Gallus is

---

[9] See the several articles on Gallus by D. Lawell: '*Qualiter vita prelatorum conformari debet vite angelice*: A Sermon (1244–1246?) Attributed to Thomas Gallus', *Recherches de théologie et philosophie médiévales*, 75.2 (2008), 303–36; 'Affective Excess: Ontology and Knowledge in the Thought of Thomas Gallus', *Dionysius*, 26 (2008), 139–74; '*Ne de ineffabili penitus taceamus*: Aspects of the Specialized Vocabulary of the Writings of Thomas Gallus', *Viator*, 40.1 (2009), 151–84; 'Thomas Gallus's Method as Dionysian Commentator: A Study of the *Glose super angelica ierarchia* (1224), Including Considerations on the Authorship of the *Expositio librorum beati Dionysii*', *Archives d'histoire doctrinale et littéraire du Moyen Âge*, 76 (2009), 89–117; '*Spectacula contemplationis*: A Treatise (1244–1246) by Thomas Gallus', *Recherches de théologie et philosophie médiévales*, 76.2 (2009), 249–85.

[10] See M. E. Crossnoe, 'Education and the Care of Souls: Pope Gregory IX, the Order of St. Victor and the University of Paris in 1237', *Mediaeval Studies*, 61 (1999), 137–72, at 165, n. 98.

[11] The abbey of St Victor was founded in Paris by William of Champeaux in 1108 and housed an Augustinian order of regular canons.

[12] Crossnoe, 'Education and the Care of Souls', p. 169.   [13] See Lawell, 'Affective Excess', p. 142.

[14] Additional treatments of Gallus's life and thought include M. Capellino, *Tommaso di San Vittore: Abate Vercellese* (Vercelli: Società Storica Vercellese, 1978); J. Barbet, 'Thomas Gallus', *DS*, vol. xv (1991), pp. 800–16; K. Ruh, *Geschichte der abendländischen Mystik*, vol. III: *Die Mystik des deutschen Predigerordens und ihre Grundlegung durch die Hochscholastik* (Munich: Beck, 1996), pp. 59–81; B. McGinn, 'Thomas Gallus and the New Dionysianism', in *The Presence of God: A History of Western Christian Mysticism*, vol. III: *The Flowering of Mysticism. Men and Women in the New Mysticism (1200–1350)* (New York: Crossroad, 1998), pp. 78–87; and B. T. Coolman, 'The Medieval Affective Dionysian Tradition', *Modern Theology*, 24.4 (2008), 615–32, reprinted in Sarah Coakley and Charles M. Stang (eds.), *Re-Thinking Dionysius the Areopagite* (Oxford: Wiley-Blackwell, 2009), pp. 85–102.

credited, or accused, of initiating an affective interpretation of the Dionysian *Mystical Theology*. That short treatise, which succinctly encapsulates the Dionysian corpus, depicts Moses's ascent of Mt. Sinai. As he proceeds, Moses leaves behind all sense-perception and intellectual cognition, and at the apex of this ascent, plunges into the 'cloud of unknowing', where he is united to God through an absolute negating and utter transcending of all intellectual capacities and cognitive activities. In Gallus's affective interpretation, however, this account of strictly intellectual transcendence is supplemented by the introduction of an affective dimension that posited love (*amor, dilectio, affectio*) as an essential feature of this ascent to and union with God. As Paul Rorem has pointed out, *The Mystical Theology* contains no references to charity, love, delight or the affections generally; yet, for Gallus and later medieval readers in this tradition, when Moses finally abandons all intellectual and cognitive activity, he is united to the unknown God *through love*. But that is not all. Gallus interpolates love into the Sinai ascent precisely at this point because, taking a cue from Hugh of St Victor, 'love surpasses knowledge and is greater than intelligence'.[15] As Gallus puts it: 'We are convinced that the affection is ineffably, more profoundly, and more sublimely drawn to God by God himself than is the intellect, because men and angels love more than they have the power to reason or understand.'[16] This affective reading, accordingly, distinguished a loving power or capacity from a knowing one within the soul, and insisted, moreover, on the superiority of the former over the latter at the highest point of the divine–human relationship.

Gallus executes this reading of Dionysius in three different treatments of *The Mystical Theology* over the span of twenty years. Both later medieval and modern readers have tended to focus on these. A prolific author, Gallus also wrote at least two extensive commentaries on the Song of Songs,[17] to which he gave an affective, Dionysian reading. In these, a much more complex picture of the relationship between love and knowledge, affect and intellect, emerges, a picture that does not square well with the traditional anti-intellectualist characterization. This is most apparent in light of his teaching on the spiritual senses.

[15] *In hierarchiam caelestem S. Dionysii* (PL 175. 1038D).
[16] *The Cloud of Unknowing*, trans. J. Walsh, SJ (New York: Paulist Press, 1981), p. 123, from Gallus's commentary on Isaiah.
[17] See J. Barbet, *Un commentaire du Cantique attribué à Thomas Gallus* (Paris and Louvain: Béatrice-Nauwelaerts, 1972). The two authentic commentaries have been edited by Barbet, in *Thomas Gallus: Commentaires du Cantique des Cantiques* (Paris: Vrin, 1967), pp. 65–104 and 105–232; references to *Comm. II* and *Comm. III* are followed by chapter, section and page designations. There is a partial English translation of *Comm. II* in D. Turner, *Eros and Allegory: Medieval Exegesis of the Song of Songs* (Kalamazoo, MI: Cistercian Publications, 1995), pp. 317–39.

GALLUS'S ORIGINAL APPROPRIATION OF THE
DIONYSIAN ANGELIC HIERARCHY

Gallus's Song commentaries pose a formidable threat to the most intrepid
reader, as the 'l'abondance des details et la luxuriance des images'[18] often
obscure its organizing principle. As Gallus himself recognized, the crucial
interpretive key to the commentaries – also the most distinctive feature
of his appropriation of the Dionysian corpus and the most jarring feature
for the modern reader – is his 'angelization' of the human mind,[19] modelled on Dionysius's description of the nine angelic orders, subdivided into
three triads, each with its own particular name, office and activity.[20] Gallus
describes the 'angelized' mind as follows. The lowest hierarchy (angels,
archangels, principalities) is the basic nature of the soul and its wholly natural activities. In the middle hierarchy (powers, virtues, dominions) is the
realm of nature assisted by grace, and involves 'effort, which incomparably
exceeds nature'. The highest hierarchy (thrones, cherubim, seraphim) is
the realm of grace above nature, and involves 'ecstasy' in the literal sense
of transcending the mind itself (*excessus mentis*).[21]

It is possible, indeed common, to read Gallus's nine-grade division of
the soul as a mystical *itinerarium mentis in Deum*, or a ladder of rungs the
traversing of which results in ecstatic union with God. On this reading,
key points along the way are identifiable. First, the transition from the
middle triad to the highest triad (that is, from rank 6 to rank 7) is a
self-transcending, literally ecstatic, movement in which the soul is drawn
above and outside itself. Yet initially even here, both the affective and the
intellective capacities of the soul are functioning. It is only at the ascent from
cherubim to seraphim (from rank 8 to rank 9) that Gallus's 'affectivizing'
fully sets in. At the cherubic rank the *intellectus* and the *affectus* 'walk hand
in hand' (*coambulant*)[22] up to the point where at 'the consummation of its
cognition and light', the intellect fails (*defectus intellectus*).[23] Then to the
ninth and seraphic rank only the 'principal affection' (*affectus principalis*)

[18] Barbet, 'Introduction', *Commentaires*, p. 43.
[19] Gallus here expands an intuition of his Victorine predecessors, especially Richard of St Victor's use
   of angelic modes of being in human contemplation. See S. Chase, *Angelic Wisdom: The Cherubim
   and the Grace of Contemplation in Richard of St. Victor* (University of Notre Dame Press, 1995).
[20] *Comm. II*, Prol. 66: 'In order to understand this explanation of the [Song of Songs], it is necessary
   to set down first the meaning of the statement in the *Celestial Hierarchy* that: "each intelligent
   being, heavenly or human, has its own set of primary, middle, and lower orders and powers".'
[21] *Comm. II*, Prol. 67.
[22] This felicitous rendering of Gallus's Latin is from Turner, *Eros and Allegory*, p. 322.
[23] *Comm. III*, Prol. 115.

is able to proceed, which alone is able to be united to God.[24] Now Gallus separates *intellectus* and *affectus*, barring the former from proceeding further into the final darkness of union with the Word: 'here is the cutting off of knowledge (*scientia*)', after which only the *scintilla synderesis*, the 'spark of the soul', remains.[25] This is Gallus's unique and influential teaching regarding the 'high point of affection' (*apex affectionis*),[26] which alone is capable of ecstatic, loving union.[27] In this climax, the love-sick night of Solomon merges with the apophatic darkness of Dionysius's Moses.[28] At the seraphic rank, the soul-bride is united to the divine spouse via the *affectus* and *not* the *intellectus*. Here is where the charge of anti-intellectualism emerges.

SERAPHIC SENSATION

But several features of Gallus's descriptions of affective, seraphic union (along with what precedes and follows it), both in the Song commentaries and in his engagement of the Dionysian corpus, trouble this account. These are most apparent in his teaching on the spiritual senses of the soul. Gallus uses the language of spiritual sensation to delineate more precisely the soul's ascent from the eighth to the ninth rank of its interior hierarchy. On the one hand, he attributes 'eye-ishness' (*oculositas*) to the cherubic order, since here the intellect has its 'highest perspicacity'.[29] It is this cherubic seeing that is blinded in the amorous darkness of seraphic union, where the soul lacks 'mental eyes' (*oculos mentes*), that is, reason and intellect (*carentes ratione et intellectu*).[30] Yet the seraphic soul is not completely senseless, for Gallus explicitly asserts that divine unknowability is overcome with some form of seraphic perception. In a remarkable passage, he collides two biblical texts with (if the term be pardoned) 'sensational' results. In Exodus, God had refused Moses's request for face-to-face vision: 'no one can see God and

---

[24] *Comm. III*, Prol. 115.   [25] *Comm. III*, 7.D, 219.

[26] See E. von Ivánka, *Plato Christianus: Übernahme und Ungestaltung des Platonismus durch die Väter* (Einsiedeln: Johannes Verlag, 1964), pp. 315–63, for the Stoic and neo-Platonic origins of the phrases *apex mentis* and *principalis affectio*.

[27] McGinn notes that Gallus was the first to use this term in the mystical sense and that his role in its subsequent medieval deployment is insufficiently investigated. See McGinn, *The Flowering of Mysticism*, p. 82, n. 51.

[28] The phrase is P. Rorem's in *Pseudo-Dionysius: A Commentary on the Texts and an Introduction to their Influence* (Oxford University Press, 1993), p. 218. This merging of the Song's spousal imagery with the Victorine to introduce a Christological dimension where it is absent in Dionysius – at the highest point of the soul's ascent to union with God.

[29] *Comm. III*, 4.A, 176: *Recte autem huic ordini attribuitur oculositas, propter precipuam attracte intelligentie perspicacitatem . . .*

[30] *Comm. II*, 1.A, 68: *. . . non habentes oculos mentes, id est cecatos, carentes ratione et intellectu . . .*

live'; but in 1 Corinthians, Paul contrasted the clouded knowledge of God
'in a mirror darkly' of this present life with the full 'face to face' vision of
God in the life to come. Gallus resolves the difficulty with an appeal to a
form of spiritual sensation:

> This [seraphic] refreshment does not occur *through a mirror* (*speculum*), but
> through the experience (*experientiam*) of divine sweetness, because taste and touch
> are not accomplished *through a mirror*..., even though vision is: 1 Cor. 13: 12:
> *now we see through a mirror*. Thus John 1:18: *No one ever sees God*; [and] Exod. 33:
> 20: *man will not see me and live*, but [Scripture] does not say: he will not taste or
> we will not taste.[31]

Thomas here describes a spiritually sensuous experience, couched in the
language of taste and touch in contrast to intellectual or rational knowing
analogous to physical sight, which allows for some form of perception of
God. Elsewhere, Gallus expands this seraphic sensorium to include an olfactory dimension, which encounters 'the sweet-smelling divine beauty'.[32] The
'sweetest, super-intellectual fragrance' is 'scattered'[33] in the soul through the
experience of seraphic union. The odour of spikenard symbolizes the soul's
experience of the 'affectual in-flowings' from the divine spouse which are
redolent and warming to the affect.[34] The Canticle's 'cup of spiced wine'
prompts the observation that 'wine' pertains to spiritual taste, while 'spiced'
refers to the 'confection of spiritual aromas'.[35] More striking perhaps is Gallus's description of seraphic touch. Commenting on the Song verse 'My
beloved put [his hand] through the key hole, and my bowels are moved by
his touch', Gallus says that bowels here signify 'the fervent affection that
loves most tenderly'. When 'moved *by the touch* of the [Spouse's] hand', this
tender affection is 'stirred' (*consternatur*) to rise up in ignorance (*ignote*) to
experience and receive the overshadowing Beloved (*superadventus divini*)

---

[31] *Comm. III*, 1.C, 124: *Hec refectio non fit per speculum, sed per divine dulcedinis experientiam, iuxta*
      quod gustus et tactus non exercetur per speculum, ... sed visus, Cor. 13: videmus nunc per speculum.
      Ideo Io. 1: Deum nemo vidit unquam; Exod 33: non videbit me homo et vivet, et non dicit: non gustabit,
      vel non gustabimus.
[32] *Explanation of the Ecclesiastical Hierarchy*, in Walsh, *Sapientia Christianorum*, p. 252.
[33] *Comm. II*, 1.G, 76: *... et suavissime superintellectualibus fragrantiis respergunt...*
[34] *Comm. II*, 4.G, 99: *Nardus redolens et calens significat puras et affectuales influitiones que ex affectuali*
      virtute proprie calent et redolent.
[35] *Comm. III*, 8.A, 224: 'It is the same thing to give the bride a cup of spiced wine, as when the bride
      was said to suck the breast of the groom; this then is the meaning: liquefied and made fit for union
      with me by devotion, I am made to taste (*sapidam factam*), which is noted by "wine", as from
      the confection of spiritual aromas, what is noted in "spiced", you will incorporate me into you by
      absorbing [me], and lead me to the more interior things and, taken up more interiorly anew, "I will
      give to you the new wine of my pomegranates", that is, having drawn you to me more intimately,
      liquefied by new fervors, I will manifest [to you]; by "new wine", understand new things (*novitas*),
      by "pomegranates", [understand] fervor.'

intimately within her, just as the blessed Virgin was troubled (*turbata*) by the angelic visitation.[36] In short, in the highest, seraphic encounter with God, 'love penetrates . . . by touching, smelling, and tasting'.[37]

Incontestably, then, Gallus deploys a doctrine of the spiritual senses to navigate the soul's ascent to and experience of union with God: 'The *affectus* tastes, touches, and smells spiritually, [but] the *intellectus* sees and hears.'[38] He thus subordinates the latter to the former. The divine ray 'offers itself to minds through a sensible and rapid fervour . . . in the *affectus*, that is, not in the *intellectus*'.[39] In its experience of 'sensing, tasting and smelling', the 'principal affection ascends into divine things infinitely above the intellect'.[40] This experience, accordingly, is in some sense ineffable and 'cannot be spoken with a mental word, much less a corporeal word'.[41] But what precisely is the nature of this seraphic sensation, and how exactly does Thomas distinguish and relate these diverse modes of 'spiritually sensuous' apprehension?

A SPIRITUAL SENSORIUM

It is already apparent in the foregoing descriptions that Gallus operates with the following anthropological assumption: the soul has two basic modalities – he can call them powers (*vis animae*) – namely, the *intellectus* and the *affectus*. These two modalities, moreover (again as in Alexander of Hales and Bonaventure), have their proper objects and acts. The *intellectus* is oriented towards the true; the *affectus* is oriented towards the good. The former delights in the *pulcro et claro*, the latter delights in the *dulci et suavi*.[42] The proper act of the *intellectus*, moreover, is *speculatio*. Gallus often refers to the 'speculative intellect' as that which engages its object in the clarity of a mirror or glass. He thus inverts the Pauline sense of seeing

---

[36] *Comm. II*, 5.C, 103.

[37] *Comm. II*, 1.A, 69: . . . *affectus qui penetrat tangendo, olfaciendo, gustando.*

[38] *Explanatio EH*, fol. 66rb–67va: . . . AD, id est, secundum, DECOREM divinum SUBSTANTIALITER BENEVOLENTEM. *Affectio siquidem gustat, tangit et olfacit spiritualiter, intellectus videt et audit.* In Lawell, '*Ne de ineffabili*', p. 169, n. 57.

[39] *Commentary on Isaiah*, ed. G. Théry, Commentaire sur Isaïe de Thomas de Saint-Victor', *La vie spirituelle*, 47 (1936), 146–62, at 155–56: . . . *raro tamen et momentanee in affectu, scilicet non intellectu supple, se offert mentibus per sensibilem et rapidum fervorem.*

[40] *Glose AH*, fol. 418a: . . . *per aliam experiendo, sentiendo, gustando et olfaciendo summa vi anime que est principalis affectio ascendens in divina in infinitum super intellectum* . . . In Lawell, '*Ne de ineffabili*', p. 174, n. 73.

[41] *Explanatio DN*, fol. 107rb/156va, in Lawell, '*Ne de ineffabili*', p. 163, n. 37: *Unde nec verbo mentis, multo minus verbo corporis dici potest.*

[42] Walsh, *Sapientia Christianorum*, Appendix 1, 9–10, pp. 93–4; Théry, 'Commentaire sur Isaïe', p. 153.

in a mirror (*speculum*), which for the Apostle suggested a certain obscurity of knowledge, interpreting it rather as clarity of intellectual knowledge, a clarity that is ultimately obscured by super-substantial darkness of loving union with God: 'For whatever super-substantially exceeds the speculative intellect, necessarily pertains to the super-mental apex of the affection.'[43] For its part, the proper act of the *affectus* is *dilectio*, which for Gallus entails a more direct contact with its object than sight or hearing. Accordingly, 'it is necessary for us to cognize divine things not by seeing or hearing intellectually. For those three senses [i.e. smell, taste, and touch] . . . are not exercised through a mirror (*per speculum*), but directly (*per speciem*).'[44] This notion that intellectual speculation is characterized by mediated distance, while affectual love has immediate contact, appears in Gallus's earliest extant work, his partial commentary on a passage from Isaiah. The soul cognizes (*cognoscit*) and apprehends (*apprehendit*) in two different ways that are analogous to the apparent difference between seeing and hearing on the one hand, and smelling, tasting and touching on the other. The former can apprehend without being affected or even by being oppositely affected: 'One can see and hear torment without [feeling] torment or see and hear delight without [feeling] delight; indeed, one can see and hear torment *with* delight and delight *with* torment.' By contrast, one cannot smell, taste or touch without being 'affected by that which we apprehend'.[45] For Thomas, the former is the proper modality of the speculative *intellectus*; the latter, that of the loving *affectus*. Clearly then, the 'distance' between subject and object is a crucial factor distinguishing these apprehensional modes. The *affectus* apprehends in some sense through direct contact, which is why Gallus ultimately identifies this power with union itself. Love 'unites us wholly to the plenitude of the divine, super-intellectually and ineffably, through the highest apex of our affectual power, which for this reason is called union'.[46]

   While he thus distinguishes the acts and objects of these two apprehending modes, Gallus nonetheless consistently attributes a *cognitio Dei* (*cognitio* having a wider connotation in the Middle Ages than the English 'cognition') to *both* the intellect and the affect. Such is true at the lower

---

[43] *Explanatio EH*, fol. 66rb–67va: *Quicquid autem supersubstantiale est intellectum speculativum excedit, unde necessario ad supermentalem affectionis apicem pertinet.* In Lawell, '*Ne de ineffabili*', p. 169, n. 57.

[44] *Explanation of the Angelic Hierarchy*, in Walsh, *Sapientia Christianorum*, p. 252

[45] *Commentary on Isaiah*, in Walsh, *Sapientia Christianorum*, Appendix I, p. 9[1], lines 8–16.

[46] *Explanatio AH*, fol. 3va: *hoc vinculum unit nos plenitudini divine superintellectualiter et penitus ineffabiliter per apicem summum nostre virtutis affectualis, que ideo vocatur unitio.* In Lawell, '*Ne de ineffabili*', p. 170, n. 59.

levels of the hierarchized soul, where these powers 'walk together' and experience their proper *cognitiones Dei*. Such is also the case at the highest level: even after the *intellectus* is arrested in its ascent at the cherubic rank, the *affectus* continues to enjoy a seraphic *cognitio Dei*. Here, the *affectus* 'cognizes God above every existing intellection and cognition',[47] however paradoxical this may seem. Gallus often associates this 'affectual cognition' with Mary of Bethany's experience of Christ: 'this *cognitio* is the portion of Mary, which for this reason "is not taken away" since it exceeds the intellect and speculum through union with God'.[48] Similarly, he explicitly attributes a form of apprehension to this union: 'the *synderesis*... apprehends supernal things'.[49]

In short, 'in so far as we thus taste, touch and embrace, and smell God, so, to that extent do we cognize him, by ineffably participating in his sweetness and suavity (*dulcedinem et suavitatem*)'.[50] This is an apprehending by 'spiritual examination (*spirituali examinacione*)', because when 'our spirit is united to the divine Spirit, it senses those things which are God's'.[51] Gallus captures this sensuous experience with the term 'wisdom' (*sapientia*), whose Latin etymology for medieval authors generally contained this notion of a 'tasted knowledge'[52] born of love: 'but that wisdom – namely cognizing God in this way – is obtained more by the burning of love into God (*multo estu dilecionis in Deum*)'.[53]

Perhaps the most striking feature, though, of Gallus's treatment of seraphic sensation (if I may put it so), and the feature which most mitigates against an anti-intellectual reading, is that he consistently orients these spiritual senses towards the divine *theoriae*, as Bonaventure will do. Though the term *theoria* is a crucial part of the Christian mystical vocabulary nearly from the beginning,[54] and is often a synonym for contemplation itself,

[47] *Comm. III*, 1.O, 141: *cognoscit eum super omnem existentem intellectum et cognitionem.* See also *Comm II*: 'Therefore the embrace of the groom, with the aforesaid mediating taste, is illuminated with a special privilege of fuller cognition after a long time, as in 1 Kings 14: 29; Ps. 34 [33]: 8: "taste and see"; and Prov 31: 18: "he has tasted and has seen".'

[48] *Explanatio AH*, fol. 3va: *Hec autem cognitio est Marie portio, que ideo non aufertur quia excedit intellectum et speculum per unitionem ad Deum.* In Lawell, '*Ne de ineffabili*', p. 170, n. 59.

[49] *Glose AH*, Paris, Bibliothèque Mazarine, MS 715, fol. 412b (in Lawell, '*Ne de ineffabili*', p. 157, n. 21): HOC ANIME etc., *id est, illam cuius ens est supernarum rerum apprehensiva, scilicet sinderesim.*

[50] *Explanation of the Angelic Hierarchy*, in Walsh, *Sapientia Christianorum*, p. 252.

[51] *Explanation of the Mystical Theology*, in Walsh, *Sapientia Christianorum*, p. 249. Echoing a theme more fully developed in twelfth-century authors, Gallus here associates this spiritual sensing with 'the senses of Christ' (*sensum Christi*).

[52] *Comm. II*, 1.A, 69: ... *unde certum est quod veram sapientiam non gustaverunt*...

[53] *Explanation of the Mystical Theology*, in Walsh, *Sapientia Christianorum*, p. 249.

[54] See A. Wilson-Nightingale, *Spectacles of Truth in Classical Greek Philosophy*: Theoria *in its Cultural Context* (Cambridge University Press, 2004) on *theoria* in its classical Greek context.

Gallus clearly means by it the divine 'ideas' or 'exemplars' which exist eternally in the divine mind. As such, for him, these *theoriae* are so many manifestations of the divine nature, apparently apprehendable in some fashion, and they flow 'down' into created minds properly disposed to receive them.[55] That Gallus should orient the *intellectus* towards these *theoriae* does not surprise; but that he should also see them as the proper object of the *affectus* is remarkable. A couple of passages will demonstrate the point. Calling them 'exemplars of the eternal Word', he describes the *theoriae* as 'sweet-smelling above the mind'[56] and 'agreeable, sweet, and of every variety' and 'most pleasing' (*gratissimam*) 'after the manner of myrrh'.[57] Frequently, he mingles the language of tasting and smelling to evoke this affective experience. Like *mandrakes*, these *theoriae* 'give a smell'.[58] Like *a cup of spiced wine*, they yield the 'most suave theoric tastings (*suavissimas theoricas degustationes*).[59] The fullest statement in this regard is prompted by the Canticle text 'smelling sweet of the best ointments' (Song 1: 2). Gallus comments: 'The best ointments are the super-intellectual *theoriae* which soothe the minds united to them and they restore and are rich in abundance for all with a kind of sweetness, beauty, clarity, suavity and every kind of desirable outpouring, as from the breast of the Word.'[60]

Consistently, then, Thomas describes the bride's affective, seraphic encounter with the groom as mediated by these *theoriae*, which engage the soul's capacity for spiritual smell, taste and touch. He is explicit about these spiritual senses at one point, when he characterizes the soul-bride's experience of union as a kind of sleep, because 'the excessive contemplation in the embraces of the bridegroom' exceeds the soul's natural capacities. In such a state, the soul-bride 'suspends the use of the exterior senses,[61] and exerts (*intendit*) and as it were diligently watches over (*invigilat*) the exercise of the interior senses'.[62]

Gallus's use of sense metaphors to describe seraphic experience and his orienting of them to the divine *theoriae* provide some insight into his claim that *affectus* in some way cognizes and apprehends God. At one point, he is quite explicit about this:

---

[55] *Comm. III*, 8.A, 224: 'And "there", persevering with you, "you shall teach me", that is, by the constant inflow of new *theoriae* . . . '

[56] *Comm. III*, 4.G, 186. [57] *Comm. III*, 1.M, 139. [58] *Comm. III*, 7.G, 222.

[59] *Comm. III*, 2.L, 153. The alternative MS gives *theoriarum* for *theoricas*, '. . . bride's most soothing tasting of the *theoria*'.

[60] *Comm. III*, 1.B, 122: *Unguenta optima sunt superintellectuales theorie que unitas sibi mentes deliniunt et universali quadam dulcedinis, pulchritudinis, claritatis, suavitatis et omnimode speciei desiderabilis effusione pollent et reficiunt, tanquam ex ubertate Verbi.*

[61] *Sensibilium.* I adopt here the alternative reading: *sensuum.* [62] *Comm. III*, 5.C, 193.

Your eyes: Even though eyes seem to be excluded from the seraphic order . . . nevertheless the Groom . . . attributes the eyes of the inferior order [i.e. the cherubim] to [the seraphic order]. Now from one consideration this [seraphic] order is said to be blinded or lack eyes, since the intelligence is not able to reach up into this order nor is it drawn [there] on account of this order's lofty eminence . . . But for another reason the Groom does attribute eyes to this order, since the eyes have an incomparably fuller cognition than all the other senses, and hence the other senses are sometimes designated by the name of vision, as when it is said: see that it smells and tastes; even so, this order exceeds the other orders inestimably by the excellence of a cognition of divine things.[63]

Though Gallus here clearly excludes an intellectual form of cognition from the seraphic experience, he just as clearly allows another. Precisely what kind of *cognitio* this entails is difficult to specify,[64] though the term has a far wider connotation for him than the modern English cognate 'cognition', as when he says of the groom: 'whom I cognize (*cognosco*) only by the most intimate experience of love (*dilectionis*)'.[65] Some indication, though, emerges from the following text:

See, he designates a twofold cognition of God, one from the comparison of creatures, which is intellective cognition, the other . . . [from] the experience of the eternal rays of wisdom, which is above intellect and every being . . . Through this [affective] power, therefore, it is necessary to understand (*intelligere*) divine things. We understand union [to be] the principal *affectus* of the soul by which we are united to God . . . [66]

Here, the distinction between forms of cognition hinges less on content than on source. The speculative intellect gathers knowledge of God indirectly through creatures, 'from below'; the adhering affect receives a direct experience of divine wisdom 'from above'. Remarkably, Gallus seems to indicate here that the *affectus* is able 'to understand' (*intelligere*) divine things in this way. Clearly, this affective *cognitio*, which 'apprehends' the divine *theoriae* – ideational in their very nature – cannot be utterly devoid of

---

[63] *Comm. III*, 7.C, 217.
[64] Perhaps Bertrand Russell's notion of 'knowledge by acquaintance' is relevant here. See his 'Knowledge by Acquaintance and Knowledge by Description', *Proceedings of the Aristotelian Society*, new series, 11 (1910–11), 108–28.
[65] *Comm. III*, 1.H, 132: *quem sola intime dilectionis experientia cognosco . . .*
[66] *Explanatio DN*, fol. 102rb: *Ecce duplicem assignat Dei cognitionem, unam ex collatione creaturarum que est intellectiva, aliam . . . experientia radiorum eterne sapientie que est super intellectum et omne ens. Secundum vero quam vim anime ista superintellectualis sapientia percipiatur, collige ex ipsius [sc. Dionysii] verbis, eodem capitulo 7h: Oportet autem videre mentem nostram habere quidem virtutem ad intelligendum per quam intelligibilia inspicit, unitionem vero excedentem mentis naturam per quam coniungitur ad ea que sunt supra ipsam. Secundum hanc vim ergo oportet divina intelligere. Unitionem autem intelligimus principalem affectum anime quo Deo coniungimur . . .* In Lawell, '*Ne de ineffabili*', p. 171, n. 61.

cognitive content. As the text quoted above suggests, it may even consum-
mate the lower form of intellectual cognition. All this raises the question
of just how radical and thoroughgoing the apparent disjunction between
cherubic intellection and seraphic affection is for Thomas Gallus.

SIMPLIFICATION: AN 'AFFECTIVIZING' OF THE INTELLECT?

Lacking an explicit articulation from Gallus himself regarding the
encounter with God at the highest reaches of the 'angelized' soul, the
reader of his Song commentaries must interpret his varied metaphors and
highly imagistic descriptions with care and caution. Tentatively, then, we
will argue that some passages scattered over the commentaries suggest that
Gallus sees the transition from the cherubic to the seraphic rank as a
transformation of the *intellectus*, rather than its complete negation. Gallus
evokes this transformation with the notion of 'simplification'. Put simply,
it appears that in some fashion the *intellectus* is taken up into or absorbed
into the *affectus* and thus the two powers are contracted or simplified into
a single cognitive modality. Here, it is crucial to recall that, as noted above,
Gallus does not confine the *affectus* to seraphic level. Rather, at every stage
of the ascent, it 'walks hand in hand' with the *intellectus*. Thus it is striking and intriguing when at one point Gallus states that in the course of
the ascent through the middle hierarchy (powers, virtues, dominions), 'the
eyes of the mind', namely, the 'movements and extensions of the affect
and intellect', are 'made simple' in order to ascend further into the highest
hierarchy (thrones, cherubim, seraphim).[67] Elsewhere, Gallus speaks of this
simplification as a response to the simplified divine nature encountered in
contemplation: 'These eyes of the bride are called "of the doves", because,
just as a dove has a simple stare, so these eyes are simplified, carried off
in contemplation of the simple bridegroom [and] are simplified from the
multitude of existing things.'[68] This simplification intensifies as the soul-
bride ascends further towards union with the simple groom: 'in the order
of the cherubim', the 'intellectual vision (*visus*) is most greatly simplified' –
not simply blinded or truncated. Finally, in the transition from cherubic to
seraphic rank, Gallus gestures at this drawing-together towards simplicity
with the language of spiritual smell: 'Spikenard is a *spicosa* plant . . . and is
especially odiferous', signifying the 'new super-infused plenitude, sweet-
smelling above the mind'.[69] This '*spicositas* of spikenard', he continues, indicates that 'the multiple cognitions of invisible divine things are

---

[67] *Comm. III*, 2.G, 153–4.   [68] *Comm. III*, 1.O, 141.   [69] *Comm. III*, 1.M, 138.

contained under that simplicity of participation', which 'is perceived in inmost contemplation of sublime *theoriae*'.[70] The overall impact of these passages suggests some form of contraction of the soul's diverse powers, *intellectus* and *affectus*, active in discrete modes at the lower parts of the soul, but increasingly simplified into a single contemplative modality, in which the power of *affectus* comes to dominate, in some sense sublimating and absorbing the power of *intellectus*.[71] In this light, it is of no little interest that such a view emerges in another commentary emanating from Gallus's community at Vercelli, *Deiformis anime gemitus*, once attributed to Gallus himself.[72] Von Ivánka argued that for this anonymous *Vercellensis*, the highest mystical experience is still the 'movement of the deiform intelligence' (*motus intelligentiae deiformis*),[73] and that 'intelligence' (*intelligentia*) is equated with (*gleichbedeutend*) the *affectio principalis* and the *scintilla synderesis*.[74]

ETERNALLY SPIRALLING INTO GOD

It is often assumed that in a straightforward manner this affective, seraphic union above intellective, cherubic knowledge – whatever the underlying relation between them – is the stopping point of Gallus's mystical theology. In fact, however, it is not. In the Prologue, after narrating the ascent through the soul's angelic hierarchies up through the seraphic union, he observes: 'It is from this order [the seraphim] that the torrent of divine light pours down in stages to the lower orders.'[75] This remark introduces a conspicuous feature of his Song commentaries, which is consistently present along with the narration of the soul's ascent to union, namely, Gallus's extensive attention to movement in the opposite direction, that is, descent. Attending to this descending dynamic grants further insight into the relation between *affectus* and *intellectus*.

Stated simply, not only does seraphic union entail some form of spiritually sensuous cognition *at that level*; for Gallus, this cognition is passed down to the lower orders of the soul. Stated otherwise, the *cognitio* received

[70] *Comm. III*, 1.M, 138.

[71] The deep background for Gallus's thinking here regarding 'simplification' may well be Hugh of St Victor's reflections on the 'liquefying' power of soul's love, which he develops in his *Commentariorum in hierarchiam Coelestem* (PL 175. 923–1154).

[72] See J. Barbet, *Un commentaire vercellien du Cantique des Cantiques: 'Deiformis anime gemitus'. Étude d'authenticité par Jeanne Barbet et Francis Ruello*, trans. Francis Ruello, Sous la règle de saint Augustin, 10 (Turnhout: Brepols, 2005).

[73] Ivánka, *Plato Christianus*, p. 341.   [74] *Ibid.* p. 355.

[75] *Comm. II*, Prol. 67. Cf. Pseudo-Dionysius, *CH* VII. 1, 205C.

by seraphic taste and smell is passed on to cherubic sight; or, what the *affectus* experiences can in some way be passed 'down' to and received by the *intellectus* in its proper modality. So the 'sweet-smelling participations of the light beyond the mind' flow 'into [the] second and lowest hierarchy'.[76] To evoke this descent, Gallus multiplies images: there is an 'inflowing of his light from the first order all the way to the last'.[77] From the seraphic abundance, *the sweet odours* waft down 'into the middle and lowest hierarchy'.[78] The lower orders are 'moistened' or 'saturated' by the highest order; 'all spiritual nutriments are received from God through the head, which 'contains all the senses (*omnes sensus*)', and are administered to the lower orders'.[79] When the Groom descends into the garden of the bride, 'that is, into the order of my seraphim', he strews 'her inferior orders with sweetness (*suavitate*), just as *the smell of a plentiful field* (Gen 27: 27)'.[80] Having received the king in her inmost part, where he now feeds and reclines, the bride says that she 'was so filled with suavity from that union', that her 'spikenard, that is, the fervent love most suavely fragrant, gave off, that is, distributed to my inferior orders, the odour of its suavity, or the odour of itself, that is, the participations of its perceived suavities according to the capacity of the individual orders'.[81] The cumulative impact of these images suggests that in some way the lower orders and capacities of the soul are fecundated by what flows down to them from seraphic affectivity. In short, although the seraphic union is exclusively affective, it nonetheless flows down and fecundates not only the *affectus* but also the *intellectus* at the 'lower' ranks of the soul.

This higher garden [of the seraphim] is made into a fountain by the water flowing down from above and from its abundance; and it pours *affectual* and *intellectual* abundance (*copias affectuales et intellectuales*) into the lower orders; but the groom commends this fountain from the principal in-flowing, namely, the *affectual* inflowing (*affectual influitio*), which is like a fountain of *intellectual things* (*intellectualium*), according to which there is an inflowing from the higher watering.[82]

Here, the exclusively affectual in-flowings pour down into the intellect and are in some way received there as intellectual things. Other passages suggest the same: 'I refill you with the fragrance of multiple

---

[76] *Comm. III*, 4.H, 188.   [77] *Comm. III*, 4.F, 183–4.   [78] *Comm. II*, 4.G, 100.
[79] *Comm. III*, 7.D, 218–19. See also *Comm. II*, 2.A, 78: '"To my palate", through which every refreshment moves from head to body, signifies the order of the seraphim, through which every true refreshment of the mind is transmitted into the inferior orders by the head of the bridegroom, by Christ.'
[80] *Comm. III*, 6.A, 206.   [81] *Comm. II*, 1.F, 75.   [82] *Comm. II*, 4.F, 98, my italics.

sweetness . . . because splendour and fragrance are in the flower on account of the refilling of the *intellect* and the affect.'[83] Again:

the words 'honey flowing from the honeycomb' are understood as the affectual in-flowings (*affectuales influitiones*) emanating from the first hierarchy into the lower ones. Likewise, by 'wine' here understand the ecstatic intellective cognition (*intellectivam cognitionem extaticam*), such as in the first hierarchy, by 'milk which flows out from the breasts' intellective cognition is understood [as] sober (*sobria*), emanating from the breast of the first hierarchy into the second.[84]

All these texts would seem to mitigate against any sharp, insurmountable break between the seraphic affect and the lower orders, including the intellect.

Finally, this overflow into the lower orders of the soul engenders a movement of return back toward seraphic union. Here too, the language of the spiritual sensorium assists Gallus. Having got the taste for the divine, the soul mounts up again for more; having caught the scent of the divine groom, the soul longs for new, richer, more intense experiences and thus surges back upwards with greater intensity: 'The experienced bride', says Gallus, 'always desires the sweetness and uplifting activity (*sursumactionem*) of the new in-flowings and always to make progress in the taste of sweetness and in being uplifted (*sursumactionem*).'[85] Again: 'by the communication of these highest and manifold graces, transfused through the seraph of the mind into the inferior orders, the natural *affectus* and *intellectus* are powerfully changed, to rise up and stretch out constantly towards the perceptions of the good and the participations in the beautiful'.[86] A circling or, better, spiralling dynamic ultimately emerges in the soul. 'However much any angelic or human mind is taken up into the interior experience and contemplation of the *theoriae*, yet that one is always circling those intimate things.'[87]

---

[83] *Comm. II*, 2.A, 77, my italics.   [84] *Comm. II*, 5.A, 101.   [85] *Comm. III*, 7.F, 221.

[86] *Comm. III*, 1.C, 124, in Walsh, *Sapientia Christianorum*, p. 253: *Ex huius igitur precipue et multiplicis gracie communicacione, per seraphim mentis in ordines inferiores transfuse, fortiter mutantur affectus et intellectus naturalis, in perceptas boni et pulchri participationes semper assurgere et extendi.*

[87] *Comm. II*, 2.E, 82: 'truly nature longs (*appetit*) for new things, because it carries natural appetites to the appetite for the highest good, in which they are always new things. Through constant ascensions of contemplation (*assiduos ascensus contemplationum*) of the lights (*luminum*) new things are constantly advancing into infinity, though those lights are ancient and eternal. Whence Augustine in the *Confessions*: "O beauty, so old and yet so new, late have I known (*cognovi*) you, late have I loved (*amavi*) you."' Again: *Comm II*, 2.E, 82: '*The vines in flower yield their sweet smell. Vines* are the speculations (*theorie*) of highest things, which contemplative minds carry into and flow the wine of the aforementioned wine cellar (Song 2: 3). They are said to flower, when new and not yet experienced suavities flow into the same mind, and this is: *Flourishing vines produce perfume*, and they are always flourishing because new things are always flowing in.'

CONCLUSION

A careful reading of Thomas Gallus's Song commentaries indicates that his affective Dionysianism is not as anti-intellectualist as is often suggested. One could also argue that Dionysius is not as non-affective or un-affective as is sometimes thought. From that angle, Gallus is simply developing the Dionysian eros (emphasized in other parts of the corpus)[88] in a more nuptial-bridal, interpersonal and affective mode, which, while deployed in un-Dionysian ways, is not asynchronous with the overall 'logic of erotic ascent'.[89] Whatever the case, it is apparent that Gallus has adopted the notion of the spiritual senses of the soul to navigate the divide between cherubic intellection and seraphic affection by equipping the latter with capacities for spiritual perception. Though in some sense blind (and deaf?) in the love-sick Dionysian night, the soul can yet smell, taste and touch its beloved in an experience that, though profoundly affective, is nonetheless a kind of knowing, a form of spiritually sensuous cognition of Christ. But, if equipping the ascending soul with seraphic affection above cherubic intellection is in some sense un-Dionysian, that Gallus uses the spiritual sensorium to span the gap may in fact reflect a deeply Dionysian intuition. In Dionysian hierarchies, the higher contains within itself all of the lower; a seraph contains all things cherubic within itself. Thus, within Gallus's hierarchically 'angelized' soul, seraphic love 'ought' to subsume cherubic knowledge within itself.[90] Admittedly, Gallus himself nowhere makes this claim explicitly. But this is precisely what his use of the spiritual sensorium – a unified continuum of diverse sense modalities – seems to accomplish. At the highest level of the soul, cherubic vision is taken up and sublimated into seraphic touch. Such a continuum can also function in reverse. What the soul perceives seraphically in its proper sense modality of touch is not confined to the high point of the affection, but in some way flows down to fecundate the cherubic modality of sight. What precisely that means or how exactly that occurs is not easy to explain.

Whatever the case, a final feature of Gallus's deployment of the spiritual sensorium merits comment in relation to recent scholarship on the spiritual senses in the patristic and medieval eras. Recently, Gordon Rudy has argued that much of the teaching on the spiritual senses in the Christian

---

[88] Thanks to Paul Gavrilyuk for pointing this out and providing the statistics: *eros* appears four times in *CH*, and frequently in *EH*; *agape* appears four times in *DN* and once in *Ep*. VIII. The cognate *agapesis* is used several times in *EH*.
[89] The phrase is from Paul Gavrilyuk, to whom I am indebted for this point.
[90] I wish to thank Paul Rorem for suggesting this point in a private conversation.

tradition is dualist and intellectualist.[91] While this tradition adopts the language of physical sensation, it does so ultimately to distance itself from the things bodily, against which it contrasts in dualistic fashion a superior spiritual realm. Rudy sees this trend epitomized in the typical ranking of the spiritual senses in a way that privileges sight, the most spiritual and least bodily of the physical senses, over taste and touch, the lowest and most bodily senses. In contrast to this majority opinion in the tradition, Rudy espies a 'minority report' stemming from Bernard of Clairvaux and Hadewijch of Antwerp, who in his reading reject the dualist and intellectualist approach by privileging the more bodily sense of taste and especially touch.[92] The larger methodological question regarding the appropriateness and usefulness of Rudy's notions of 'dualism' and 'intellectualism' cannot be pursued here. What should be noted is that neither Alexander of Hales (a monastically minded scholastic, treated in Chapter 7) nor Thomas Gallus (a scholastically trained monastic) fits comfortably into Rudy's framework. As a simple matter of fact, both prioritize taste and touch over sight and hearing in the soul's encounter with God; neither, moreover, can be interpreted as 'intellectualist' in Rudy's sense of the term. In fact, both seem keen to refuse the dichotomy, and, in their distinctive ways, to employ the notion of a spiritual sensorium precisely in order to do so.

It is certainly the case that both Thomas Gallus and Alexander of Hales sharply distinguish the spiritual senses from their physical counterparts. But this fact must be carefully interpreted. It is arguable that traditional doctrines of the spiritual senses reflect a profound, right-headed, though not fully articulated, intuition that beatifying 'knowledge of God' must have the directness, immediacy, pleasure and assimilation between knower and known, that characterizes physical sense perception. Accordingly, the self-conscious and explicit distancing of the spiritual senses from the physical senses is not ultimately an unhappy intrusion of Platonic mind–body, spirit–matter dualisms; rather, it reflects the awareness that in our present condition neither physical sensation nor rational (conceptual, ideational, notional) knowledge is adequate for beatifying apprehension of God, but that each in its own way is an analogue of it. A genuinely beatific *apprehensio Dei* must eventually, eschatologically, entail something like both. That is, the *visio Dei* must be an encounter of created embodied spirit with uncreated spirit that is marked by the direct immediacy of physical sensing, but that is also a genuine act of spiritual intelligence; again, both

---

[91] G. Rudy, *Mystical Language of Sensation in the Later Middle Ages* (New York and London: Routledge, 2002), 35.

[92] *Ibid.* pp. 45–65.

physical sensation and noetic conceptualization in the present state are partial, discrete anticipatory analogues of an eschatological apprehension that surpasses but in some fashion integrates and assimilates them. Eschatologically, all genuinely human knowledge of God must be embodied and sensuous, but also spiritual and intellectual; that is, it must bear the marks of embodied sense knowledge, even as that is transposed and subsumed into something transcending it, of which we now have only the faintest intimation. In this light, the 'disjunctive thesis' rightly acknowledges that at present we have only a vague, meagre intuition of beatific apprehension, but have no way of conceiving how it is an act of spiritual intelligence that has the directness of physical sensation – apart from an admittedly awkward doctrine of the spiritual senses. It is at present a kind of 'place holder' or marker that both affirms but also relativizes all human modes of sensing and knowing in this present life.

CHAPTER 9

Bonaventure

Gregory F. LaNave

Bonaventure's name is invariably cited today when one speaks of the doctrine of the spiritual senses in Christian history. Early twentieth-century treatments of the spiritual theology of this 'prince of mystical theology'[1] referred to the spiritual senses as an integral part of that theology,[2] and his doctrine became more famous thanks to a seminal article by Karl Rahner[3] – and an indirect response to that article by Hans Urs von Balthasar.[4] More recently, Fabio Massimo Tedoldi has published a monograph on the subject.[5]

In his earliest reference to the spiritual senses, Bonaventure notes that one may speak of them broadly or more strictly. Broadly, they refer to 'any perfect use of grace'; strictly, they refer to the 'use of interior grace with respect to God himself according to a proportion to the five senses'.[6] Similarly, there can be broader or stricter accounts of Bonaventure's doctrine on the subject, depending on whether one confines oneself to his explicit references to the spiritual senses or casts one's net more widely to encompass many other themes and texts concerning the experience of God. Strictly speaking, Bonaventure locates the spiritual senses fairly precisely within his doctrine of grace and of religious knowledge.[7] However, there are only a dozen or so explicit references to the spiritual senses

---

[1] Title given to Bonaventure by Pope Leo XIII in an allocution on 11 October 1890.

[2] See, e.g., E. Longpré, 'Bonaventure', *DS*, vol. 1 (1937), pp. 1832–3; E. Longpré, 'La théologie mystique de S. Bonaventure', *Archivum Franciscanum historicum*, 14 (1921), 51–3; D. Dobbins, *Franciscan Mysticism: The Mystical Theology of the Seraphic Doctor* (New York: J. F. Wagner, 1927), pp. 51–4; J.-Fr. Bonnefoy, *Le Saint-Esprit et ses dons selon saint Bonaventure*, Études de philosophie médiévale, 10 (Paris: J. Vrin, 1929), pp. 210–15; É. Gilson, *The Philosophy of St. Bonaventure*, trans. D. I. Trethowan and F. J. Sheed (London: Sheed & Ward, 1940), pp. 452–3.

[3] K. Rahner, 'La doctrine des "sens spirituels" au Moyen-Âge, en particulier chez saint Bonaventure', *RAM*, 14 (1933), 263–99.

[4] See esp. Balthasar, *GL*, vol. 1, pp. 371–3; vol. 11, pp. 315–26. See also S. Fields, 'Balthasar and Rahner on the Spiritual Senses', *Theological Studies*, 57 (1996), 224–41.

[5] F. M. Tedoldi, *La dottrina dei cinque sensi spirituali in San Bonaventura* (Rome: Pontificium Athenaeum Antonianum, 1999).

[6] III *Sent.* d. 13, dub. 1.   [7] III *Sent.*, d. 34, p. 1, a. 1, q. 1; *Brev.* v. 6.

scattered throughout his corpus.[8] Building a complete doctrine on them presents a challenge, since most of them do not seem to be construed in any systematic fashion. Tedoldi gives the most comprehensive account of a broader reading, arguing that the doctrine of the spiritual senses is implied whenever Bonaventure speaks of spiritual knowledge.[9]

The focus of this chapter is on a stricter account. There are several advantages to be gained from this approach. First, one may verify the consistency of Bonaventure's account of the spiritual senses, a point sometimes contested.[10] Second, it is thereby possible to see why Bonaventure evokes the spiritual senses when he does, and why many of his most important works on spiritual knowledge – *De triplici via, Lignum vitae, Christus unus omnium magister* and the disputed questions *De scientia Christi* – contain no reference to the spiritual senses at all. Third, it facilitates a strict delineation of the essential subjective and objective components of the doctrine.

The bulk of this chapter is divided into three parts. In the first, I set out the elements of Bonaventure's teaching on the topic, particularly the nature of the act of the spiritual senses, how they compare with the other senses of the human person and the identification of five distinct spiritual senses. In the second, I define the object of these senses. In the third, I consider St Francis as the exemplar of the subject of these senses. I close by addressing some of the debates concerning Bonaventure's doctrine, and by showing the connection between my reading and certain elements of Bonaventure's general understanding of theology.

The heart of Bonaventure's teaching on this subject can be summarized in one point. One might think that if there really is something like a spiritual sensorium in the human person, a capacity to perceive a spiritual reality in a sense-like way, then it will be discovered by a thoroughgoing analysis of the powers and actions of the human soul, natural and graced – in other words, the doctrine of the spiritual senses is chiefly a doctrine of the human subject. Such is not the case in Bonaventure. He does deal with the pertinent questions here, but the heart of his doctrine is its attention to the object of the spiritual senses. God makes himself present in such a

---

[8] Tedoldi identifies the following passages: III *Sent.* d. 13, dub. 1; III *Sent.* d. 34, p. 1, a. 1, q. 1; *Brev.* v. 6; *Itin.* IV. 3–7; *De red.* 8–10; *Hex.* III. 22; *De plantatione paradisi*, 9 and 16; *Soliloquium*, I. 12–17; *De quinque festivitatibus pueri Iesu*, IV. 1; *Sermo 9 in Epiph.*; and *Sermo 14 in Epiph.* Other passages that some have argued should be included in such a consideration are *Sermo 2 in Dom. 12 post Pentec.*; *Sermo 2 de S. Agnete*; *Sermo 6 in Circumc.*; *Commentarius in librum Sapientiae*, I. 1; *Comm. in Ioan.* I. 43; *Hex.* XV. 20. See Tedoldi, *La dottrina dei cinque sensi spirituali*, pp. 137–82 and 138, n. 2.

[9] Tedoldi, *La dottrina dei cinque sensi spirituali*, p. 248.

[10] See esp. Bonnefoy, *Le Saint-Esprit et ses dons*, pp. 210–15; cf. Rahner, 'The Doctrine of the "Spiritual Senses" in the Middle Ages', esp. pp. 110–11; Balthasar, *GL*, vol. II, pp. 315–26. I address this in the conclusion to this chapter.

way that he can be spiritually sensed; it is when one is attentive to that presence that one understands what the spiritual senses are.

PHYSICAL AND SPIRITUAL SENSATION

There is no doubt that 'spiritual senses' sounds like an oxymoron. 'Senses' strictly speaking have to do with the way we receive the corporeal world. Realities that are purely spiritual can influence us, but they cannot be corporeally sensed; therefore, 'spiritual senses' seems to be a metaphor at best.[11] I will first treat Bonaventure's distinction between the exterior and the interior senses, and then address the subject of the spiritual senses.[12]

Exterior and interior senses

Bonaventure speaks of man being created with a double *sensus*: one exterior, one interior.[13] The 'exterior sense' is the five corporeal senses, the acts of the sense organs as they are engaged by suitable corporeal objects. One may loosely speak of the capacity of the sense organs as the senses, but Bonaventure follows Aristotle in saying that 'sense' properly speaking refers to an act (or use, *usus*) of a potency, rather than the potency itself.[14] The corporeal senses are philosophically and theologically significant for Bonaventure, for they are the means whereby the outside world enters into man, speaks to him, forms him by means of its latent ability to lead him to God.[15] In the world as first created, sensible things were suitable to lead man to a true knowledge of God.[16] This 'book of the world' has been made obscure to us because of sin, but its potency to lead us to God remains.

The 'interior senses' are the acts of the soul – memory, intellect and will – that apprehend divine things.[17] Man is made to be oriented towards

---

[11] Dobbins insists on this, and argues that the only point of talking about spiritual senses at all is to highlight the intensity of the experience of grace (*Franciscan Mysticism*, pp. 53–4).

[12] On this point my approach differs significantly from that of Tedoldi. Tedoldi conflates the interior senses and the spiritual senses (*La dottrina dei cinque sensi spirituali*, pp. 196–202). This is not without reason, as he rightly sees that Bonaventure's doctrine demands an integrated anthropology. The spiritual senses are defined not only by analogy to, but also by a connection to, the corporeal senses. However, such an approach runs the risk of obscuring the precise *ratio* of the spiritual senses, as will become apparent.

[13] *Brev.* II. II. I; *Itin.* I. 10; *De red.* 8.   [14] III *Sent.* d. 13, dub. 1; see Aristotle, *De an.* II. 5.

[15] See esp. the account of sensation in *Itin.* II. 2–6.

[16] Not, though, without the elevation of man by grace: *Brev.* II. 12. 4.

[17] Bonaventure certainly recognizes the category of Aristotelian inner powers of the soul that are related to the exterior senses – such as imagination, memory or the estimative power (e.g. *Brev.* II. 9. 5; *Hex.* V. 24). One can rightly call these 'interior senses'. But when he speaks of the *interior sensus* he generally has in mind not these powers, but the powers of the soul as they can be related to divine things (in this way, the angels are said to have 'an internal sense' (*Brev.* II. II. 2)).

God. The natural functioning of his cognitive faculties brings him in touch with the divine. This is precisely what it means for man to be made in the image of God: 'a creature is called an "image" insofar as it has *conditiones* which point to God not only as cause, but as object, which are memory, intelligence, and will'.[18] Needless to say, the interior senses are philosophically and theologically significant, for if we do not understand the soul's natural orientation towards God we do not rightly understand the powers of the soul.[19]

The spiritual senses and the habits of sanctifying grace

In the first text in which Bonaventure speaks of the spiritual senses he gives something like a definition: the spiritual senses are the 'use of interior grace with respect to God himself according to a proportion to the five senses'.[20] Elsewhere he describes them as the 'use of spiritual speculations'[21] and 'mental perceptions of the truth being contemplated'.[22]

Bonaventure raises the topic of the spiritual senses in two texts that purport to be laying out the systematic essentials of theology: his commentary on the *Sentences* of Peter Lombard and the *Breviloquium*.[23] The general context is the same. He is unfolding his doctrine of sanctifying grace, which includes three types of habits – the virtues, by which the soul is rectified; the gifts of the Holy Spirit, by which the soul is advanced;[24] and the beatitudes, by which the soul is perfected – and beyond these a state of delight (the fruits) and a 'use' (*usus*) which he calls a 'spiritual perception' (i.e. the spiritual senses).[25]

---

[18] I *Sent.* d. 3, p. I, a. un., q. 2. See also *De sc. Chr.* q. 4.

[19] For details about what it is that the soul knows about God by means of these powers, see *Itin.* III. 2–4.

[20] III *Sent.* d. 13, dub. I.   [21] *Brev.* V. 6. I.

[22] *Brev.* V. 6. 7; see also III *Sent.* d. 34, p. I, a. I, q. I.

[23] III *Sent.* d. 34, p. I, a. I, q. I; *Brev.* V. 6.

[24] The verb consistently used with reference to the gifts of the Holy Spirit is *expedire*, which is difficult to translate smoothly. The idea is that the gifts enable the soul to move towards its perfection more quickly and easily, especially by removing impediments that remain even after the rectification of the soul through the virtues.

[25] To this schema he adds, in the *Sentences* commentary, the category of the sacraments, which assist all the other forms of grace, especially healing the soul of the wounds of sin. In the *Collationes de septem donis Spiritus Sancti* Bonaventure speaks of grace that heals (the sacraments, the seven works of justice and the seven works of mercy), grace that strengthens (the virtues and the gifts of the Holy Spirit) and grace that brings to completion (the beatitudes and the seven endowments). *De donis,* I. 17–18. The absence of the spiritual senses from this text is significant; it suggests that although Bonaventure's most formal articulation of a doctrine of the spiritual senses lies in his overall doctrine of sanctifying grace, it has to do more specifically with the intersection of this doctrine and his teaching on cognition.

Bonaventure brings an order to this doctrine by associating the habits of sanctifying grace with one another. Each of the virtues is associated with a distinctive gift, and each gift is associated with a distinct beatitude.[26] For example, the virtue of faith believes, the gift of understanding understands what is believed, and the beatitude of purity of heart attains the vision of what is understood.[27] Furthermore, the spiritual senses are associated with distinct virtues[28] and therefore by implication with distinct virtue–gift–beatitude trajectories among the habits. Thus the trajectory of faith, understanding and purity of heart is associated with the spiritual senses of sight and hearing. The trajectory of hope, counsel and mercy is associated with spiritual smell. The trajectory of love, wisdom and peace is associated with spiritual taste and touch.[29]

Strictly speaking, again, 'sense' names the act of a potency, not the potency itself. The spiritual senses are not habits; they do not, in themselves, make the soul capable of salvific or perfective acts. Rather, they are the acts whereby the soul perceives that which is given to it by the graced habits. Yet they are not the only acts that emerge from these habits. The habits of sanctifying grace all have acts that are appropriate to them. Thus, to know that God is a Trinity is an act of the virtue of faith, to understand and contemplate that truth is an act of the gift of understanding, and to see the Trinity in light of one's perfect conformity to it is an act of the beatitude of purity of heart.[30] But to be struck by the splendour of the uncreated Word is the act of spiritual sight.[31] The distinction makes sense only if one is speaking strictly, according to 'a proportion to the five senses'. 'To sense' is 'to know a thing as present'.[32] Thus, 'putting on the mind of Christ' might be a suitable description of an intellectual act that results from a likeness to God produced by grace, but knowing God as present and something to be 'sensed' is the act of the spiritual senses.

The spiritual senses and sensation

Bonaventure leaves no doubt that our experience of God can be such that it must be described in terms of sensation. His first clear evocation of the theme of a connection between the corporeal and the spiritual senses occurs in the discussion of sense perception in *De reductione artium ad theologiam*:

---

[26] See esp. *Brev.* v. 4. 3.   [27] *Brev.* v. 4. 3.   [28] *Itin.* iv. 3.

[29] See Rahner, 'The Doctrine of the "Spiritual Senses" in the Middle Ages', p. 113. The differentiation between sight and hearing, or taste and touch, comes not from the habits with which they are associated, but, as we will see, from the object of the senses.

[30] See esp. *Brev.* v. 4. 3; v. 6. 3, 6.   [31] See, e.g., *Sermo 9 in Epiph.*; *Sermo 14 in Epiph.*

[32] III *Sent.* d. 34, p. 1, a. 1, q. 1.

Every sense seeks its proper sense object with longing, finds it with delight, and never wearied, seeks it again and again ... In the same way, our spiritual senses must seek with longing, find with joy, and time and again experience the beautiful, the harmonious, the fragrant, the sweet, or the delightful to the touch. Behold how the Divine Wisdom lies hidden in sense perception and how wonderful is the contemplation of the five spiritual senses in the light of their conformity to the senses of the body.[33]

The connection is largely suggestive: if we consider the delights that our souls find in the bodily senses, and their union with their desired object, we find an analogy to a spiritual delight in what is most truly beautiful, harmonious and so on. Bonaventure affirms the existence of five spiritual senses here, indicating that they are analogous to the five physical senses and emphasizing the delight one finds in the apprehension of the noncorporeal reality of the divine wisdom.

The argument is elaborated in the *Itinerarium*, written a few years later.[34] Corporeal and spiritual sensation are divided. Corporeal sensation involves three activities – apprehension, delight and judgement – that are 'vestiges in which we can see our God'.[35] It thereby opens up a window on the divine. Spiritual sensation, by contrast, follows the infusion of grace and involves the apprehension of a spiritual object, namely, the uncreated, incarnate and inspired Word, and the delight we have in it.[36]

When the soul by faith believes in Christ as in the uncreated Word, who is the Word and the brightness of the Father, she recovers her spiritual hearing and sight, hearing to receive the words of Christ, and sight to view the splendors of that Light. When the soul longs with hope to receive the inspired Word, she recovers, because of her desire and affection, the spiritual sense of smell. When she embraces with love the Incarnate Word, inasmuch as she receives delight from Him and passes over to Him in ecstatic love, she recovers her sense of taste and touch. Having recovered the spiritual senses, the soul now sees, hears, smells, tastes, and embraces her beloved.[37]

---

[33] *De red.* 10, trans. E. T. Healy, rev. Z. Hayes, OFM, *Works of Saint Bonaventure*, vol. 1 (St Bonaventure, NY: Franciscan Institute, 1996), p. 49.

[34] The dating of *De red.* has been a point of some dispute, but it has recently been definitively determined. See J. C. Benson, 'Identifying the Literary Genre of the *De reductione artium ad theologiam*: Bonaventure's Inaugural Lecture at Paris', *Franciscan Studies*, 67 (2009), 149–78; J. M. Hammond, 'Dating Bonaventure's Inception as Regent Master', *Franciscan Studies*, 67 (2009), 179–226.

[35] *Itin.* II. 7, trans. P. Boehner, rev. Z. Hayes, OFM, *Works of Saint Bonaventure*, vol. II (St Bonaventure, NY: Franciscan Institute, 2002), p. 69.

[36] I have argued that chapters II, IV and VI of the *Itin.* should be read as a single trajectory of a kind of knowledge of God for which the model is sensation. See G. F. LaNave, 'Knowing God through and in All Things: A Proposal for Reading Bonaventure's *Itinerarium mentis in Deum*', *Franciscan Studies*, 67 (2009), 267–99.

[37] *Itin.* IV. 3, trans. Boehner, rev. Hayes, *Works of Saint Bonaventure*, vol. II, pp. 99–101.

God is knowable to us through creation. But he can also be present in such a way – namely, in the form of the Word – that he can be more strictly speaking sensed.

Five spiritual senses

Nevertheless, even if it is appropriate for us to speak of 'sensing God', one must enquire as to whether there is any real significance to the delineation of five spiritual senses. We speak of five corporeal senses because there are five distinct sense organs with different ways of apprehending sensible objects. But since we do not see God with our bodily eyes, hear him with our bodily ears and so on, this is not sufficient grounds for a strict division of spiritual senses.

Bonaventure connects the division of the spiritual senses to the spiritual powers of the soul: 'Each of these senses, as Bernard has it, has its root in the intellect and in the *affectus*, so that they might be called "experiential cognition" (*cognitionem experimentalem*). But some belong more to the intellect, such as sight and hearing, while others belong more to the *affectus*, namely, smell, taste, and touch.'[38] Following this principle, we may regard the spiritual senses as being on a continuum, from the most remote and intellectual sense of sight to the most intimate and affective sense of touch. But one may wonder, is there any strong reason to insist on five senses? Would it not be better to speak of two, one more intellectual and the other more affective? This would accord well with other texts in Bonaventure that speak of wisdom, the type of experiential cognition. Wisdom perfects the intellect 'as it is extended to the *affectus*',[39] and is juxtaposed with a knowledge that is purely intellectual, remote, marked by something like the clarity of sight. Thus the affectivity of theological wisdom is contrasted with the intellectuality of philosophical wisdom,[40] and the affective intellectuality of the Holy Spirit's gift of wisdom is contrasted with the pure intellectuality of the gift of understanding.[41] Applying this to the spiritual senses, one could speak of the contemplative knowledge of God that is

---

[38] III *Sent.* d. 13, dub. 1. Bernard aligns the modalities of spiritual perception with *intellectus* and *affectus* in a way similar to Thomas Gallus. See Chapter 8 in this volume.

[39] I *Sent.* pro. q. 3.   [40] I *Sent.* pro. q. 3.

[41] III *Sent.* d. 35, p. 1, a. un., q. 1. Etymologically, it is natural to link wisdom with the spiritual senses, for if one regards *sapientia* as deriving from *sapore* – 'to taste' – wisdom could be said to be a 'tasted knowledge'. On Bonaventure's use of the etymology of *sapientia*, see III *Sent.* d. 27, a. 2, q. 5. Indeed, in several places Bonaventure speaks of wisdom when he talks about spiritual taste (*Sermo 9 in Epiph.*; *Sermo 14 in Epiph.*). It is not only spiritual taste that is so described; Bonaventure speaks of such knowledge as an apprehension *per modum tactus* (III *Sent.* d. 27, a. 2, q. 1, ad 6).

spiritual sight passing over to the experience of ecstatic knowledge that is spiritual touch.

Such a reading, however, does not take account of the fact that Bonaventure does not always, in speaking of the spiritual senses, privilege the affective over the intellective. If he did, there would in fact be little point in talking about the spiritual sense of sight, or even that of hearing; the real point of the doctrine would be to exalt the spiritual senses of taste and especially touch. Taste and touch would be to sight, as it were, much as wisdom is to understanding.[42] It is certainly true that in terms of intimacy the senses of taste and touch have primacy.[43] But not all those passages that speak most explicitly of the five spiritual senses display the same kind of privileging.[44]

Two (non-exclusive) ways of more strongly justifying a fivefold division suggest themselves. First, Bonaventure speaks of a *proportio*[45] and a *conformitas*[46] between the spiritual senses and the corporeal senses. Given his broader point that 'the wisdom of God is hidden in all knowledge',[47] we are justified in seeing a great deal of continuity between different forms of cognition. The remarkable point of Bonaventure's doctrine is thus that we can and must speak of five spiritual senses because there is something about their grasp of God that is very like the grasp of truth – and in a hidden way the grasp of God – in the corporeal senses. Specifically, there is an immediacy to the knowledge of God in the spiritual senses that is best understood in comparison to the immediacy of corporeal sensation.[48]

Second, one may argue that as the corporeal senses are differentiated not only by the sense organs but also by the kinds of things that they perceive (e.g. one does not 'hear' that which is visible or 'smell' that which is audible) – what Aristotle termed 'proper sensibles'[49] – so the spiritual senses may be understood as distinguished by what they apprehend. The point is not that spiritual sight is surpassed by spiritual touch, but that these senses are different kinds of perception – that they are engaged by different aspects of the object that is perceived. The delineation of five spiritual senses is justified by a distinction in the object known by these

---

[42] The gift of wisdom 'begins in cognition and ends in affection' (III *Sent.* d. 35, p. 1, a. un., q. 1).

[43] III *Sent.*, d. 13, dub. 1. See Longpré, 'La théologie mystique de S. Bonaventure', 53; Rahner, 'The Doctrine of the "Spiritual Senses" in the Middle Ages', pp. 116–17.

[44] In those texts in which Bonaventure mentions each of the spiritual senses, he typically gives the order of sight, hearing, smell, taste and touch. That 'touch' comes last accords well with its intimacy, but 'sight' and 'hearing' are not presented as propaedeutic to touch in the way understanding is sometimes presented as propaedeutic to wisdom.

[45] III *Sent.* d. 13, dub. 1.   [46] *De red.* 10.   [47] *De red.* 26.

[48] This is Tedoldi's argument; see *La dottrina dei cinque sensi spirituali*, pp. 250–60.

[49] *De an.* II. 6, 418a.

senses.[50] If one follows this view, as I do here, it thus becomes all-important to identify the object of these senses.

THE OBJECT OF THE SPIRITUAL SENSES: THE WORD

In some texts, Bonaventure does not specify the object of the spiritual senses.[51] In the texts from book III of the *Sentences* commentary, God is the object. But in the majority of texts, the object specified is Jesus Christ, or the Word. The most explicit text in this regard is *Itinerarium*, IV. 3, quoted earlier. There we read that the uncreated Word is associated with the spiritual senses of sight and hearing, the inspired Word with the spiritual sense of smell, and the incarnate Word with the spiritual senses of taste and touch. In the *Breviloquium*, Christ as Splendour is seen by spiritual sight, as Word is heard by spiritual hearing, as Wisdom is apprehended by spiritual taste, as inspired Word is smelled by spiritual smell and as incarnate Word is embraced by spiritual touch. *Sermo 9 in Epiphaniam* repeats this division. *Hexaëmeron*, III. 22 has something of the same division, but locates the whole in the context of talking about the inspired Word. And *Sermo 6 in Circumcisionem Domini, Soliloquium* I. 12–17, and *De quinque festivitatibus pueri Iesu*, IV. I speak in a general way about the spiritual senses apprehending Jesus.

Behind this language is Bonaventure's understanding of the Word – arguably the centre of his theology.[52] Within the Trinity itself, the Word is the 'expressive likeness' of the Father.[53] We may call this the 'uncreated Word', which is one of the proper names of the second person of the Trinity. This inner-trinitarian reality is also the principle for the communication of God outside himself. Because the second person is the self-expression of the Father, he is also the one in whom resides the exemplary truth of all created things. To know any created thing is to know, in some measure,

[50] The next section discusses Bonaventure's delineation of a fivefold distinction in the object known by the spiritual senses. One may wonder whether there is a kind of circularity here: there are five spiritual senses because there are five relevant aspects of the object known; but we say that there are five and only five distinct relevant aspects because there are five spiritual senses to be engaged. It is fair to say that Bonaventure does not demonstrate the existence of only five relevant aspects of the Word. My point is that nevertheless he understands the distinction of the spiritual senses with reference to the object known, not simply the existence of five corporeal senses.

[51] *De red.* 10; *Sermo 2 de S. Agnete.*

[52] See Z. Hayes, 'Christology and Metaphysics in the Thought of Bonaventure', *The Journal of Religion*, 58, suppl. (1978), 82.

[53] The second person of the Trinity is called the Son (signifying his hypostatic likeness to the Father), the Image (as expressed likeness) and the Word (as expressive likeness) (*Brev.* I. 3. 8; see *Comm. in Ioan.* I. 6, q. I).

its eternal exemplar – the uncreated Word in whom all things were made. But there are other kinds of expression of the Word in the world as well.[54] The Word became flesh; there is a distinctive expression of the divine in human form in Jesus Christ – the incarnate Word. Moreover, Christ on the cross is a distinctive expression of the divine, for the crucifixion is the ultimate outpouring of divine love for our sakes; we may therefore speak of the crucified Word.[55] Finally, the Word is present to us in the special infusion of grace that allows us both to know divine revelation and to conform ourselves to it; this is the inspired Word, present in scripture and especially the prophets, but also expressed in the conformity of a life to the revelation of the gospel.[56]

To contemplate the incarnate and crucified Word, to be infused with the inspired Word, to see the uncreated Word behind all created things – as the *Itinerarium* presents it, each one of these activities involves receiving the self-expression of God. Knowing God in this way is not the same as reasoning from an effect to the first cause. It is to apprehend an object as an expressive likeness of God. In order for this to occur, certain objective and subjective elements have to be in place. Objectively, God has to make himself present to us through his self-expression. In order for this to be received, subjectively, it must engage that capacity of the human soul that is able to receive it, namely, the spiritual powers of man, transformed by the infusion of the habits of sanctifying grace. The resulting act is the spiritual sensation: the act of the transformed powers of man apprehending the self-expressive presence of God in the Word.

The differentiations of the spiritual senses follow upon the differentiations in God's self-expression. The *Breviloquium* suggests as much. We can apprehend the glory of God's eternal self-expression, seeing the splendour of the light of the uncreated Word. We can rejoice that this Word is to be communicated to us, hearing its wondrous harmony. We can be moved by the lure of God's coming to us, smelling the fragrance of the inspired Word and becoming ourselves 'the good odour of Christ poured forth in every place' (2 Cor 2: 14–15). We can savour his real, concrete presence,

---

[54] The theme of the 'uncreated, inspired and incarnate Word' occurs several times in his major theological works: *Itin.* IV. 3; *Brev.* IV. 1; *Hex.* III and IX. Other texts speak simply of the uncreated and the incarnate Word (e.g. *Christus unus omnium magister*, 12–13; *De red.* 20; *Comm. in Ioan.* 1. 1).

[55] *De donis*, 1. 8.

[56] For Bonaventure, the Franciscan imitation of Christ is justified not by the literal sense of the gospel, but by its spiritual meaning; the guide for this imitation is not only the incarnate Word, but the inspired Word. See, e.g., Bonaventure, *Legenda Sancti Francisci*, 1. 3; 11. 8; IV. 5. On the 'inspired Word', see P. Maranesi, *Verbum inspiratum: Chiave ermeneutica dell'Hexaëmeron di San Bonaventura* (Rome: Istituto storico dei Cappuccini, 1996).

tasting the goodness and learning from the wisdom of the incarnate Word. And we can be united with the one who is the absolute delight of our soul, touching or embracing the incarnate Word – ultimately, as the *Itinerarium*, *Legenda maior* and *Hexaëmeron* have it, being impressed with the touch of the crucified Word.[57]

There is an interior aptitude for the spiritual on the part of man, but the spiritual senses come into play only when the spiritual, the divine, expresses itself in such a way that it is able to be received by the properly attuned human subject. This is why Bonaventure speaks of them only rarely. The reason why he does not advert to the spiritual senses at all in most texts in which he speaks of the highest possible knowledge of God is that he does not need to. When we consider the fact that the soul can be rapt to an earthly anticipation of the beatific knowledge of God, what is important is that the soul participates in the divine light in a superhuman way, and experiences a kinship with God. When we consider the ecstatic wisdom at the height of Christian knowledge, Bonaventure emphasizes especially that such knowledge is felt (*sentitur*) more than it is known (*cognoscitur*).[58] One comes to talk about the spiritual senses only when the question becomes how we grasp God in his ultimate self-expression – what it is about what is known that engages our ability to know.

THE SUBJECT OF THE SPIRITUAL SENSES: THE ONE
WHO HAS EXPERIENCED GOD

The relation of the spiritual senses to the expressivity of God in the Word has implications for identifying the subject of the spiritual senses. What can be said about the one who possesses these senses?

When it comes to sanctified knowledge the Seraphic Doctor holds up many models.[59] None of them, however, does he describe as possessing the

---

[57] Cf. the passing over with Christ on the cross in *Itin.* VII. 2 and the touch of the Crucified that impresses St Francis with the stigmata in *Legenda Sanctus Francisci*, XIII. *Hexaëmeron*, II, in speaking of the highest form of Christian wisdom (*sapientia nulliformis*) does not advert explicitly to the Crucified, but it describes the passing over to wisdom in much the same terms as *Itin.* VII.

[58] See *Comm. in Ioan.* I. 43; *De sc. Chr.* Epilogue.

[59] In the *Sentences* commentary he praises the acumen of Peter Lombard (I *Sent.* pro., q. 4) and Alexander of Hales (II *Sent.* pro.); Christ himself is the great model in the disputed questions *De sc. Chr.*; the *Itinerarium* highlights the example of Daniel and especially of Paul and Francis (*Itin.* pro. 3); Augustine is the master of science and wisdom in *Christus unus omnium magister*, 19; *De red.* holds up the examples of Augustine, Anselm, Gregory, Bernard, Dionysius, Richard of St Victor and especially Hugh of St Victor (*De red.* 5); and the *Hexaëmeron* goes so far as to talk about an order of 'seraphic men' (*Hex.* XXII. 23) – to say nothing of the examples Bonaventure provides of such qualities in his sermons.

spiritual senses.[60] This is in keeping with his tendency not to invoke the spiritual senses to speak generally of the height of spiritual knowledge. To speak of the spiritual senses is not the same as seeing Augustine as a great exemplar of wisdom, or Dionysius as prototypical of the one who possesses negative mystical knowledge.[61]

Tedoldi argues at length that Bonaventure's doctrine of the spiritual senses finds its practical exemplar in the picture of Francis in the *Legenda maior*.[62] There are several levels to this. First of all, there is the verification of a spiritual sensorium. Francis's road to God required a proper subjugation of his bodily senses, for the body is tempted by a *pronitas sensuum*. Yet the result is not the disappearance nor the irrelevance of the bodily senses; indeed, when the body is made perfectly obedient to the spirit, God provides service to the saint by the things of the world. The senses are to be not so much abandoned as transformed. Second, there is the ample testimony in the *Legenda maior* to the sensate experience of the *Poverello* as he was advancing on his spiritual journey. Tedoldi identifies the role of each of the five spiritual senses in Francis's itinerary, exactly mirroring the doctrine in the *Sentences* commentary concerning the relative play of the intellect and the *affectus* in each of the senses. Francis sees visions, and learns to move from them to the invisible reality they represent; he hears revelations from on high, and also receives the name of the Lord in a way close to that of taste; he follows the Lord with desire, drawn by the smell of the fragrance of the Beloved; he tastes the divine things; and he comes to the experience of union pre-eminently through the sense of touch. Third, the culmination of Francis's experience in the stigmata is emphatically a sensate experience – indeed, one that involves all five senses, most especially the sense of touch. The body has not been abandoned; it has rather been made the recipient of the impression of the divine, that is, the Crucified.

The last point is entirely in keeping with what we have already seen in a strict account of Bonaventure's doctrine of the spiritual senses. Francis dramatically exhibits Bonaventure's understanding of revelation occurring through the expressivity of the Word. The pinnacle of Francis's experience of God, in Bonaventure's view, is his reception of the stigmata. The Crucified is the final, best instance of the expressivity of God in the world, for there is no better expression of God's love. And Francis received the stigmata precisely by being impressed with the wounds of the Crucified.

---

[60] With the exception of Christ – but this only by inference (see III *Sent.* d. 13, dub. 1).
[61] See *De triplici via*, III. 11.　　[62] Tedoldi, *La dottrina dei cinque sensi spirituali*, pp. 287–324.

Ultimately, it is in Francis that Bonaventure sees the expressive relationship of God to the world.[63]

Bonaventure does not explicitly refer to the spiritual senses as such in the *Legenda maior*. However, his sense of Francis's relation to God's revelation does indicate the significance of the kind of knowledge and delight he does associate with these senses.

THE SPIRITUAL SENSES, MYSTICAL EXPERIENCE AND THEOLOGY

Since some of the debates concerning Bonaventure's doctrine of the spiritual senses are well known, it is worthwhile to comment on them very briefly here.

The charge that Bonaventure sometimes identifies the spiritual senses as acts (sensations) and sometimes as faculties (senses) was levelled by Jean-François Bonnefoy.[64] Later scholars denied that there is any real inconsistency here, maintaining that even when a text such as the *Itinerarium* seems to speak of the senses as faculties, they can still be understood as acts.[65] Bonnefoy did, however, highlight some difference between the major texts on the spiritual senses – the passages from the *Sentences* commentary, the *Breviloquium* and the *Itinerarium* – which was developed in the debate between Rahner and Balthasar. Rahner understands the spiritual senses as the acts of the soul as it moves from a unitive contemplation (contuition) to a unitive experience (ecstasy), thus combining the texts from the *Sentences* commentary with a reading of Bonaventure's more general spiritual doctrine. The Christocentrism of the *Itinerarium* and the *Breviloquium* does not fit in well here, as Rahner maintains that the object of the spiritual senses is properly God in his transcendence, and finds the attempt to delineate five distinct spiritual senses 'rather forced'.[66] Balthasar, by contrast, emphasizes the doctrine of the *Itinerarium* and *Breviloquium*, extending the meaning of the spiritual senses to encompass a whole range of acts between faith and ecstasy. For Balthasar, the spiritual senses have to do with the Christiformity of Christian experience; any attempt to locate it solely in the 'unitive way' of the spiritual life lessens its distinctive

---

[63] See E. R. Daniel, 'Symbol or Model? St. Bonaventure's Use of St. Francis', in F. de Asis Chavero Blanco, OFM (ed.), *Bonaventuriana: Miscellanea in onore di Jacques Guy Bougerol OFM*, 2 vols., Bibliotheca Pontificii Athenaei Antoniani, 27–8 (Rome: Edizioni Antonianum, 1988), vol. 1, pp. 56–7.

[64] Bonnefoy, *Le Saint-Esprit et ses dons*, pp. 210–15.

[65] See Longpré, 'Bonaventure', 1832–3; and Dobbins, *Franciscan Mysticism*, pp. 51–4. Dobbins especially excoriates those who would speak of an entire spiritual sensorium in the human person.

[66] Rahner, 'The Doctrine of the "Spiritual Senses" in the Middle Ages', pp. 113–17.

Christian meaning.[67] Tedoldi sides more with Balthasar than with Rahner, but attempts some reconciliation in distinguishing between the 'use' and the 'perfect use' of grace: the spiritual senses more strictly have to do with the latter, but by extension include the former.[68] Tedoldi also strongly emphasizes the text from *De reductione*, with its continuity between the corporeal senses and the spiritual senses.

What I have called my own 'strict' account adjudicates the Balthasar–Rahner debate and Tedoldi's attempted reconciliation not through a wider applicability of the notion of spiritual senses, but through attention to the objective pole of the doctrine. On this point, Balthasar gives a better account of Bonaventure's teaching. But there is no need to downplay the association of the spiritual senses with the highest degrees of the infusion of sanctifying grace. One should simply note that to speak of the knowledge or experience that comes with such grace is different from speaking of the spiritual senses; as I have said, the latter come into play only when one considers the way the soul knows God when it apprehends him in his self-expression.

One thing is clear: having a 'sense' for God is not, for Bonaventure, a matter of rarefied spiritual experience only. Spiritual sensation has theological consequences, as one can see when one looks at two well-known Bonaventurean themes: the theological argument *ex pietate* and the idea that theology is an affective knowledge.

Theological reasoning will frequently uncover several possible explanations of a truth of faith. How is one to judge between them? Some arguments are useful in a practical sense in fostering the devotion, love, virtue and so on of the theologian, and may be preferred for that reason. A different kind of adjudication, however, comes from the argument *ex pietate*.[69] An argument *ex pietate* springs from 'thinking of God most piously' – thinking of him in a way that accords with one's highest knowledge of him.

The same distinction must be made with respect to the fact that theology involves an 'affective cognition'.[70] When Bonaventure talks about theology as perfecting the intellect as it is extended to the affect,[71] he does not simply mean that there are affective consequences proper to theology.

[67] Balthasar, 'Bonaventure', pp. 319–26; see also Balthasar, *GL*, vol. I, p. 373.
[68] Tedoldi, *La dottrina dei cinque sensi spirituali*, p. 301; see also pp. 258–60.
[69] See esp. G. H. Tavard, *Transiency and Permanence: The Nature of Theology according to St. Bonaventure* (St Bonaventure, NY: Franciscan Institute, 1954), p. 203; cf. J. G. Bougerol, *Introduction to the Works of Bonaventure*, trans. J. de Vinck (Paterson, NJ: St Anthony Guild Press, 1964), p. 81.
[70] See Chapters 7 and 8 in this volume.   [71] I *Sent.* pro., q. 3.

Theology involves a kind of affective knowledge; indeed, this is theology at its most perfect. The chief characteristic of this kind of knowledge is that it is directed at an object to whom one stands in an affective relation.[72] By faith, I assent to the revelation in Jesus Christ. In theology, the real, affective relation I have towards Christ gives me a sense for him that helps me to determine, among a variety of ways to understand his revelation, which are most in accord with who he is. The result is thinking of God 'most piously'. Moreover, as my affective relation to Christ grows, so my sense for him, and therefore my sense for the principles that guide me in my knowledge of him, grows and deepens.

In the end, Bonaventure's doctrine of the spiritual senses is of a piece with his general approbation for the ancient idea of Christian gnosis, the idea that the understanding of the faith requires a real and ongoing transformation of the intellect, that what the theologian can know is dependent upon his transformation in grace. He modifies this according to his Franciscan inclinations and insights, especially with respect to the sense for God that comes from receiving his self-expression, but the result is the same: only insofar as the theologian knows God through the spiritual senses does he recognize the deeper truth of revelation.

---

[72] See G. LaNave, *Through Holiness to Wisdom: The Nature of Theology according to St. Bonaventure* (Rome: Istituto storico dei Cappuccini, 2005), pp. 60–5.

CHAPTER 10

Thomas Aquinas

Richard Cross

THEORETICAL PRESUPPOSITIONS AND *DESIDERATA*

What is in some sense philosophically surprising about the spiritual senses is not that they are absent in much high scholastic theology (though this certainly is the case); it is that anyone should have posited them in the first place. God, after all, is an immaterial being, and we might be forgiven for supposing that the senses have to do merely with corporeal or material things. We might think that there is some further faculty – the mind or the intellect – that has to do with immaterial things, be they universals or particulars (such as God). Indeed, the distinction between intellect and sense is commonplace in both Platonic and Aristotelian philosophy: the intellect has to do with the intelligible (immaterial) realm, and the senses to do with the material. Admittedly, the way this distinction works out in the two traditions depends on radically different metaphysics. For Plato, the intelligible is fundamentally distinguished from the sensible: the realm of the intelligible is extrinsic to the realm of the sensible since immaterial universals are extrinsic to sensible particulars.[1] For Aristotle, intelligible universals are immanent in the sensible particulars, and cognition is fundamentally a case of *abstracting* universals from the particulars.[2] Given these distinctions between intellect and sense, it is perhaps no surprise that some philosophically rigorous thinkers saw no need to posit spiritual senses. The intellect, on either view, is required to cognize any immaterial object, and no further mental faculty is necessary.

---

[1] The distinction between sense and intellect and their objects is ubiquitous in Plato. The most well-known account is *Resp.* VI, 509D–513E. For the extrinsicity claim, see e.g. Plato, *Parm.* 133C, cf. 132A, 133B, 134B; Aristotle, *Met.* A. 9, 991a13.

[2] See Aristotle, *De an.* II. 5, 417b 20–28; III. 4, 429a 29 – b 4. Aristotle's thought is that intelligibility requires universality, and universality – be it something merely conceptual or not – is not straightforwardly the result of our sense experience of particulars. Some merely conceptual operation has to be performed on the particulars for the intelligible universality to be made evident.

In one of the most important moves in the history of cognitive theory in the West, Plato made the fundamental objects of cognition simple, non-compositional, Forms. Since the Forms are simple, knowledge of them is non-propositional, more akin to acquaintance or intuition than to description.[3] God is simple in this sense, and thus, in the kind of Christianized Platonism that forms the relevant background to scholastic notions of our knowledge of God, is something that is ideally cognized non-propositionally. Now, non-compositional forms are generally understood to be *universals*, whereas God is a *particular*. So it might be thought for this reason that God is not an appropriate object for properly intellectual encounter. In fact, although the scholastics were not directly acquainted with Plato's views, it is notable that Plato may have thought of universals as objects with numerical identity, and thus as (in this sense) *indivisible*, and hence particular.[4] Plato himself assumes that our cognition of his universals is something we in principle gain by direct intellectual experience, and he sometimes talks of this experience as a kind of 'seeing'.[5] But this is a metaphor for an entirely intellectual operation: the difference from his successor, Aristotle, is merely that Plato does not believe that this kind of cognition needs to be, or even can be, gained by straightforward *abstraction* from material particulars. Whatever the philosophical merits of Plato's position here, it was not open to the scholastics, since they did not know the relevant texts; and in any case, there is no reason to believe that they would have found the general psychological claim convincing, since they rejected the metaphysics underlying Plato's cognitive claims.[6] But my point is that the claim that there are intelligible particulars is not new, or particularly unexpected – provided that the particulars are of the right kind (i.e. immaterial objects). Against this background, the motivation for positing spiritual senses is reduced or even eliminated.

In terms of the role of affect and emotion, Aquinas holds that our cognitive experiences lead to appetitive acts, and that both cognitive and appetitive acts lead further to what we might call affective or emotional responses. Such responses are experiential, with phenomenal content, and so relevant here. According to Aquinas, passions are things that happen to us: they are automatic responses, inherent in the sense appetite, to cognitive and appetitive acts of the material or bodily sense powers.[7] Passions are contrasted with *will*. The will, an immaterial faculty of an immaterial

---

[3] See e.g. Plato, *Resp.* VII, 517–518B.   [4] Plato, *Parm.* 131B–C.
[5] See e.g. the texts cited at nn. 1 and 3 above.   [6] See e.g. Aquinas, *ST* I. 84. 1 c.
[7] *ST* I-II. 22. 3 c.

substance, the soul, elicits acts – of (deliberately) *wanting* or *desiring* – in response to goals presented by the intellect.[8] But there are also responses analogous to passions in the will. Aquinas sometimes uses the term *affectus* to talk about them.[9] Such responses – I shall label them 'emotions' – are 'act[s] of the will, having a similar effect [to that had by a passion], but without passivity (*passione*)'[10] – where the effect of passion is to aid in moving us to certain sorts of action.[11] We could think of emotions as 'quasi-passions': and I take it that Aquinas would not talk of a fully fledged act of the will in just this way. Perhaps what Aquinas means is that the emotion is as it were one step removed from the act of wanting or desiring: it is not itself our seeking some goal, though it may motivate in the seeking of a goal, and it could even be a goal of activity.

Let me give an example of two closely related acts, one an emotion, the other an active willing: *delectatio* and *fruitio*. Now, *delectatio* is equivocal, referring to both the passion of the sensitive appetite and the 'emotion' in the will. The passion in the sensitive appetite follows the cognitive realization of having achieved something good: from this realization, 'there is caused a motion of the soul in the sensitive appetite'[12] – a 'taking pleasure'[13] or 'resting'[14] in the thing achieved. The emotion, inherent in the will, is much the same as this, but it inheres in the will without the relevant physiological or bodily change: it is the state of resting or taking pleasure in the goal achieved.[15] Although Aquinas relates the act of *fruitio* closely to this, he does not identify it as *delectatio*. Rather, he follows Augustine: *fruitio* is willing something for its own sake, not for the sake of anything else.[16] Now, the reason why one might want to will in this way could be that the thing willed 'stills the appetite with a certain sweetness and *delectatio*';[17] but the willing or *fruitio* itself is clearly distinguished from the affective state or *delectatio* which somehow here explains (is the final cause of) the *fruitio*. We will the *delectatio* (or the thing which causes the *delectatio*), not the *fruitio*, on pain of infinite regress, since *fruitio* just *is* the relevant active willing.[18]

---

[8] See e.g. *ST* I. 82. 4; I-II. 9. 1. For the requirement that the act be *deliberate*, see *ST* I-II. 1. 1 c.
[9] See e.g. *ST* II-II. 180. 1 c.   [10] *ST* I-II. 22. 3 ad 3.   [11] See e.g. *ST* I-II. 24. 3 c.
[12] *ST* I-II. 31. 1 c.   [13] *ST* I-II. 11. 1 ad 3.   [14] *ST* I-II. 4. 1 c.   [15] *ST* I-II. 31. 4 c.
[16] *ST* I-II. 11. 1 *sed contra*, referring to Augustine, *De doctrina christiana*, I. 4. 4 and *De trin*. X. 10. 13; X. 11. 17.
[17] *ST* I-II. 11. 3 c.
[18] For a good account of *fruitio* in Aquinas, see S. Kitanov, *Beatific Enjoyment in Scholastic Philosophy and Theology: 1240–1335*, unpublished doctoral thesis, Faculty of Theology, University of Helsinki, 2006, pp. 72–8. Kitanov argues, wrongly in my view, that Aquinas does not distinguish *delectatio* from *fruitio*; but this is a mistake, based on a confusion between an affective response (*delectatio*) and an appetitive act (*fruitio*).

In what follows I hope to show that Aquinas can give a full and richly textured account of all these sorts of experience without appealing to spiritual senses – and I hope that the virtues of his account from the perspective of theological anthropology will become clear. In short, Aquinas's more fully developed account of human nature and emotion – a more fully developed theological anthropology – allows him to dispense with spiritual senses. And my claim is not that he rejected them simply because they were superfluous; rather, his alternative account of religious experience satisfies an anthropological *desideratum*: that human beings are genuinely bodily, and the faculties that they have – primarily directed to knowing and experiencing material things,[19] not God[20] – are nevertheless suitable for other sorts of knowledge and experience too. So a consequence of my argument in this chapter is that we should think of Aquinas's tendency in anthropology as being strongly *holistic* or *integrative*: the same emotions inform our responses to the divine as inform our responses to the created realm, and the same cognitive powers are responsible for both sorts of cognition. One might add too that the same appetitive powers function in the same way in the two cases. Given this holistic approach, taking very seriously the capacities of our embodied nature as sufficient for all of our experience – taking very seriously, in other words, the psycho-physical unity of human existence – there is simply no reason to posit spiritual senses: indeed, given that holism is *ceteris paribus* a *desideratum* of theological anthropology, Aquinas's position constitutes a powerful argument against the existence of such senses.

INDIRECT DIVINE ENCOUNTER

In this section, I consider experience of God distinct from our direct encounter of him in the beatific vision, whether in our current embodied state or in heaven. I take it that the distinctive contents of such experiences will be fundamentally affective, and so focus on those responses here. Now, any talk of encounter with God seems to require some account of God's unity with the person encountering him. Aquinas is explicit about this: even indirect divine encounter requires some kind of union with God.[21] But Aquinas is clear, and persistently so, that talk of God's union with anything created is to be understood wholly in *causal* terms. Aquinas holds that God is generally present to the creation in the sense that everything is subject to his causal control (presence by 'power'); he holds too that God is

---

[19] *ST* I. 85. 8 c.   [20] *ST* I. 88. 3 c.   [21] *ST* I-II. 26. 2; see too I. 43. 5 ad 3.

present in the sense that he has cognitive access to creation (his being in the creation by 'presence'), and he holds too that God is present to everything by being the first cause of its existence (presence by 'essence').[22] God is present as something known and loved by his giving grace to people.[23] This kind of union makes people *like* God (similar to God) in certain crucial ways.[24] Fundamentally, grace unites people in a particular way to God, and to the extent that one believes oneself to be so united, and desires this, certain positive emotional or affective states follow. Aquinas describes these in ways that bear some relation to the functions ascribed by other thinkers to the spiritual senses. Indeed, grace has built into it a certain kind of cognitive component:

The soul is conformed to God by grace. Therefore, for a divine person to be 'sent' to someone through grace, it is necessary that there is some assimilation of that [person], through some gift of grace, to the divine person who is sent ... Augustine notably says that the Son is sent 'when he is known and perceived by someone': for 'perception' means a certain experimental knowledge.[25]

Still, it is important to stress that the relevant states follow directly merely from our beliefs and desires, since Aquinas does not believe it possible to *know* that one has grace, or has the requisite union with God. Still, he believes that the presence of such beliefs and desires provides the believer with good evidence that God is indeed present to her through grace,[26] and presumably he would maintain that for the relevant affective responses to be what they seem to be, they must be the result of such union.

Aquinas posits two ways in which, *in via*, we can come to have true beliefs about God's existence. The first is simply by natural reason: we can know him through his general causal relation to creatures,[27] and we can know too in this way that God is the goal of our existence.[28] This kind of knowledge is something for which we have a natural desire.[29] Aquinas seems to suggest that even this kind of knowledge generates some kind of affective response,[30] though I do not know of any passage where he explores this in any detail. But of more interest to him, in any case, are the affective consequences of our supernatural cognition of God, resulting from the theological virtue of faith.[31] This kind of graced cognition is what

---

[22] *ST* I. 8. 3 c.   [23] *ST* I. 8. 3 ad 4.   [24] *ST* I-II. 112. 3 c.   [25] *ST* I. 43. 5 ad 2.
[26] *ST* I-II. 112. 5 c.   [27] *ST* I. 12. 12 c; see too I. 2. 3 c.   [28] *ST* I-II. 2. 1–8 c.
[29] *ST* I-II. 94. 2 c; I. 12. 1 c.
[30] *ST* II-II. 180. 7 c. As we shall see, Aquinas holds that practising virtue leads to a good affective response, and he doubtless would not deny that Aristotle and the philosophers legitimately had such an affective response in their contemplation of the first principle of material being.
[31] *ST* I. 12. 13 c.

seems to him to generate the kinds of affective reaction that are relevant to a discussion of the psychological states that others would perhaps ascribe to spiritual senses.

Prior to these affective responses, we need certain cognitive and appetitive acts. The relevant acts are important, because they are specifically what generate the affective responses. The first is the cognitive act of *beatitudo*: the act that makes God, as the goal of our activity, present to the will,[32] whether directly or (as in the indirect cases in which I am interested in this section) through the supernatural virtue of hope.[33] God's being present to our will leads to certain appetitive acts. The ultimate appetitive response to *beatitudo* is *fruitio*, an act of the will somehow actively directed to the goal of our activity (I discussed this above). But on the way to *fruitio* we have acts of love (*amor*), willing the good for the object of our desire,[34] *dilectio* (those acts that result from our deliberation about our rational responses to what is presented by the intellect)[35] and *caritas* (loving something on the grounds of its intrinsic value).[36] *Caritas* is caused by hope in the case that we currently lack our goal;[37] and the relevant hope can be a passion or emotion in the case of a natural goal,[38] or a theological virtue (a habit, not an act), in the case of a supernatural goal.[39]

Aquinas holds that certain cognitive acts automatically involve appetitive acts: in particular, that our cognition of some goal automatically generates an appetitive act towards that goal[40] – and especially when that goal is the ultimate goal: namely, the vision of the divine essence, which generates *fruitio*.[41] So built into Aquinas's account of religious experience is a strongly appetitive component, such that there is no way that our cognitive experiences of God – howsoever obtained – do not *ipso facto* involve an appetitive component. These cognitive and appetitive acts automatically generate certain *affective* responses: in particular *delectatio*, our resting in the good we seek, enjoying the satisfaction of our desire.[42] We can experience *delectatio* if we achieve (even through hope) what we desire through our intellective appetite, even if this rational desire is not properly directed.[43] *Gaudium* is a species of *delectatio*: it consists in the pleasure that we take specifically in

---

[32] *ST* I-II. 3. 1 c, 8 c.   [33] *ST* II-II. 17. 1 c, 2 c; I-II. 11. 1 c.   [34] *ST* I-II. 26. 4 c.

[35] *ST* I-II. 26. 3 c.   [36] *ST* I-II. 26. 3 c.   [37] *ST* I-II. 40. 7 c.   [38] *ST* I-II. 40. 7 c.

[39] *ST* II-II. 18. 8 c. *Caritas* can of course refer too not to an act but to a theological virtue, and in this case it gives us the relevant spiritual union by which we are transformed to suitability to our ultimate supernatural goal. See *ST* I-II. 62. 3 c; II-II. 24. 8 c; II-II. 25. 1 c. *Caritas* results, furthermore, in the gift of wisdom, *uniting* us with God: on this, see Andrew Pinsent, 'The Gifts and Fruits of the Holy Spirit', in Brian Davies and Eleonore Stump (eds.), *The Oxford Handbook of Aquinas* (Oxford University Press, forthcoming).

[40] *ST* I. 82. 4 c.   [41] *ST* I. 82. 2 c.   [42] *ST* I-II. 4. 1 c; I-II. 11. 1 ad 3; II-II. 180. 1 c, 7 c.

[43] *ST* I-II. 32. 2 c.

the satisfaction of our rational appetite.[44] So, as a species of *delectatio*, it is, like *delectatio*, a kind of resting in the object of love.[45] In the case of someone with grace, *gaudium* is an effect of the theological habit of charity.[46] The emotions themselves generate further responses in us. Aquinas says the most about the act of *amor*. If we are in the presence of something that satisfies our desire, then *amor* leads to *delectatio*, characterized as a kind of union with the object of our desire;[47] it leads also to ecstasy, our having *delectatio* in something external to ourselves;[48] and it leads to zeal, our being very strongly attached to the object of our love.[49] Aquinas's overall position is nicely focused in his discussion of contemplation. Aquinas holds that the act of contemplation *in via* is an intellectual act that aims at the truth: in so doing, it generates the *affectus* of *delectatio*.[50] The relevant truth is *divine* truth;[51] we are led to this truth by contemplating God's effects[52] (presumably, though Aquinas does not say so here, this contemplation will be both richer and more emotionally rewarding in the case of someone with the virtue of faith). Indeed, both contemplation itself, and the fact that the act is directed to divine truth, generate *delectatio*.[53]

A CHRISTOLOGICAL LACUNA?

Thus far the account has not made use of specifically Christian theological resources, and it might be thought that Aquinas's account proceeds independently of Christology. Now, it is certainly the case that Aquinas's general theoretical account of experience of the divine does not put Christ at its heart. But this does not mean that he does not believe there to be space for specifically Christian encounters with the living Jesus. Aquinas, perhaps unsurprisingly, deals with this most fully in the case of the Eucharist, and what he highlights is our affective response:

We can consider the effect of this sacrament from the manner in which this sacrament is given, because it is given in the manner of food and drink. And for this reason, every effect which food and drink bring about in bodily life – namely sustaining, increasing, restoring and giving pleasure (*delectat*) – this sacrament does in relation to spiritual life.[54]

The idea is that the sacrament can bring about this emotional response – *delectatio* – only on condition that the recipient believes it to be Christ's

---

[44] *ST* I-II. 31. 3 c, 4 c, 5 c, 7 c; II-II. 70. 3 c; I-II. 25. 4 c. The distinction is a commonplace, deriving from Avicenna; see *De anima*, IV. 5, ed. S. van Riet, *Liber de anima seu Sextus de naturalibus*, IV–V, in *Avicenna Latinus* (Louvain: Éeditions Orientalistes, and Leiden: Brill, 1968).
[45] *ST* II-II. 28. 3 c; see I-II. 5. 1 c, 2 c.   [46] *ST* II-II. 28. 3 c.   [47] *ST* I-II. 28. 2 c; I-II. 25. 2 c.
[48] *ST* I-II. 28. 3 c.   [49] *ST* I-II. 28. 4 c.   [50] *ST* II-II. 180. 1 c.   [51] *ST* II-II. 180. 3 c, 4 c.
[52] *ST* II-II. 180. 4 c; I. 12. 12 c.   [53] *ST* II-II. 180. 7 c.   [54] *ST* III. 79. 1 c.

body and blood, and thus that it offers some kind of encounter with Jesus himself.[55]

But Aquinas also considers the relationship between Christ and the believer from a rather different angle. When talking about Christ's status as head of the church, Aquinas suggests not that the Christian life fundamentally consists in some kind of personal encounter of Jesus, but rather that it is the means whereby the believer is enabled to take on Christ's way of 'looking' at things: Christ gives the believer a 'spiritual sense' – a Christ-like capacity to make proper judgements about the values of things. Aquinas argues that the human head is responsible for all the motion and sensation of the whole body; analogously, Christ is responsible for the spiritual motion and sensation of the members of the church: Christ 'pours spiritual sense and motion' into the believer.[56] We should not understand this to imply any doctrine of the spiritual senses. Rather, it refers to the believer's capacity to judge matters with the mind of Christ:

It is necessary that someone is incorporated into Christ as a member of his through baptism. But just as the members [of a body] derive sense and motion from the natural head, so from the spiritual head, which is Christ, his members derive spiritual sense, which consists in the *cognition* of the truth, and spiritual motion which is through the prompting of grace.[57]

So a 'spiritual sense' here is not understood as any kind of special faculty. Aquinas uses the term to refer to an *act* of cognition: an act that has the truth as its object, and the catalyst for the language is not Aquinas's religious epistemology, but rather Paul's metaphor of the body. The claim is startling, nevertheless: that being a member of Christ's body enables the believer to look at things with the eyes of Christ, as it were. I return in the final section to consider further material on Christ's grace of headship, since, as we shall see, it forms one of the classic loci for the discussion of the spiritual senses.

DIRECT DIVINE ENCOUNTER

Aquinas's discussion of the beatific vision provides the general principles of his account of our direct cognitive access to God, and he sees any experience of God that we have in this life as continuous with the general account he gives of the beatific vision – though, as we shall see, he clearly believes that there are different degrees of such beatific vision. The beatific

---

[55] *ST* III. 75. 1 c.
[56] *ST* III. 8. 2 c; I discuss the remaining relevant texts in the last section of this chapter.
[57] *ST* III. 69. 5 c, my italics.

vision is an act of our intellectually cognitive power (an 'operation of the intellect'):[58] the senses, as directed merely to material particulars, cannot be involved in it, since God is not such a particular.[59] Now, it is important to realize that the mind is naturally inclined merely to know universals abstracted from material particulars. In order to know the very special kind of immaterial object that God is, there is required some means to make this kind of cognitive content accessible to mind. Aquinas talks of this as a 'created light', and calls it the 'light of glory'.[60] The analogy is with our abstractive knowledge of universals. In order to abstract, the mind requires some way of discovering the intelligible content – the universal – in the particular, and so God has structured the mind in such a way that, although it has no cognitively accessible contents of universals prior to abstracting, its abstractive power nevertheless somehow contains a 'light' that includes such contents.[61] As an account of abstraction, this is far from satisfactory, but for my purposes here the important point is that intelligible content needs to be made clear to the mind: it is not immediately accessible. The same is the case with our knowledge of the immaterial particular that is God. Our cognitive powers are not, of themselves, able to see God's essence. The reason is that cognition of an essence requires in some sense the union of the knower and the known, and God's essence is not something that can be in us naturally.[62] So to have such cognition, we require some intrinsic – though accidental – modification to our minds. As intrinsic, such a feature is of course created: it is something inherent in us.[63]

But, given the Aristotelian requirement that our intellectual acts have to do with universals, why should Aquinas not posit that there are required certain spiritual senses in order for us to cognize God – an immaterial *particular* – directly? The answer has to do with just what it is that direct encounter with God involves, and how this encounter relates to our standard cognitive processes. Basically, what we encounter of God is his essence:

---

[58] *ST* I. 12. 1 c; I. 12. 3 ad 3.   [59] *ST* I. 12. 3 c; I. 12. 11 c.
[60] *ST* I. 12. 5 c.   [61] *ST* I. 84. 5 c.   [62] *ST* I. 12. 4 c.
[63] *ST* I. 12. 5 c. Aquinas's position here is somewhat vulnerable, as Scotus later spotted, because his official line is that the proper object of the human intellect is the essence of material substance (see *ST* I. 84. 7 c). Now, one reason for positing some kind of cognitive mechanism over and above the intellect – be it a spiritual sense or some wholly non-sensory faculty – would be that there is some kind of constraint on the kinds of thing that the intellect can cognize: in particular, a constraint that restricts the intellect to cognizing material things. And this is precisely what Aquinas holds. As Scotus points out, powers are individuated by their objects: if the object of the intellect is material substance, then a power that includes in its object immaterial substance is simply a different power. For this objection, see my 'Duns Scotus on Religious Experience', in R. Cross (ed.), *John Duns Scotus, Theologian: Proceedings of 'The Quadruple Congress' on Duns Scotus*, part II, *Archa verbi, Subsidia*, vol. V (Münster: Aschendorff, forthcoming).

and the faculty of ours that engages with the *essences* of things is our intellect. The fact that God's essence is not repeatable in the way creaturely essences are makes no difference to the general cognitive model. Intellectual cognition conveys something of the *kind* of thing that is the object of cognition: and beatific cognition, even in Aquinas's apophatic account of these matters, gives this sort of knowledge.[64]

Aquinas's account of any mystical encounter with God *in via* assumes exactly this model. In the case of someone who has, *in via*, a direct encounter with God, that encounter is (as all direct encounters with God are) cognitive, and is thus an operation of the intellect:[65] after all, the intellectual powers are properly human in the way the sensitive powers are not.[66] Any such encounter entails an affective response – namely, *delectatio*.[67] In line with Aquinas's general view about the beatific vision, the senses – which are directed to material objects – can play no role.[68] Indeed, our currently embodied state makes it impossible for us to encounter God directly, since it requires that we know things through sense images.[69] So any direct encounter with God requires that we do not exist in our usual embodied way: at the very least, we are somehow released from our embodied reliance on the senses for our knowledge.[70] Furthermore, in line with standard scholastic teaching, Aquinas holds that the enjoyment of the beatific vision by someone embodied (e.g. after the resurrection of the body) standardly has certain bodily effects, rendering the body immortal, impassible, agile and somehow translucent. The case of someone experiencing direct encounter with God *in via* is not like this: Paul, for example, when he encountered God, 'was not simply beatified, such that there was brought about the redounding [of glory] onto his body; rather, he was beatified only in a certain respect. For this reason, his rapture was something like prophecy.'[71] Whatever we make of Paul's experience, it is clearly different in kind from cases of beatific vision after the general resurrection.

Aquinas talks of 'vision' in this context. This traditional language should not be taken to entail any spiritual sense. But still, why use the metaphor of vision in this cognitive context at all – rather than, say, that of hearing, or any of the other senses? Aquinas's account of the exterior senses provides an immediate answer. Vision is, in Aquinas's view, the only sense that

---

[64] *ST* I. 12. 1 c. [65] *ST* II-II. 175. 2 c. [66] *ST* I. 78. 1 c.
[67] *ST* II-II. 175. 2 c. [68] *ST* II-II. 175. 4 c. [69] *ST* I. 12. 3 c; II-II. 175. 5 c.
[70] *ST* II-II. 175. 5 c. Note that in this late account Aquinas has abandoned his earlier claim that it may be that direct encounter with God requires complete separation from the body: see e.g. *Super II Cor.* 12. 2, n. 457, ed. R. Cai, *Super epistolas S. Pauli lectura*, 2 vols. (Turin and Rome: Marietti, 1953), vol. 1, 543b.
[71] *ST* II-II. 175. 3 ad 2.

does not require any natural or physical change either in the organ or in the thing sensed (hearing involves vibrations in the ear; smell requires the object of the sense to be heated in order to release its odour; touch involves the heating or cooling of the skin by the object; and taste involves the moistening of the tongue by the thing tasted).[72] So vision is simply the best available metaphor, because its immateriality makes it closest to immaterial intellectual cognition. That said, it might still be thought that the metaphor of different physical senses is required on the grounds that they convey different kinds of cognitive content – what we learn through one sense is perhaps not replicable through what we gather through another. So perhaps we might think that our various experiences of God should be as cognitively rich as our sense experiences, and somehow convey different content. But I doubt this: there are not irreducibly different kinds of semantic content conveyed in our experiences of God, since there are not different kinds of object (as there are in the cases of our external senses): even though God can be represented to us in different ways,[73] he is, according to Aquinas, wholly simple and undifferentiated.[74] Equally, the distinction between different external senses is necessitated by the low level of semantic differentiation of which each sense is capable, not by the rich variety of input. The human intellect is one power, and the external senses five, precisely because of its more highly refined and wider-ranging capacity.

Clearly, Aquinas regards cases in which someone has a direct experience of God in this life as highly exceptional. Aquinas's focus is clearly more on the practical notion of living the Christian life in hope than on any kind of mysticism, something that he clearly regards as highly unusual. But Aquinas's theology nevertheless includes an account of direct encounter with the divine, and the account is entirely in line with his general anthropology and cognitive theory. Thus, it requires no special spiritual senses, and can be accounted for, psychologically, in ways precisely analogous to both other kinds of spiritual experience and our general encounter with the material world. And this is in line with his overriding anthropological holism.[75]

---

[72] *ST* I. 78. 3 c. In saying that vision involves no natural change, Aquinas does not mean to imply that it involves no change at all: it consists of what he calls a 'spiritual' change, one in which the form of the thing sensed 'is received in the receiver according to spiritual existence', such that 'the intention of the sensible form is brought about in the organ of sense' without actually making the organ an instance of the received form: in seeing something blue, the eye is not *really* made blue (*ST* I. 78. 3 c).

[73] *ST* I. 13. 2 c.   [74] *ST* I. 3. 7 c.

[75] I have tried to show the extent to which Aquinas believes emotions and affective responses to be involved in divine encounter. As far as I know he never considers the physical senses to have any specific role in such cases.

'O TASTE AND SEE THAT THE LORD IS SWEET' (PSALM 34 [33]: 8)

Now, by way of problematizing what I have just argued, I should like to consider passages where Aquinas refers to spiritual senses. The first point to note is that these passages are few in number: just fifteen or so in all of Aquinas's massive oeuvre. Furthermore, as we shall see, they largely recur in very specific contexts: discussions of the church as the body of Christ (and more specifically, Christ's headship), and discussions of the sin of *stultitia*. In both cases the catalyst for the discussion are things quite extrinsic to Aquinas's theories of cognition and religious experience. With one clear exception, they largely conform to an explicit definition that Aquinas gives of 'spiritual sense', and we shall see too that, again with two possible exceptions, what he says is wholly consistent with what I have argued thus far.

The first group of texts deals with Christ's grace of headship, and his relation to the body of Christian believers.[76] Aquinas persistently analyses these bodily metaphors in terms of the relative functions of head and body. I have discussed one such text, in which he gives his definition of 'spiritual sense', above. As we saw, Aquinas's exegesis of Paul focuses on the way in which the believer comes to take on the mind of Christ. This reading is confirmed by consideration of Aquinas's discussion of the sin of *stultitia*. The foolish person allows his senses to plunge him into worldly pleasures, and as a result he loses a 'spiritual sense' that allows him to formulate true beliefs and judgements about spiritual things.[77] What does Aquinas mean by 'spiritual sense' here? On the face of it, it is not anything other than the intellect capable of making good judgements in religious matters. The language is odd, because Aquinas talks of the relevant sense as though it is just the external senses (something he cannot in any case mean, since he denies that the external senses have any role in the discrimination of spiritual things).[78] But the oddity is in fact explained, as it so often is in Aquinas, by the fact that he is working with a pre-existent definition of *stultitia*. In this case, he supposes that *stultitia* is the same as *insipientia* (lack of wisdom), and according to Isidore of Seville, whose definition Aquinas is glossing, *insipientia* is 'contrary to wisdom, because it lacks the *savour* of discretion and sense'.[79] So the sensory language comes from an

---

[76] *ST* III. 8. 2 c; III. 69. 5 c; see too *In Sent.* III. 13. 2. 3 obj. 2; IV. 5. I. 3. 2 c; *De ver.* 27. 3 obj. 5; 27. 4 c; *Super I Cor.* II. I; *Super I Cor.* 12, v. 17 (I briefly discuss this text below); *Super II Cor.* II. I (again, I discuss this passage briefly below); *Super epistolam ad Ephesios lectura*, I. 8. I return to the remaining passage, *In Sent.* III. 13. 3. 2. 3 *expos. textus*, in greater detail below.
[77] *ST* II-II. 46. I c; II-II. 46. 2 c.   [78] *ST* II-II. 46. 2 c.
[79] *ST* II-II. 46. I ad I, discussing Isidore of Seville, *Etymologiarum libri XX*, 10 (PL 82. 393C), my italics.

authority, and is glossed by Aquinas in a way that effectively removes any connotations of an internal spiritual sense. Aquinas, in short, is saving an authority, and his policy in cases like this is to adopt authoritative definitions and then give them his own distinctive spin in a way that often bears scant relation to the original definition. One relevant case, for example, is his adoption of Jerome's talk about the 'eyes of the mind' as the relevant power allowing us to enjoy the beatific vision.[80] Aquinas talks of the 'incorporeal eye' cognizing both material and immaterial entities, and tacitly assumes that Jerome's language is nothing more than a way of talking about our intellect. Thus the incorporeal eye performs all the functions that the intellect performs: it knows material things abstractively and God beatifically;[81] and Aquinas treats the contrast between the corporeal eye and incorporeal eye as equivalent to the contrast between the corporeal eye and the intellect.[82]

What we learn from the account of *stultitia* is that talk of spiritual senses is a way of talking about our actually using our intellect to judge correctly in spiritual matters, and the sense is, in effect, the correct *act* of intellectual judgement. This is borne out by other texts on Christ's headship too. For example, in Reginald of Piperno's *reportatio* of Aquinas's commentary on chapters 11 to 13 of 1 Corinthians, Aquinas is reported as commenting on 1 Corinthians 12: 17 ('If the whole body were an eye, where would the hearing be? If the whole were hearing, where would the smelling be?') as follows: 'Smell is a spiritual sense, and serves in spiritual people to distinguish good from evil.'[83] So the spiritual person is able better to distinguish the morally good from the morally bad: in the light of Aquinas's explicit account of spiritual senses (as intellectual acts of discrimination), the sensory language is not evidently anything other than metaphorical: it is the metaphor of the body that leads to the sensory language. Elsewhere, Aquinas identifies spiritual senses as acts of faith and hope.[84] In these cases, the context (again generally the question of Christ's headship) is more specifically Augustine's claim in Letter 187 that all senses can be found in the head, whereas only touch is located throughout the body:[85] a passage that Aquinas, in his *Sentences* commentary, uses as the basis of an objection to the effect that Christ is not the head of the church since he lacks certain spiritual senses.

---

[80] *In Sent.* IV. 49. 2. 2 *sed contra* 2, referring to Jerome's commentary on Isaiah 3 (*super* 6.1) (PL 24. 93A).

[81] *In Sent.* IV. 49. 2. 2 ad 4.

[82] Compare *In Sent.* IV. 49. 2. 2 ad 4 with *In Sent.* IV. 49. 2. 2 ad 7.

[83] *Super I Cor.* 12, v. 17 (for the text, see conveniently www.corpusthomisticum.org/c1r.html, accessed 23 April 2009).

[84] *De ver.* 29. 4, obj. 15.   [85] Augustine, *Ep.* 187. 13 (CSEL, 57. 117).

The specific context is relevant here, since it forms a crucial component in a discussion of Christ's headship in Peter Lombard.[86] Peter Lombard's account of Christ's headship makes Augustine's claim central, and it provides the context for the more important of Aquinas's two discussions of Origen on the issue of spiritual senses. Peter Lombard appeals to Augustine to argue that, since Christ is the head of his mystical body, the members of the body have only limited grace, whereas Christ has the fullness of grace: since all senses are in the head, Christ has (on the analogy of senses to grace) the fullness; since only touch is in the other members, believers have (on the same analogy) only limited grace.[87] Aquinas disagrees, and comments as follows:

'In the Saints there is only touch.' This seems to be false, because Origen, *On Leviticus*, distinguishes five spiritual senses, saying that spiritual sight occurs when we see God; hearing when we hear who speaks; smell, by which we smell the good odour of Christ; taste, when we taste his sweetness; touch, when we touch, with John, the Word of life. All of these things are in all the saints. So they do not have merely touch. I reply by saying that the spiritual senses can be distinguished [1] by likeness to the acts of corporeal senses, and thus they are in all the saints, as Origen says, and [2] by likeness to certain properties of the senses, according to which touch is necessary, and the others not, and in this way, because there are in the saints all things necessary to salvation, whereas in Christ there are all things which simply pertain to the perfection of grace, it follows that all the senses are said to be in Christ, whereas in others there is only the sense of touch.[88]

The second of Aquinas's two proposed readings follows Lombard's metaphor. But the first abandons the metaphor, and straightforwardly notes that both Christ and all saints have all five spiritual senses. (Aquinas's talk about the 'saints' here leads me to suspect that the discussion is focused on the beatific vision of the *comprehensor*, and not on divine encounter *in via*). On the metaphor, the point of the first interpretation would be that we should not infer from Christ's grace of headship that the members of his body lack any other possible kind of grace. But the claim that the members do not lack other possible kinds of grace is supported by the literal claim

---

[86] The notion of spiritual discernment or judgement crops up in a rather different context too. Aquinas is reported by Leodigardius Bissuntinus as commenting on 'He who has ears, let him hear' (Mt 13: 9), that Jesus is 'arousing [us] to spiritual sense': the 'ears' Jesus is talking about are 'interior' ears (*Lectura super Matthaeum*, 13: 3; see www.corpusthomisticum.org/cml13.html, accessed 23 April 2009). But there is no theory of spiritual senses here: the point (as I take it that it is in the gospel too) is simply that we should be able to understand Jesus' message.

[87] Peter Lombard, *Sent.* III. 13, n. 2, in Spicilegium Bonaventurianum, 4–5, 3rd edn (Grottaferrata: Collegium Sancti Bonaventurae ad Claras Aquas, 1971–81), vol. II, p. 84.

[88] *In Sent.* III. 13, *expos. textus*. For the second discussion, see *Catena in Luc.* 12. 2.

that both Christ and all the saints have all other kinds of grace – all spiritual senses. The first point to note is that Aquinas does not in fact think that it is true that both Christ and saints have all possible kinds of grace, since they are all *comprehensores* and thus lack both faith and hope.[89] This already suggests that exegetical pressure is leading Aquinas to claim things that he does not generally hold. But, more importantly, I think we should be very wary of interpreting this passage to mean that Aquinas, even here, adopts a doctrine of the spiritual senses. For in this passage he does not tell us how we should integrate Origen's claim into his general theories of cognition and religious epistemology (which are clearly and fully worked out). The passage, in fact, signally fails to be anything like a *theory* of the spiritual senses; even if Aquinas accepts them, they remain functionally redundant (given that he has a clear theory of religious experience that does not require such senses).

The issue of *tasting* God occurs elsewhere too, commenting on Psalm 34 [33]: 8. The context is an account of our religious experience *in via*:

When he [David] says 'taste and see, because sweet', we are exhorted to experience [God] . . . [In relation to tasting], he does two things. First, he encourages us to experience. And secondly he posits the effect of the experience: 'and see, *because*'. Therefore he says 'taste and see' etc. An experience of a thing arises from sense, but in one way of something present, and in another of something absent – because, of something absent, through sight, smell and hearing, and of something present through touch and taste; and of something present that is extrinsic through touch, and of something intrinsic through taste. But God is not far from us, or outside us, but in us . . . And therefore the experience of divine goodness is called 'taste' . . . Now, the effect of experience is posited to be twofold. The one is the certainty of the intellect, the other the security of the affect. With regard to the first, he says 'and see'. For in corporeal things, something is first seen and then tasted, but in spiritual things something is first tasted and then seen, because no one knows who does not first taste: and for this reason he first says 'taste', and then 'see'.[90]

I assume that 'the certainty of the intellect' refers to the certainty that Aquinas takes to obtain in the case of someone with faith,[91] and that 'the security of the affect' refers to the believer's affective response to her faith, as discussed above.[92] Taste is a metaphor for this affective response, and the key claim in the passage is that we can usefully employ certain similarities to our standard sense experience to illustrate our experiences of God. Overall,

---

[89] See *ST* III. 7. 3 c and III. 7. 4 c.
[90] *In psalmos* 33, n. 9, ed. S. Fretté, *Doctoris angelici divi Thomae Aquiatis opera omnia*, 34 vols. (Paris: Vivès, 1871–80), vol. XVIII, p. 419.
[91] *ST* II-II. 1. 4 c; II-II. 2. 1 c.   [92] See e.g. Aquinas, *ST* I-II. 112. 5 c.

it is hard to avoid the impression that Aquinas's exposition is again driven by exegetical purposes, and that it should not be taken as giving insight into his more theoretically driven accounts – much as I have argued above for other passages.

Space does not allow me to extend this analysis to include later scholastic thinkers. But it is certainly the case that even many of those who would disagree with Aquinas on a large number of points in both the philosophy of mind and the certainty of the Christian faith would agree with him that there is no need to posit spiritual senses.[93] Aquinas did not hold at the time the kind of paradigmatic place in medieval philosophy that later historiography has assigned to him. But the continuing assumption and development of Aristotelian principles in cognitive psychology and theories of will and the emotions, in mainline medieval philosophy, eliminated the need to posit spiritual senses in addition to our standard cognitive, appetitive and affective capacities.

---

[93] I consider Duns Scotus's teaching on the question of our experience of God in my 'Duns Scotus on Religious Experience' (see n. 63 above).

CHAPTER 11

Late medieval mystics

Bernard McGinn

The mid-thirteenth-century German Franciscan David of Augsburg wrote one of the most popular handbooks of spiritual guidance of the late Middle Ages, whose title, *The Composition of the Interior and Exterior Man according to the Triple State of Beginners, Proficient and Perfect*, demonstrates its traditional approach. David expressed concern about the emphasis on visions and ecstatic experiences typical of many late medieval mystics, in part because these authors seemed to blur the distinction between interior experience and external sensation. At one point he singles out erotic visions of kissing and embracing that could even involve 'being caressed by other less decent deeds and acts, so that just as the interior spirit is consoled by Christ or Mary, so too the exterior flesh is caressed in a physical way and carnally consoled by a sensation of delight fitted to it'.[1] David is a witness to aspects of late medieval mysticism that seem to challenge the traditional distinction between external, bodily sensation and a separate set of interior, spiritual senses seen as organs of affective intentionality directed to God and the heavenly world.[2]

The evolution of the category of spiritual sensation is long and varied, as the chapters of this volume demonstrate. To what extent did at least some late medieval mystics present teachings on perceiving God that tended to undermine, or negate, the distinction between inner and outer sensation, so that encountering the divine was presented as perceived in a corporeo-spiritual totality?[3] Any adequate answer to this question would need a book,

---

[1] David of Augsburg, *Fr. David ab Augusta: De exterioris et interioris hominis compositione secundum triplicem statum incipientium, proficientium et perfectorum* (Grottaferrata: Collegium Sancti Bonaventurae ad Claras Aquas, 1899), III. 66. 1–5.

[2] On this issue, see B. McGinn, 'The Language of Inner Experience in Christian Mysticism', *Spiritus*, 1 (2001), 156–71. For a more complete acount of some late medieval mystics on spiritual sensation, see G. Rudy, *Mystical Language of Sensation in the Later Middle Ages* (New York and London: Routledge, 2002).

[3] In dependence on the teaching of K. Barth (*Church Dogmatics*, III/2), H. U. von Balthasar presents a holistic biblical anthropology that undercuts any separation between sense and spirit and contends

not a single chapter, to investigate the evidence.[4] What follows is only a sounding in the capacious sea of late medieval mystical views on the role of sensation, inner and outer, in the path to God. To gain some sense of the teaching of some mystics in this domain, it is helpful to keep in mind a series of questions. First, what kind of language does the mystic use for describing how God is perceived? Second, does this language involve an explicit or implicit distinction between inner and outer sensation? If the distinction is explicit, does this mean that the spiritual senses are to be conceived of as a second set of senses, primarily as ways of describing interior cognition? Third, how does the mystic relate the various forms of sensation (inner and outer, or both together)? Is there, for example, a distinct form of knowing ascribed to each form of sensation? Is there a prioritizing of the senses? Finally (and this was increasingly important in the late Middle Ages), is there a discussion of how to discern the difference between true and false perceptions of God? To pursue each of these questions, even with regard to only a few mystics, would be a large task. My observations here will begin to sketch out something of this large terrain.[5] Despite many helpful studies, we are still at the beginning of in-depth consideration of this central theme in the history of mysticism.

TWO FORERUNNERS

We start with two Cistercians, Bernard of Clairvaux and William of Saint-Thierry, not only because they represent the beginnings of important shifts in late medieval mysticism, but also because they were among the masters of mystical teaching for those who followed.[6] Bernard is one of the mystics who provides explicit discussions of the spiritual senses, treatments that largely follow tradition, especially in giving priority to seeing. Bernard

that for the biblical view of humanity: 'What is at stake is always man as a spiritual-corporeal reality in the concrete process of living.' *GL*, vol. i, p. 384.

[4] For example, we lack adequate studies of even the Latin terminology for interior sensation and perception. Without this, it is difficult to know exactly how different authors made use of terms that are all too often considered as having the same meaning – *sensus interiores, sensus animae, sensus spirituales.*

[5] I will leave out of account those mystics, such as Meister Eckhart, who adopt a strong anti-experiential, or anti-sensate, approach to mystical consciousness. Eckhart, of course, was aware of the existence of visions and ecstatic states of perception, and recognized their possible usefulness, but he felt that they were often misleading, and always secondary to what was essential in the pursuit of union with God.

[6] I have summarized the teaching of these two great mystics in B. McGinn, *The Growth of Mysticism: Gregory the Great through the Twelfth Century* (New York: Crossroad, 1994), chaps. 5–6, which contain references to the teaching of each on the role of sensation in the mystical path, as well as to the secondary literature on the topic.

relates the five exterior senses to five modes of affective loving within the soul, noting that just as 'in the bodily senses seeing is more worthy than the others and hearing is preferred to the other three', so too 'in the senses of the soul' the love that is more worthy than others and guides all the rest is 'holy or devout love toward God'.[7] Nonetheless, Bernard's actual practice of using sense language, in his exegesis of the Song of Songs,[8] as well as in the rare accounts of his own experience, is more complicated. For one thing, although the abbot says that the soul has its senses, just as the body does,[9] his use of the language of sensation undercuts any simple division between bodily sensing, necessary at both the beginning of the path to God (the stage of *amor carnalis Christi*) and at its conclusion in the resurrection of the body, and the inner activation of a set of purely spiritual senses. Although he often emphasizes that the heavenly reward will be a clear *visio Dei*,[10] the bliss of heaven will also involve tasting and touching God (*SSCC* 50. 8). Contact with God in this life begins with hearing, both the outer word of preaching and hearing in the heart. In using sensory language to describe the progress of the soul to union with God, Bernard, in fact, makes use of a wide range of inner and outer senses, often without clear distinction. At times some kind of seeing is described as the goal;[11] at other times the emphasis is on perception through touch, in line with the abbot's delight in the tactile images of kissing and embracing taken from the Song of Songs. For example, in exegeting Song of Songs 1: 4, where the bride is spoken of as 'black but beautiful', Bernard uses Mary Magdalene as a model for those who initially reach out to touch Christ 'by desire not by hand, by wish not by eye, by faith not by senses'. If the soul perseveres in the life of faith, however, she will be able to touch Christ's 'deep and mystical breast'. At this point, Bernard tells his audience, 'You will touch with the hand of faith, the finger of desire, the embrace of devotion; you will touch with the eye of the mind.' Here synaesthetic spiritual touching with the mind's eye combines the highest and the lowest forms of sensation.[12] In his account of how the Word sometimes visited his soul in *Sermones super Cantica Canticorum*, 74, Bernard again speaks

---

[7] *De div.* 10. 2–4, ed. Jean Leclercq et al., *Sancti Bernardi opera* (Rome: Editiones Cistercienses, 1957–77), vol. VI. 1, pp. 122–4. Bernard has two other discussions of the *sensus animae* in *De div.* 116 and *Sententia*, 3. 73 (*Opera*, vol. VI. 1, pp. 393–4; vol. VI. 2, pp. 108–12). The latter text makes use of the term *sensus spirituales* (vol. VI. 2, p. 109, lines 1–4). On Bernard's teaching on the spiritual senses, see Rudy, *Mystical Language*, chap. 3.

[8] Bernard's *SSCC* are found in *Opera*, vols. I–II.

[9] For example, Bernard, *De div.* 10. 4; *SSCC* 24. 6.

[10] See e.g. *SSCC* 38. 3, 52. 5–6.   [11] For example, *SSCC* 23. 15–16, 41. 3, 45. 5–6.

[12] *SSCC* 28. 9–10 (*Opera*, vol. I, pp. 198–9).

primarily in the language of feeling, not of seeing or hearing. 'As often as he would enter into me, I didn't perceive the different times when he came. I perceived he was present; I remembered that he had been there . . .' Bernard insists that Christ does not enter by way of any of the exterior senses, nor 'by any kinds of motions sent down to my most inward parts'. No, it is only in the melting feeling of the heart set afire with love that the Word's presence is known.[13]

The Song of Songs contains a wide range of sense images, not only of seeing, hearing, and touching, but also of smelling (e.g., Song 1: 2 and 11–12, 2: 13, 3: 6, 4: 10, 6: 1, 7: 13) and tasting (Song 1: 2, 2: 3–5, 5: 1, 7: 9, 8: 2). A favourite Psalm text of Bernard, as of many mystics, emphasizes tasting God (Ps 34 [33]: 9: *Gustate et videte quoniam suavis est Dominus*). Hence, it is no surprise that the abbot often employs smelling and tasting images to describe the experience of God.[14] In short, Bernard's biblical rhetoric on perceiving God cannot be put into any simple, or simply hierarchical, pattern. It also tends to undercut, in practice if not as much in theory, any sharp distinction between inner and outer sensation.

William of Saint-Thierry's *The Nature and Dignity of Love* contains a discussion of the relation of the five interior and exterior senses that repeats what he found in Bernard,[15] but other aspects of his mysticism are more important for our theme. Like Bernard, William uses the language of perceiving God in such varied ways that any simple account would be misleading.[16] If the *Meditative Orations* can be said to privilege seeing, especially the face-to-face vision of God, William's late mystical treatises, such as the *Exposition on the Song of Songs*, follow the poem of love in highlighting taste and touch. A crucial element in his teaching, however, is how William analyses the relation between physical sensation in general (*sensus*) and the perception of God that culminates in what he terms the *intelligentia amoris* or *intellectus amoris*, and also *sensus amoris*.[17] For William

---

[13] *SSCC* 74. 5–6 (*Opera*, vol. II, pp. 242–3). For other texts on touching (embracing) as the supreme form of union, see, e.g., *SSCC* 83. 3 (*Opera*, vol. II, p. 299) and *Sermo in 'Qui habitat'*, 15. 2 (*Opera*, vol. IV, p. 476). Touching, as well as tasting, implies an immediate contact not found in the other senses.

[14] On smelling and tasting God, see, e.g., *SSCC* 9. 6, 19. 7 (*Opera*, vol. I, pp. 46, 112); *SSCC* 67. 6, 85. 8–9 (*Opera*, vol. II, pp. 192, 312–13); and *De diligendo Deo*, 9. 26 (*Opera*, vol. III, p. 141). For a survey of spiritual tasting, see P. Adnès, 'Gout spirituel', *DS*, vol. VI (1967), pp. 626–44.

[15] William, *De natura et dignitate amoris*, VII (PL 180. 391–3).

[16] On William's teaching on the spiritual senses, J. Walsh, 'Guillaume de Saint-Thierry et les sens spirituels', *RAM*, 35 (1959), 27–42; and D. Bell, *The Image and Likeness: The Augustinian Spirituality of William of Saint Thierry* (Kalamazoo, MI: Cistercian Publications, 1984), pp. 160–5.

[17] This dimension of William's thought was first highlighted by L. Malevez, 'La doctrine de l'image et de la connaissance mystique chez Guillaume de Saint-Thierry', *RSR*, 22 (1932), 178–205, 257–79.

there is a real analogy between the immediate, concrete and transformative nature of sense perception and the higher, supra-rational transformation that occurs when the soul comes to 'know' God through love.

Gregory the Great was the first to use the expression 'love itself is a form of knowing', thus emphasizing the importance of affective intentionality in contact with God.[18] The meaning of this formula was explored by many twelfth-century mystics, especially the Cistercians and Victorines. William was the most penetrating in his analysis of how sense-knowledge functions as the paradigm for the process by which the soul comes to know the Divine Lover in a mode of perception that produces an intellectual-affective connaturality of a cognitive, though not conceptual, nature. What is crucial to note is that for William, probably because of his sense of the understanding available only through faith (what he called the *ratio fidei*), the connection between sense-knowledge and knowing God by love is not a bottom-up, rational analysis that uses the lower to understand the higher, but rather a top-down analogy in which revelation teaches us that because both forms of knowing and perceiving come from God, faith allows us to see their inner connection.

In describing the process of sensation in his work on *The Nature of the Body and Soul* (*c.* 1140?) William highlights three aspects of sense perception that remained constant in his teaching: (1) there must be a similarity between knower and what is known; (2) in the act of perception knower and known become in some sense one; and (3) this process involves a transformation on the part of the knower.[19] William's mystical works, especially the *Mirror of Faith* and the *Exposition on the Song of Songs*, extend this analogy to mystical knowing. William describes three stages in the progressive transformation of love in the *Mirror of Faith*. 'This process takes place more powerfully and more worthily when the Holy Spirit . . . so draws the human will to himself that [1] the soul loving God, [2] and perceiving him in the act of loving, [3] is transformed suddenly and totally, not indeed into the nature of divinity, but still into a form of beatitude above what is human but below what is divine . . . '[20] This itinerary of love begins as an *affectus*, that is, an attraction or desire planted in us by God, presumably in both the external and the internal aspects of human intentionality. It progresses under the

---

What follows depends on my treatment of William in B. McGinn, *The Growth of Mysticism: Gregory the Great through the Twelfth Century* (New York: Crossroad, 1994), pp. 234, 243, 250–60.

[18] Gregory the Great, *Hom. Evang.* XXVII. 4 (PL 76. 1207A).

[19] *De natura corporis et animae*, I. 8 (PL 180. 705D–706A). There are similar discussions in *Meditativae orationes*, 3. 7–8 (PL 180. 213BC) and *Speculum fidei*, 97 (SC 301. 168).

[20] *Speculum fidei*, 101 (SC 301. 170). See also *Expositio in Canticum Canticorum*, 21 and 94 (SC 82. 96, 218–20).

action of the Holy Spirit to the stage where it can be called both a *sensus amoris* and an *intellectus amoris*. Though the two terms are never explicitly defined or differentiated, it seems that the *sensus amoris* is used to express the concrete and existential nature of this intimate contact with God, while the *intelligentia amoris* or *intellectus amoris* highlights its cognitive character. William insists that this mode of knowing and uniting with God is like sense-knowledge. In the *Exposition on the Song of Songs* he says: 'At times, when grace overflows to secure and manifest experience of God, in a new way something sensible is suddenly present to the sensation of enlightened love (*fit repente sensui illuminati amoris modo quodam novo sensibile*), something that no corporeal sense could hope for, no reason conceive, no intellect be fit for save the intellect of enlightened love.'[21] So, the *intellectus amoris*, while not a corporeal act of sensing, is more like it than it is like conceptual knowing. How far this penetrating analysis was known to late medieval mystics is difficult to determine, but William's quasi-sensate notion of the *intelligentia amoris* provides an important backdrop to much that was to come among the vernacular mystics of the late Middle Ages.

THREE LATE MEDIEVAL VERNACULAR MYSTICS

In the world of the 'New Mysticism' originating about 1200 the efforts of mystics to express their consciousness of God's action provide a rich source for presentations of the role of inner and outer sensation. Two important factors in this new stage in the history of mysticism were the move into the vernacular languages and the spread of highly somatic language about encountering God. The nascent vernaculars of the late Middle Ages offered new possibilities for experimentation in trying to convey incommunicable forms of consciousness, ones that went beyond those available in the technical Latin of academic discourse. The rapid growth of mystical literature in Dutch, German, French, Italian and English during the thirteenth and fourteenth centuries, as well as the flexibility of the new vernaculars, created linguistic possibilities that the mystics, many of them women, were happy to develop. Among these experiments in language was an outpouring of highly emotional, sensate (often sexual) descriptions of the delights of loving encounter with God, as well as of the inner torment of unfulfilled desire for the Divine Beloved. Descriptions of feelings, sensations and states of emotion are notoriously difficult to evaluate, not only for contemporaries,

---

[21] *Expositio*, 94 (SC 82. 218).

but especially for those separated by many centuries from the original context, so it is all too easy to read these texts in a naively 'experiential' way, as attempts to record 'what actually happened' (*wie es eigenticlich gewesen war*). Perhaps. But late medieval religious rhetoric was designed to fulfil many purposes, often of a didactic and theological nature, although even the doctrine presented in much late medieval vernacular mysticism was expressed in forms of language that were emotionally excessive, charged with immediate expressions of sense feelings that invited the reader to participate in a direct perception of God on the level of corporeal sensation, just what David of Augsburg and others found problematic and dangerous. A look at three authors from different vernacular traditions will help illustrate this claim.

The Dutch beguine Hadewijch of Antwerp, who appears to have lived in the mid-thirteenth century, is a good example of medieval treatment of the spiritual senses, especially because she has been seen as one of the foremost exponents of a view of contact with God that eschews a clear distinction between outer and inner perception, insisting that God becomes present to humans in a 'single sensorium', that is, as an embodied spirit in which there is a strong continuity between external acts of sensation (looking, hearing, smelling, tasting and touching) and interior perceptions directed to realities that, while less physical, have no less direct an effect on the human person.[22] The holistic character of Hadewijch's view of how God moves her, both to weal and to woe, is unmistakable. Knowing how to interpret it is more difficult. Without denying that Hadewijch and many other late medieval mystics reject a strong distinction between inner and outer forms of sensation, we must recognize that their views of sensation are complex, and often challenge our modern conceptions of ways to envisage the totality of human sensory experience.

Hadewijch's mystical corpus is unique in embracing accomplished poetry in two forms, a collection of visions, and didactic letters of a quasi-Pauline character addressed to a community of beguines.[23] Her visions, such as Vision 7, which is recorded as happening one Pentecost at Matins,

---

[22] The fullest argument is made by Rudy, *Mystical Language*, chap. 4; but see also J. Milhaven, *Hadewijch and her Sisters: Other Ways of Knowing and Loving* (Albany: SUNY Press, 1993), pp. 34–5, 44–5, 70, 101–10; and C. Bynum, *Holy Feast and Holy Fast: The Religious Significance of Food to Medieval Women* (Berkeley: University of California Press, 1987), pp. 153–61. For the wider background of the treatment of the body by women in the late Middle Ages, see Bynum, 'The Female Body and Religious Practice in the Late Middle Ages', in M. Feher et al. (eds.), *Fragments for a History of the Human Body*, vol. 1 (New York: Zone, 1989), pp. 160–219.

[23] For a summary of Hadewijch's mysticism, see B. McGinn, *The Flowering of Mysticism: Men and Women in the New Mysticism, 1200–1350* (New York: Crossroad, 1998), pp. 200–22.

are often directly somatic. In this showing she sees Christ first as a child and then as a mature man who gives her full fruition of his divine and human natures in an erotic embrace that is a powerful evocation of a sexual encounter with God. 'Then he himself came to me', she says, 'and took me completely in his arms and pressed me to him. And all my limbs felt his limbs in the full satisfaction that my heart and my humanity desired. Then I was externally completely satisfied to the utmost satiation.'[24] In such texts, Hadewijch seems to go out of her way to insist that the fruition she experienced involved both inward transformation to another state and external corporeal satisfaction – exactly what disturbed David of Augsburg.

When we look at what Hadewijch sets forth in her courtly 'Songs' (*Liederen*, formerly called *Strofische Gedichten*), we find both a confirmation and a qualification of the sensate language of Vision 7.[25] What is important for Hadewijch in these poems is not any *theory* of how Christ becomes present to outer or inner consciousness, but rather how to put into words the concomitance of fruitive satisfaction and unsatisfied hunger that marks all contact with God in this life. The message was not new; the mode of expression was.

Throughout her works Hadewijch mentions the senses (*sinne*) as a general category rarely. In the Songs she concentrates on how God's presence as the overwhelming power of love (*minne*) takes over the whole person in often paradoxical ways. For example, Song 25 opens with an invocation of how the lover must be prepared to receive both gladness and fear when surrendering to love's command. Stanza 3 then turns to the language of sweetness and sound:

What amazes me about sweet love is that her sweetness overcomes all, and [that] she so consumes me from within, and she so little realizes my heart's pain. She has brought me into such woe that I feel that I cannot believe it. The hidden ways along which love sends me, they totally rob me of myself. The high gift of the clamour of the deep silence deafens me.

---

[24] The most recent edition of the Visions is by F. Willaert, *Hadewijch: Visioenen* (Amsterdam: Uitgeverij Prometheus, 1996). Vision 7 can be found on pp. 78–83. This translation is from B. McGinn, *The Essential Writings of Christian Mysticism* (New York: Random House, 2006), pp. 103–4. For a recent study of the Visions, see V. Fraeters, 'Gender and Genre: The Design of Hadewijch's *Book of Visions*', in T. de Hemptinne and M. E. Góngora (eds.), *The Voice of Silence: Women's Literacy in a Men's Church* (Turnhout: Brepols, 2004), pp. 57–81.

[25] The new edition of Hadewijch's forty-five Songs is V. Fraeters and F. Willaert (eds.), *Hadewijch: Liederen*, with a reconstruction of the melodies by L. Grijp (Groningen: Historische Uitgeverij, 2009). There are two earlier English versions of these poems: M. Hart (trans.), *Hadewijch: The Complete Works* (New York: Paulist Press, 1980); and M. Baest (trans.), *Poetry of Hadewijch* (Leuven: Peeters, 1998). I have consulted the translations of Hart and Baest in making my own version.

The paradox of 'silent clamour' invoked here is a sensate image for describing the mysterious action of *minne* at work 'from within', but still affecting the whole person.

The sense of strangeness and emotional turmoil is heightened in the next paragraph, where the beguine combines the paradox of noiseless sound with the sensations of touch and taste.

> Her [love's] deep silence is inaudible, however loud the noise she makes, except by him who has experienced it and whom love has wholly drawn into herself, and has stirred so intimately with her deep touch that he feels he is totally in love. When she also fully contents him with the wonder of her taste the clamour ceases for a moment with that. Ah! Soon desire awakens, that wakes with a new storm the inner senses (*de inneghe sinne*).[26]

Another mention of the inner senses occurs in Song 42. 4, where the tactile experiences of feeling and smelling *minne* like 'oil poured out' (Song 1: 2) unite the inner and outer dimensions of mystical consciousness: 'It is as if your lofty name is like oil poured out, Love, sweet and soft, very pleasing. But above all you are a delight to the inner senses.'[27] In these texts, and in mentions of the inner senses in her Letters,[28] Hadewijch seems to be expressing a kind of depth perception of love's power, an experience that begins with physical sensation and concludes with a total appropriation of *minne* in the deepest cognitive and affective realms of the person.

Other evocations of the term 'senses' also suggest a connection between the outer and the inner. Song 29, for example, opens with the lover's complaint that because of 'the love of high faithfulness all his senses are in manifold pain' (*Doer hogher trouwen minne, / soe sijn al mine zinne / in menechfoude pine*). In the second stanza the lover asks 'high love' to maintain or preserve his senses, 'So then I am certain, with an inward understanding, that the lover of our love / is entirely perfect.'[29] Sensation here is not divided into inner and outer: it is through love's guardianship of what happens in 'all the senses' that one gains inner understanding. The senses also are mentioned in Song 7, where Hadewijch relates them to one of the main themes of her mysticism – *oerewoet*, the madness and ferocity

---

[26] Lieder, 25. 3–4 (ed. Fraeters, pp. 204–6).

[27] Lieder, 42. 4 (ed. Fraeters, p. 304): *Het es ghelijc uwe hoghe name / alse olie uteghegoten, minne, / suete ende saechte, verwale bequame. / Maer boven al sidi ghenoechte den inneghen sinne.* The *inneghen sinne* are also mentioned in Lieder, 36. 5 (ed. Fraeters, p. 272).

[28] The term *inneghe sinne* appears in Letter 22. 17–18; Letter 28. 156–7 speaks of *die sinnen miere zielen*. See J. Mierlo, SJ (ed.), *Hadewijch: Brieven. I. Tekst en Commentaar* (Amsterdam: Standaard Boekhandel, 1947), pp. 188 and 235.

[29] Lieder, 29. 2 (ed. Fraeters, p. 228): *Sal mi hogher minne / behouden minen sinne, / soe ben ic seker des, / met verstane van binnen, / dat die minnare onser minnen / wel volmaket es.*

of love that consumes everything by its overwhelming force. 'Where is new love now with her new goodness?' asks Hadewijch at the beginning of stanza 4. She explains: 'Because my distress brings me into much new pain, my senses melt away in the madness of love (*oerewoet*). The abyss into which she hurls me is deeper than the sea, for her new deep abyss renews my wound. I look for healing no more until I again experience her fully.'[30]

In describing how God acts on the human lover throughout the Songs, Hadewijch uses a variety of sense images. Some involve synaesthesia, as when she speaks about 'tasting the hidden word' that is experienced by those who receive silence in the midst of clamour.[31] Hadewijch tends to privilege the language of taste and touch above hearing and seeing. As Gordon Rudy has pointed out, taste and touch imply an immediacy of contact, a reciprocity of action between lover and beloved, and also, at least for touching, a sense of force and movement, even of turbulence.[32] In Hadewijch's Songs the language of tasting God comes first in number of occurrences, closely followed by evocations of touch.[33] At times the two are used together. Song 5. 3, for example, speaks of love's unheard-of way of acting. 'He cannot find rest whom love touches', she says, 'he tastes many nameless hours'.[34] Although taste is appealed to more often than touch,[35] most of the images used for the ways *minne* acts upon the beloved are tactile: wounds, blows, embraces and kisses.[36] The importance of touching

---

[30] Lieder, 7. 4 (ed. Fraeters, p. 102): *Ay, waer es nu nuwe minne / met haren nuwen goede? / Want mi doet mini ellende / te menich nuwe wee. / Mi smelten mine sinne / in minnen oerewoede. / Die afgront daer si me in sende / die es dieper dan die zee, / want hare nuwe diepe afgronde, / die vernuwet me de wonde. / Ic en sueke meer ghesonde/ eer icse mi nuwe al kinne.* For other appearances of *oerewoede*, see Lieder, 15. 2; 18. 13; 23. 11; 24. 3; 28. 3, 4 and 6; 32. 9; 36. 10; 38. 5; and 44. 3.

[31] Lieder, 4. 4 (ed. Fraeters, p. 86).

[32] Rudy, *Mystical Language*, p. 67. The note of immediacy and reciprocity is present whether the touch is described as a person reaching out to touch God or, as is more frequently the case, God touching the person. On this major theme in mysticism, see Pierre Adnès, 'Toucher, touches', *DS*, vol. xv (1995), pp. 1073–98.

[33] According to my calculations, the forty-five Songs use the language of tasting some twenty-three times, while touch is invoked about sixteen times. On the role of tasting in late medieval mysticism, see R. Drage, '"Taste and See, for God is Sweet": Sensory Perception and Memory in Medieval Christian Mystical Experience', in A. C. Bartlett (ed.), *Vox Mystica: Essays on Medieval Mysticism in Honor of Professor Valerie M. Lagorio* (Cambridge and Rochester, NY: D. S. Brewer, 1995), pp. 3–14.

[34] Lieder, 5. 3 (ed. Fraeters, p. 90): *Hi ne can ghedueren, / dien minne gheraect. / Hi ghesmaect / vele onghenoemeder uren.* The 'nameless hours' are explained in stanzas 4–7 as the antitheses of the nature of *minne*.

[35] With respect to tasting, it is worth noting that in her Letters Hadewijch sometimes warns against pursuing 'sweetness' (*soeticheiden*) rather than God himself; see e.g. Letters 4. 77–9 and 15. 75–80. Letter 10. 15–50 (ed. Mierlo, pp. 86–8) contains an analysis of the difference between perfect and imperfect appropriations of the sweetness God sends to the soul, affirming: '. . . love is not measured by sweetness but by the possession of virtues with charity'.

[36] My calculations give seventeen appeals to the wound of love (Song 2: 4), five references to love's blows and three each to kisses and embraces.

is also confirmed by a text in Hadewijch's Letter 20 recounting the twelve nameless hours of love, that is, the activities 'which fling love forth from herself and carry her back again into herself'. The seventh hour reveals that 'The most secret name of love is touch (*ghereinen*) and this is a nature that springs from love herself. For love is always desiring, touching, and devouring in herself. Nonetheless, she is entirely perfect in herself.'[37] To be sure, the beguine calls upon the language of all the senses in describing the effect of *minne* on those who have surrendered themselves to her power. There are descriptions of hearing, especially the paradox of loud sounds that also are silence, already noted above.[38] Appeals to sight and seeing God also occur,[39] and there is a reference to following the 'odour' of Christ (see Song 1: 2).[40] Nevertheless, Hadewijch's mystical language favours tasting and touching.

Hadewijch is not the only, nor even the first, Dutch mystic to give major attention to the role of the senses in the encounter with God. The Cistercian nun Beatrice of Nazareth, whose writings make her the earliest surviving Dutch mystic, provides a comparable teaching in her short treatise, the *Seven Manners of Loving*. The central figure of Dutch mysticism, Jan van Ruusbroec (d. 1381), has a rich doctrine of the role of the senses that cannot be discussed here. What is important for this brief sketch is to see how mystics from other vernacular traditions of the late Middle Ages dealt with the issue of inner and outer sensation. Do their teachings suggest that the Dutch mystics form a special case, or are they representative of a broad shift in medieval mysticism?

In the realm of fourteenth-century and fifteenth-century German mysticism Henry Suso (d. 1366) would make a good test case for investigating how sense-experience relates to transcendent consciousness of God, especially in his *Life of the Servant* and the two works he devoted to eternal wisdom.[41] German mystics were also among the first to discuss the rules for discernment of spirits (*discretio spirituum*) that were needed to distinguish false from true mystical experiences.[42] Nevertheless, the mystic who offers

---

[37] Letters, 20. 64–70. On the use of 'touch' (*ghereinen*) in Dutch mysticism, see L. Reypens, 'Ruusbroec-Studien, I: Het mystieke "gherinen"', *Ons Geestelike Erf*, 12 (1938), 158–86.

[38] On hearing, see Lieder, 4. 3, 4; 25. 3–4; 31. 4–6.

[39] On sight, see, e.g., Lieder, 10. 5; 11. 4–6; 14. 4; 16. 7; 26. 1. Obviously, the language of seeing is far more prevalent in Hadewijch's visions.

[40] On being drawn by the odour of love, see Lieder, 45. 2.

[41] Suso first composed his *Büchlein der ewigen Weisheit c*. 1328–30. A few years later he used much of the same material, but with additions and changes, in his Latin *Horologium sapientiae*.

[42] The Augustinian Henry of Friemar the Elder (d. 1340), the author of two mystical works in Latin, also wrote the first formal treatise on discernment of spirits, entitled *Tractatus de quatuor instinctibus*, which survives in over 150 manuscripts.

the greatest affinity to Hadewijch is Mechthild of Magdeburg, whose life spanned much of the thirteenth century and who died as a member of the Cistercian nuns of Helfta about 1280.[43] Mechthild is a woman of one book, but a great one. Her visions, poems and dialogues were collected during her lifetime and put together in the collection entitled *The Flowing Light of the Godhead*.[44]

Mechthild offers revealing comparisons with Hadewijch, but the differences between the two are as instructive as their similarities. As for Hadewijch, for Mechthild *minne* is a polyvalent category, referring to the love that is God, love as a cosmic force, love as a personification and also love as a human emotion.[45] Also like Hadewijch, Mechthild does not engage in theoretical discussions of the relation of the outer and inner senses.[46] Her practice of sense language, however, is somewhat different from Hadewijch's. Like Hadewijch, Mechthild makes considerable use of the language of tasting God,[47] but she rarely talks explicitly about 'touching God',[48] although *The Flowing Light* abounds in highly sensate, even sexualized, accounts of God's contact with the soul, employing a wide range of tactile erotic images found in both the Song of Songs and in courtly literature.[49] She makes use of the language of odour and smell more often

---

[43] A number of writers have compared Hadewijch and Mechthild (and often a third beguine, the French Marguerite Porete). See, e.g., F. Gooday, 'Mechthild von Magdeburg and Hadewich: A Comparison', *Ons Geestelijk Erf*, 48 (1974), 305–62; K. Ruh, 'Beguinenmystik: Hadewijch, Mechthild von Magdeburg, Marguerite Porete', in *Kleine Schriften*, 2 vols. (Berlin: Walter de Gruyter, 1984), vol. ii, pp. 237–49; and B. Newman, *From Virile Woman to Woman Christ: Studies in Medieval Religion and Literature* (Philadelphia: University of Pennsylvania Press, 1995), chap. 5.

[44] Mechthild van Magdeburg, *Mechthild von Magdeburg: Das fliessende Licht der Gottheit*, ed. H. Neumann, 2 vols. (Munich: Artemis, 1990–93). I will use the translation by F. Tobin, *The Flowing Light of the Godhead* (New York: Paulist Press, 1998). There is a rich literature on Mechthild; for an introduction, see B. McGinn, *The Flowering of Mysticism*, pp. 222–44. Among more recent works, see S. S. Poor, *Mechthild of Magdeburg and her Book: Gender and the Making of Textual Authority* (Philadelphia: University of Pennsylvania Press, 2004).

[45] Gooday, 'Mechthild von Magdeburg and Hadewijch of Antwerp', p. 321, estimates that *minne* occurs about 2,000 times in Hadewijch's writings and about 500 times in Mechthild's book.

[46] For Mechthild's teaching on the spiritual senses, see M. Schmidt, 'Elemente der Schau bei Mechthild von Madgeburg und Mechthild von Hackeborn', in P. Dinzelbacher and D. R. Bauer (eds.), *Frauenmystik im Mittelalter* (Ostfildern: Schwabenverlag, 1985), pp. 123–51; and 'Versinnlichte Transzendenz bei Mechthild von Magdeburg', in Dietrich Schmidtke (ed.), *'Minnichiu gotes erkennusse': Studien zur frühen abendländische Mystiktradition* (Stuttgart and Bad Cannstatt: Frommann-Holzboog, 1990), pp. 61–88.

[47] On tasting God, see, e.g., *FL* 2. 3, 2. 15, 2. 19, 4. 12 and 6. 1, as well as the remarks in Schmidt, 'Elemente der Schau bei Mechthild von Magdeburg', pp. 131, 137–45. Schmidt considers *gustus* as the supreme spiritual sense in Mechthild, but this position seems to undervalue the role of spiritual seeing. Of course, it would be a mistake to freeze Mechthild's rich imagistic presentations of sense language into a rigid system.

[48] See e.g. *FL* 2. 3, 6. 1.

[49] Among the erotic images used are the pursuit of the lover, courtly dancing, the kiss, the embrace, the wound of love, the bed of love, undressing and coition. Some key passages can be found in

than Hadewijch does,[50] and she emphasizes hearing and especially seeing, which is ranked above the other senses.[51] For example, *The Flowing Light*, 2. 19 features a poetic dialogue between Lady Knowledge and Lady Soul in which Knowledge reveals the existence of three heavens in the soul. The first is described as 'made by the devil with his alluring false cunning', a place where 'the soul remains unconsoled and the simple senses (*einvaltigú sinne*) are deceived'. This heaven seems to be the realm of the fallen senses (therefore in a sense 'made' by the devil). 'The second heaven', she says, 'was created by the longing of the senses (*gerunge der sinne*) and by the first stage of *minne*'. Here God is not seen, but the soul 'tastes an indescribable sweetness that permeates all her members. She hears as well a voice speaking of certain things that she really wants, for she is still joined to her earthly senses (*mit irdischen sinnen*).' The hearing invoked here recalls another characteristic of Mechthild's accounts of God's action in her life – the beguine often speaks of the initiation of ecstatic contact with God as receiving God's special 'greeting' (*gruos*), that is, an outflowing from the Trinity that is perceived by the soul as a kind of inner hearing.[52] If the soul attains perfect humility in the second heaven, Mechthild says, 'she shall travel on to the third heaven where the true light is given her'. At this point the senses themselves break in saying: 'Our Lady, the Soul, has slept since childhood. Now she has awakened in the light of open love.' Finally, the narrative voice sums up the third heaven of seeing God: 'In this light she looks around herself to discover who it is that reveals himself to her and what that is that one is saying to her. Thus does she see truly and understand how God is all things in all things.'[53] Seeing and, to a lesser extent, hearing are the sense activities exercised in the third heaven, which fits the dominant symbol of Mechthild's presentation of God as 'flowing Light'.

Is the seeing of God that exists in the third heaven corporeal or spiritual? If the second heaven finds the soul still joined to the earthly senses, then

---

FL I. 22, I. 44, 2. 15, 2. 19, 2. 22, 2. 23, 2. 25, 3. 1, 3. 10, 4. 15, 5. 4 and 5. 25. Books 6 and 7, composed in Mechthild's final years, generally avoid erotic images, though not the theme of *minne*.

[50] See Schmidt, 'Versinnlichte Transzendenz bei Mechthild von Magdeburg', pp. 63–9.

[51] For some representative passages on seeing God, consult *FL* 2. 19, 4. 2, 4. 14, 6. 33, 6. 41, 7. 2, 7. 8 and 7. 11.

[52] In *FL* 4. 2 Mechthild reveals that she first received God's *gruos* ('greeting') at the age of twelve, and the term occurs often (see, e.g., *FL* I. 2, I. 5, I. 14, 2. 3, 5. 17–18 (a mutual greeting between Mechthild and God), 6. 1 and 6. 39). See W. Haug, 'Grundformen religiöser Erfahrung als epochale Positionen: Vom frühmittelalterliche Analogiemodell zum hoch- und spätmittelalterliche Differenzmodell', in W. Haug and D. Mieth (eds.), *Religiöse Erfahrung: Historische Modelle in christlicher Tradition* (Munich: Fink, 1992), esp. pp. 94–100.

[53] *FL* 2. 19 (ed. Neumann, vol. 1, pp. 51–2), trans. Tobin, pp. 83–4. I have slightly modified Tobin's version here.

Mechthild seems to be invoking a spiritual seeing for the third heaven. In other places she clearly refers to a spiritual seeing, using the traditional term of 'the eye of the soul' (*mit meinen selen ougen*),[54] and even speaking of 'the spiritual eyes of the loving soul' (*mit geistlichen ougen der minnenden sele*).[55] It is clear that the German beguine knew and appealed to interior sense-perception in line with the tradition of the spiritual senses. The issue that confronts us here, however, is how she related spiritual perception and external perception, the realm of the bodily senses. Is external sensation, with its risks of diabolical deception, so dangerous and deceiving that it needs to be denied or negated for the soul seeking true love of God? This question goes to the heart of Mechthild's anthropology.

There are, to be sure, many passages in which the beguine highlights the difference, even strife, between body and soul. A dialogue between soul and body at the beginning of *The Flowing Light* has the body complain to the soul after soul has had to return from an ecstatic union with God in the following words: 'Well, woman, just where have you been? You come back so love-struck, lovely, vibrant, free and witty. Your carrying on has cost me my appetite, sense of smell, color, and all my strength.' The soul responds, 'Shut up, murderer! Quit your bellyaching. I'll always be on my guard with you around.'[56] A later passage says: 'What one is able to see with the eyes of the flesh, hear with the ears of the flesh, and say with one's fleshly mouth is as utterly different from the open truth of the loving soul as light from wax is from the bright sun.'[57]

Despite such passages, Mechthild's anthropology is really an interactive and holistic one which insists that exterior sense-perception, despite its present fallen condition, can be cleansed, renewed and even deified.[58] Before the fall, Adam and Eve were able to see God with their corporeal eyes.[59] Nevertheless, the indissoluble link of outer and inner sense-perception has a deeper root than the prelapsarian state – an incarnational one founded on Mechthild's teaching that from all eternity the transcendent *minne* that is the Trinity decreed that the second person was to take on human nature in Jesus Christ and join body and soul to divinity so that the inner and

[54] *FL* 4. 2; see also *FL* 4. 13, 6. 1, 6. 29, 6. 31, 7. 37.   [55] *FL* 7. 1; cf. 7. 7.
[56] *FL* 1. 2 (ed. Neumann, vol. 1, p. 8), trans. Tobin, p. 41. For other passages expressing conflict between body and soul, see, e.g., *FL* 1. 4–5, 1. 46, 2. 1, 2. 5, 2. 25, 3. 1, 3. 3, 3. 5, 4. 2, 4. 12 and 6. 19.
[57] *FL* 6. 36 (ed. Newmann, vol. 1, p. 244), trans. Tobin, p. 261.
[58] On the holistic character of Mechthild's anthropology, see McGinn, *Flowering of Mysticism*, pp. 233–4, and 240; and Amy Hollywood, *Soul as Virgin Wife: Mechthild of Magdeburg, Marguerite Porete, and Meister Eckhart* (University of Notre Dame Press, 1995), pp. 23–25 and 71–86.
[59] *FL* 4. 14.

the outer person and the physical senses can share in divine love.[60] In *The Flowing Light*, 4. 14 Mechthild says that she saw and still sees the 'three Persons in the eternal heights before God's Son was conceived in the body of St. Mary', and also sees that the 'Second Person had become one nature with Adam's humanity before he debased himself in sin'. This is why 'Man has a complete nature in the Holy Trinity and God saw fit to fashion it with his own divine hands.' The ultimate dignity of humanity is founded in the fact that the 'divine nature now includes bone and flesh, body and soul', so that 'the soul alone with its flesh is mistress of the house of heaven, sits next to the eternal Master of the house, and is most like him. There eye reflects in eye, there spirit flows in spirit, there hand touches hand, there mouth speaks to mouth, and there heart greets heart.'[61] Thus, as Mechthild says, although the seraphim are superior to humanity in their spiritual being, human nature is higher than the angels as enfleshed spirit united with God.[62]

Mechthild's view of the transformation being wrought by divine *minne* on the human person is a process involving mutual love and reciprocity between body and soul and their related modes of sensation. In this life the soul has to look after and care for the body, to act as the 'inner housewife of the body', as one passage puts it.[63] Body and its senses serve the soul, though perhaps with some trepidation. It is only in heaven, especially after the resurrection of the body, that body and soul will be in perfect harmony.[64] In the deification process now under way we can discern something like a single sensorium – a continuum of outer sensing and inner perception in which the effects of sin on both aspects of the person are being gradually overcome by the reciprocal motions of soaring up to God and sinking down in pain and dereliction after the model of Christ on the cross. These are the essential modalities of Mechthild's mysticism, and both body and soul are involved in this dynamic process, though in differing ways.[65] In a number of texts it is even difficult to determine whether Mechthild is talking about a sensation of God's action that is corporeal or spiritual,

---

[60] Mechthild shares this teaching, often called Christ's eternal predestination, with a number of other theologians. For passages on the eternal decision regarding the incarnation made in the *consilium trinitatis*, see *FL* 1. 22 and 4. 14.

[61] *FL* 4. 14 (ed. Newmann, vol. I, pp. 127–29), trans. Tobin, pp. 156–8. For other passages linking the incarnation with the nature of humanity as enfleshed spirit, see *FL* 2. 22, 5. 6, 6. 16, 6. 31 and 7. 1.

[62] *FL* 2. 22, 4. 14.

[63] See *FL* 7. 7 (ed. Newmann, vol. I, p. 263): . . . *die husvrowe inwendig des lichamens, die sele* . . .

[64] For example, *FL* 5. 25, 7. 65.

[65] On the need for both body and soul to share in the graces of *minne*, see esp. *FL* 4. 12–15 (ed. Newmann, vol. I, pp. 123–30; trans. Tobin, pp. 152–8). Other passages include *FL* 5. 4, 5. 25, 6. 5, 6. 13, 6. 26, 6. 29, 6. 36, 7. 7, 7. 47, 7. 63 and 7. 65.

owing to the way in which her language expresses, in Margot Schmidt's phrase, a 'sensualized transcendence'.[66] Other passages highlight a more distinct reciprocal activity between outer and inner.

Mechthild describes several kinds of divine action on the enfleshed psyche. For example, God sometimes speaks in the soul without the activity of the external senses,[67] but the action of divine *minne* can also be first experienced in the outer senses and pass up into the soul.[68] Finally and perhaps most important, Mechthild says that the delights felt first in the soul should flow down into the body and its senses to help in overcoming the effects of sin. Thus, *The Flowing Light*, 6.1 describes how the soul gradually conquers sin as the Lord casts his radiance on her:

Then she begins to taste his sweetness and he begins to greet her with his Godhead so that the power of the Trinity penetrates fully her soul and her body . . . And then he begins to caress her so that she becomes weak . . . And then he begins to give her full knowledge. And then she begins to taste with delight his love on her flesh.[69]

Once again, David of Augsburg would not have approved of such fleshly taste.

The fourteenth century was the golden age of English mysticism with the appearance of four major figures: the anchorite Richard Rolle (*c.* 1300–1349); the Augustinian Walter Hilton (d. 1396); the anonymous cleric who wrote *The Cloud of Unknowing* and its related treatises (active *c.* 1380–90); and finally the anchoress Julian of Norwich (1343–*c.* 1416). Here we shall only consider Rolle, becase he is an exponent of a particularly vivid, some have thought excessive, sensory language about encountering God.[70] Rolle wrote extensively in both Middle English and in Latin, but we can get a good sense of his mysticism from his most famous work, the

---

[66] Schmidt, 'Versinnlichte Transzendenz bei Mechthild von Magdeburg', pp. 61–2, 83.

[67] *FL* 6. 23.

[68] *FL* 5. 4. This appears to be what Mechthild means by referring to the senses as the 'chamberlains of the soul' in the love drama in *FL* 1. 44.

[69] *FL* 6. 1 (ed. Newmann, vol. 1, p. 206; trans. Tobin, p. 227): . . . *und so beginnet er ir die volle bekantnisse ze gebende, und so beginnet si denne vroeliche ze smekende an irme vleisch sine liebi* . . .

[70] Many scholars have commented on Rolle's sensory language. From the perspective of a comparison with the other English mystics, see W. Riehle, 'The Experience of God as a Spiritual Sense Perception', in W. Riehle (ed.), *The Middle English Mystics* (London: Routledge & Kegan Paul, 1981), pp. 104–27. Riehle summarizes: 'He [Rolle] constantly strives to express the transcendental world in concrete terms by introducing sensual details even when they may not be particularly relevant theologically' (p. 125). I would like to acknowledge insights from two unpublished papers prepared by students in my seminars on late medieval mysticism: R. Coyne, 'Presence, Perception, and Language in Richard Rolle', University of Chicago, 2002; and L. Blackburn, 'Sensing the Love of God: The Anthropology of Richard Rolle's *Incendium amoris*', University of Notre Dame, 2005.

Latin treatise called *The Fire of Love* (*Incendium amoris, c.* 1340).[71] In this book, an exposition of the contemplative life, the anchorite adopts such concrete language about God's action in his life that students of English mysticism like David Knowles dismissed his accounts of sensible devotion as dubious phenomena that were, 'in technical mystical terminology, the experiences of a "beginner"'. The result, according to Knowles, is that Rolle 'has little or nothing to teach . . .'[72] As Thomas Merton pointed out in a review of Knowles, the English Benedictine was so deeply embued with neoscholastic views of mysticism that he could not really appreciate a deeply somatic mystic like Rolle. Merton asks: 'But is it, after all, realistic to cling arbitrarily to a single set standard in such things as mysticism, in which the great rule is that there are no rules?'[73]

The disagreement between Knowles and Merton can be illustrated by a look at some texts in *The Fire of Love* where Rolle discusses the central theme of his mysticism, the role of the gifts of 'heat, song and sweetness' (*fervor, canor* and *dulcor*) in the path to union with God. In a discussion in chapter 14, Rolle begins by evoking the authority of scripture, not just his own experience: 'Insofar as I have been able to study the scriptures, I have discovered and recognized that the highest love of Christ consists in three things: in heat, in song, and in sweetness.' Counselling that these gifts are best received when one is seated in a state of repose and 'the highest devotion', he describes the three graces in a way that stresses their effect on the inner person. 'I call it "heat" when the mind is truly set afire by eternal love, and the heart in the same manner finds itself now burning with love, not by guess but in reality.' Song is the next state, 'when, as the fire grows, the soul now receives the sweetness of eternal praise and thinking is turned into singing and the mind lingers in its honeyed melody'. Finally, these two gifts combine in their action to 'cause marvelous sweetness in the soul . . .'[74] This all seems to describe an internal event, but the opening

---

[71] The best current edition is Richard Rolle, *The* Incendium amoris *of Richard Rolle of Hampole*, ed. M. Deanesly (Manchester University Press, 1915). There are many English versions, but I will make my own translations. For an introduction to Rolle, see N. Watson, *Richard Rolle and the Invention of Authority* (Cambridge University Press, 1991), which treats the *Incendium amoris* in chap. 5 (pp. 113–41).

[72] D. Knowles, *The English Mystical Tradition* (London: Burns & Oates, 1961), p. 54.

[73] T. Merton, 'The English Mystics', in *Mystics and Zen Masters* (New York: Dell, 1967), p. 148.

[74] Richard Rolle, *Incendium amoris*, cap. 14 (ed. Deanesly, pp. 184–5), trans. B. McGinn, *The Essential Writings of Christian Mysticism*, pp. 342–3. The most detailed treatment of the three mystical graces is in Watson, *Richard Rolle and the Invention of Authority*, chaps. 5–7 (pp. 113–91). Rolle's contemporary Henry Suso also frequently speaks of sharing in the angelic song of heaven (e.g. *Life of the Servant*, chaps. 5, 11, 23, 35, 36, 41). Rolle's notion of *canor* can be compared to the mystical wordless song, or *iubilus*, well attested among continental mystics. He himself often uses *iubilus* to describe his singing (e.g. chap. 35).

words of the Prologue of *The Fire of Love* make it clear that although the heat comes from within, it has an effect on the entire person. Here Rolle speaks in a personal way:

'I was in a state of wonder, more than I can tell, when I felt my heart grow warm within me for the first time. And this burning was not imaginary, but like an actual fire (*quasi sensibile igne*). I was amazed at how the heat leapt up in my soul and about the unaccustomed comfort I had because of my lack of experience of this abundance. I had to keep feeling my breast to see if there was some external cause for this heat.[75]

Later in the Prologue Rolle says that 'I have called the flame a fire by way of a metaphor, because it burns and illumines', but he also specifically notes that he is desolated when 'I no longer have that feeling of internal fire that I am used to, which everything of body and of soul delight in and in which they know they are secure' (*dum sensum illum ignis interni, cui cuncta corporis et spiritus applaudunt, et in quo secura se sciunt, non habeo ut solebam*).[76]

Passages such as that in chapter 14 might seem to place the taste of sweetness (*dulcor*) at the acme of the mystical path. Nevertheless, it is clear that although the three gifts always operate in reciprocal fashion, Rolle's notion of progress in the contemplative life begins with *fervor*, moves on to *dulcor* and culminates in hearing and singing, that is, participation in heavenly *canor*, which is the supreme mystical gift.[77] This emphasis on ecstatic sound and singing was not new, but few medieval mystics put more stress on it than the English hermit. The language of seeing also occurs, but rarely, as for example in chapter 19: 'Then, indeed, he [the mystic] rouses up his powers in a strong way and with heaven open as it were beholds the citizens above with his intellectual eye (*oculo intellectuali*) . . . '[78] There are also passages relating to smelling heavenly odours. Few late medieval

---

[75] Richard Rolle, *Incendium amoris*, Prologus (ed. Deanesly, p. 145). Rolle returns to the autobiographical description in cap. 15 (ed. Deanesly, pp. 187–91), which Watson sees as the centre of the book.

[76] Richard Rolle, *Incendium amoris*, Prol. (ed. Deanesly, p. 146). For another text explicitly asserting that both body and soul share in the experience of fire, see cap. 2 (ed. Deanesly, p. 208): . . . *cor in igne amoris conversum supernum sensibiliter sentit calorem* . . .

[77] Watson's account in *Richard Rolle and the Invention of Authority* shows that this progression connects Rolle's mature works, culminating in the treatise called the *Melos amoris*, his most detailed treatment of mystical song. In the *Incendium amoris* the song is most emphasized in the third part of the work (caps. 31–42). The three mystical gifts appear throughout the treatise: caps. 15, 19, 22, 25, 31, 32–36 passim, 37, 40, 41 and 42 (ed. Deanesly, pp. 188–91, 201–2, 207–9, 215, 232–3, 236–53, 256–7, 270, 273 and 277–8).

[78] *Incendium amoris*, cap. 19 (ed. Deanesly, p. 202), see also caps. 34, 35 and 36 (ed. Deanesly, pp. 241, 243, 245, 249).

mystics rival Rolle in the range and in the density of his appeals to sense language.

At the beginning of the reception of the mystical gifts, Rolle emphasizes the divide between *fervor, canor* and *dulcor* and carnal flesh and its concupiscence. In chapter 11, for example, he says: 'The death of evil affections is the goal of those who open themselves to contemplation and whose inner person (*interior homo*) is already being changed into another glory and form.'[79] Nevertheless, the English anchorite, like Mechthild, does not divide the external senses as good creations of God from the forms of interior perception that enhance their activity in the spiritual realm. What starts with a gift from God felt within and described in sensate language is meant to flow outward towards and be transformative of ordinary physical sensation. The internal experience of *fervor, canor* and *dulcor* enables us to begin to turn away from our sinful fixation on merely created beauty to begin to concentrate on transcendent divine beauty.[80]

The necessity of the corporeal element in this process is evident from Rolle's distinction of two kinds of rapture in chapter 37. The first mode of rapture is where a person, like Paul in his rapture to the third heaven (2 Cor 12), 'is so carried outside fleshly sensation that during the time of the rapture he does not feel anything in the flesh or what is done by the flesh'. The second mode of rapture is 'an elevation of the mind to God through contemplation' in which the body maintains its control and sensation, just as Christ never lost control of his body and its senses. This 'being raptured in the midst of fleshly sensation (*rapi in sensu carnis*)' is the supreme height of love possible in this life. Rolle describes it again in sensate language without appealing to 'spiritual' senses – 'feeling the heat of uncircumscribed light'; 'panting for Christ with great ardour'; 'drinking down an absolutely marvelous draft from the heavens'; and 'melting into song in honeyed sweetness'.[81] Thus Rolle believes that it is possible to unite inner spiritual delight with everyday conscious experience, as he expressly teaches in chapter 40.[82] The English hermit, like Hadewijch or Mechthild, is a witness to forms of mystical language that are concretely sensate in expression and that teach that the unification of the inner and outer dimensions of the person is the goal of the mystical life.

---

[79] *Incendium amoris*, cap. 11 (ed. Deanesly, p. 176).
[80] On the reordering of our drive towards beauty, see e.g. *Incendium amoris*, caps. 5, 28 and esp. 35.
[81] *Incendium amoris*, cap. 37 (ed. Deanesly, pp. 254–6), trans. McGinn, pp. 344–5.
[82] *Incendium amoris*, cap. 40 (ed. Deanesly, pp. 267–8).

CONCLUSION

The five mystics discussed here are not representative of all late medieval mysticism – a phenomenon too varied to be summarized by easy generalizations. Despite their differences, however, they show that there was an impetus during these times towards presenting an integrated notion of the mystical self that saw the outer and inner aspects of sensation – feeling, desiring, perceiving and knowing – as part of a continuum of conscious and progressive reception of divine gifts. Like all Christian mystics, these figures insisted that because of Adam's fall, the initiative for redirecting the senses back towards their original goal comes from God alone. In various ways they also rooted their conviction about the necessity of harmonizing and integrating the outer and inner dimensions of perception of God in Christology, that is, in belief that in Jesus Christ, the incarnate God, body, soul and divinity are one and undivided. This tendency towards integration does not seem to be dependent on a developed faculty psychology, because the two Cistercians looked at here do have such a psychology, whereas it is not important for the three vernacular mystics considered (though this is not the case for other vernacular theologians, such as Ruusbroec). The integration of the outer and inner senses is also deeply eschatological, in the sense that the full attainment of the bliss of the corporeo-spiritual human totality will not be realized until the resurrection of the body, though it is under way now in the interim period, the time of *transitus*, during which the senses have begun to be reformed by the action of grace on the whole human faculty of sensation. Such forms of embodied mystical teaching may even find resonance among spiritual seekers today.

CHAPTER 12

Nicholas of Cusa

Garth W. Green

INTRODUCTION

In *De quaerendo Deum*, Nicholas of Cusa – at the origin of a mystical ascent – writes of the way in which an external object is 'taken up into consciousness', from the five external senses, through the 'common sense', to the imagination and the intellect.[1] In *De visione Dei* – when depicting the culmination of a mystical ascent – Cusa used this same theme of the *ordo cognoscendi* in order to establish his claim both for a *visio Dei* and for only a *pregustus* thereof.[2]

In these two texts and passages, I will suggest, an important confluence obtains. In the first, Cusa presents an Aristotelian model of the nature of sensible cognition, or aesthetic. In the second, Cusa presents a neo-Platonic, and specifically Origenist, aesthetic. Cusa, I will suggest, inherits and synthesizes the Aristotelian doctrine of the common sense (*sensus communis*) and inner senses (*sensus interiores*) with the Origenist doctrine of the spiritual senses (*sensus spirituales*). These aesthetics, I will suggest, respond to distinct experiential exigencies, propose distinct faculties and imagine distinct ends of cognition, and thus are incongruent. For this reason, a disaggregation of these doctrines is essential to a comprehension of Cusa's theological aesthetics. Once their particular character and role is set out, we will be able to appreciate the way in which Cusa establishes their *coincidentia* within his account of the theological significance of sensibility. For in Cusa's superposition of an Origenist theological aesthetic over an Aristotelian theory of cognition, neither escapes in its original, Aristotelian or Origenist, form.

---

[1] *DQD* 1. 24. Herein, I cite J. Hopkins (trans.), *Complete Philosophical and Theological Treatises of Nicholas of Cusa*, 2 vols. (Minneapolis: A. J. Banning Press, 2001). I also cite text, section and paragraph numbers in *Nicolai de Cusa opera omnia iussu et auctoritate Academiae Litterarum Heidelbergensis* (Hamburg: Meiner, 1932–); *DQD* is found in vol. IV, *Opuscula*, 1, ed. P. Wilpert (1959).
[2] *DVD* Preface, 1, trans. Hopkins, vol. II, p. 680. For the term *pregustus*, see also *Idiota de sapientia*, I. II.

ARISTOTLE AND CUSA: THE *SENSUS COMMUNIS*

Aristotle's doctrine of the *sensus communis* in *De anima*, III,[3] is set out in the context of an account of the nature of sensation. In *De anima*, II. 4, 417a, Aristotle had depicted sensation as a 'process of movement or affection from without'. This process Aristotle traced from the 'individual and external objects' that 'excite to activity the sensory powers'[4] to the sensible faculty itself. An enumeration of the five external senses and a depiction of 'the objects perceptible by each' followed. This correspondence between each individual sense and its sphere of objects could be secured insofar as 'each sense', on the basis of its particular constitution, 'has one kind of object which it discerns'.[5] Each particular or 'special' sense reveals for sensation the 'special objects' attributable uniquely thereto; 'the object of sight', for example, is 'the visible'. Each particular sense functions within a single sensible horizon, established by the 'common sensibles' (movement, rest, number, figure, magnitude). These, Aristotle continues, 'are not peculiar to any one sense, but are common to all', as those characteristics by means of which individual senses discern their respective properties and objects.[6] While, Aristotle suggests, there is 'no special sense-organ for the common sensibles', there is 'a general sensibility', αἴσθησις κοινή, in which 'all [special senses] form a unity'.[7] The synthesis of 'white' and 'sweet' as data of sight and taste, respectively, must be attributed not to each sense individually but to that 'common sense' that provides the synthetic context for the inclusion of such particular data within a single sensible experience.[8]

[3] Aristotle's doctrine is exposed at *De an.* III. 1, 425a 27, *DMR* 1, 450a 10 and *De partibus animalium*, IV. 10, 686a 31. See D. K. W. Modrak's comprehensive *Aristotle: The Power of Perception* (University of Chicago Press, 1987) and P. Gregoric's *Aristotle on the Common Sense* (New York: Oxford University Press, 2007). Gregoric adds *De an.* III. 7, *Historia animalium*, I. 3, 489a 17 and *Met.* I. 1, 981b 14 to this shorter list of commonly discussed passages; see Gregoric, *Aristotle on the Common Sense*, pp. 65–7.

[4] *De an.* II. 5, 417b 27 and 417b 20 respectively.   [5] *De an.* II. 6, 418a 15.

[6] *De an.* II. 6, 418a 18.   [7] *De an.* III. 1, 425a 28.

[8] In *DMR*, common sense also appears as 'the primary faculty of perception' and as effective in memory as both the 'faculty whereby we perceive time' (*DMR* 1, 451a 19) and that faculty in which we possess and present the recollection of past events as past (*DMR* 1, 450a 12). Thus the common sense both combines the individual accomplishments of the five senses and provides a form for their recollection. The common sense also functions as a power of self-consciousness; in and through it, we apprehend not *what* we apprehend, but *that* we apprehend. Inner sense thus yields a second-order perception of a first-order perception. In this apperceptive function, *sensus communis* is not only the 'common power that accompanies all the senses' (Aristotle, *De somno et vigilia*, II, 455a 14 – 455b 2), but is also 'the master sense organ to which all sense organs lead' (*ibid.* II, 455a 33–4). For the latter dynamic, see, e.g., T. K. Johansen, 'In Defense of Inner Sense: Aristotle on Perceiving that One Sees', *Proceedings of the Colloquium on Ancient Philosophy*, 21 (2005), 235–76.

More importantly for our purposes, the *sensus communis* functions within the order of cognition, the process by means of which material is progressively informed. Only upon the reception of sensible data by the five external senses does the common sense possess material for synthesis, and only as synthesized by the common sense can such data be determined by, for example, imagination and intellection. Thus, in *De anima*, Aristotle's order of exposition follows this order of cognition, as it moves from intuition to imagination[9] and to intellection.[10] It is this last characteristic function of the common sense in the *ordo cognoscendi* that I wish to isolate. Identifying the function of the *sensus communis* will allow us to show its incongruence with the spiritual senses doctrine, and thus establish the necessary problem-context for our address of Cusa's theological aesthetics.

In his excellent review of key moments within the subsequent history of this doctrine, Nicholas Steneck enumerates those cognitive faculties or 'actions that... follow in the order of knowing the actions of the five external senses'.[11] The first of these, the common sense, is thus placed 'within a graded hierarchy... on the basis of a progressive abstraction'.[12] Steneck uses Avicenna's account to illustrate the way in which five 'internal senses' (common sense, imagination, estimation, fantasy and memory) interact functionally within the process of cognition.[13] The common sense is situated at the first level of this process: 'common sense receives the forms of an object from the five proper or external senses... and composes and divides these forms one with another'.[14] While distinct from the five external senses, nonetheless the common sense functions together with them and within a doctrine of sensible cognition. Then, such intuitive data 'pass to imagination where they are stored'.[15] Imagination thus obtains at a

---

[9] *De an.* III. 3, 427b 15.   [10] *De an.* III. 4, 429a 10.
[11] N. H. Steneck, 'Albert the Great on the Classification and Localization of the Internal Senses', *Isis*, 65.2 (June 1974), 193–211. See also Steneck, 'The Problem of the Internal Senses in the Fourteenth Century', unpublished Ph.D. diss., University of Wisconsin, 1970.
[12] Steneck, 'Albert the Great', p. 209.
[13] In 'The Internal Senses in Latin, Arabic, and Hebrew Philosophical Texts', *HTR*, 28 (1935), 69–133, H. A. Wolfson recalls that 'through the Latin translations from the Arabic in the 12th and 13th centuries, the Avicennian and Averroian classifications of the internal senses became known to the scholastics', such that 'Albertus Magnus, Thomas Aquinas, and Roger Bacon' were able to integrate 'these Arabic sources in their discussion of the internal senses' (pp. 114–15). For Albert's transformation of Avicenna's theory, see Steneck, 'Albert the Great', p. 198, nn. 15–17, and U. Dähnert, *Die Erkenntnislehre des Albertus Magnus gemessen an den Stufen der 'abstractio'* (Leipzig: Gerhardt, 1933). Wolfson reports that he is 'unable to find the use of "internal senses" prior to Augustine', but claims that 'when the term "internal sense" first appears in Latin philosophic texts it is used (e.g. Augustine, *Conf.* I. 20 and VII. 17; *De lib. arbit.* II. 3–5) 'as synonymous with Aristotle's "common sense" in terms of its function'. Dähnert, *Die Erkenntnislehre*, p. 269.
[14] Steneck, 'Albert the Great', p. 196.   [15] *Ibid.* p. 197.

second level of abstraction, as 'the power that accepts the form of an object even when the object is not present', while fantasy and estimation obtain at a third level of abstraction, for their active generation of qualities are related but not reducible to sensible impressions. In other words, in and through the common sense we both synthesize discrete data into a perceptual unity (of *what* we know) and achieve its apperceptive representation (in order *that* we know what we know). The common sense functions herein as a point of synthesis for the diversity of the discrete data of the five external senses, and towards the presentation of sensible objects as sensible and as present.[16]

The central point is that the inner sense(s) is inseparable from, and serves within, an account of the *ordo cognoscendi* and the process of abstraction, in which the material object outside us is transmuted in distinct stages into an immaterial idea. It answers the question of the nature and limits of knowledge. This directionality of the *sensus interiores* doctrine raises the question of the stability of any *sensus spirituales* doctrine erected on its basis. Within the sphere of possible cognition opened up by the Aristotelian account, Origen's famous and foundational depiction of the five spiritual senses would be impossible. Origen's assertion that 'there is, as the scripture calls it, a certain generic divine sense' (Prov 2: 5) or *sensus divinitatis* in *Contra Celsum*, 1. 48 would have to be accepted not on analogy with the natural fivefold *sensorium*, but as a strained metaphor. Origen enumerated 'several [five] forms of this [divine] sense'. He depicted 'a sight which can see things superior to corporeal being', a 'hearing which can receive impressions of sounds that have no objective existence in the air' and a 'taste which feeds on living bread that has come down from heaven and gives life to the world'. So, too, did Origen lay claim to 'a sense of smell which smells spiritual things' and 'a sense of touch in accordance with which John says that he has handled with his hands "the Word of life"' (1 Jn 1: 1). Thus, Origen attributes to the five spiritual senses both the internal unity and the correspondence between sense and sensed that Aristotle attributes to the five external senses.

---

[16] Inner senses posterior to the common sense cannot yield objective, sensible presence. Steneck, *ibid.* p. 202, n. 32, depicts the way in which (1) 'by composing and dividing the forms and intentions received in the internal senses, *fantasy* is able to conjure up such images as a gold mountain, which we obviously have never seen', (2) *estimation* 'receives intentions that are not sensed in the senses', in order to direct the individual to particular actions, and (3) *memory* 'apprehends an object through a [inner sensory] form that it has stored rather than a form that it receives de novo' from the external senses, in a merely reproductive presence. This depiction of the limits of sensible presence will not be inconsequential to the capacity and range of an Aristotelian aesthetic to yield the conditions necessary for a theological aesthetic.

However, the sensible conditions for the possibility of these aesthetic claims would be absent from, rather than present within, the structure of the (neo-)Aristotelian account. When Aquinas thus argues that 'in this life, material and sensible things form our proper natural objects', he argues against both Augustine's understanding of our 'knowledge of incorporeal things'[17] and the very possibility of a spiritual sensation.[18] As noted by Richard Cross in Chapter 10 above, there is, in Aquinas's neo-Aristotelian aesthetic, 'simply no reason to posit spiritual senses'. But Aquinas offers for our consideration not only an indifference to but a critique of a spiritual sensorium. If Cusa inherited from Origen a hope or an intention, he inherited from Aquinas a challenge, a strong argument against the existence of spiritual senses.

Thus, I introduce Cusa through Aristotle not only in order to provide context for the passage from *De quaerendo Deum* with which we started,[19] but to suggest also that Cusa's own theological aesthetics cannot be understood in abstraction from this double inheritance. The Aristotelian doctrine – 'one of the most successful and resilient of Aristotelian notions' for Gregoric[20] – that leads Aquinas to dispense with an Origenist theological aesthetic will be inherited by Cusa, as well. But while Cusa also assumes basic Aristotelian epistemic principles,[21] he nonetheless will recover and recapitulate a form of the doctrine rejected by his fellow Dominican. Cusa will no longer posit parallel and fivefold physical and spiritual faculties. Rather than a second, spiritual, sensorium, Cusa will discover a hidden theological significance within the shadows of the physical sensorium.[22]

---

[17] Aquinas, *ST* I. 87, ob. 1.   [18] *ST* I. 87.

[19] Cusa advances the doctrine of the common sense and explores its philosophical and theological significance in a series of texts and passages throughout his writings. See, e.g., the much longer account of the role of sensibility and the common sense in the order of cognition in the late *Compendium*, 6, trans. Hopkins, vol. II, p. 1394.

[20] Gregoric, *Aristotle on the Common Sense*, p. 12.

[21] At *DVD* XIV. 107 (trans. Hopkins, vol. II, p. 732), and as we will see, Cusa claims that, 'because the intellect is united to the body through the medium of the sensible [power], it is not perfected apart from the senses. For whatever comes to it proceeds to it from the sensible world through the medium of the senses.' For Cusa, as I will suggest, the theological significance of sensibility will have to be derived from out of this sensible structure of experience. For this reason, Cusa writes that when 'the pilgrim sets out on his journey', he must not 'close off for himself the pathway [of ascent]' that begins necessarily from the sensible, even if this pathway ultimately will 'surpass the limits of every mode of intuition' for the latter's intrinsic connection to finite objectivity. *DFD* I, trans. Hopkins, vol. I, p. 342. One is to both begin with and leave behind or transcend the limits of the (neo-)Aristotelian aesthetic.

[22] The Aristotelian inner senses are active in, and tied to, the determination of outer sensory objects, and thus could not be separated from the outer senses. Origen, instead, supposed that 'the eye of the soul of any genuine Christian is awake and that of the senses [i.e. the body] is closed', such that 'in proportion to the degree in which the superior eye is awake and the sight of the senses is closed,

Cusa transforms the Aristotelian aesthetic from within, in order that it yield or conform to an Origenist intention. But in neither case (either in Aquinas's rejection or in Cusa's reformation) will the doctrine emerge from this confrontation unchanged.

The question for us, then, becomes: how can Cusa extract an Origenist aesthetic from this Aristotelian epistemology? By contextualizing our address of Cusa in this way, we will be able (1) to recognize and negotiate the effects of a pressure that the spiritual senses doctrine undergoes, as Aristotelian accounts of the nature and limits of sensible cognition are assimilated into Christian theology,[23] and (2) to recognize the constitutive role of sensibility within Cusa's theology, the way in which it provides a model or pattern evident at each stage of his mystical ascent.

THE SYNTHESIS OF *SENSUS COMMUNIS* AND *SENSUS SPIRITUALIS* IN *DE QUAERENDO DEUM*

Cusa employs the language of the spiritual senses throughout his corpus. Iris Wikström, for instance, in 'On Tasting the Sweetness of Wisdom', has attended closely to Cusa's use of the analogy of taste in *De visione Dei*.[24] In that text, Cusa does indeed utilize the analogy of taste, in writing, for example, of '[God's] incomprehensible sweetness'.[25] He also employs the

---

the supreme God and His Son . . . are comprehended and seen by each man.' *Contra Celsum*, VII. 39, trans. H. Chadwick, *Contra Celsum* (Cambridge University Press, 1965), 427. See also *ibid.* VII. 39: '. . . the eye of the soul of any genuine Christian is awake and that of the senses is closed' (trans. Chadwick, p. 427). The Origenist disjunction between the physical and spiritual senses will be amended by Cusa: the spiritual significance of sensibility will not be derived from a turn away from external sensible experience, but from the theological amplification thereof.

[23] This suggests that we incorporate post-Bonaventuran transformations of the spiritual senses into a wider history of theological aesthetics. Notably, Rahner insisted on the fivefold nature of the spiritual senses as a criterion for 'proper' or 'authentic' expositions thereof; 'one can only speak properly of an idea or doctrine of spiritual faculties when these . . . expressions; "to touch" God, "to open the eyes of the heart", etc. are found in a complete system in which five instruments are involved in the spiritual perception of immaterial realities'. 'The "Spiritual Senses" According to Origen', p. 82. However, this criterion of a correspondence between sense and sensed within a necessarily fivefold sensorium may prove unhelpful. Cusa provides a test-case; according to Rahner's criterion, Cusa's 'doctrine' may fail. But Cusa recovers (rather than rejects, with Aquinas) the significance of sensibility. A criterion that orients analysis from this more general aesthetic context would concern itself less with the letter of the doctrine than with its wider, animating intention.

[24] Iris Wikström, 'On Tasting the Sweetness of Wisdom', in K. Reinhardt, H. Schwaetzer and O. Dushin (eds.), *Nicolaus Cusanus: Ein bewundernswerter historischer Brennpunkt: Philosophische Tradition und wissenschaftliche Rezeption. Akten des Cusanus-Kongresses vom 20. bis 22. September 2006 in St. Petersburg* (Regensburg: Roderer, 2008), pp. 34–44. Cusa's doctrine of intuition has attracted less scholarly attention than has his doctrine of intellection; see, however, G. Santinello, *Il pensiero di Nicolò Cusano nella sua prospettiva estetica* (Padua: Liviana, 1958).

[25] *DVD* XXVI. 71, 74, trans. Hopkins, vol. II, p. 713.

analogy of smell – recalling the 'sweet savour of Christ unto God' of Paul's 2 Corinthians 2: 15 – in writing of Jesus Christ as 'the fragrance of the food of delight' that attracts us to, and sustains us in, mystical contemplation.[26] However, Cusa also asserted therein the limits of such sensible but non-visual analogies. The prominence attributed to sight already in the title of the work is reinforced by its structure, its thematic content and its assertion of the superior capacity of vision to express Cusa's comprehension of sensibility's proper role in theology.[27] Cusa thus will suggest that 'revelation falls short of a savoring' and can be characterized only as a *pregustus*, a foretaste.[28] It is in this context, then, that Cusa suggests that 'to taste of You' is 'not other than . . . to see Absolute Form'.[29] The *sapor* of our *sapientia* of God is apparently best understood through, and as, a *visus*; the mediate discursivity of vision replaces the consummated immediacy, and enjoyment, of a tasting, or a touch.[30] For this reason, I would like to suggest that the distinctive feature of Cusa's theological aesthetics lies in the predominance of visuality therein. But how is this latter to be understood, and why does Cusa suppose that it best situates the theological significance of sensibility?

In *De quaerendo Deum*, Cusa proposes 'an analysis of God's name', in order that we may be brought to a 'clear recognition' thereof.[31] The treatise begins with a depiction of the problem-context for any such analysis.[32] Cusa recalls the situation of Paul, who taught of an 'Unknown God', in order that his auditors 'might seek him, to see whether they could gropingly find him'.[33] Paul admits, and emphasizes, that 'in men's thoughts there can be no likeness at all to God'. However, this absence or negation is fecund;

---

[26] *DVD* xx. 91, trans. Hopkins, vol. II, p. 723.
[27] The central figure of the work – the *sensibilis apparentia* that occasions Cusa's *sensibile experimentum* (*DVD* I. 5) – is a painting or icon of an omnivoyant Christ. This painting, however, is only the principal and orienting visual image in *De visione Dei*: thirteen out of twenty-five chapter titles employ visual terms. In the text's chapters, Cusa discusses absolute sight (1–2), God's vision (4–5, 8–9), our vision of God (6–7, 10–11, 13) and thus the seeing of the invisible Father through the visible image thereof (12, 21, 25, 18, 21). On these and related points see A. Stock, 'Die Rolle der "icona Dei" in der Spekulation "De visione Dei"', in R. Haubst (ed.), *Das Sehen Gottes nach Nikolaus von Kues: Akten des Symposions in Trier vom 25. bis 27. September 1986, Mitteilungen und Forschungsbeiträge der Cusanus-Gesellschaft*, 18 (Trier: Paulinus-Verlag, 1989), pp. 50–68, and H. L. Bond, 'The "Icon" and the "Iconic" Text in Nicholas of Cusa's *De visione Dei* I–XVII', in T. Izbicki and C. Bellitto (eds.), *Nicholas of Cusa and his Age: Intellect and Spirituality* (Leiden: Brill, 2002), pp. 177–95. For Cusa's solicitation to 'pass . . . from hearing to seeing' see *DI* III. 11. 245, p. 141; for his assertion of the 'superiority' of vision, see *DC* II. 14, trans. Hopkins, vol. I, p. 236.
[28] *DVD* xvii. 80, trans. Hopkins, vol. II, p. 716.   [29] *DVD* v. 14, trans. Hopkins, vol. II, p. 686.
[30] For Dorothy Koenigsberger, 'the Cusan taste of wisdom refers to an apprehension that men never really taste', but rather infinitely defer. See her *Renaissance Man and Creative Thinking: A History of Concepts of Harmony, 1400–1700* (Atlantic Highlands, NJ: Humanities Press, 1979), p. 132. See *Idiota de sapientia*, 18 (Hopkins, vol. I, pp. 493–526) for Cusa's insistence upon such a 'deferral'.
[31] *DQD* I. 16.   [32] *DQD* I. 17–18.   [33] *DQD* I. 17.

'God is therefore made known by the fact that every intellect is too small to befigure or conceive him'.[34] Problematically, however, 'Paul names him God – or *Theos* in Greek'. This naming of the unnamed or unknown God will itself be productive for Cusa's own analysis, for it contextualizes the problem to which *De quaerendo Deum* offers itself as a response; 'since man cannot conceive of any likeness to God, as Paul said, then how is it that God can be sought in order to be found?'.[35]

Cusa responds to this question with the materials set out already.[36] He suggests that we 'now determine whether the name *Theos* itself offers us any assistance'. Self-evidently, '*Theos* is not that name of God which excels every concept', but is instead a concept, 'the name of God insofar as God is sought', and conceived, 'by human beings in this world'.[37] In the name, Cusa continues, 'there is enfolded (*complicatio*) a certain way-of-seeking whereby God is found'.[38] Cusa suggests that '*Theos* is derived from *theoro*, which means both 'I see' and 'I hasten'.[39] In order that we may seek, then, in order that we may then find, we 'ought to hasten by means of sight'. In this *venatio*, 'vision bears a likeness to a pathway, by means of which a seeker ought to advance'. Along this pathway, or 'ladder of ascent', Cusa suggests that we first engage and analyse (1) 'the nature of sensible vision', in a *sensible* theological moment, as a step towards (2) an analysis of the nature of 'intellectual vision', that of the *ratio* in a *symbolic* theological moment, in order that we then be in a position to 'attain unto God, who sees all things', in a *speculative* theological moment.[40] As Cusa will state later in this text: 'we are not moved toward what is altogether unknown'.[41] In order to set up his 'theory's ladder of ascent' and its three principal moments, Cusa solicits us to 'examine sight'.[42]

Cusa next gives an account of the nature and dynamics of vision.[43] The theme of the *ordo cognoscendi* is only an occasion, only the necessary first step in an 'ascent of our intellects'.[44] Cusa's intention is to delimit vision

---

[34] *DQD* I. 17.   [35] *DQD* I. 17.   [36] *DQD* I. 19.   [37] *DQD* I. 19.   [38] *DQD* I. 19.

[39] For the way in which Cusa 'parte dalla etimologia del nome *theos* derivato da *theoro* cioè vedo e corro', see M. T. Liaci, 'Significato di immanenza e trascendenza nel *De quaerendo Deum*', in *Nicolò Cusano agli inizi del mondo moderno*, Congresso Internazionale Nicolò Cusano (Florence: G. C. Sansoni, 1970), pp. 399–407. See also J. Hopkins, *Nicholas of Cusa's Dialectical Mysticism: Text, Translation, and Interpretive Study of* De visione Dei (Minneapolis: Arthur Banning Press), p. 18.

[40] *DQD* I. 19.   [41] *DQD* II. 32.

[42] *DQD* II. 32. For the 'three spheres' of sensible, symbolic and speculative theology, see, e.g., *DI* II. 1 (trans. Hopkins, vol. I, p. 59). For the threefold ascent through each, see *DVD* XIV. 10 (trans. Hopkins, vol. II, p. 732). For the 'three cognitive modes', the perceptual, the intellectual [rational], and the intelligential, see *DB* 5 (trans. Hopkins, vol. II, p. 793); *DC* II. 14 (trans. Hopkins, vol. I, p. 235); and *De possest*, 62 (trans. Hopkins, vol. II, p. 947).

[43] *DQD* I. 20.   [44] *DQD* I. 16.

and the sphere of the visible. He argues that 'in the realm of visible things, only color is found'. Thus, 'sight [itself] is not of the realm of visible things', but is 'above all visible things'. Vision 'stands above' its objects as its *principium*; 'within the circumference of its realm [the world of visible things] does not find sight or anything similar to sight, or analogous to sight, it cannot attain to sight'.[45] We do not see vision, but rather only those objects seen by means of acts of vision. This conclusion is not merely negative, but is again productive. The recognition that 'it cannot attain unto [the knowledge] that sight is something' gives rise to the comprehension that 'it judges that whatever is not-colored is not anything'.[46] Thus, Cusa concludes that 'no name among all the names that can be named in that realm [of visible things] befits sight'. The 'name and essence of sight' are invisible to the analysis that orients itself only from the sphere of visible objects themselves, and turns away from the act that stands above such objects as their possibility-condition.[47]

The delimitation of a sphere of vision allows for the production of the concept of the invisible, already at the level of our sensible faculty, of that which sees and is not seen. We are thus to 'ascend, then, by means of a similarity of relation from sight to hearing and to taste, smell, and touch – and, therefore, unto the communal sense (*sensus communis*), which is situated above all [five] senses'.[48] Just as vision possesses an objective structure that allows for the distinction between the invisible *terminus a quo* and the visible *terminus ad quem* of an act of vision, so too 'hearing is above things audible, taste above things tastable, smell above things discernible by smell, and touch above things tangible', as the acts by which such correlates can be made manifest and experienced.[49] Vision, as both one of and a synecdoche for the five senses, is thus placed within the higher sensible faculty of the common sense. The latter 'enfolds in its power all the power of the aforementioned senses', and thus contains within itself 'the form of the sensible world'.[50]

Here, then, the Aristotelian *sensus communis* functions within a neo-Platonic process of ascent. Just as each discrete sense, for example vision, makes manifest a relation between an invisible ground and a visible image, so too the common sense lies 'above', and is 'invisible' to, each discrete sense, as the site of a synaesthetic plenitude that the discrete senses cannot as such imagine. But Cusa does not depict vision in this way in order to arrest his analysis at this Aristotelian notion. Cusa intends instead to

---

[45] *DQD* I. 22.   [46] *DQD* I. 22.   [47] *DQD* I. 22.
[48] *DQD* I. 24.   [49] *DQD* I. 24.   [50] *DQD* I. 28; I. 30.

advance past, and use the results of the analysis of sensibility, 'in order to continue upward to the intellect'.[51] In the latter ascent, vision will continue to play a role in Cusa's theological aesthetics not as a single sense within a second, spiritual sensorium, but as that sensible modality uniquely capable of evincing the basic figures of Christian self-understanding, across and within each of the three levels of mystical ascent.

The analysis of intuitive or sensible vision[52] is propaedeutic to the analysis of the objective or projective structure of reason and the 'intellectual vision' thereof.[53] The former provides a model for the latter. As the insufficiency of the eye was discovered by the intellect, so now the latter will delimit *scientia*, the scope of *ratio*, in order to open up the possibility of and space for an *excessus mentis*. While in the latter case both subject and object, or *principium* and *principiatum*, are internal to the mind (whereas the objective correlate of any act of vision is external thereto), Cusa asks us nonetheless to 'apprehend how the intellect is like unto free sight' (*apprehendas quomodo intellectus est ut visus liber*).[54] Just as the act of vision served as a *principium* or source for objects of vision that could not be reduced to such objects, so now, 'within the entire realm of reasons the intellect [itself, *qua* source or fount for the production of ideas, concepts, judgements] is unattainable'.[55]

Just as we could derive 'no name' for the source of vision from within the sphere of objects of vision, so now 'the intellect [itself] is not found in the realm of rational things' as the principle of genesis for such formal objects. The mind, too, cannot understand itself except by means of the relative position between an invisible origin and a visible image or manifestation

---

[51] *DQD* I. 25. Cusa begins by adopting an Aristotelian aesthetic, and endorses Aristotelian-Thomistic principles – e.g. that 'there cannot be in the intellect anything which is such that it was not first in the senses' (*DVD* XXIV). But he holds that on questions regarding the form of intellectual contemplation, '[the Peripatetics] are surely wrong'. *DI* II. 9, 148, trans. Hopkins, vol. I, p. 85. Aristotle, Cusa suggests, 'shunned the truth' and 'failed to arrive at the Spirit', of the unity of the invisible and visible, as did 'the Platonists'. *DB* 42, trans. Hopkins, vol. II, p. 811. Cusa attributes the method of ascent to Plato in *DVS*, and sets out Proclus's agreement and 'the Peripatetics' disagreement' therewith (*DVS* 8, 20–22; see also 26). For condemnation of 'the Aristotelian sect [that] now prevails', and its 'ignorance' of the theme of invisibility that can propel mystical ascent, see *ADI* 6 (trans. Hopkins, vol. I, pp. 459–92, at p. 462). Cusa's integration of Aristotelian psychology into the first stage of the mystical ascent has led several scholars to situate Cusa in an Aristotelian context: C. Giacon, 'Il "possest" del Cusano e le dottrine aristotelico-tomistiche dell'atto e potenza e dell'essenza ed esistenza', in *Nicolò Cusano agli inizi del mondo moderno*, pp. 375–84, writes not only of 'affini di Aristotele e di S. Tommaso', but of 'una sostanziale identità' (p. 375). The theme of the *visio Dei*, however, shows the neo-Platonic, and not neo-Aristotelian, direction of Cusa's theology. Its task is to elicit from an Aristotelian beginning an Origenist intention and end, a theological aesthetics.

[52] *DQD* I. 20–3.   [53] *DQD* I. 25–7.   [54] *DQD* I. 25.   [55] *DQD* I. 25.

thereof.[56] This point is amplified in *De filiatione Dei* (1445). Therein, Cusa continues to suggest that the intellect, which expresses itself by means of conceptual activity, 'cannot be sufficiently expressed' *qua* source in such activity. The intellect remains a power expressed in, but not reducible to, its modes, accomplishments or manifestations. While all such productions express its effectivity, all such productions are, with respect to their source, 'nothing other than a manifestation' of it. This source is 'present or signified' in each manifestation and yet only *as* absent or unsignifiable.[57]

Cusa's ascent incorporates both sensible and intellectual vision, and does so by means of their isomorphism. In both cases, Cusa applies the distinction between the visible (manifestation, result) and the invisible (principle, origin) in order to evince the necessary insufficiency of the analysis thus far conducted, to propel the reader further upon her ascent. For this reason, Cusa repeats that his task is to establish the methodological structure in which the reader 'will be able to hasten along that pathway through which God is found', towards a satisfaction not yet realized.[58] And if God will be situated 'above all sight, hearing, taste, touch, smell, speech, sense, reason, and intellect' in an ascending series as the excess to each such attempt at determination, it will be only by means of Cusa's delimitation of each faculty, both intuitive and intellectual.[59] This series of delimitations is made by Cusa not to deny but to establish the significance of sensibility, to establish the sensible figure of vision at each level of mystical ascent.

Within the early period and in this same thematic context, Cusa begins the *Apologia doctae ignorantiae* with the injunction from Psalm 46: 10 to 'be still and see that I am God'.[60] Cusa suggests that, here, 'He commands that our sight be redirected unto Himself'.[61] Such a *visio Dei*, however, could 'not remain in a mere cognitive seeing, which puffs us up'.[62] In such a 'vision of the invisible God', we must see that we do not see. We are to see that 'God is not this or that',[63] a determinate objectivity, but rather an 'Ineffable Form,

---

[56] This necessary excess, both sensible and rational, will be applied, of course, in a further theological context, as (1) the source of sensible vision cannot itself be seen, and as (2) the mind 'cannot be either participated in, or attained unto' except through its productions – the 'mental words' or concepts of intellectual life – so, in a third stage of ascent, (3) God 'cannot be participated in [as] the Fount of intelligible beings' except through his visible manifestation. *DFD* IV. 76, trans. Hopkins, vol. I, p. 352. For a similar *processus*, cf. *De aequalitate*, 18–31 (trans. Hopkins, vol. II, pp. 839–77); *De ludo globi*, 101–10 (trans. Hopkins, vol. II, pp. 1236–42); *De possest*, 43–54 (trans. Hopkins, vol. II, pp. 932–42). On the connection between vision and Cusa's ascent see B. H. Helander, *Die visio intellectualis als Erkenntnisweg und -ziel bei Nikolaus Cusanus* (Stockholm: Almqvist & Wiksell, 1988).

[57] *DFD* IV. 75, trans. Hopkins, vol. I, p. 352.   [58] *DFD* I. 27.   [59] *DFD* I. 27.

[60] *ADI* 7, trans. Hopkins, vol. I, pp. 457–92, at p. 463.   [61] *ADI* 7, trans. Hopkins, vol. I, p. 463.

[62] *ADI* 7, trans. Hopkins, vol. I, p. 463.   [63] *ADI* 8, trans. Hopkins, vol. I, p. 464.

which surpasses every concept'.[64] The frustration of *visio* is propaedeutic to the frustration of *ratio*, and to a theological vision of the limits of physical and philosophical vision. Both frustrations are, now, preparatory for a higher satisfaction. The significance of sensibility is attained only when we demonstrate the necessary limits thereof, when sensibility yields of itself to what it cannot bring to presence. The opposition between visible and invisible, at each stage of the mystical ascent, is fecund for Cusa insofar as it provides an impetus to the *investigatrix* and a clue to the way in which 'we better grasp the Inaccessible's greater distance from us the closer we come to [this] Inaccessibility'.[65] Cusa terms this demonstration of the impossibility of an encompassing vision or a consummating *ratio* of God a 'stratagem'.[66] By its means, we are 'elevated, as by a high tower, so that we may see'.[67] But this elevation or ascent does not yield a new visibility, but rather yields necessarily limits thereto. We see that we do not see, and then 'know that we don't know'.[68]

It is for this reason, I suggest, that Cusa argues that 'revelation falls short of savoring', of the immediacy of a taste or a touch.[69] Vision is the most exalted sense for Cusa insofar as it can attest not only to revelation as a re-vealing, but also and equally as a re-veiling. Vision, it seems, best positions presence in terms of absence. Vision does so, of course, in order that the 'visible image' be positioned through the 'invisible ground' thereof, the God 'whom none have ever seen' (Exod 33: 23).[70] The goal of all theological pursuit and comprehension is situated within Cusa's account precisely as that which is not, and cannot be, brought fully to sensible presence. The significance of sensibility is transformed by a negation and an absence. Vision, uniquely, presents the ingredience of invisibility within visibility, their co-presence and reciprocal determination within the spheres of sensible, symbolic and speculative experience. The spiritual significance of sensibility is, for this reason, positioned principally through the analogy of vision rather than the direct presence and consummated delight intimated by a *tactus* or a *sapor*. This latter significance is found neither in a

---

[64] *ADI* 9, trans. Hopkins, vol. I, p. 465.   [65] *ADI* 13, trans. Hopkins, vol. I, p. 468.

[66] *ADI* 14, trans. Hopkins, vol. I, p. 468.   [67] *ADI* 18, trans. Hopkins, vol. I, p. 472.

[68] *ADI* 18, trans. Hopkins, vol. I, p. 472.   [69] *DVD* XVII. 80, trans. Hopkins, vol. I, p. 716.

[70] With this deduction of a vision *that* we do not see, at each of the three levels of ascent, Cusa reports that he 'now sees the faith [the "evidence of things unseen" – Heb 11: 1] which the Catholic Church holds by revelation of the Apostles' to be neither paradox nor scandal. *DVD* XIV. 84, trans. Hopkins, vol. II, p. 84. Cusa hopes to make manifest a 'hidden truth', that '(1) a man cannot understand You who are Father except in Your Son, the Understandable One and Mediator'. *DVD* XIX. 86, trans. Hopkins, vol. II, p. 720. Only in the latter, 'as Son of God, [do] I see the Father', since 'a son cannot be seen *as* son unless the father is seen' and vice versa. The Father, of course, is seen precisely 'as' invisible, and 'through' the Son who reveals him. *DVD* XX. 89, trans. Hopkins, vol. II, p. 721.

synaesthetic plenitude as in Origen nor in the rejection thereof by Aquinas, but in the reception and transmutation of both into a novel theological aesthetic. Of course, the significance of this 'privilege' of vision could be personal as well as principled; it is not irrelevant that, in a letter to Gaspard Aindorffer, abbot of Tergensee, Cusa wrote: 'if I write or say something about [mystical union], it will be all the less sure in that I have never tasted the full sweetness of the Lord [i.e. had a personal mystical experience]'.[71]

Our conclusion, then, echoes the Preface of *De quaerendo Deum*, with which we began our analysis of Cusa. But whereas the latter began problematically, the former ends assertorically, no longer with Paul's problematic proclamation, but with its systematic explication.[72] Cusa began with the presupposition that 'to attempt to depict as visible You who are invisible' was a scandal and a paradox. He ends with the supposition that this attempt is not only possible, but necessary.[73] Cusa's early disclosure of God's essence and relation to us, the way in which *Deus absconditus* is equally *Deus revelatus*, may indeed, as some commentators have suggested, privilege the former hiddenness and invisibility. One may question Cusa's depiction of their relation in *De quaerendo Deum*. Cusa's most sustained reflections on the theological significance of sensibility and of vision are found only in the meditation on the icon of Christ in the middle-period *De visione Dei* and the still more dialectically determined later texts.[74] But even in

---

[71] For this citation, see Michel de Certeau, 'The Gaze: Nicholas of Cusa', *Diacritics*, 17.3 (Fall 1987), 2–38, at 25.

[72] *DQD* I. 17–18, and above.

[73] *DVD* XVII. 80, trans. Hopkins, vol. II, p. 717. See *De aequalitate*, 43–4 and 47–9 (trans. Hopkins, vol. II, pp. 862–6), for Cusa's most explicit depiction of the scriptural bases of his concern with visibility, and *De possest*, II (trans. Hopkins, vol. II, p. 914), for the Pauline sources. With Paul, Cusa would ask how 'the invisible things of Him from the creation of the world' can be 'clearly seen from the things that are made' (Rom 1: 20). Cusa would also ask with Paul, in a specifically Christological context, how we can understand 'the visible image of the invisible God' without either scandal or paradox (Col 1: 15–16; 1 Cor 2: 9–14). Cusa would provide, then, a theological account of Paul's vision *per speculum et in aenigmate*, in order that 'the eyes of your understanding be enlightened, so that you may know . . .' (Eph 1: 18). This account proceeds necessarily by means of and through an account of the nature and limits of vision. In its attempt to resolve these questions, *De quaerendo Deum* reveals Cusa's contribution to the history or development of theological aesthetics as such.

[74] *Compendium*, 9–15 and 20–28 can be appreciated in this context (trans. Hopkins, vol. II, pp. 1386–1419). In the middle and late periods of his work, Cusa will determine the interrelation between visible and invisible with increased dialectical precision. Regarding Cusa's development, Cranz, 'The Transmutation of Platonism in the Development of Nicolaus Cusanus and of Martin Luther', in *Nicolò Cusano agli inizi del mondo moderno*, pp. 73–102 argues that only in the 'late works beginning with the *De principio* of 1459 through the *De apice theoriae* of 1464' can one detect such a dialectical advance. For Cranz, only in *De non aliud* (1462) does Cusa bring to fruition 'that seeing, which I refer to God [and which] is the seeing of the invisible *in* the visible' (p. 93). Caramella, instead, sees this development 'già nel *De visione Dei*' of 1453, in which 'i valori dell'implicito e dell'esplicito', both in the context of sensible vision and with regard to 'i limiti della ratio',

Cusa's earliest attempts, one may recognize a real theological exigence and a genuine and consistent effort to determine the theological significance of sensibility.

CONCLUSION

In this chapter I have argued that two distinct aesthetics obtain within the basic structure of Cusa's work. I have suggested that Cusa synthesizes these aesthetic doctrines, Aristotelian and Origenist respectively. I have suggested that he first employed the Aristotelian doctrine of the *sensus communis* in order then to transcend its limits, and to arrive at the spirit, if not the letter, of the Origenist doctrine of the *sensus spiritualis*. Neither aesthetic, however, remained in its inherited form. Cusa's assimilation of Aristotelian psychology disallowed the position of a second, fivefold faculty for a parallel set of objects and properties. Nevertheless, this absence was as significant as a presence for the history of the doctrine: it reflects the way in which Cusa reformulates the Origenist construal of the theological significance of sensibility. By retaining, while recasting, the doctrine of the spiritual senses, Cusa offers an essential moment within the history of theological aesthetics.

are already fully articulate. See S. Caramella, 'Il problema di una logica trascendente nell'ultima fase del pensiero di Nicola Cusano', in *Nicolò Cusano agli inizi del mondo moderno*, pp. 367–74. See also W. Beierwaltes, '*Visio facialis* – Sehen ins Angesicht: Zur Coincidenz des endlichen und unendlichen Blicks bei Cusanus', in R. Haubst (ed.), *Das Sehen Gottes nach Nikolaus von Kues: Akten des Symposions in Trier vom 25. bis 27. September 1986, Mitteilungen und Forschungsbeiträge der Cusanus-Gesellschaft*, 18 (Trier: Paulinus-Verlag, 1989), pp. 91–118.

CHAPTER 13

Jonathan Edwards and his Puritan predecessors

William J. Wainwright

Jonathan Edwards is known for his insistence on a 'practical' or 'experimental' religion that engages the human heart. At its core is a sense of God's excellence and loveliness or the beauty and splendour of divine things.

The savingly converted enjoy 'gracious discoveries' of 'God, in some of his sweet and glorious attributes manifested in the Gospel, and shining forth in the face of Christ . . . In some the truth and certainty of the Gospel in general is the first joyful discovery they have . . . More frequently Christ . . . is made the object of the mind, in his all-sufficiency and willingness to save sinners.'[1] Recalling his own conversion, Edwards says:

The first instance that I remember . . . of that sort of inward, sweet delight in God and divine things that I have lived much in since, was on reading those words, 1 Tim. 1: 17. 'Now unto the King eternal, immortal, invisible, the only wise God, be honor and glory for ever and ever, Amen.' As I read the words, there came into my soul, and was as it were diffused through it, a sense of the glory of the divine being; a new sense, quite different from any thing I ever experienced before. Never any words of scripture seemed to me as these words did. I thought with myself, how excellent a Being that was; and how happy I should be, if I might enjoy that God, and be rapt up to God in heaven, and be as it were swallowed up in him.[2]

Some express their new experiences by the terms 'sight or discovery', others by 'a lively or feeling sense of heart'.[3] Both refer to a new understanding of spiritual notions. Those who have these experiences find that such phrases as 'a spiritual sight of Christ', 'faith in Christ', 'poverty of spirit' and so on had not previously conveyed 'those special and distinct ideas to their minds which they were intended to signify; in some respects

---

[1] Jonathan Edwards, *A Faithful Narrative of the Surprising Work of God, in the Conversion of Many Hundred Souls . . .* , ed. C. C. Goen, *The Great Awakening, The Works of Jonathan Edwards* (New Haven, CT: Yale University Press, 1957–), vol. IV, p. 171.
[2] Edwards, 'Personal Narrative', in *Letters and Personal Writings*, ed. G. S. Claghorn, *Works*, vol. XVI, p. 792.
[3] Edwards, *A Faithful Narrative*, pp. 171–2.

no more than the names of colors are to convey the ideas to one that is blind from birth'.[4]

Edwards's language was not new. That conversion involved the bestowal of a new spiritual sense was a Puritan commonplace. In what follows I shall argue that Puritans use 'sense of heart' in three different ways. It is often used for a feelingful conviction of gospel truths which carries no implication of direct or immediate cognitive contact with the divine. But its use more frequently reflects the conviction that a converted heart involves a direct cognitive contact with God or 'holy things'. There were at least two models for this. The first is a 'Platonic' model which construes the contact as the immediate intuition of a reason thought of as essentially having an affective dimension. The second model is sense-perception.

While it is often difficult to determine just which of these three senses is intended, I shall argue that John Smith rather clearly intended the second (a Platonic affect-laden intellectual intuition) while Edwards intended the third (a direct cognition modelled on sense-perception).

I shall also argue that Edwards's attempt to systematically model the spiritual senses on ordinary sense-perception is less successful than Smith's deployment of a Platonic model.[5]

PURITANS AND THE SPIRITUAL SENSES

Commenting on Philippians 1: 9 ('I pray that your love may abound more and more in knowledge and all judgment'), Thomas Brooks (*c*. 1608–1686) said that 'the Greek word that is here rendered *judgement* signifies sense, not a corporal, but a spiritual sense and taste, an inward experimental knowledge of holy and heavenly things', which he calls 'heart knowledge', and which, 'for Brooks . . . corresponds especially to the sense of taste, while "seeing" is associated with speculative knowledge. "It was not Adam's seeing, but his tasting of the forbidden fruit that made him miserable; and it is not your seeing of Christ, but your experimental tasting of Christ that will make you truly happy."'[6] Or consider Thomas Shepard (1605–1649), who said, 'Saints have an experimental knowledge of the work of Grace, by virtue of which they come to know it for a certainty . . . as by a

---

[4] *Ibid.* p. 174.
[5] Although because Edwards's failure is partly due to his acceptance of John Locke's influential analysis of sense-perception, it is at least abstractly possible that a more accurate analysis of sense-perception could provide the basis for a more adequate perceptual model of spiritual 'sensing'.
[6] B. Walton, *Jonathan Edwards*, Religious Affections *and the Puritan Analysis of True Piety, Spiritual Sensation, and Heart Religion* (Lewiston, NY, Queenston, Ont., and Lampeter: Edwin Mellen Press, 2002), pp. 101–2.

feeling heat, we know that the fire is hot; by tasting honey, we know it is sweet'.[7]

The Puritan's talk of spiritual senses should be placed in the context of devotional practices that were strikingly similar to those of contemporary Roman Catholics. According to Charles Hambrick-Stowe, the Puritans 'knew and used classic Catholic devotional works'. Among 'the most popular, judging from the number of editions were the works of St. Augustine, St. Bernard of Clairvaux' and 'Thomas a Kempis's . . . *The Imitation of Christ* . . . To a large extent, the Puritan devotional literature that blossomed in the early seventeenth century was modeled on earlier Roman Catholic devotional literature.' 'Continuity' also 'existed in the area of techniques . . . Most important was the use of the imagination and the senses in the exercise known as composition of place', that is, placing oneself within the scenes of the salvation story on which one is meditating. John Downame 'in his directions for the stages of meditation', for example, enjoins his readers 'to let [their] hearts [be] affected with a lively taste, sense, and feeling of the things whereon we meditate'.[8]

For Richard Baxter (1615–1691), meditation involved (1) using the sensory images of the scripture to visualize (as well as to imaginatively hear, smell and touch) divine things while at the same time recognizing the images' inadequacy, together with (2) a single-minded concentration on the excellences of heaven or other objects of meditation, with the penultimate aim of eliciting and strengthening holy thoughts, desires and feelings, and (as for other Puritans) the ultimate aim of achieving 'union with Christ, a union that was [typically] expressed in mystically erotic imagery from the Song of Songs and Jesus' parable of the ten virgins'.[9]

Regular times were set aside for meditation in a place 'free from company and noise' and from other distractions.[10] Baxter, for instance, admonishes his reader to

Get thy heart as clear from the world as thou canst. Wholly lay by the thoughts of thy business, troubles, enjoyments, and everything that may take up any room in thy soul. Get it as empty as thou possibly canst, that it may be the more capable of being filled with God . . . say to thy worldly business and thoughts, as Christ to his disciples, "Sit ye here, while I go and pray yonder."[11]

It is difficult to overemphasize the importance which Puritans placed on these spiritual practices. 'Regular secret prayer' was regarded as 'the

---

[7] *Ibid.* p. 98.   [8] *HS*, pp. 28–33 and 36.   [9] *HS*, p. 189.   [10] *HS*, p. 163.
[11] Richard Baxter, *The Saint's Everlasting Rest* (abridged) (New York: American Tract Society, 1840), reproduced online by the Christian Classics Ethereal Library, 1999, www.ccel.org/ccel/baxter/saints_rest.html, chap. xiii, p. 6 (accessed 15 December 2009).

primary and most necessary means' of grace. John Cotton (1585–1652), for example, argued that 'the end of preaching' was that one 'may learn to pray'.[12] Richard Baxter urged that meditation on heaven, that is, on 'the ravishing glory of saints, and the unspeakable excellencies of the God of glory, and the beams that stream from the face of his Son', is the 'duty by which all other duties are improved, and by which the soul digests truth for its nourishment and comfort'. Meditation of this sort involves 'the acting of all the powers of the soul', the will and the affections as well as the understanding. For

what the better had we been for odoriferous flowers, if we had no smell . . . or what pleasure should we have found in meats and drinks, without the sense of taste? So what good could all the glory of heaven have done us, or what pleasure should we have had in the perfection of God himself, if we had been without the affections of love and joy?.[13]

'Prayer brings us to communion with God.'[14] Thomas Shepard observed, 'I have seen God by reason and never been amazed at God . . . I have seen God himself [in prayer] and have been ravished to behold him.'[15] Cotton Mather (1663–1728) spoke of being 'inexpressibly irradiated from on high', of being 'exceedingly ravished', 'raised up into Heaven', of 'delights and raptures', and reported an experience in which he was transported 'into the Suburbs of Heaven', where he was filled with a 'Joy unspeakable and Full of Glory. I cannot utter, I may not utter the Communications of Heaven, whereto I have been this Day admitted: but this I will say, I have tasted that the Lord is gracious.'[16]

But while talk of spiritual senses is common, it is unclear how literally it was intended. In some cases it may simply refer to knowledge by acquaintance (with holiness, for instance, the 'things of God', or his gifts). When Thomas Goodwin (1600–1680) says that faith 'hath all senses annexed to it, and found in it . . . seeing, hearing, tasting, smelling, so faith conduceth to the discerning of things spiritual, which are not taken by reason only, but by a spiritual sense joined thereunto', he seems principally concerned to distinguish speculative knowledge of divine things from an 'experimental' or 'acquired knowledge in matters spiritual, founded on . . . a collection of conclusions from what we have sense of, as all artists gather conclusions from experiments made'. For example, the saints 'come to have experience with hope or assurance from the love of God shed, not manifested or apprehended by knowledge so much as shed, whereof the subject is said

---

[12] *HS*, p. 177.　　[13] Baxter, *The Saint's Everlasting Rest*, chap. xiii, pp. 1–2.
[14] *HS*, p. 179.　　[15] *HS*, p. 179.　　[16] *HS*, p. 285.

to be in the heart rather than the understanding'.[17] Goodwin's language suggests that, in this case at least, the spiritual senses are metaphors for a deeply affective knowledge by acquaintance.

What kind of acquaintance, though? Our authors' language sometimes rather strongly suggests that the most appropriate model is ordinary sense-knowledge. Thus Richard Sibbes (1577–1635) asserts that 'the spiritual life of a Christian is furnished with spiritual senses. He hath a spiritual eye and a spiritual taste to relish spiritual things, and a spiritual ear to judge of holy things, and a spiritual feeling. As everyday life, so this excellent life hath senses and motions suitable to it.' The unconverted lack 'spiritual senses; as Saint Austin saith of men that complain that they do not taste and relish these things. Surely, saieth he, thou wants a spiritual palate to taste these things.'[18] Or consider the Puritan mystic Francis Rous (1579–1659):

After we have tasted those heavenly things . . . from this taste there ariseth a new, but a true, lively, and experimental knowledge of the things so tasted . . . For even in natural fruits there are certain relishes . . . which nothing but the tast it self can truly represent and shew to us. The West-Indian Piney [pineapple] cannot be so expressed in words, even by him that hath tasted it, that he can deliver over the true shape and character of that taste to another that hath not tasted it.[19]

On the other hand, while John Preston (1587–1628) and John Owen (1616–1683) also employ the language of the spiritual senses, it is not clear that either intends more than an affective *intellectual* understanding or intuition of divine things. (These are not equivalent. An intellectual intuition entails direct or immediate cognitive contact. Intellectual understanding or grasp as such does not.) Thus Preston distinguishes between 'a teaching by men, and a teaching by God; that is when God shall enable a man to see things in good earnest, otherwise it will be but as a man sees things when his mind is upon another matter: so we shall see, and not see . . . you may hear oft enough of these things, but your hearts will be minding other matters [such as your] profits [or] pleasures'. When the Spirit 'presents' divine things to us, however, 'he draweth the heart from minding other things, to seek after Christ, to long after him, and not to' be content until it is 'united to him'.[20]

Or consider Owen, who identifies the heart with the soul's governing 'bias' or 'inclination', the principle or ground of all its 'moral operations'.[21]

[17] Walton, *Jonathan Edwards*, pp. 90–1. [18] *Ibid.* p. 198.
[19] Quoted in G. Nuttall, *The Holy Spirit in Puritan Faith and Experience* (Chicago and London: University of Chicago Press, 1992), p. 139.
[20] Walton, *Jonathan Edwards*, pp. 201–2. [21] *Ibid.* p. 108.

Its importance can not be overestimated, for 'the great contest of heaven and earth is about the affections of the poor worm which we call man'. The 'recovery' of our affections towards God is the 'chief design' of his 'effectual grace', and the basis of any proper understanding of divine things.[22] 'A spiritual light into, and discovery of the revelation and declaration made in the gospel' of God's love in Christ 'is not a mere assent unto the truth of the revelation or authority of the revealer' but 'a spiritual discerning, perception, and understanding of the things themselves revealed and declared . . . a spiritual sense of [their] power, glory, and beauty'.[23]

Owen is by no means averse to the language of the senses: spiritual discernment involves

a complacency of mind, from that gust, relish and savour, which it finds in spiritual things, from their suitableness unto its [the soul's] constitution, inclinations and desires. There is a salt in spiritual things, whereby they are conditioned and made savoury unto a renewed mind, though to others, they are as the white of an egg that hath no taste or savour in it. In this gust and relish lies the sweetness and satisfaction of spiritual life.

By contrast, 'speculative notions about spiritual things, when they are alone, are dry, sapless and barren. In this gust we taste by experience that God is gracious, and that the love of Christ is better than wine, or whatever else hath the most grateful relish unto a sensual appetite'.[24]

When placed in the context of his thought as a whole, however, Owen's talk of the spiritual senses is arguably a metaphor for an affect-laden intellectual insight or intuition: 'The true nature of saving illumination consists in this, that it gives the mind such a direct intuitive insight and prospect into spiritual things as that, in their own spiritual nature, they suit, please and satisfy it, so that it is transformed into them, cast into the mould of them, and rests in them'.[25] We must therefore 'labor to possess the mind with the beauty and excellency of spiritual things, that so they be presented lovely and desirable to the soul'. For these excellencies 'have an infinite beauty, goodness, and amiableness in them, which are powerfully attractive to spiritual affections, and which alone are able to fill them, to satisfy them, to give them rest and aquiescency'.[26]

I believe that John Smith's talk of the spiritual senses should also be understood in this way. Merely 'historical' or intellectual knowledge of

---

[22] *Ibid.* p. 113.
[23] J. Owen, *Gospel Grounds and Evidences of the Faith of God's Elect* [1695], electronic resource http://biblestudy.churches.net/CCEL/O/OWEN/FAITH/FAITH.TXT, p. 11 (accessed 15 December 2009).
[24] Walton, *Jonathan Edwards*, pp. 111–13. [25] *Ibid.* p. 202. [26] *Ibid.* pp. 204–5.

divine things is insufficient. 'We must not think we have ... attained to
the right knowledge of truth, when we have broke through the outward
shell of words and phrases that house it up; or when by a logical analysis
we have found out the dependencies and coherencies of them one with
another'; or when we have succeeded in guarding it 'with the ... strength
of our demonstration[s]' against those who would challenge it.[27] 'The best
and truest knowledge of God' is not that 'wrought out by the labor and
sweat of the brain but', rather, 'that which is kindled within us by an
heavenly warmth in our hearts', that is, by love of the good.[28]

Smith is no more averse to employing the language of the spiritual
senses than Owen. He speaks, for example, of 'the senses of the soul', and
with Plotinus of an 'intellectual touch' of God, and says that 'the soul it
self hath its sense as well as the body'.[29] 'There is', he says, 'an inward
sweetness and deliciousness in divine truth, which no sensual mind can
taste or relish ... Divinity is not so well perceived by a subtle wit ... as by
a purified sense, as Plotinus phraseth it'.[30]

Smith's spiritual sensation is best thought of as an *intellectual* intuition,
though, an act of 'that *reason* that is within us'.[31]

We must shut the eyes of sense, and open that brighter eye of the *understanding*,
that other eye of the soul, as the philosopher calls our *intellectual faculty* ... the
light of the divine world will then begin to fall upon us ... and in God's own light
shall we behold him. The fruit of this knowledge will be sweet to our taste, and
pleasant to our palates ... How sweet and delicious that truth is which holy and
heaven-born souls feed upon in their mysterious converses with the Deity, who
can tell but they that taste it. When *reason* once is raised by the mighty force of the
Divine Spirit into a converse with God, it is turned into sense ... whereas before
we conversed with him only ... with our discursive faculty ... combating with
difficulties, and sharp contests of divers opinions, and laboring ... in its deductions
of one thing from another; we shall then fasten our minds on him ... with such a
serene *understanding* ... such an *intellectual* calmness and serenity, as will present
us with a blissful, steady, and invariable sight of him. [What] before was only
faith ... now becomes vision.[32]

But if Smith's 'spiritual sensation' *is* best thought of as intellectual intuition, why employ the language of the physical senses? Partly because it
was traditional. But also because our ordinary senses are apt metaphors
for the intuition's directness or immediacy and affective overtones. Other
analogies are at least as apt, however. The spiritual cognition's directness,
for example, is strikingly similar to our immediate recognition of the

[27] John Smith, SD, p. 8, spelling and capitalization modernized.   [28] SD, p. 3.
[29] SD, pp. 5, 3.   [30] SD, p. 15.   [31] SD, p. 15, my italics.   [32] SD, pp. 15–16, my italics.

prima facie rightness of an instance of justice or kindness on a view like W. D. Ross's, or our immediate acquaintance with numbers, universals, values and other so-called 'Platonic' entities. Nor are intellectual intuitions always affectless. Kant's respect for the moral law is the affective resonance of the recognition of its obligatoriness in rational beings with inclinations, while Platonists think that reason itself has an affective dimension. Knowing the good involves loving it, delighting in it and putting it into practice – a view which Smith shares.[33]

JONATHAN EDWARDS AND THE SPIRITUAL SENSATION

Edwards's language was not new. What was new was his attempt to provide a philosophically sophisticated and illuminating articulation of Puritan ideas about the spiritual senses that would remove some of the unclarity we've uncovered in the first section by explicitly modelling the new spiritual sensation(s) on ordinary sense-knowledge rather than on an intellectual insight or intuition.

The objects of a sense or feeling of the heart are (1) 'actual [i.e. lively, clear and distinct] ideas', (2) of things pertaining to the will or affections, (3) that involve a 'feeling of sweetness or pleasure, bitterness or pains'. They include (the ideas of) (1) 'beauty and deformity', 'good or evil', as well as 'excellency', 'value', 'importance' and their opposites, (2) delight and pleasure, and pain and misery, (3) affective and conative attitudes, dispositions and states ('desires and longings, esteem . . . hope, fear, contempt, choosing, refusing . . . loving, hating, anger'), (4) 'dignity', 'terrible greatness, or awful majesty', 'meanness or contemptibleness' and so on and (5) the non-evaluative characteristics on which beauty and deformity, pleasure and pain, and attributes like dignity or majesty depend.[34] The object of a sense or feeling of the heart is, in essence, good and evil, and what pertains to them. Natural good or evil is 'good or evil', which is agreeable or disagreeable to 'human nature as such'. Spiritual good or evil is what is agreeable or disagreeable to people with 'spiritual frames', that is, those

---

[33] *SD*, p. 20: 'Intellectual life, as [the Platonists] phrase it' is a non-discursive 'knowledge . . . [that] is always pregnant with divine virtue, which ariseth out of an happy union of souls with God, and is nothing else but a living imitation of a Godlike perfection drawn out by a strong fervent love of it. This divine knowledge . . . makes us amorous of Divine beauty . . . and this divine love and purity, reciprocally exalts divine knowledge.'

[34] Why regard these as objects of a sense or feeling of the heart? Presumably because a perception of beauty or importance involves a perception of the non-evaluative features on which beauty or importance depend, or because one cannot fully grasp or understand the nonevaluative properties without perceiving their beauty or importance, or both.

who, because the Spirit dwells within them, love being in general (i.e., God and the beings that derive from him, are absolutely dependent on him, and reflect him).[35]

The direct or 'immediate object of this spiritual sense' is 'the beauty of holiness',[36] 'true moral or spiritual beauty'[37] – a 'new simple idea' that cannot be produced by the 'exalting, varying, or compounding of that kind of perceptions or sensations which the mind had before'.[38] However, the spiritual sense also has an *indirect* object – spiritual facts or truths. There are two cases to consider.

In the first, the spiritual sense enables us to recognize the truth of propositions that are logically or epistemically related to the excellency of divine things. For example: our apprehension of Christ's beauty and excellency produces a conviction of his sufficiency as a mediator.[39] To grasp the appropriateness of God's end in creation, namely, the communication of his glory *ad extra*, one must perceive its beauty. Again, one must see the beauty of holiness to appreciate the 'hatefulness of sin'[40] and thus be convinced of the justice of divine punishment and our inability to make satisfaction.[41] The spiritual sense, then, enables us to grasp the truth of a number of important doctrines.

But it also helps us grasp the truth of the gospel scheme as a whole.[42] A conviction of the gospel's truth is an inference from the beauty or excellency of what it depicts, namely, 'God and Jesus Christ . . . the work of redemption and the ways and works of God'.[43] 'There is a divine and superlative glory in these things' that distinguishes 'them from all that is earthly and temporal',[44] and a spiritual person 'truly sees' this glory:[45] his perception of it is as immediate and direct as a perception of colour or the sweetness of food.[46] (This was not, of course, a new idea. Richard Sibbes, for instance, said, 'God . . . causeth him to see a divine majesty shining forth in the scriptures, so that there must be an infused establishing by the Spirit to settle the heart in this first principle . . . that the Scriptures are the word of God'. Or again, 'How do you know the word to be the word? It carrieth proof and evidence in itself. It is an evidence that the fire is hot to him that feeleth it, and that the sun shineth to him that looks on it; how

[35] Edwards, *Miscellany*, 782, in *The 'Miscellanies' 501–832*, ed. A. Chamberlain, *Works*, vol. XVIII, pp. 458–63.
[36] Edwards, *RA*, p. 260.   [37] Edwards, *TV*, p. 548.   [38] *RA*, p. 205.
[39] *Miscellany*, 782; *RA*, pp. 272, 302.   [40] *RA*, pp. 274, 301.
[41] *RA*, p. 302.   [42] *RA*, pp. 291–2.
[43] Edwards, 'A Divine and Supernatural Light', in *Sermons and Discourses, 1730–1733*, ed. M. Valerie, *Works*, vol. XVII, p. 413.
[44] *Ibid.* p. 413.   [45] *RA*, p. 298.   [46] 'A Divine and Supernatural Light', p. 422.

much more doth the word . . . I am sure I felt it, it warmed my heart, and converted me.'[47])

A conviction of the gospel's truth is thus 'an effect and natural consequence of this perception'.[48] The perception and conviction are nonetheless distinct. The mind *infers* the truth and reality of the things depicted in the gospel from its *perception* of their spiritual beauty. There is, however, no 'long chain of arguments; the argument is but one, and the evidence direct; the mind ascends to the truth of the gospel but by one step, and that is its divine glory'.[49] And because only one step is involved, we can truly say that the divinity or reality or truth of the gospel is 'as it were' known intuitively, that 'a soul may have a kind of intuitive knowledge of the divinity [or truth or reality] of the things exhibited in the gospel'.[50]

The mind's object differs in the two cases, however. In the first, it is a comparatively specific doctrinal proposition that is logically or epistemically connected with other propositions that affirm that some person or characteristic or activity or state of affairs is truly amiable or beautiful or excellent. Our spiritual sense enables us to *perceive* the truth of the latter, and from this we *infer* the truth of the former. In the second, the mind's object is the content of the gospel as a whole – what Paul Ricoeur has called 'the world of the text'. The central or controlling features of this world – God, Christ and the scheme of salvation – are *perceived* to be truly beautiful. On the basis of this perception one immediately concludes that the biblical world is not fictional like those depicted in *The Brothers Karamazov* or *Moby-Dick*, but *real*.

If my interpretation is correct, the new spiritual sense does not typically involve a direct or immediate or quasi-perceptual awareness of God himself. Rather, God's reality is *inferred* from the excellency and beauty of the things depicted in scripture. But as we have just seen, the inference 'is without any long chain of arguments; the argument is but one, and the evidence direct'. Because of the inference's spontaneity and immediacy, a person can even be said to have 'a kind of intuitive knowledge' of divinity.[51] Edwards's interpretation of the redeemed's knowledge of God's reality is thus strikingly similar to Descartes's and Locke's account of our knowledge of other minds and physical objects. While other minds and physical objects are not directly perceived on their view, their reality *is* spontaneously and immediately inferred from sensations or impressions that *are* directly apprehended. Edwards thinks our knowledge of God is

---

[47] Nuttall, *The Holy Spirit*, pp. 23, 29.　　[48] 'A Divine and Supernatural Light', p. 413.
[49] *RA*, pp. 298–9.　　[50] *RA*, p. 298.　　[51] *RA*, p. 298.

similar. Even though God is not *directly* perceived, his reality is no more remote or uncertain than other minds or physical objects are on views like Descartes's and Locke's.

But what *kind* of idea is the idea of true beauty? There is textual evidence for the claim that Edwards identified true beauty with the delight or pleasure which holy things evoke in people with spiritual 'frames' or 'tempers', or with the tendency of holy things to evoke this pleasure in the savingly converted. There is also evidence for the claim that he identified true beauty with a love of being in general, the consent of being to being in which holiness consists. Both views appear incompatible with some of Edwards's other positions. The first seems inconsistent with his belief that the apprehension of beauty is a 'perception' of something existing 'without' the mind,[52] while the second is inconsistent with his conviction that beauty is a simple idea. Can a coherent position be constructed from Edwards's remarks?

He may have been driving at this: beauty is identical with benevolence or agreement in somewhat the same way in which water is identical with H_2O or in which (according to physicalism) consciousness is identical with certain arrangements of matter. But benevolence is also the objective or 'physical' basis of a dispositional property, the tendency to produce a new simple idea in those with converted hearts. The new idea is a delight or pleasure in being's consent to being which somehow 'represents' or is a 'perception of' it.

On this interpretation, the idea of true beauty resembles Locke's ideas of primary and secondary qualities. Spiritual delight is, in Locke's words, a simple 'sensation or perception in our understanding' like our ideas of colour or solidity.[53] The dispositional property is what Locke calls a 'quality', a 'power to produce those ideas in us'.[54] Benevolence is the objective configuration underlying this power and corresponds to the microstructure of bodies that underlie their tendency to excite ideas of primary and

---

[52] The philosophers who most influenced Edwards (Locke and the Cartesians) denied that ideas of pleasure and pain tell us anything about the nature of the objects that produce them. See John Locke, *HU*, pp. 2, 8. See also Francis Hutcheson, who says that moral approbation (i.e. the disinterested delight in morally good dispositions and actions) 'cannot be supposed an image of anything external, more than the pleasures of harmony, of taste, of smell'. *Illustrations on the Moral Sense* (Cambridge, MA: Harvard University Press, 1971), p. 164. The idea of true beauty does. Edwards explicitly rejects the suggestion that 'the idea we obtain by this spiritual sense could in no respect be said to be a knowledge or perception of anything besides what was in our own mind', or that it is 'no representation of anything without'. On the contrary, the idea of spiritual beauty is 'the representation and image of the moral perfection and excellency of the Divine being . . . of which we could have no true idea without it'. *TV*, pp. 622–3.
[53] Locke, *HU* II. 8. 8.   [54] *HU* II. 8. 8.

secondary qualities in minds like ours. Like simple ideas of primary and secondary qualities, the new spiritual sensation 'represents' or is a 'perception' of its object. Just as 'extension' or 'red' can refer to the idea, the power or the physical configuration that is the base of the power, so 'beauty' can refer to the sensation, to the relevant dispositional property or to benevolence.[55]

Why does Edwards speak of the new cognition as a kind of *perception* or *sensation*? Partly of course because Puritans commonly did so. But while Edwards may have been indebted to his predecessors for the *idea* of a spiritual sensation, his development of it was strongly influenced by empiricists such as Locke and (probably) Francis Hutcheson.

The object of the spiritual sense is a new simple idea, and Edwards shared Locke's conviction that simple ideas come 'from experience'.[56] As Hutcheson said, 'reasoning or intellect seems to raise no new species of ideas but [only] to discover or discern the relation of' ideas 'received by some immediate powers of perception internal or external which we may call sense'.[57]

Spiritual understanding also involves a kind of relish or delight, and Edwards follows Locke and Hutcheson in thinking that being pleased or pained, like a feeling of tactual pressure or being appeared to redly, is a kind of sensation or perception. All three believe that pleasure and pain are simple ideas.

Then again, the new simple idea occurs involuntarily, and Edwards associated sensation with passivity.[58] This too was a commonplace. For example, Hutcheson said that a sense is 'a determination of the mind to receive any idea from the presence of an object...independent on our will'.[59]

Finally, the mind's apprehension of true or spiritual beauty is immediate (non-inferential). As Edwards says, 'this manner of being affected with the' beauty of a thing 'depends not...on any reasonings...but on the frame

---

[55] Does the idea of beauty not only 'represent' but also 'resemble' its object, as Locke's ideas of extension, figure and motion 'resemble' the objective configurations that cause them? Edwards never explicitly says it does. (That the idea is a 'perception' of 'something without' only distinguishes it from ideas of tertiary qualities such as pleasure or pain.) In calling it 'knowledge', however, and in insisting that we can have no true idea of its object without it, Edwards implies that the idea *accurately* represents (some aspect of) its object. This suggests that the idea of beauty should be assimilated to Locke's ideas of primary qualities.

[56] *HU* II. I. 2.   [57] Hutcheson, *Illustrations*, p. 135.

[58] Cf. Edwards, 'Subjects to be Handled in the Treatise on the Mind', no. 29, in *Scientific and Philosophical Writings*, ed. W. E. Anderson, *Works*, vol. VI, p. 390.

[59] Francis Hutcheson, *An Inquiry into the Original of our Ideas of Beauty and Virtue* (London: 1725), II. I. I.

of our minds whereby they are so made that' as soon as we perceive or cognize it, it 'appears beautiful'.[60] A comparison with Hutcheson is again instructive, for Hutcheson argued that the power of receiving the idea of beauty should be called a 'sense' because 'we are struck at the first with the beauty'.[61]

It is thus clear *why* Edwards speaks of the new cognition as a perception or sensation. Whether he *should* have done so is another matter.

The third and fourth considerations are far from decisive. Our sensations (and the beliefs directly based on them) appear involuntary and immediate, but so too does our recognition of the fact that $2 + 2 = 4$. Passivity and immediacy are not peculiar to ideas derived from (internal or external) sensation.

The first two considerations carry more weight. Locke and Hutcheson identify reason with reasoning. Reason is sharply distinguished from the will and its affections and from the senses. Its sole function is to manipulate ideas received from other sources. Edwards sometimes indicates that he shares these views.[62] Reason does not have an affective dimension and is not the source of new simple ideas. The cognition of true beauty, on the other hand, has an affective dimension since it involves relish or delight, and its object is a new simple idea. Spiritual cognition must therefore be construed as a kind of sensation or perception.

Edwards's account of spiritual perception is subject to some of the same difficulties as Locke's account of sense-perception.[63] Is it in any way *less* satisfactory? It may be in one respect. If I am right, the idea of true beauty is both a kind of delight or relish *and* an apparent cognition. Can something be both? It is not sufficient to argue that perceptions of objectively real value properties can be inherently affective (and thus pleasurable or painful), for Edwards does not think of pleasure and pain in this way. Pleasures and pains in his (and Locke's and Hutcheson's) view are not qualities or affective dimensions of more complex experiences. They are discrete internal sensations. But if spiritual pleasure *is* a kind of internal thrill or delight, how can it *also* be a true 'representation' of something existing 'without'?[64] Ordinary pleasures and pains differ from visual or auditory

[60] *TV*, p. 619.   [61] Hutcheson, *Inquiry*, II. 1. 12.

[62] 'If we take reason strictly – not for the faculty of mental perception in general [which would include sense-perception], but for ratiocination . . . the perceiving of spiritual beauty and excellency no more belongs to reason, than it belongs to the sense of feeling to perceive colors . . . Reason's work is to perceive truth and not excellency' ('A Divine and Supernatural Light', p. 422).

[63] It is not clear that the mind's immediate objects are ideas, how they represent or resemble their objects, and so on.

[64] *TV*, pp. 622–3.

impressions in lacking what Berkeley called 'outness;' they do not seem to point beyond themselves. Either spiritual pleasure is radically unlike ordinary pleasure in this respect, or it is not an apparent cognition.

The final chapter of *The Nature of True Virtue* implicitly addresses this issue by attempting to show that 'the frame of mind, or inward sense... whereby the mind is disposed to' relish true virtue for its spiritual beauty is not 'given arbitrarily' but agrees 'with the necessary nature of things'.[65] But the 'frame of mind' that disposes a person to delight in true beauty (i.e. to be pleased with benevolence) is benevolence itself. Edwards thinks that it will therefore be sufficient to show that *benevolence* agrees with the nature of things.

Edwards's strategy, in other words, is this. True benevolence is the 'mechanism' underlying the new spiritual sense. If we can show that benevolence has a foundation in the nature of things, we can conclude that the spiritual sense, too, is aligned with reality. Edwards's task, then, is to prove that benevolence agrees with the 'necessary nature of things', and he offers four arguments to show that it does.[66] They vary in their persuasiveness, however, and a more convincing argument can be derived from his doctrine of the indwelling of the Holy Spirit.

Like his medieval and Reform predecessors, Edwards thinks that God is present to his creatures in virtue of his knowledge, causal activity and substance. Yet because he is an occasionalist like Malebranche, an idealist like Berkeley and a mental phenomenalist like Hume, God's presence is more intimate on Edwards's view than on more traditional accounts. What are 'vulgarly' called causal relations are mere constant conjunctions. True causes necessitate their effects. Because God's will alone meets this condition, God is the only true cause. He is also the only true substance. Physical objects are collections of 'corporeal ideas' (ideas of colour, for example, or solidity, resistance and so on). Minds are series of 'thoughts' or 'perceptions'. Now any substance underlying perceptions, thoughts and corporeal ideas would be something that 'subsisted by itself, and stood underneath, and kept up' mental and physical properties. But God alone subsists by himself, and stands underneath and keeps up thoughts, perceptions, solidity, colour and other corporeal qualities (ideas). 'The substance of [minds and] bodies', therefore, is 'either nothing, or nothing but the Deity acting in that particular manner... where he thinks fit.' The only real cause and

---

[65] *TV*, p. 620.
[66] For a discussion of these arguments, see my *Reason and the Heart* (Ithaca, NY: Cornell University Press, 1995), pp. 34–8.

the only real substance are thus God himself. 'How truly, then is it in him that we live, move, and have our being.'[67]

God's relation to his elect is even more intimate, however. The Holy Spirit 'dwells' in the saints 'as a vital principle in their souls [and] there produces those effects wherein he exerts and communicates himself *in his own proper nature*'.[68] 'True saving grace is no other than the very love of God; *that is, God in one of the persons of the Trinity*, uniting himself to the soul of a creature as a vital principle, dwelling there and exerting himself by the faculties of the soul of man, in his own proper nature, after the manner of a principle of nature.' The saints are thus 'not only partakers of a nature that may in some sense be called Divine, because "tis conformed to the nature of God; *but the very Deity does in some sense dwell in them.*'[69] (There were Puritan precedents for this. Calling 'attention to Paul's emphatic "The Spirit itself" or "the Spirit himself, *auto to pneuma*"', Samuel Petto says, 'if it were only *to pneuma* . . . it might be by a proxie, gifts and graces; but seeing it is *auto to pneuma*, the Spirit himself, this argueth it to be a peculiar work of the Spirit, requiring its own more immediate presence.' And Baxter claims that 'the Spirit itself is given to true believers, and not only grace from the Spirit . . . The Spirit itself is present as the immediate Operator: not so immediate as to be without means [e.g. preaching, scripture, feelings of love and consolation, etc. (?)], but so immediate as to be no distant agent, but by proximate attingency . . . performeth his operations.'[70])

Edwards is making two claims. First, the new spiritual disposition and tastes which God bestows on the soul are divine. The difference between God's love and joy and the love and the joy that he bestows on his saints is a difference of degree, not of nature or kind. Second, God does not act on the soul from without, but dwells within it, 'as a principle of new nature', living, acting and exerting itself in the exercise of the soul's faculties. The 'mechanism' underlying the new spiritual sense thus ultimately turns

[67] Jonathan Edwards, 'Of Atoms', *Works*, vol. VI, pp. 215–16. While Edwards is explicitly discussing God's relation to corporeal qualities, he clearly thinks that similar considerations show that God is also the only substance underlying mental qualities.

[68] *RA*, p. 201, my italics.

[69] Edwards, *Treatise on Grace*, in *Writings on the Trinity, Grace, and Faith*, ed. S. H. Lee, *Works*, vol. XXI, p. 194, my italics. Cf. *Discourse on the Trinity*, *Works*, vol. XXI, p. 124, where Edwards says that in communicating 'divine love to the creature . . . God's spirit or love doth but communicate of itself. *'Tis the same love*, so far as a creature is capable of being made partaker of it.' My italics.

[70] Nuttall, *The Holy Spirit*, pp. 49–50.

out to be God himself. Hence, since God in some sense *is* reality or being itself,[71] it follows that the spiritual sense is necessarily aligned with reality.[72]

Another problem is not so easily overcome, however. That spiritual cognition is best thought of as a kind of sensation or perception (on the model of sensory seeing, hearing, tasting and the like) seems inconsistent with other aspects of Edwards's position. A number of Hutcheson's critics took exception to his moral sense theory because they believed that (1) at least some moral propositions are necessarily true, and that (2) necessary truths are discerned by reason.[73] Hutcheson maintained that the moral sense grasps the goodness of benevolent actions and dispositions, that is, perceives that benevolence is (morally) good. His critics objected that 'benevolence is good' is *necessarily* true and that necessary truths are apprehended by *reason*, not sense. It is therefore significant that Edwards, too, apparently believed that basic moral truths are necessary.[74] Nor is he likely to have thought that the connection between benevolent actions and dispositions and spiritual beauty is only contingent – that holiness or benevolence might not have been truly beautiful. But if 'holiness is beautiful' *is* necessarily true, Edwards seems committed to the implausible view that our knowledge of at least some necessary truths is derived from a sense, that is, that some necessary truths are perceived by a kind of sensation.

One *may* be able to apprehend the redness of a table without apprehending *that* the table is red. (Perhaps animals and infants do.) But *can* one apprehend the moral goodness of a benevolent action without apprehending *that* the action is morally good or apprehend its spiritual beauty without apprehending *that* it is truly beautiful? Not clearly. The idea of beauty derives from experience in the sense that one acquires it by encountering beautiful objects. But the idea of beauty does not seem to be a discrete feeling or sensation (like a feeling of sexual pleasure or a raw sensation of redness) that is *first* received from experience and *then* incorporated

---

[71] God 'is in effect being in general': *TV*, p. 621. Since God is the only true substance and the only true cause, created beings are no more than God's 'shadows' or 'images', absolutely and immediately dependent on him for both their being and their qualities.

[72] For some difficulties in this solution see my 'Jonathan Edwards, God, and "Particular Minds"', in the fortieth anniversary issue of the *International Journal for Philosophy of Religion*, 68.1 (2010), 201–13.

[73] See, e.g., the correspondence between Hutcheson and Gilbert Burnet.

[74] Edwards clearly thinks that at least some moral truths are necessary. See *Freedom of the Will*, ed. P. Ramsey, *Works*, vol. I, p. 153. Edwards's example is: 'It is . . . fit and suitable, that men should do to others, as they would that they should do to them.' It is worth observing that Locke, too, thinks that basic moral truths are necessary. See *HU* III. II. 15–18; IV. 3. 18–20; and IV. 4. 7–10.

in a judgement. On the contrary, receiving the idea of beauty appears to *be* judging that what one is contemplating is beautiful. Edwards seems committed to claiming that this judgement if true is necessarily true. If it is, then it is doubtful that one should speak of apprehending a thing's beauty as a kind of internal or external *sensing*.

One could avoid this problem as well as one raised earlier if one were to interpret spiritual cognition as an intellectual intuition with affective overtones in the manner of Smith. A view like Smith's sidesteps two of the most pressing problems confronting Edwards – how a feeling of delight can also be an apparent cognition and how a necessary truth can be grasped by a kind of sensation. It sidesteps them because (1) on Smith's view, the 'sensation' or 'feeling' is not the cognition itself but, rather, its accompaniment or (better) its affective dimension or resonance, and because (2) there is no mystery in necessary truths[75] being objects of intellectual intuition.

The Puritans' talk of spiritual senses sometimes seems to be a metaphor for nothing more than a deeply feelingful conviction of gospel truths. On the whole, however, the Puritans clearly want to say more – that the spiritual senses are new cognitive faculties involving a direct cognitive acquaintance with spiritual realities. Edwards, though, implicitly recognized that in a sceptical age claims like these need defending, and proceeded to do so by showing that the new spiritual sense has as much right to be regarded as a cognitive faculty as ordinary sense-perception. I have argued that Edwards's attempt is unsuccessful, and that a more promising model can be found in John Smith.

Smith's implicit solution of the problem should have been a live option for Edwards. For Edwards belonged to a Puritan tradition that contained an important Platonic strand, and was himself influenced by Henry More, Ralph Cudworth and John Smith. But Edwards's commitment to empiricism precluded this solution. Philosophers like Locke identified reason with ratiocination and insisted that simple ideas originate in experience (internal or external sensation). Because Edwards accepted these theses, he could not construe spiritual cognitions as rational intuitions. Whether they are essential to his overall epistemology, however, is doubtful.[76]

---

[75] For example, those of logic, mathematics or morality.

[76] For one thing, as John E. Smith and others have pointed out, the line between will or affections on the one hand and understanding on the other is more flexible in Edwards than in Locke or Hutcheson.

CHAPTER 14

John Wesley

Mark T. Mealey

As the other chapters of this collection attest, the language of spiritual sensation has a wide range of expressions and a variety of possible references. John Wesley explicitly recognizes this idiom in patristic, medieval, Reformation and early modern sources.[1] Consider Wesley's sprawling anthology, *A Christian Library*, which includes writings from dozens of authors employing this language.[2] Among others, he includes the pseudo-Macarian *Homilies*, Pascal's *Pensées* and many examples from seventeenth-century Puritan and Anglican authors, including John Smith, Henry Scougal, William Beveridge, Richard Baxter and John Owen. The language of spiritual sensation serves diverse theologies in these various sources; in some cases such language refers to the act of the mind contemplating spiritual truths or grasping the true sense of the scriptures; in some cases it refers to intention, love or affect in the soul that longs for God; in some cases it seems to refer to a capacity distinct from natural reason or affect. Elsewhere Wesley cites Origen and Augustine on the spiritual senses, but he also comments on his contemporary Francis Hutcheson, who proposes a separate moral sense and aesthetic sense. He translates Moravian hymns that are soaked in the language of spiritual sensation and he publishes his own abridgement of Jonathan Edwards's *Treatise Concerning Religious Affections*. The diversity of this partial list of the tradition of spiritual sensation with which he had contact underlines the need to understand Wesley on his own terms. Nevertheless, it is clear that his understanding of spiritual sensation is shaped by this tradition.

---

[1] For a discussion of Wesley's contact with the tradition of spiritual sensation, see M. T. Mealey, 'Taste and See that the Lord is Good: John Wesley in the Christian Tradition of Spiritual Sensation', Ph.D. diss., University of St Michael's College, Toronto, 2006, pp. 20–49.

[2] John Wesley (ed.), *A Christian Library: Consisting of Extracts from and Abridgments of the Choicest Pieces of Practical Divinity which have been Published in the English Tongue*, 50 vols. (Bristol: Farley, 1749–55).

In an important early theological essay, his *Earnest Appeal to Men of Reason and Religion*, Wesley sets out an explicit account of a theological category of spiritual sensation:

Now faith (supposing the Scripture to be of God) is πραγμάτων ἔλεγχος οὐ βλεπομένων, 'the demonstrative evidence of things unseen', the supernatural evidence of things invisible, not perceivable by eyes of flesh, or by any of our natural senses or faculties. Faith is that divine evidence whereby the spiritual man discerneth God, and the things of God. It is with regard to the spiritual world, what sense is with regard to the natural. It is the spiritual sensation of every soul that is born of God.[3]

Faith, according to the scriptural account, is the eye of the new-born soul. Hereby every true believer in God 'seeth him who is invisible'. Hereby (in a more particular manner, since life and immortality have been brought to light by the gospel) he 'seeth the light of the glory of God in the face of Jesus Christ'; and 'beholdeth what manner of love it is which the Father hath bestowed upon us, that we', who are born of the Spirit, 'should be called the sons of God'. It is the ear of the soul, whereby a sinner 'hears the voice of the Son of God, and lives'; even that voice which alone wakes the dead, 'Son, thy sins are forgiven thee'. It is (if I may be allowed the expression) the palate of the soul; for hereby a believer 'tastes the good word, and the powers of the world to come'; and 'hereby he both tastes and sees that God is gracious', yea, 'and merciful to him a sinner'. It is the feeling of the soul, whereby a believer perceives, through the 'power of the Highest overshadowing him', both the existence and the presence of Him in whom 'he lives, moves, and has his being'; and indeed the whole invisible world, the entire system of things eternal. And hereby, in particular, he feels 'the love of God shed abroad in his heart'.[4]

We may observe here several typical features of Wesley's use of this language. First, he freely refers to spiritual senses by an analogy with the five natural senses (and names the sense of touch with the verb 'feel'). Second, this quotation is quite characteristic of Wesley's constant use of biblical sentences as the material for his language of spiritual sensation. Third, what is known through the spiritual senses comprises specifically theological truth, which here includes the knowledge of God, of redemption in Christ, of personal salvation and of the work of the Spirit in the believer. Fourth, since '*every* true believer in God "seeth him who is invisible"', the experience belongs not only to a mature stage of faith, but to every stage of faith. Fifth, the spiritual senses are not to be identified with 'any of

---

[3] *Earnest Appeal to Men of Reason and Religion* (1743), §6, in *The Appeals to Men of Reason and Religion and Certain Related Open Letters*, ed. Albert Outler et al., *Bicentennial Edition of the Works of John Wesley* (Oxford: Clarendon Press, 1975), vol. xi.

[4] *Earnest Appeal* (1743), §7.

our natural senses or faculties'. Sixth, the particular object of the spiritual senses is identified both as 'him who is invisible' and as 'the love of God shed abroad in [the believer's] heart'.

Wesley uses the term 'spiritual sensation' at least three times, speaks of 'spiritual senses' or 'spiritual sense' at least sixteen times, and once speaks of 'faculties capable of discerning things invisible';[5] and he has other related terms. Yet these are by no means his only terms to name spiritual sensation, or even his most important terms. Wesley prefers to use biblical phrases or words to name his theological terms.[6] If a text refers to tasting or seeing, feeling or hearing, to the blind receiving sight, to sweetness, to those who hear but hear not, or see but see not, or to light or to darkness, or in effect makes any reference related to the senses, then Wesley will use it to express his category of spiritual sensation.[7] Among these biblical sentences certain expressions stand out both for their frequency in Wesley's writing and because Wesley takes them as explicit warrants for the theology of a direct, immediate spiritual sensation which he asserts that they name. These too are quite numerous, but we may mention three here as representative: 'seeth him who is invisible' (Heb 11: 27); 'seeth the light of the glory of God in the face of Jesus Christ' (2 Cor 4: 6; Wesley frequently refers to several texts in the entire passage, 2 Cor 3: 13 – 4: 18); 'the same Spirit beareth witness with our spirit, that we are the children of God' (Rom 8: 16). The whole set of biblical terms and phrases that he takes as terms implying spiritual sensation are ubiquitous in his sermons, letters, journals and hymns.[8]

---

[5] These terms appear in the following significant discussions of spiritual sensation: S17, *The Circumcision of the Heart* (1733), §§2–3, I. 1–2, 6–9, 13, II. 2, 4–10; S3, *Awake, Thou that Sleepest* (1742), I. 8–12, II. 7–11, III. 1–3, 5–9, 15; *Earnest Appeal* (1743), §§6–12, 32–5, 49–52, 57–60; *Minutes of 1744 Conference* (1744) ed. Albert Outler, *John Wesley* (New York: Oxford University Press, 1964); S9, *The Spirit of Bondage and Adoption* (1746), §1, I. 1–6, II. 1–6, 9–10, III. 1–8; S10, *The Witness of the Spirit* (1746), I. 5–12, II. 8–14; S12, *The Witness of Our Own Spirit* (1746), §§18–19; S19, *The Great Privilege of Those that are Born of God* (1748), I. 1–10; *Letter to Conyers Middleton* (1749), VI. 2. 1–12; S30, *Upon our Lord's Sermon on the Mount, X* (1750), §17; S45, *The New Birth* (1760), II. 1–5; S43, *The Scripture Way of Salvation* (1765), II. 1–4, III. 7, 14–18; S119, *Walking by Sight and Walking by Faith* (1788), §§1–21; S130, *On Living without God* (1790), §§1–16. In this chapter I will use the numbering and suggested dating of the sermons in the *Bicentennial Edition*, vols. I–IV, *Sermons* (Nashville: Abingdon, 1984–7). The sermon numbers mostly coincide with the traditional numbering; the numbering of the sections within the sermons is the same as in previous editions.

[6] It is however clear in various contexts that he thinks of 'spiritual senses' as a biblical term which he would derive (as Origen among others also did) from Heb 5: 14: 'senses exercised to discern both good and evil'.

[7] For a study of the vocabulary of the spiritual senses in the passages cited in n. 5 see Mealey, 'Taste and See', pp. 64–87.

[8] The language of spiritual sensation is the characteristic idiom of both Charles Wesley's hymns and John Wesley's translations of Pietist hymns. Here are lines from the first two hymns of *A Collection of Hymns for the Use of the People Called Methodists* (1781): 'See all your sins on Jesus laid' (Hymn 1, stanza 7); 'Awake from guilty nature's sleep, And Christ shall give you light' (Hymn 1, stanza 8); 'Ye

Among his biblical terms for spiritual sensation the most important is *elenchos*, a term he often simply transliterates from the definition of faith in Hebrews 11: 1, *pragmatôn elenchos ou blepomenôn*.[9] The following expressions appear as terms for spiritual sensation and as equivalents for *elenchos*: 'spiritual sensation'; 'demonstrative evidence'; 'supernatural evidence'; 'divine evidence'; 'evidence'; 'divine consciousness'; 'divine evidence and conviction'; 'witness of the Spirit'; 'sure trust and confidence'.

Wesley's readers demonstrate that the language of spiritual sensation so prominent in his writings may be understood in a wide variety of ways. The language is an important background for the categories of 'experience' and 'feeling' in Methodist piety and theology. The language of spiritual sensation might refer to intention, or a state of the will or emotion in the experience of love for God, and these meanings have been read back into Wesley.[10] In the wider tradition of spiritual sensation, the language might be taken as a reference to the operation of the intellect in its knowledge of God's grace – supernaturally assisted and oriented, but still the operation of the natural intellect. This meaning has also been found in Wesley.[11]

All of these approaches share the same difficulty as interpretations of Wesley: whereas each of these interpretations locates the spiritual senses in a natural capacity, Wesley himself denies that what he means by spiritual sensation is in any way a natural capacity. We have already seen this in his description of the spiritual senses as 'the supernatural evidence of things invisible, not perceivable by eyes of flesh, or by any of our natural senses or faculties'.[12] He elaborates on the epistemology which leads him to this distinction between 'natural' senses and 'spiritual' senses later in the same text:

And seeing our ideas are not innate, but must all originally come from our senses, it is certainly necessary that you have senses capable of discerning objects of this

---

then shall know, Shall feel, your sins forgiven' (Hymn 1, stanza 9); 'Come, and partake the gospel feast; Be saved from sin; in Jesus rest: O taste the goodness of your God, And eat his flesh, and drink his blood!' (Hymn 2, stanza 4).

[9] See the quotation above from *Earnest Appeal* (1743), §6. Important texts that explicitly define *elenchos* as spiritual sensation include: S3, *Awake, Thou that Sleepest* (1742), 1. 11; *Earnest Appeal* (1743), §§1–12; *Minutes of 1744 Conference* (1744), q. 4, ed. Outler, p. 136; S5, *Justification by Faith* (1746), IV. 2; S43, *The Scripture Way of Salvation* (1765), II. 1–4; S119, *Walking by Sight and Walking by Faith* (1788), §10–11. For a discussion of *elenchos* as spiritual sensation see Mealey, 'Taste and See', pp. 76–9, 138–49.

[10] G. Clapper, *John Wesley on Religious Affections: His Views on Experience and Emotion and their Role in the Christian Life and Theology* (Metuchen, NJ, and London: Scarecrow Press, 1989).

[11] D. J. Luby, *Perceptibility of Grace* (Rome: Pontificia Studiorum Universitas A. S. Thomas Aquinas in Urbe, 1994).

[12] *Earnest Appeal* (1743), §6.

kind: Not those only which are called natural senses, which in this respect profit nothing, as being altogether incapable of discerning objects of a spiritual kind; but spiritual senses, exercised to discern spiritual good and evil. It is necessary that you have the hearing ear, and the seeing eye, emphatically so called; that you have a new class of senses opened in your soul, not depending on organs of flesh and blood, to be 'the evidence of things not seen', as your bodily senses are of visible things; to be the avenues to the invisible world, to discern spiritual objects, and to furnish you with ideas of what the outward 'eye hath not seen, neither the ear heard'.

And till you have these internal senses, till the eyes of your understanding are opened, you can have no apprehension of divine things, no idea of them at all. Nor, consequently, till then, can you either judge truly, or reason justly, concerning them; seeing your reason has no ground whereon to stand, no materials to work upon.[13]

Wesley's empiricism is on display in this quotation: reason depends on sensation. Wesley frequently asserts the principle that *nihil est in intellectu quod non fuit prius in sensu* – nothing is in the intellect which was not first in the senses.[14] The intellect requires the content of sensation to reason. When the intellect attempts to grasp spiritual objects – the strictly supernatural objects of spiritual sensation – on the basis of the content of natural sensation alone, it grasps in the dark, its conclusions are open to debate and doubt. This is not simply scepticism, but reflects Wesley's version of Aristotelian epistemology, described in various sources.[15] He suggests here that reason can operate on the basis of natural sensation or spiritual sensation; but the natural senses and natural reason apart from the spiritual senses cannot grasp the spiritual realities known by the spiritual senses; in fact, 'we have no idea of them at all'. Spiritual senses grasp spiritual reality which is otherwise outside the purview of natural faculties. Spiritual reality is grasped by spiritual sensation prior to any act of the intellect.

There is an important connection to notice here between Wesley's doctrine of spiritual sensation and his doctrine of the reception of grace. In an exchange of letters with the anonymous 'John Smith' on the topic of

---

[13] *Ibid.* §§32–33.

[14] See S119, *Walking by Sight and Walking by Faith* (1788), §10; cf. §§7–8 for the contrast between spiritual sensation and the intellect.

[15] For his Aristotelian account of sensation and cognition, see his translation of Henry Aldrich's Aristotelian logic, in T. Jackson (ed.), *Works of John Wesley*, vol. xiv, pp. 161–89; his abridgement of Peter Browne's *The Procedure, Extent, and Limits of Human Understanding* (London, 1728, 1729) in the Appendix to *A Survey of the Wisdom of God in the Creation: Or, a Compendium of Natural Philosophy: In Five Volumes*, 3rd edn (1777), vol. v, pp. 172–4; and his comments on Locke, in which he rejects Locke's account of cognition in favour of the Aristotelian account of his education, Jackson (ed.), *Works of John Wesley*, vol. xiii, pp. 455–64.

'perceptible inspiration' (as 'John Smith' terms Wesley's doctrine of spiritual sensation), Wesley defends his position that 'faith, hope, and love are
not the effect of any, or all, our natural faculties'.[16] These supernatural
gifts are completely out of the reach of all natural faculties: 'supposing a
man to be now void of faith, hope, and love, he cannot effect any degree
of them in himself by any possible exertion of his understanding, and of
any or all his other natural faculties, though he should enjoy them in the
utmost perfection'. What is required is a 'distinct power from God' that
is 'created anew' by 'the operation of the Spirit of God'. It is clear in the
exchange of letters that this 'distinct power from God' is the capacity for
the perceptible inspiration of grace.[17] We should note Wesley's claim here
that faith, hope and love are possible only when we receive a capacity for
spiritual reality through the gift of spiritual sensation; and the reception
of spiritual sensation is this act of new creation, the reception of a 'distinct
power from God'. As I will argue below, Wesley's doctrine of spiritual sensation functions as his doctrine of the reception of the supernatural habit
of grace.

We may point to several other texts between 1743 or earlier and Wesley's
death in 1791 which assert the same supernatural origin of the capacity for
spiritual sensation as we have seen in the letters to 'John Smith', and which
sharply distinguish it not only from the natural senses and from natural
reason, but from all natural capacities whatsoever.[18] Wesley certainly does
not deny that natural human reason, aided by grace, can contemplate the
spiritual realities known through the spiritual senses – this is the implication
of the quotation above from the *Earnest Appeal*. And Wesley does not deny
an emotional or affective or intentional response to the grace known in
spiritual sensation: quite the contrary. But he does deny that spiritual
sensation can be identified with the activity of any natural capacity.

Although the spiritual senses are a distinct faculty from natural sensation
and reason, Wesley understands the operation of this faculty by an analogy
from his understanding of natural sensation. The term 'spiritual senses'
already makes this analogy.

---

[16] Letter to 'John Smith', 25 June 1746, §7.   [17] See e.g. *ibid.* §§6, 9.
[18] See e.g. S11, *The Witness of the Spirit, II* (1767), III. 4; S70, *The Case of Reason Impartially Considered*
(1781), II. 10; S110, *On the Discoveries of Faith* (1788), §1–4, and passim. Again, see the quotation
above from *Earnest Appeal* (1743), §6: 'the *supernatural* evidence of things invisible, not perceivable
by eyes of flesh, *or by any of our natural senses or faculties*'. Or see S43, *The Scripture Way of Salvation*
(1765), II. 1: 'A *supernatural* evidence of God and of the things of God, a kind of spiritual light
exhibited to the soul, and a *supernatural* sight or perception thereof... We have a prospect of the
invisible things of God. We see the spiritual world, which is all round about us, and yet *no more
discerned by our natural faculties than if it had no being*'. My italics.

Wesley gives an account of natural sensation in his *Survey of the Wisdom of God*.[19] The most informative text for our purposes is in the Appendix to the *Survey*, a highly condensed excerpt from Peter Browne's *The Procedure, Extent, and Limits of Human Understanding*[20] that includes an account of the relation of sensation and cognition.[21] 'Ideas' are images of sensible objects in memory; we have no 'idea' of God, 'as he is in himself', then, but in our natural knowledge of him we reason from our sensible experience in the visible creation. Sensible ideas have three properties: they are *original*, meaning that they are antecedent to any operation of the mind, that the mind is passive in the reception of sensation and that without sensible images thought is impossible in an embodied soul; they are *simple*; and they are *direct and immediate*, arising simply from the proximity of the material object and a person with the appropriate capacity for sensation. We may speak of sensation as a kind of knowledge: 'this is a knowledge direct, immediate, and intuitive, and carries in it the highest certainty'; it admits of no proof from reason, for reason depends on sensation. As a kind of 'evidence', sensation demands an immediate assent. 'When the sensation is regular and perfect, the assent of the intellect necessarily follows all at once; though in a manner quite different from demonstration, which extorts it by intermediate proof.' It does not yield even to the clearest demonstration, 'when the organ is rightly disposed, and exercised upon its proper object, at a just distance, and in a due medium'. If sensation were not 'immediate, clear, and undoubted' we would be confined to scepticism; without certainty in sensation, certainty is impossible in reasoning.

Here is a recognizably Aristotelian, realist account of sensation,[22] as opposed, say, to a Lockean or modern empiricist account of sensation. And here too is the background to Wesley's doctrine of spiritual sensation as an evidence or *elenchos*. As 'the demonstrative evidence of things unseen' or 'the supernatural evidence of things invisible' spiritual sensation is a direct, immediate experience of the spiritual object prior to any act of reason or affective response; by contrast with reasoning about God from the sensible world, it is not a conclusion based on evidence, but is an original and direct form of evidence that demands an immediate assent. He speaks of spiritual sensation as 'immediate', but not without 'means', by which he seems to mean that spiritual sensation has no middle term – is

---

[19] For a brief discussion of sensation in one of the sermons, see S117, *On the Discoveries of Faith* (1788), §2.
[20] *Survey* (1777), vol. v, pp. 171–224.   [21] *Ibid.* pp. 172–83.
[22] The use of 'sensible ideas' in an Aristotelian tradition probably derives from Aristotle's own phrase in *De an.* III. 8, 432a 4–5, and his discussion of 'image' in *De an.* III. 3–8.

not discursive – but requires means, which include the scriptures.[23] Only
as we make contact with the reality of God through the spiritual senses
do we have something to reason about. Once we see God by the spiritual
senses it is possible for us to respond in our natural capacities, whether
intentionally, affectively or rationally.

One of the obstacles to a proper understanding of Wesley's epistemology,
and therefore to grasping the analogy from natural sensation to spiritual
sensation, is the widespread opinion that Wesley's epistemology is Lockean.
Elsewhere I explain why I believe this opinion is profoundly misguided.[24]
Again, several scholars of Wesley have fallen into the mistake of viewing
Browne's epistemology as a kind of Lockean account. In fact, his *Procedure*
is a fierce repudiation of Locke, as one of Wesley's friends, Vincent Perronet,
recognized.[25] For our purposes the key difference between Locke and the
Aristotelian tradition in which Wesley was expert is the level of realism in
which sensation is understood. In Locke's representational epistemology,
the proper object of sensation is not the object we suppose that we sense,[26]
but the idea of sense that we experience; whereas in Aristotelian epistemology, the person who senses becomes one with that which is sensed in a real
way, so that the proper object of sensation *is* the object we suppose that
we sense.[27] We also need to mention that Locke's apparent materialism in
his account of sensation and cognition would have a fatal implication for
any doctrine of spiritual sensation such as Wesley's, with its high degree of
theological realism.

To this point we have dealt only with preliminary questions in understanding Wesley's theological category of spiritual sensation. The meaning
of spiritual sensation as a theological category emerges in its most important uses in his theology. He defines three of his central doctrines by means
of spiritual sensation as an explanatory theological category – faith, new

---

[23] 'You thought I had meant "immediate inspiration". So I do, or I mean nothing at all. Not indeed
such inspiration as is *sine mediis*. But all inspiration, though by means, is immediate.' *Farther
Appeal, I* (1745), v. 28. For a discussion of the relation between immediate spiritual sensation and
the whole array of 'means of grace', including scripture, see S16, *The Means of Grace* (1746), v. 1. For
a suggestion that 'immediate' means without a middle term or a process of argument, and another
avowal that spiritual sensation is antecedent 'to any reasoning whatsoever', see S11, *The Witness of
the Spirit, II* (1767), III. 4.
[24] M. T. Mealey, 'Tilting at Windmills: John Wesley's Reading of John Locke's epistemology', *Bulletin
of the John Rylands University Library of Manchester*, 85.2–3 (2003), 331–46. For a discussion of the
Aristotelian character of Wesley's epistemology and of the relation to Locke, see R. Matthews,
'"Religion and Reason Joined": A Study in the Theology of John Wesley', Th.D. diss., Harvard
University, 1986, pp. 255–80.
[25] See Mealey, 'Tilting at Windmills', pp. 337–9.   [26] See, e.g., *HU* II. 8. 15–18.
[27] See Aristotle, *De an.* III. 2, 425b 27–9: 'The activity of the sensible object and of the sensation is
one and the same, though their essence is not the same'. Trans. W. S. Hett, *Aristotle: On the Soul*
(Cambridge, MA: Harvard University Press, 2000), 147. Cf. *De an.* III. 2, 426a 16–18.

birth and the witness of the Spirit. These themes together with his doctrine of justification constitute his account of conversion. Further, his doctrine of justification depends on his doctrine of faith; his doctrines of sanctification and Christian perfection depend on his doctrine of new birth; his doctrine of the assurance of faith is contained in his doctrine of the witness of the Spirit.

Over the course of his career, Wesley defines faith in three main ways: as an assent to the truths of the faith on the warrant of revelation alone; as a sure trust and confidence; and as the spiritual sensation of God and the things of God or, equally, as an *elenchos*, the demonstrative evidence of things unseen.[28] The first definition belongs to an early period in his theology, from the time of his ordination in 1725 to some point in the mid 1730s, perhaps up to 1738. He uses the second definition, taken from the wording of an Anglican formulary (Cranmer's sermon on faith), as one of his characteristic definitions of faith from 1738 to his death in 1791. He first formally makes the third definition of faith in 1743 in the definition of faith quoted above from the *Earnest Appeal*.[29] From 1743 to 1791 this is his main definition of faith,[30] and I have argued elsewhere that the second and third definitions are coordinated under his category of spiritual sensation throughout his mature theology.[31]

In order to understand this definition of faith as an *elenchos* or spiritual sensation, we need to grasp the order of the *via salutis* in Wesley's theology. His expression of this order is invariable in his mature theology. We may outline the main features of his *via salutis* by reference to his sermon *The Scripture Way of Salvation*.[32] Faith is the principle of Christian life from which all the benefits of grace flow.[33] Faith has two consequences that necessarily exist wherever true faith exists: justification, which is God's forgiveness of our sins or pardon and can be considered a change in our relation to God;[34] and sanctification, which is a real change in us, a process of gaining all Christian tempers or virtues with the goal that all of our

[28] For discussions of the history of Wesley's definitions of faith, see Matthews, 'Religion and Reason Joined', pp. 184–246; R. Maddox, *Responsible Grace: John Wesley's Practical Theology* (Nashville: Kingswood, 1994), pp. 127–28; Mealey, 'Taste and See', pp. 112–14, 122–38. On faith as spiritual sensation see Mealey, 'Taste and See', pp. 104–62; Matthews discusses several relevant issues in chaps. 3, 4 and 5 of his 'Religion and Reason Joined'.

[29] See n. 3 above.

[30] For a list of relevant references, see Mealey, 'Taste and See', p. 124, n. 208. For examples, see S4, *Scriptural Christianity* (1744), I. 1–2; *The Witness of Our Own Spirit* (1746), §8; S132, *On Faith, Heb. 11:1* (1791), §1.

[31] Mealey, 'Taste and See', pp. 122–38.

[32] The following paragraph is adapted from *ibid.* pp. 117–18.

[33] S43, *The Scripture Way of Salvation* (1765), II. 1–4; III. 1–18.

[34] *Ibid.* III. 1–2. Maddox's contention that Wesley 'was inclined to view justification as effecting faith, more than vice versa' (*Responsible Grace*, p. 173) cannot be sustained.

desires and affections be transformed by our love for God.[35] He thinks of 'new birth' or 'regeneration' as the first moment in the life-long process of sanctification.[36] In the very moment in which a person acquires faith, his or her sins are forgiven (justification), and he or she is made a new creation, and the healing of his or her soul in the image of God is begun (new birth). Since true faith necessarily implies both of these consequences, justification and the new birth must begin in the same moment as faith;[37] but since faith is the condition in us of justification and new birth, it is prior to both of them in reality. They are simultaneous in time, but faith is prior in reality. 'Salvation' is comprised by these three terms: it means to have faith, and therefore to be justified and to have experienced the new birth, and therefore to be in the way of holiness that has its proper term in the holiness of Christ.[38]

Wesley is able to explain why faith has this originative priority in his *via salutis* through his understanding of the definition of faith as an *elenchos* or spiritual sensation. We can follow his reasoning by examining another significant text from *The Scripture Way of Salvation* in which Wesley explains *elenchos* by a clear analogy with his account of sensation.[39] Wesley argues that the *pragmatôn elenchos ou blepomenôn* implies both an objective 'supernatural evidence of God' and the 'supernatural sight or perception therof', the human experience of faith:

Faith, in general, is defined by the Apostle, ἔλεγχος πραγμάτων οὐ βλεπομένων – 'an evidence', a divine 'evidence and conviction' (the word means both) 'of things not seen' – not visible, not perceivable either by sight, or by any other of the external senses. It implies both a supernatural *evidence* of God, and of the things of God, a kind of spiritual *light* exhibited to the soul, and a supernatural *sight* or perception thereof.[40]

But the human experience of faith, the act of 'spiritual sight or perception', is not the focus of Wesley's discussion. Instead, this reference to the human experience of faith leads him to focus on another condition for the experience, apart from the 'supernatural evidence of God': 'Accordingly, the Scripture speaks of God's giving sometimes light [i.e. evidence], sometimes a power of discerning it.'[41]

Thus, apart from the gift of light, the 'supernatural evidence of God', the act of spiritual sight implies a faculty for spiritual sight. In another

---

[35] S43, *The Scripture Way of Salvation* (1765), III. 3, 13–18.
[36] *Ibid.* I. 4; cf. S45, *The New Birth* (1760), II. 5; IV. 3.
[37] S43, *The Scripture Way of Salvation* (1765), I. 4.   [38] *Ibid.* I. 3–4, II. 1–4; III. 1, 3.
[39] This paragraph is adapted from Mealey, 'Taste and See', pp. 150–1.
[40] S43, *The Scripture Way of Salvation* (1765), II. 1.   [41] *Ibid.* II. 1.

text, Wesley draws the same inference: 'Faith implies both the perceptive faculty itself, and the act of perceiving God and the things of God. And the expression, "seeing God", may include both; the act, and the faculty, of seeing him.'[42] Prior to the human experience of faith, God must both give light and give the capacity to receive the light. The faculty of being able to perceive is not a human act but a divine creation, as much as any of the natural powers, such as sensation and mind, are given by God. The 'supernatural evidence of God' is the presence of God and the illumination of God that makes the spiritual world available to spiritual sensation, and is also a sheer act of God. These two prior conditions for the human experience of faith are the 'two-fold operation of the Holy Spirit':

So St. Paul: 'God, who commanded light to shine out of darkness, hath shined in our hearts, to give us the light of the knowledge of the glory of God in the face of Jesus Christ.' And elsewhere the same Apostle speaks of 'the eyes of' our 'understanding being opened'. By this two-fold operation of the Holy Spirit – having the eyes of our soul both *opened* and *enlightened* – we see the things which the natural 'eye hath not seen, neither the ear heard'.[43]

Faith as spiritual sensation has been analysed into three elements: the reception of a new power or capacity in us which makes spiritual sensation possible; the evidence, light, or enlightenment of 'God and the things of God' that makes the spiritual world visible to someone who has the capacity; and the human act of spiritual sensation or the experience of faith, on account of this God-given capacity. In this definition of faith as *elenchos* or spiritual sensation the focus of his discussion is on the first two elements of the meaning of faith, entirely the act of God, on which the human act of faith depends.

For Wesley, then, faith as *elenchos* implies both the original ground of the knowledge and love of God and also the human experience of faith or knowledge of God. This is to say that faith as spiritual sensation functions in Wesley's theology both as the reception of the supernatural habit of grace, the source of all the habits and acts which flow from it, and as a doctrine of the perception of grace.[44] What Wesley means to describe here is not Christian perfection or the final stages of mystical experience but

---

[42] Letter to Mr Richard Tompson, 16 March 1756.
[43] S43, *The Scripture Way of Salvation* (1765), II. I.
[44] For an argument that Wesley operates with distinctions between created and uncreated grace, operative and cooperative grace, and actual and habitual grace (including the supernatural habit of grace), but does so under other terms and expresses these distinctions in his category of spiritual sensation, see Mealey, 'Taste and See', pp. 229–30, 236–9. Here I use these terms for the sake of concision in analysis, while recognizing the need for an argument about how appropriate the terms are in a discussion of Wesley.

the foundation of every Christian life. It is for this reason that faith as spiritual sensation is the principle both of justification and of new birth or sanctification, in his *via salutis*. Further, just as for Wesley natural sensation is understood in a realistic manner as an 'immediate' and 'direct' contact with the visible world, and our only source of contact with the visible world, faith as spiritual sensation is an immediate and direct contact with the reality of God.

Wesley elaborates on his doctrine of the perception of grace in his doctrine of 'the witness of the Spirit' as spiritual sensation. He clearly distinguishes between a perception of God's love, which is to say of uncreated grace, by the spiritual senses alone, and a perception of the graces worked in us, of created grace, through the testimony of scripture and reason acting together. He calls the first 'the witness of God's own Spirit to my spirit'; and he calls the second the 'witness of our own spirit'.[45] He represents the witness of our own spirit as a syllogism: 'The Word of God says everyone who has the fruit of the Spirit is a child of God. Experience, or inward consciousness, tells me that I have the fruit of the Spirit. And hence I rationally conclude: therefore I am a child of God'.[46] Wesley explains in the passages cited that the premises and conclusion draw on a combination of the testimony of scripture, 'inward consciousness' and the operation of reason. The first premise requires recognition of the meaning of the Bible; and the second premise requires experience of the 'fruit of the Spirit' in me; but the conclusion is drawn discursively through the act of reason presented in this syllogism; thus, the witness of our own spirit requires both scriptural testimony and the operation of natural reason.

By contrast, the 'witness of God's own Spirit' is a non-discursive and direct experience of God's love: 'By "the testimony of the Spirit" I mean an inward impression on the soul, whereby the Spirit of God immediately and directly witnesses to my spirit that I am a child of God, that "Jesus Christ hath loved me, and given himself for me"; that all my sins are blotted out, and I, even I, am reconciled to God'.[47] This is indeed an experience not of a created grace in me, but of God's own love through the operation of the Spirit of God:

That 'the testimony of the Spirit of God' must, in the very nature of things, be antecedent to 'the testimony of our own spirit', may appear from this single consideration: we must be holy in heart and life before we can be conscious that we

---

[45] For a discussion see *ibid.* pp. 248–56.

[46] S11, *The Witness of the Spirit, II* (1767), II. 6. Also see S10, *The Witness of the Spirit, I* (1746), I. 4, II.

[47] S11, *The Witness of the Spirit, II* (1767), II. 2, quoting with a few elaborations from *The Witness of the Spirit, I* (1746), I. 7.

are so. But we must love God before we can be holy at all, this being the root of all holiness. Now we cannot love God till we know he loves us: 'We love him, because he first loved us'. And we cannot know his love to us till his Spirit witnesses it to our spirit. Till then we cannot believe it; we cannot say, 'The life which I now live, I live by faith in the Son of God, who loved me, and gave himself for me'. 'Then, only then we feel Our interest in his blood, And cry, with joy unspeakable, Thou art my Lord, my God.' Since therefore the testimony of his Spirit must precede the love of God and all holiness, of consequence it must precede our consciousness thereof.[48]

Wesley determines, then, the following order: God reveals his love in an objective *elenchos* or evidence; we experience that love by the spiritual senses (described here as 'the testimony of the Spirit'); we love God as a consequence; that love leads to acquired habits and acts of love, to holiness in heart and life.

Clearly, a non-discursive, immediate experience of God might easily become unmoored from and privileged over the Bible as God's testimony. Various theological traditions that emphasized spiritual senses in modernity discovered this fate, including that of many Methodists. For Wesley himself, as we have noted, this 'immediate' testimony is not without 'means', especially those available in the scriptures.[49] Wesley's typical procedure, on display in the quotations above, is to use biblical sentences almost exclusively to describe spiritual sensation. Likewise, the Bible provides the whole vocabulary and grammar for the spiritual senses in Wesley's procedure. More work needs to be done on the relation between spiritual sensation and the reading of the Bible in Wesley.

We note that his definition of 'the witness of God's own Spirit with our spirit' coincides exactly with his definition of faith as spiritual sensation and his analysis of it in *The Scripture Way of Salvation*, II. 1.[50] And we note that this explanation of faith and the witness of the Spirit as spiritual sensation reveals an intrinsic reason why, in the *via salutis*, faith is the origin in us of holiness at the new birth.[51]

In the most important sermons on his doctrine of new birth, Wesley describes new birth as the opening of the spiritual senses.[52] As we see in his

---

[48] S11, *The Witness of the Spirit, II* (1746), III. 5. [49] See n. 23 above.
[50] Mealey, 'Taste and See', pp. 256–60. On this identity, see, for example, the conference minutes for 25 June 1744, in *Minutes of 1744 Conference*, q. 4.
[51] There is no space here to explain the complex and lengthy development of Wesley's use of the 'witness of the Spirit' as a doctrine of the assurance of faith. His doctrines of faith and the witness of the Spirit as spiritual sensation drive the development in two ways: by setting the problem (how can a lack of assurance be accounted for if faith is spiritual sensation?); and by setting the assumptions for the solution. See Mealey, 'Taste and See', pp. 256–82.
[52] See S19, *The Great Privilege of Those that are Born of God* (1748), I. 1–10, III. 2–3; and S45, *The New Birth* (1760), II. 4. Also see S130, *On Living without God* (1790), §§1–5, 8–11, 16 ('This change

explanation, the metaphor of opening does not point to a latent natural capacity, but to the original state of humanity in union with God: humanity was created to 'dwell in God', a spiritual rather than a natural condition. He cites the fall of humanity as the background for this doctrine. Since God is love, and humans are created in the image of God, 'man at his creation was full of love, which was the sole principle of all his tempers, thoughts, words and actions'.[53] To be 'full of love' is to have the life of God. But the fall breaks union with the life of God: ' . . . he died to God, the most dreadful of all deaths. He lost the life of God: he was separated from him in union with whom his spiritual life consisted. The body dies when it is separated from the soul, the soul when it is separated from God'.[54] This spiritual death requires a spiritual rebirth that will restore us to 'the life of God'. In extended passages, Wesley outlines an analogy between sensation in natural birth and new birth.[55] In our natural birth we gain the use of our natural senses; in our supernatural birth we regain the capacity and the use of our spiritual senses, lost in the fall. 'His whole soul is now sensible of God . . . all his spiritual senses being now awakened . . . thus the veil being removed which before intercepted the light and voice, the knowledge and love of God, he who is born of the Spirit, dwelleth in love, "dwelleth in God, and God in him".'[56] In Wesley's *via salutis*, new birth is the first moment of sanctification, sanctification is growth in holiness, in habit and act, and holiness is defined as the love of God and man. New birth is the insertion of a principle of holiness that makes growth in holiness possible,[57] and this principle is to 'dwell in love', which is to say for the believer to 'dwell in God, and God in him'. New birth as the recovery of spiritual sensation restores love as the principle of thought, word and action; and this principle is the restored life of God.

As we have just seen, in his *via salutis* Wesley thinks of faith as the one necessary and sufficient condition in us of new birth; and faith as *elenchos* intrinsically leads to the new birth. 'We must love God before we can be holy at all, this being the root of all holiness. Now we cannot love God till we know he loves us: "We love him, because he first loved us." And we cannot know his love to us till his Spirit witnesses it to our

from spiritual death to spiritual life is properly the new birth', §11). See Theodore Runyon, *The New Creation: John Wesley's Theology Today* (Nashville: Abingdon, 1998), pp. 71–81, 146–67; and Mealey, 'Taste and See', pp. 167–212.
[53] S45, *The New Birth* (1760), I. 1.   [54] *Ibid.* I. 2.
[55] *Ibid.* II. 4; S19, *The Great Privilege of Those that are Born of God* (1748), I. 1–10, II. 1, III. 2–3; S130, *On Living without God* (1790), §§2–12.
[56] S19, *The Great Privilege of Those that are Born of God* (1748), I. 8–10.
[57] S45, *The New Birth* (1760), III. 1.

spirit.'[58] With the highest degree of theological realism, faith as *elenchos* is the reception of union with God: we do not come into contact with an idea about God or an emotion about God, but with God's love. Because God *is* love, this is a direct and immediate contact with God. As a consequence of this contact with God's love by an *elenchos*, we immediately begin to be transformed by God's love, which now exists in us as a principle for all holiness.[59] New birth is the reception of the very life of God as a principle of holiness in us, as a consequence of faith. The realism of his account of sensation underwrites by analogy this theological realism in his doctrine of new birth as spiritual sensation. If the sense in act is the sensible in act, there is a real union between the one who senses and that which is sensed: on account of faith as *elenchos* we dwell in God, and God dwells in us; our life is hidden with God in Christ; the Spirit of God dwells in us.

Thus, Wesley's doctrine of new birth as spiritual sensation expresses a doctrine of union with God or participation in the divine nature which he names almost exclusively under biblical terms:[60]

'Hast thou received the Holy Ghost?' If thou hast not, thou art not yet a Christian. For a Christian is a man that is 'anointed with the Holy Ghost and with power'. Thou art not yet made a partaker of pure religion and undefiled. Dost thou know what religion is? that it is a participation of the divine nature; the life of God in the soul of man; Christ formed in the heart; 'Christ in thee, the hope of glory?' happiness and holiness; heaven begun upon earth? 'a kingdom of God within thee; not meat and drink', no outward thing; 'but righteousness, and peace, and joy in the Holy Ghost?' an everlasting kingdom brought into thy soul; a 'peace of God, that passeth all understanding;' a 'joy unspeakable, and full of glory?'

Knowest thou, that 'in Jesus Christ, neither circumcision availeth anything, nor uncircumcision; but faith that worketh by love;' but a new creation? Seest thou the necessity of that inward change, that spiritual birth, that life from the dead, that holiness?[61]

His doctrines of sanctification and Christian perfection express a doctrine of participation in the divine nature as a *telos*; his doctrine of new birth expresses a doctrine of participation in the divine nature as an *archē*.

It is difficult to imagine a doctrine of salvation that would stand in greater contrast with the great Enlightenment critiques of Christian theology than Wesley's doctrine of faith, the witness of the Spirit and new birth as spiritual sensation. Although the category of spiritual sensation

---

[58] S11, *The Witness of the Spirit, II* (1746), III. 5.
[59] *Farther Appeal, II* (1745), III. 8; *The New Birth* (1760), I. 1.
[60] For a full discussion, see Mealey, 'Taste and See', pp. 177–91.
[61] S3, *Awake, Thou that Sleepest* (1742), II. 10, 11. This sermon was composed by Charles Wesley, but John Wesley included it in his sermon collections.

was now being understood by others around him in senses less offensive to the canons of modernity, he retained its meaning in a mode of theological realism that belonged to pre-modern theology.[62] Not only is his doctrine antithetical to Locke, but it resembles the Macarian homilies much more than it does, say, John Smith the Cambridge Platonist. For this reason it is difficult for his followers and his interpreters to avoid the pull towards re-appropriating this theology within modern understandings of 'experience' and 'feeling', which is to say within a natural psychology or epistemology. Nevertheless, we can also understand Wesley's doctrine of spiritual sensation as a kind of alternative proposal for persons dealing with sceptical Enlightenment critiques of religion. Whereas Hobbes, Locke and Hume demand an appeal to sensible experience, Wesley offers an appeal to sensible experience in another key. Where Enlightenment critiques called into question traditional evidences for religion, Wesley almost entirely forgoes these, but stresses another more convincing form of evidence. Where Enlightenment scepticism cuts us off from contact with that which we know, Wesley retains real union between the knower and the known, even with God. Where Enlightenment critiques denied that reason could establish the particular doctrines of the Christian faith, Wesley agrees, but then insists that we are not bound by natural reason, since we may have a direct and immediate contact with the realities named by the doctrines.

[62] As an example, Gregory Palamas's account of spiritual senses is remarkably similar to Wesley's, though it is very unlikely that Wesley had read Palamas. See John Meyendorff's description of Palamas's doctrine of spiritual sensation in *A Study of Gregory Palamas*, trans. G. Lawrence (London: Faith Press, 1964), pp. 162–75.

CHAPTER 15

Karl Rahner and Hans Urs von Balthasar

Mark J. McInroy

The fact that the 'doctrine of the spiritual senses' serves an important function for numerous patristic and medieval theologians may not surprise contemporary scholars. What might be unexpected, however, is the high level of significance the doctrine has for the two most influential Catholic theologians of the twentieth century: Karl Rahner and Hans Urs von Balthasar. In his 1996 article on the topic, Stephen Fields draws long-overdue scholarly attention to the versions of the doctrine found in Balthasar and Rahner, highlighting their divergent readings of Bonaventure as his key point of contrast.[1] At the conclusion of his study, however, Fields indicates that more work needs to be done on this subject. Most intriguingly, he suggests that Rahner's investigations into the spiritual senses 'may have inspired [his] idea of the pre-apprehension', referring to Rahner's notion of the *Vorgriff auf esse*, first developed in *Spirit in the World*.[2]

Although I make some qualifications regarding this hypothesis below, I argue in this chapter that the spiritual senses do eventually come to inform a reworked version of this aspect of Rahner's theology. This claim not only suggests that one of the core features of Rahner's theological anthropology was influenced by his study of the spiritual senses; it also helps to account for the seeming disappearance of the doctrine from Rahner's theological considerations after 1934, as I suggest that it had an ongoing, albeit 'subterranean', influence on Rahner's thought.

For Balthasar, one need not argue *that* the spiritual senses are important; that much is overtly stated, especially in his theological aesthetics.[3] What remains under-studied, however, is the systematic significance of the spiritual senses for *The Glory of the Lord*. Here I demonstrate that the

---

[1] S. Fields, 'Balthasar and Rahner on the Spiritual Senses', *Theological Studies*, 57 (1996), 241.

[2] K. Rahner, *Geist in Welt: Zur Metaphysik der endlichen Erkenntnis bei Thomas von Aquin* (Innsbruck: Rauch, 1939), published in English as *SW*.

[3] H. U. von Balthasar, *Herrlichkeit: Eine theologische Ästhetik*, 3 vols. (Einsiedeln: Johannes Verlag, 1961–9), published in English as *GL*.

spiritual senses occupy a prominent position as the anthropological correlate requisite to the reception of divine revelation. Or, to use Balthasarian
parlance: it is precisely through the spiritual senses that one performs the
epistemologically central task of 'seeing the form'.

Last, I suggest in this chapter that the spiritual senses provide a lens
through which to appreciate similarities between Balthasar and Rahner in
a time when their differences are often accentuated. The most noteworthy point of contrast between Balthasar and Rahner is often said to be
that whereas Rahner is concerned with philosophically accounting for the
transcendental structure of the human subject, Balthasar is deeply critical of this approach, and he instead focuses his theological attention on
the 'appearing phenomenon' beyond the human being. The investigation
of the spiritual senses offered here challenges both characterizations. In
short, when each figure is viewed through his use of the doctrine, we see
that Rahner is much less dictated by his philosophical influences than is
often thought to be the case, and we also observe that Balthasar is more
concerned with theological anthropology than is typically assumed.

KARL RAHNER AND THE SEARCH FOR A VIABLE
DOCTRINE OF THE SPIRITUAL SENSES

Rahner's articles on the spiritual senses are routinely acknowledged as
among the most important studies of the doctrine in the twentieth century.
And yet a question has haunted academic work on the spiritual senses that
follows in his wake: does Rahner simply cease to engage with the doctrine
after his essays from the 1930s, or does it continue to influence his theology
later in his career? The question is acutely felt in the present setting, as
Rahner's seeming lack of interest in the doctrine after 1934 has cast some
doubt on its potential for contemporary theology. Indeed, the apparent
abandonment of the topic by one of its foremost scholars has inclined
many to view the spiritual senses as a mere artifact of intellectual history.
This chapter, however, argues for the enduring significance of the spiritual
senses for Rahner's thought, and in so doing it charts avenues for the
relevance of the doctrine for contemporary systematic theology.

Although Rahner's articles treat of a number of figures in the history
of the spiritual senses, his lengthiest examinations take up Bonaventure's
articulation of the idea.[4] Strangely, however, whereas Rahner insists in his

[4] K. Rahner, 'La doctrine des "sens spirituels" au Moyen-Âge'; 'Der Begriff der Ecstasis bei Bonaventura', *Zeitschrift für Aszese und Mystik*, 9 (1934), 1–19. In 1975, K. Neufeld combined the 1933 and

1932 essay on Origen that a fivefold understanding of spiritual perception is necessary for a 'proper' doctrine of the spiritual senses,[5] in his 1933 and 1934 treatments of Bonaventure he emphasizes spiritual touch to a disproportionate degree. Crucially, too, in distorting Bonaventure's model of the spiritual senses so as to give undue priority to spiritual touch, and in reformulating spiritual touch such that it grants one an *immediate* experience of God, Rahner's ostensibly historical investigation betrays an interest in the constructive value of the spiritual senses for systematic theology, as I will argue below.

The most curious feature of Rahner's position involves his assertion that spiritual touch in Bonaventure's thought should be equated with 'ecstasy'. Rahner claims that when Bonaventure speaks of spiritual touch in his writings, one should understand him to be speaking of an ecstatic form of union characterized by a dark, obscure 'contact' with God.[6] As Rahner puts this point, 'In brief one may say that spiritual touch is nothing else than the act by which the soul grasps the substance of God in ecstasy.'[7] Following Pseudo-Dionysius and certain earlier medieval theologians, Bonaventure believes that the intellect is surpassed in the final stage of contemplation,[8] and a form of union that is non-intellectual is then achieved. This *excessus ecstaticus*, most often translated simply as 'ecstasy', is, in Rahner's terms, 'the experience of the will, the union with God of a more direct love'.[9]

Rahner enlists four citations from Bonaventure's works as support for his contentious claim that spiritual touch and ecstasy are the same: two from the *Sentences* commentaries, one from the *Breviloquium* and one from the *Itinerarium*. The two passages from the *Sentences* commentaries, however, simply indicate that touch is the highest spiritual sense, but they

---

1934 articles and published them in German as 'Die Lehre von den "geistlichen Sinnen" im Mittelalter', in K. Neufeld, SJ (ed.), *Schriften zur Theologie*, vol. XII: *Theologie aus Erfahrung des Geistes* (Zürich: Benziger Verlag, 1975), pp. 137–72. This German article was then translated into English as 'The Doctrine of the "Spiritual Senses" in the Middle Ages', in *Theological Investigations*, vol. XVI, pp. 104–34.

[5] Rahner here has a key hand in perpetuating Poulain's definition of the 'doctrine of the spiritual senses'. See Chapter 1 in this volume.

[6] 'La doctrine des "sens spirituels" au Moyen-Âge', p. 290 (English, p. 126).

[7] 'La doctrine des "sens spirituels" au Moyen-Âge', p. 289 (English, p. 126).

[8] The one exception to this rule is the exceedingly rare instance of *raptus*, which Rahner summarizes as follows: '"raptus" . . . is a direct, clear vision of God through the intellect, and is a foretaste of the beatific vision as an "actus gloriae". This is a privileged and exceptional state which Bonaventure thinks, for instance, St. Paul enjoyed, but not Moses'. 'La doctrine des "sens spirituels" au Moyen-Âge', p. 279 (English, p. 117).

[9] 'La doctrine des "sens spirituels" au Moyen-Âge', p. 279 (English, p. 117).

do not make any mention of ecstasy.[10] The *Breviloquium* mentions both
ecstasy and spiritual touch, but Rahner's use of the passage in question is
highly misleading. Rahner quotes Bonaventure's *Breviloquium* as follows:
'The supreme delightfulness [of Christ] can be touched in that He is the
Incarnate Word dwelling bodily in our midst, offering Himself to our
touch, our kiss, our embrace, through ardent love which makes our soul
pass, by ecstatic rapture, from this world to the Father.'[11] On the basis of
this text, Rahner insists that ecstasy and spiritual touch are one and the
same in Bonaventure's thought.

However, immediately prior to this passage we actually see that Bonaventure speaks of all *five* of the spiritual senses, not just touch:

> The supreme beauty of Christ the spouse is seen in that he is resplendence, his
> supreme harmony heard in that he is the Word, his supreme sweetness tasted in
> that he is Wisdom comprising both Word and resplendence, his supreme fragrance
> inhaled in that he is the Inspired Word within the heart, his supreme delightfulness
> touched in that he is the Incarnate Word dwelling bodily in our midst, offering
> himself to our touch, our kiss, our embrace, through ardent love which makes our
> soul pass, by ecstatic rapture, from this world to the Father (*quae mentem nostram
> per ecstasim et raptum transpire facit ex hoc mundo ad Patrem*).[12]

The passage does mention 'ecstatic rapture', of course, but the precise
relationship between spiritual touch and this state remains unclear. It could
very well be the case, for example, that all five of the spiritual senses – and
not exclusively spiritual touch – function to bring the individual to ecstasy.
Whereas Rahner's tendency is to single out one spiritual sense as the object
of his attention, then, Bonaventure's text describes the operation of all
of the spiritual senses in relation to Christ. More significantly, it is not
at all obvious from this passage that the spiritual senses are active *within*
ecstatic rapture.[13] Instead, this passage arguably suggests that the spiritual
senses perform the function of making one *ready* for ecstasy, but that they
do not continue to function as the soul is vaulted to this ecstatic state.
Bonaventure could certainly be more straightforward about the matter,
but taken in conjunction with the following portion of Bonaventure's
Itinerarium, this alternative interpretation seems likely.

---

[10] 'La doctrine des "sens spirituels" au Moyen-Âge', p. 289 (English, p. 126). Latin from the Quaracchi
edition of Bonaventure's works: *Opera omnia* (Rome: Quaracchi, 1882–1902, 10 vols.). See III *Sent.*
d. 13, dub. 1 (ed. Quaracchi, vol. III, p. 292a); III *Sent.* d. 27, a. 2 q. 1 (ed. Quaracchi, vol. III,
p. 604b).

[11] 'La doctrine des "sens spirituels" au Moyen-Âge', pp. 289–90 (English, p. 126). Bonaventure, *Brev.* v.
6 (ed. Quaracchi, vol. v, p. 258b), trans. J. de Vinck, *The Works of Bonaventure*, vol. II: *Breviloquium*
(Paterson, NJ: St Anthony Guild Press, 1965), p. 205.

[12] *Brev.* v. 6 (ed. Quaracchi, vol. v, p. 258b), trans. de Vinck, p. 205.

[13] See P. Gavrilyuk's treatment of the spiritual senses in Pseudo-Dionysius in Chapter 5 in this volume.

Rahner quotes the *Itinerarium* as saying that the soul 'is transported to Him (the Word) in ecstatic love and recovers... touch'.[14] However, Rahner's editorial hand is acutely felt here. First, the ellipses that he uses above exclude the words *gustus ut*. That is, the passage actually says that the soul 'is transported to him in ecstatic love and recovers *taste and* touch' (*ut transiens in illud per ecstaticum amorem, recuperat gustum et tactum*).[15] If Rahner wants to use this text to support his claim that spiritual touch should be identified with ecstasy, then spiritual taste should be included in his assessment as well. Additionally, as we saw above in Rahner's use of the *Breviloquium*, so too does the passage here indicate that all five senses function in regard to the relationship with ecstasy:

When it [the soul] believes in Christ as the uncreated Word and splendor of the Father, it recovers the spiritual senses of hearing and sight (*spiritualem auditum et visum*): its hearing, in order to listen to the teachings of Christ; and sight, in order to behold the splendor of his light. When, through hope, it longs to breathe in the inspired Word, by this aspiration and affection it recovers spiritual olfaction. When, through charity, it embraces the incarnate Word, by receiving delight from him and passing into him in ecstatical love, it recovers taste and touch.[16]

Again, Rahner has given disproportionate emphasis to Bonaventure's remarks regarding spiritual touch. Most significantly, however, the strong suggestion of this portion of Bonaventure's text is that the spiritual senses are not so much active within ecstasy as they function *prior to* ecstasy. In the very same section of the *Itinerarium* as that used by Rahner, Bonaventure makes even clearer that the spiritual senses serve this preparatory function in relation to ecstasy. Bonaventure writes, 'It is at this step, where the interior senses (*sensibus interioribus*) have been restored to see what is most beautiful, to hear what is most harmonious, to smell what is most fragrant, to taste what is most sweet, and to embrace what is most delightful, that the soul is prepared (*disponitur*) for spiritual ecstasies.'[17] Even more plainly than in the *Breviloquium*, then, this passage indicates that the spiritual senses are active in a stage of preparation that is distinct from ecstasy itself.

---

[14] Rahner leaves Bonaventure's text in its original Latin, quoting it as follows: 'ut *transiens* in illud (Verbum) per *ecstaticum* amorem recuperat... tactum' (Rahner's italics). Rahner uses this passage to claim, 'ecstasy... arises from peace and this is expressly referred to spiritual touch'. Both passages taken from 'La doctrine des "sens spirituels" au Moyen-Âge', p. 289 (English, p. 126). Bonaventure, *Itin.* IV. 3 (ed. Quaracchi, vol. V, p. 306b), trans. J. de Vinck, *The Works of Bonaventure*, vol. I: *Mystical Opuscula* (Paterson, NJ: St Anthony Guild Press, 1960), p. 37.

[15] *Itin.* IV. 3 (ed. Quaracchi, vol. V, p. 306b, my italics), trans. de Vinck, p. 37.

[16] *Itin.* IV. 3 (ed. Quaracchi, vol. V, p. 306b), trans. de Vinck, p. 37.

[17] *Itin.* IV. 3 (ed. Quaracchi, vol. V, p. 306b), trans. de Vinck, p. 37.

Why does Rahner so massage Bonaventure's texts to fit his thesis? Part of the issue has to do with genuine ambiguities in Bonaventure's writings. Bonaventure makes a wide range of comments on the spiritual senses throughout his works that are not easily synthesized into a coherent whole. In fact, the interpretive difficulties involved with this topic had led Jean-François Bonnefoy to conclude in his 1929 monograph that Bonaventure uses the term *sensus spiritualis* equivocally throughout his writings, and that he is simply inconsistent on the matter of the spiritual senses.[18] It is in direct response to Bonnefoy, then, that Rahner advances his own reading, and he evinces a clear desire to cull a coherent doctrine of the spiritual senses from Bonaventure's works.[19] This drive to find a consistent doctrine provides some explanation for Rahner's tendency to gloss over certain ambiguities in Bonaventure's texts.

This still leaves the question, of course, of why Rahner chooses the specific interpretive option that he follows. Instructively for our examination, he writes the following about the fivefold nature of the spiritual senses in Bonaventure's texts: 'This description of the object of the spiritual senses undeniably possesses both depth and beauty, but it must also be admitted that the attempt to discover a special object for every sense, a "ratio" through which it perceives the Word, is rather forced (*un peu forcé*).'[20] Crucially, then, Rahner is inclined to emphasize spiritual touch alone over a fivefold articulation of the doctrine not from an internal assessment of tensions and ambiguities within Bonaventure's texts, but rather from Rahner's own presupposition that the notion of a fivefold doctrine of the spiritual senses is a bit artificial. It is certainly surprising to witness a moment in which the contemporary viability of Bonaventure's thought seems to be dictating Rahner's purportedly historical study.

By contrast, Rahner does find resources with which to articulate a viable doctrine of the spiritual senses when Bonaventure's model of spiritual touch is equated with ecstasy. Rahner clearly holds that Bonaventure's idea of a dark, mystical encounter with God has contemporary theological potential. In particular, Rahner is drawn to the immediate, non-intellectual experience of God involved in the *excessus ecstaticus*. Unlike the fivefold version of the spiritual senses, this apophatic model of union is sustainable in the contemporary setting, according to Rahner.

[18] J.-F. Bonnefoy, *Le Saint-Esprit et ses dons selon saint Bonaventure*, Études de philosophie médiévale, 10 (Paris: J. Vrin, 1929), p. 214.
[19] 'La doctrine des "sens spirituels" au Moyen-Âge', pp. 269–70 (English, pp. 110–11).
[20] 'La doctrine des "sens spirituels" au Moyen-Âge', p. 276 (English, p. 115).

Most significantly for our comparison with the *Vorgriff auf esse* below, spiritual touch confers an immediate experience of God that takes place in the *apex affectus*, the 'deepest' part of the human being. Rahner describes this encounter as follows:

> If God touches this deepest point from within, giving form to it, as it were, then the 'apex affectus' will become conscious of this direct union of love without the intellect taking any active part. The soul experiences God directly (*immédiatement*) in the ground of its being only as the motive power of ecstatic love which leaves all knowledge behind it, and in consequence the experience remains obscure . . . God is here the dark fire of love.[21]

It is this quest for a direct experience of God that drives Rahner's rereading of Bonaventure on the spiritual senses. The notion that the encounter with God occurs in the *apex affectus* makes it of a fundamentally different order than everything else. It is a place where God can be immediately present. 'The "apex affectus" in which God is present is not merely a capacity of the same order as the intellect. As the highest and most interior element in the soul it belongs to a deeper level of reality than the intellect and all that is related to it.'[22] The significance of this idea of the experience of God taking place at a level deeper than conceptual thought will come into view as we examine Rahner's notion of the *Vorgriff auf esse*.

SPIRITUAL TOUCH AND THE *VORGRIFF AUF ESSE*

Fields mentions that 'Bonaventure's mysticism may have inspired Rahner's notion of the pre-apprehension', and as support for this claim he gestures towards the similar time frame within which Rahner was occupied with both topics. Rahner's articles on Bonaventure were published in 1933 and 1934; he wrote his dissertation from 1934 to 1936 at the University of Freiburg (it was later published as *Geist in Welt* in 1939). From a biographical standpoint, then, it is certainly striking that Rahner begins to develop his idea of the *Vorgriff auf esse* immediately after having completed his treatments of the spiritual senses.

The term *Vorgriff*, loosely borrowed from Heidegger, is most often translated in English as 'pre-apprehension', although 'pre-grasp', 'anticipation' and 'dynamic transcendence' are also useful renderings. The *Vorgriff* is

---

[21] 'La doctrine des "sens spirituels" au Moyen-Âge', p. 288 (English, p. 125).
[22] 'La doctrine des "sens spirituels" au Moyen-Âge', p. 288 (English, p. 124). This Rahnerian interpretation of Bonaventure situates him in a broader tradition of affective mysticism, which draws extensively from both Pseudo-Dionysius and Thomas Gallus. See Chapters 5 and 8 in this volume.

frequently regarded as a pre-understanding of being, an ever-receding horizon about which one cannot have conceptual knowledge. It is the condition for the possibility of knowledge, but the *Vorgriff* itself is always unthematic. As Rahner describes this feature of his thought, 'This transcending apprehension of further possibilities, through which the form possessed in a concretion in sensibility is apprehended as limited and so is abstracted, we call "pre-apprehension" (*Vorgriff*).'[23] The pre-apprehension, then, is the 'background' against which all objects of knowledge appear. As such, it is a pre-thematic knowledge of a different order from all other things known by human beings. Francis Schüssler Fiorenza helpfully describes Rahner's *Vorgriff* as 'a pre-apprehension of God . . . a knowledge of God, but God as the undefined and absolute mystery . . . This pre-apprehension is both the condition of the search and the impetus for the search.'[24]

One might be tempted at this point to draw a seemingly clear parallel between Rahner's idea of the *Vorgriff* and the understanding of spiritual touch outlined above. Especially suggestive is the similarity between, on the one hand, the *Vorgriff* as a pre-apprehension of an undefined, mysterious God and, on the other hand, spiritual touch as granting an experience of God deeper than conceptual thought. I suggest, however, that caution should be exercised in making such a comparison between spiritual touch and the notion of the *Vorgriff* as it is articulated at this early point in Rahner's career. Most important in this connection is the fact that Rahner makes a specifically *philosophical* argument in *Spirit in the World*, and it is on the basis of the method by which Rahner derives his early notion of the *Vorgriff* that it should be distinguished from spiritual touch, as I will show below.

In *Spirit in the World*, Rahner begins his philosophical argument for the *Vorgriff* with the metaphysical question: what is being? Rahner's key claim regarding this question is that when we ask the question of being, we ask not just about particular beings, but rather being as a whole. Being human involves being constituted so as to have a 'compelling necessity to ask about being in its totality'.[25] We cannot avoid asking this question, even if only implicitly. And yet, Rahner insists, the very fact that we can ask about being indicates that we have some sort of prior knowledge about it. 'We cannot ask about reality as a whole without thereby affirming the fundamental knowability of reality as a whole.'[26] This affirmation of the

[23] *SW*, p. 142.
[24] F. S. Fiorenza, 'The New Theology and Transcendental Thomism', in J. Livingston (ed.), *Modern Christian Thought: The Twentieth Century* (Upper Saddle River, NJ: Prentice Hall, 2000), p. 210.
[25] *SW*, p. 59.   [26] *SW*, p. 68.

intelligibility of being is always pre-thematic, but for Rahner it represents a genuine contact with reality.

Methodologically, then, Rahner begins his process of reasoning with the fact that we have knowledge of particular things in the world, then on the basis of that fact *infers* that we have a pre-apprehension of being. The idea that we have this pre-apprehension is therefore a logical conclusion derived from the knowledge of finite things. It is what we know must be the case on the basis of an experience of something besides the pre-apprehension of being itself. By contrast, of course, spiritual touch according to Rahner involves the immediate experience of God's presence. This pre-apprehension of being is clearly distinct from an experience of the God who embraces human beings with 'the dark fire of love' as described in his account of Bonaventure's model of spiritual touch.

However, as a number of Rahner scholars have recently argued, key differences obtain between the notion of *Vorgriff* advanced in *Spirit in the World* and the version of the idea articulated in Rahner's later writings.[27] Most significantly, whereas Rahner's early works articulate detailed philosophical defences for the pre-apprehension, one does not observe such sustained philosophical arguments in his later writings. Instead, the pre-apprehension in these works is posited for distinctly theological reasons. Later in his career, for example, Rahner indicates that he is uninterested in defending this notion of the experience of transcendence:

> It is of course no part of our task to show with the aid of an epistemological and existential ontological reflection that the experience of transcendence (which forms our present theme) actually exists as such in man, to show that, in its transcendental necessity with which it is present as a condition of human knowledge as a whole, it also includes an equally necessary and irreversible dependence on the mind (in knowledge and freedom) on that which or him whom in Christian terminology we call God. All this is simply presupposed here.[28]

On the basis of this passage and others, Karen Kilby argues that Rahner's method moves in a theological direction during the course of his career. She maintains that 'the *Vorgriff* ought to be understood to function more as a theological proposal than as a prior philosophical claim'.[29] Francis

---

[27] See F. S. Fiorenza, 'Rahner on Method', in D. Marmion and M. E. Hines (eds.), *The Cambridge Companion to Karl Rahner* (Cambridge University Press, 2005), pp. 65–82; K. Kilby, *Karl Rahner: Theology and Philosophy* (New York: Routledge, 2004), esp. pp. 19–31; P. Endean, *Karl Rahner and Ignatian Spirituality* (Oxford University Press, 2001).

[28] K. Rahner, 'Experience of Transcendence from the Standpoint of Catholic Dogmatics', in *Theological Investigations*, vol. XVIII: *God and Revelation*, trans. E. Quinn (New York: Crossroad, 1983), pp. 173–4; Kilby, *Karl Rahner*, p. 84.

[29] Kilby, *Karl Rahner*, p. 103.

Schüssler Fiorenza similarly observes a shift from the early to late Rahner, and he indicates a problematic trend in the interpretation of Rahner's thought: 'Rahner's method is analysed almost exclusively in relation to its philosophical foundations in *Spirit in the World* ... Such approaches disregard significant innovations within Rahner's theological writings in the ensuing decades.'[30] In particular, Fiorenza observes, 'Rahner moves from the language of being in his early philosophical writings to the language of mystery. Whereas his early philosophical writings emphasized the intelligibility of being, his theological writings underscore the mystery of God.'[31]

Last, and most significant for our purposes, Philip Endean maintains that Ignatian spirituality had an enduring impact on Rahner's theology, and that the *Vorgriff* is actually rearticulated in accord with this influence later in Rahner's career. Endean points to an essay of 1956 (published in 1958) indicative of this shift. Whereas Rahner's early writings regard the *Vorgriff* as an inferential knowledge of God based on finite objects in the world, in this essay he discusses a different notion of the pre-apprehension. This version of the *Vorgriff*, in Rahner's words, has 'a function which is no longer simply that of making possible the apprehension of objects of knowledge belonging to this world and of God by means of concepts formed from such objects, but designates in contrast to these modes of cognition an immediacy and independence in the pre-apprehension of God (*eine Unmittelbarkeit und Fürsichstandigkeit dieses Vorgriffes auf Gott*)'.[32] As is true for Rahner's notion of spiritual touch, then, so too in this version of his *Vorgriff* do we observe an emphasis on the immediate presence of God. The awareness of absolute being is no longer inferred; instead, it is directly experienced.

Remarkably, later in the same essay Rahner actually draws on the language of perception used in the spiritual senses tradition to describe the characteristics of this *Vorgriff*, or immediate experience of God.

This experience lays hold of the soul completely, opens the soul in a way in which it is clearly not generally open, in ordinary or even in reverent and devout knowledge of God. We are, therefore, dealing with an experience in which the very centre of the spiritual person as such comes into action and expressly so, experienced as such. This actual concrete central experience is identical with a 'perception' or

---

[30] Fiorenza, 'Rahner on Method', p. 68.　　[31] *Ibid.* p. 69.
[32] Rahner, 'Die Logik der existentiellen Erkenntnis bei Ignatius v. Loyola', in *Das Dynamische in der Kirche* (Freiburg: Herder, 1958), p. 127, trans. W. J. O'Hara as 'The Logic of Concrete Individual Knowledge in Ignatius Loyola', in *The Dynamic Element in the Church* (New York: Herder & Herder, 1964), p. 146, translation emended. Endean, *Karl Rahner*, p. 129.

'sense' (*Wahrnehmung*). For theological reasons we must exclude an interpretation that would make this a *visio beata immediata* in the doctrinal sense. Nevertheless, it has an immediacy about it that makes it possible and necessary to term it a 'perception' or 'sense' of God, on account of its clearly experienced difference from other pious sentiments in thought and love. It is consequently clear too that the 'immediate' (*unmittelbare*) derivation of this consolation from God is inwardly 'perceived', and also how and why this is so. The source itself is perceived, the divine origin of the consolation is not merely inferred.[33]

In this extraordinary passage, we can clearly see Rahner's reading of Bonaventure on spiritual touch influencing his account of the experience of God. First, and most obviously, Rahner describes an experience during which one 'perceives' or 'senses' (*wahrnehmen*) God. Second, this perception is not one of clear vision, but it is instead an opaque awareness of God's presence that brings to mind the dark 'contact' with God that Rahner describes in his work on Bonaventure. Third, Rahner here speaks of an immediate experience, which is of course what he takes great pains to affirm in his reading of Bonaventure on spiritual touch. Fourth, and last, in this description, God is not only present to the human being, but present in a manner that is utterly unique, as is the case in Rahner's interpretation of Bonaventure when spiritual touch is equated with the *excessus ecstaticus*.

On the one hand, then, I suggest that it would be too strong to say that Rahner's study of Bonaventure 'inspired' his notion of the *Vorgriff auf esse*. The version of the idea that Rahner formulates between 1934 and 1936 manifests noteworthy differences from the notion of spiritual touch that he describes in his Bonaventure study. Most particularly, this philosophical notion of the *Vorgriff* offers only inferential knowledge of the absolute. At this early point in Rahner's career, it seems most reasonable to regard him as having come to his initial idea of the *Vorgriff* via independent means that were not especially impacted by his reading of Bonaventure.

On the other hand, however, one cannot help but notice that Rahner changes his idea of the *Vorgriff* during his career, and that it is eventually brought in line with his understanding of spiritual touch to a remarkable extent. Furthermore, Rahner's obvious interest in articulating a viable doctrine of the spiritual senses makes it unlikely that the idea would wholly vanish from his theological considerations. Last, Rahner explicitly uses the language of the spiritual senses later in his career than has been recognized in previous scholarship on this topic. It seems likely, therefore, that the

---

[33] Rahner, 'Die Logik der existentiellen Erkenntnis', p. 134 (English, pp. 153–4).

constructive potential that Rahner saw in the idea of spiritual touch had a slow, subterranean influence on his rearticulation of the notion of *Vorgriff* that eventuated in the notion of the pre-apprehension as the dark, immediate presence of God. Although the doctrine of the spiritual senses could not rightly be said to have inspired Rahner's notion of the *Vorgriff*, then, it does seem to have been in ongoing relationship with the idea of the pre-apprehension of being that subtly changed it over time.

BALTHASAR'S USE OF THE DOCTRINE OF THE SPIRITUAL SENSES

Balthasar closely studies Rahner's work on the spiritual senses in the early 1930s,[34] and he refers to the spiritual senses tradition in a number of his writings throughout his career.[35] With the publication of his theological aesthetics in the 1960s, however, Balthasar makes full systematic use of the doctrine.[36] At the heart of Balthasar's aesthetics stands the task of perceiving the glory of the divine form (*Gestalt*) through which God is revealed to human beings. Although extensive scholarly attention has focused on Balthasar's understanding of both revelation and form, what has not been sufficiently addressed is his model of the perceptual faculties by which the human being is made capable of beholding the form that God reveals. I suggest that this lacuna in contemporary scholarship can be addressed by looking at the role played by the spiritual senses in *The Glory of the Lord*. To appreciate the significance of the doctrine for his theological aesthetics, however, it will first be necessary to look at the contours of Balthasar's project through his central categories of beauty and form.

To Balthasar, much of modern theology has neglected the beauty of God's revelation. He describes his project as an 'attempt to develop a

---

[34] In October 1934 Balthasar writes a letter to Josef Pieper in which he makes overt mention of Rahner's studies. Quoted in M. Lochbrunner, *Hans Urs von Balthasar und seine Philosophenfreunde* (Würzburg: Echter Verlag, 2005), p. 15.

[35] See esp. H. U. von Balthasar (ed.), *Origenes, Geist und Feuer: Ein Aufbau aus seinen Werken* (Salzburg: Otto Müller, 1938), trans. R. Daley, *Origen, Spirit and Fire: A Thematic Anthology of his Writings* (Washington, DC: Catholic University of America Press, 2001); Balthasar, *Kosmische Liturgie: Maximus der Bekenner: Höhe und Krise des griechischen Weltbilds* (Freiburg: Herder, 1941), later published as *Kosmische Liturgie: Das Weltbild Maximus' des Bekenners* (Einsiedeln: Johannes Verlag, 1961), trans. B. Daley, SJ, *Cosmic Liturgy: The Universe According to Maximus the Confessor* (San Francisco: Ignatius Press, 2003); *Das betrachtende Gebet* (Einsiedeln: Johannes Verlag, 1955), trans. G. Harrison, *Prayer* (San Francisco: Ignatius Press, 1986); *Sponsa verbi: Skizzen zur Theologie II* (Einsiedeln: Johannes Verlag, 1961), trans. A. V. Littledale, A. Dru, B. McNeil et al., *Explorations in Theology*, vol II: *Spouse of the Word* (San Francisco: Ignatius Press, 1991); *Christlich meditieren* (Freiburg: Herder, 1984), trans. M. Skerry, *Christian Meditation* (San Francisco: Ignatius Press, 1989).

[36] See esp. *GL*, vol. I, pp. 365–425.

Christian theology in the light of the third transcendental, that is to say: to complement the vision of the true and the good with that of the beautiful'.[37] As is thoroughly documented in expositions of his thought, 'beauty' for Balthasar is not merely ornamental; talk of 'the beautiful' does not pertain to surface appearance.[38] Rather, as a transcendental property of Being, beauty permeates all of reality at its very roots (as do the other transcendentals, truth and goodness). In witnessing true beauty, therefore, one comes into contact with the shimmering depths of Being as it shines forth to the human person.

Additionally, as Balthasar never tires of repeating, the beauty of God must not be 'Platonized' or 'demythologized' into something essentially spiritual, separable from the material medium of its expression.[39] As he puts this point, 'The original of beauty lies not in a disembodied spirit which looks about for a field of expression and, finding one, adjusts it to its own purposes as one would set up a typewriter and begin typing, afterwards to abandon it.'[40] The notion of beauty against which Balthasar writes would regard the union of the beautiful with the material form as merely incidental. For Balthasar, by contrast, beauty is fundamentally conjoined with the concrete medium of its expression.

Balthasar's notion that beauty is always concretely manifested leads to his claim that beauty must take a form (*Gestalt*). That is, the beautiful does not 'begin', so to speak, as an incorporeal spirit that then takes form upon itself in a second movement of sorts. Instead, all beauty is shown through the form. Balthasar puts this idea succinctly when he writes, 'Only through form can the lightning-bolt of eternal beauty flash.'[41] Moreover, the materiality of the form does not in any way compromise or diminish the beauty that shines through it. To Balthasar,

Visible form not only 'points' to an invisible, unfathomable mystery; form is the apparition of this mystery, and reveals it while, naturally, at the same time protecting and veiling it. Both natural and artistic form have an exterior which appears and an interior depth, both of which, however, are not separable in the form itself. The content (*Gehalt*) does not lie behind the form (*Gestalt*), but within it.[42]

Form, then, could be said to have two distinct yet ultimately inseparable components in Balthasar's aesthetics. There is the materially manifested

---

[37] *GL*, vol. I, Foreword.
[38] See, for example, A. Nichols, *The Word has been Abroad: A Guide through Balthasar's Aesthetics* (Edinburgh: T. & T. Clark, 1999), pp. 1–33.
[39] *GL*, vol. I, p. 411.   [40] *GL*, vol. I, p. 20.
[41] *GL*, vol. I, p. 32.   [42] *GL*, vol. I, p. 151, translation emended.

form, which is visible and concrete, and then there is the content of the
form, which although 'invisible', shines forth as mystery and depth through
the material form. 'We are confronted simultaneously with both the figure
and that which shines forth from the figure, making it into a worthy, a
loveworthy (*liebenswürdig*) thing.'[43] Balthasar uses the Thomistic categories
of *species* (or *forma*) and *lumen* (or *splendor*) to develop these two aspects
of the manifestation of beauty.[44] Whereas *species* refers in its strictest sense
to the actual material form itself, *lumen* indicates the glory of Being that is
shown through it.

Of course, if we think of *species* and *lumen* as separable from each
other, then we lapse into dualism, in Balthasar's estimation. In such a case,
Balthasar says,

We still remain within a parallelism of ostensive sign and signified interior light.
This dualism can be abolished only by introducing as well the thought-forms and
categories of the beautiful. The beautiful is above all a form, and the light does
not fall on this form from above and from outside, rather it breaks forth from the
form's interior. *Species* and *lumen* in beauty are one.[45]

Balthasar, then, holds a deeply non-dualist understanding of form in which
the splendour of *Gestalt* is inextricable from its material aspect. He further
writes:

The appearance of the form, as revelation of the depths, is an indissoluble union
of two things. It is the real presence of the depths, of the whole of reality, *and* it is
a real pointing beyond itself to these depths... both aspects are inseparable from
one another, and together they constitute the fundamental configuration of Being.
We 'behold' the form; but, if we really behold it, it is not as a detached form,
rather in its unity with the depths that make their appearance in it. We see form
as the splendour, as the glory of Being. We are 'enraptured' by our contemplation
of these depths and are 'transported' to them. But, so long as we are dealing with
the beautiful, this never happens in such a way that we leave the (horizontal) form
behind us in order to plunge (vertically) into the naked depths.[46]

The luminosity of being remains 'tied', as it were, to the particular, concrete
form through which it shines.

The ultimate form, of course, or super-form (*Übergestalt*), to use
Balthasar's terminology, is that of Christ. The form of Christ displays
absolute beauty, to which all other worldly beauty is relative. Building
from the above treatment of *Gestalt*, we can see how Balthasar's theory of
form lends him resources with which to treat the reality of God's presence

---

43 *GL*, vol. I, p. 20.   44 *GL*, vol. I, pp. 117–18.
45 *GL*, vol. I, p. 151.   46 *GL*, vol. I, pp. 118–19.

in the world. In Christ, we do not see a mere pointer to the divine; Christ is not a sign. Instead, in the Christ-form, we encounter the divine presence in the very midst of creaturely reality.[47] The person of Jesus is the medium through which God is made known. Knowledge of God, then, is inextricably linked to this concrete form.

Much more could be said about Balthasar's notion of form. For our immediate purposes, however, the most significant points to observe are, first, the fact that the form is the necessary medium through which the glory of God and the depths of reality are made present to the human being and, second, the manner in which the visible, sensory aspects of *species* and the invisible, supersensory aspects of *lumen* inextricably cohere as a unity-in-duality on Balthasar's ontology of aesthetic form.

PERCEPTION IN BALTHASAR'S THEOLOGICAL AESTHETICS

If the glory of God is mediated to the human being through the form, then perceiving this form stands out as an absolutely essential task for Balthasar's theological aesthetics. Balthasar himself makes clear that perception is central to his project: 'A "theological aesthetics" . . . has as its object primarily the perception of the divine self-manifestation.'[48] And yet this notion of perception is distinct from the status ordinarily granted the category. Balthasar here resists, for example, the Kantian division of reality into a phenomenal realm that can be perceived and a noumenal realm that is wholly inaccessible to the senses. Instead, he has in mind a more robust idea of what 'perceiving' means. Balthasar holds that 'one must possess a spiritual eye capable of perceiving (*wahrnehmen*) the forms of existence with awe. (What a word: "Perception" [Wahr-nehmung]! And philosophy has twisted it to mean precisely the opposite of what it says: "the seeing of what is true!")'[49] For Balthasar, then, perception belongs at the very centre of our grasp of truth. Balthasar hints at the specific sort of perception that his project will require in this same portion of his theological aesthetics. He writes, 'For this particular perception of truth, of course, a "new light" is expressly required which illumines this particular form, a light which at the same time breaks forth from within the form itself. In this way, the "new light" will at the same time make seeing the form possible and *be itself seen along with the form*.'[50] On the basis of the foregoing analysis of Balthasar's understanding of *Gestalt*, we can see that this 'new light' of which he speaks

---

[47] *GL*, vol. I, p. 432.   [48] *GL*, vol. I, Foreword.
[49] *GL*, vol. I, p. 24. See also *GL*, vol. I, p. 120.   [50] *GL*, vol. I, p. 120, italics added.

corresponds to the invisible splendour of the form; I will next demonstrate that it is precisely through the spiritual senses that this new light is seen.

THE ROLE OF THE SPIRITUAL SENSES IN BALTHASAR'S THEOLOGICAL AESTHETICS

Given the terms that Balthasar has set for his theological aesthetics, the crucial role played by the spiritual senses should now be coming into view. We have seen that the form, on Balthasar's model, consists of both sensory and supersensory dimensions, both visible and 'invisible' aspects, and we have seen the centrality of perceiving the form for Balthasar's project. Balthasar attempts to rehabilitate perception for theology, but mere sensory perception alone will not suffice for the task Balthasar has set for himself. Balthasar writes, 'Eyes are needed that are able to perceive the spiritual form.'[51] In order for the supersensory, invisible splendour of the form to be perceived, a notion of perception that exceeds the corporeal realm must be developed. It is precisely at this juncture that Balthasar makes his appeal to the doctrine of the spiritual senses. He writes, 'We will do this by taking our lead from the concept of the "spiritual senses" ... these constitute the final word on the specificity of the subjective evidence with regard to the Christian object.'[52] Balthasar describes the need for this model of the perceptual faculties of the human being as follows: 'In Christianity God appears to man right in the midst of worldly reality. The centre of this act of encounter must, therefore, lie where the profane human senses, making possible the act of faith, become "spiritual".'[53] Human perception requires a transformation for the subjective conditions of the receipt of revelation to be fulfilled. As Balthasar memorably captures this transition, 'Our senses, together with images and thoughts, must die with Christ and descend to the underworld in order then to rise unto the Father in an unspeakable manner that is both sensory and suprasensory.'[54] The spiritual senses, then, lie at the very centre of the encounter between the human being and God.

At the outset of this chapter I claimed that it is through the spiritual senses that one performs the task of seeing the form. We are now sufficiently familiar with the terms used in Balthasar's theological aesthetics for a more precise formulation of this idea: although the corporeal senses perceive the material form, it is the spiritual senses that behold the splendour and luminosity of being as it is revealed in the supersensory aspect of the form.

---

[51] *GL*, vol. I, p. 24.   [52] *GL*, vol. I, p. 365.   [53] *GL*, vol. I, p. 365.   [54] *GL*, vol. I, p. 425.

Of course, it should immediately be said that Balthasar's ontology of form forbids a separation of the material from the splendour that shines forth from it, and it should also be mentioned that Balthasar's anthropology forbids a separation of the corporeal from the spiritual.[55] In truth, then, both aspects of form are perceived in simultaneity by both the corporeal and the spiritual perceptual faculties in the human being. This formulation, however, is of service to us inasmuch as it allows us to put a finer point on the exact role of the spiritual senses in Balthasar's theological aesthetics.

From this vantage point, then, we can see the significance of a doctrine of the spiritual senses for the fulfilment of Balthasar's goals as he puts them forward in his theological aesthetics. That is, inasmuch as Balthasar calls for perception of the form, and inasmuch as that form consists of both sensory and 'supersensory' aspects (i.e. a material component and a 'spiritual' dimension), some account of the way in which this human perception exceeds the material realm is absolutely essential to the success of Balthasar's project. In other words, it is precisely because the form itself is possessed of both sensory and supersensory aspects that the perception of that form must be both sensory and supersensory. Balthasar's theological aesthetics thus demands a doctrine of the spiritual senses; in fact, one could go so far as to claim that if such a doctrine did not already exist, then for purposes of his theological aesthetics Balthasar would need to invent it.

CONCLUSION

The above examination has argued that the spiritual senses are highly significant for the theologies of Karl Rahner and Hans Urs von Balthasar. In Rahner's case, I claimed that the spiritual senses function as an ongoing, 'subterranean' influence on his rearticulation of the *Vorgriff auf esse* that takes place later in his career. This notion not only helps to explain the otherwise curious disappearance of the spiritual senses from Rahner's theological considerations after 1934; it also, of course, indicates that the doctrine should be regarded as more than an item of historical interest in Rahner's early writings on Christian spirituality. Moreover, looked at through the lens of the spiritual senses, we see that Rahner is much less preoccupied with 'philosophy' than is often thought to be the case. If Rahner's understanding of spiritual touch comes to significantly shape his understanding of the point of contact between the human being and God,

---

[55] For an exposition of Balthasar's 'non-dualist' anthropology, see *GL*, vol. 1, pp. 380–3, 406–7, 425.

then concerns about Rahner's anthropology being overly dictated by his philosophical starting point will need to be reconsidered.

In Balthasar's case, we see that the spiritual senses occupy a position of noteworthy prominence in his theological aesthetics, and indeed that his project actually requires such an account of spiritual perception for its success. If the form is to be perceived, then spiritual senses are necessary for the task. Furthermore, Balthasar's rearticulation of the spiritual senses indicates that he does in fact focus on the epistemological capacities of the human being more than is typically thought to be the case among commentators on his texts. Through Balthasar's appropriation of the spiritual senses tradition, then, one observes that he develops an anthropological structure that precisely mirrors the sensory and supersensory dimensions of the form, accounting for the perception of both aspects for his theological aesthetics.

CHAPTER 16

Analytic philosophers of religion

William J. Abraham

In 1901 Robert Campbell Moberly (1845–1903), the distinguished Anglican theologian, published a lengthy book on the atonement entitled *Atonement and Personality*.[1] Buried in the middle of it is a chapter that sketches an interesting analysis of the concept of reason in theology. The vision of reason is nicely sandwiched between an account of human agency and of the capacity to love in a chapter entitled 'The Holy Spirit in Relation to Human Personality'. This trinity of topics fitted neatly together for Moberly in two distinct ways. First, he insisted that in each case a proper understanding of these concepts begins with our initial and inchoate grasp of these notions and then moves to a richer account engendered by his robust trinitarian theology. Second, the proper functioning of human agency, human reason and the capacity to love are intimately related, so that reason, as applied in theology, depends on proper human self-realization brought about by radical submission to Christ through the Spirit and resulting in an emancipation that brings true love to expression in human relations.

Moberly is operating in a tradition that depicts reason as a faculty. In its initial manifestation the exercise of this 'rational' faculty takes the prosaic form of question and answer, comparison, inference and discovery. This is reason operating in the early stage of development. Reason at this level is infantile; using it in this manner is like acquiring the capacity to walk; it is really the 'grating and creaking of the machinery'[2] in its initial operations. Thus this cannot be the essence of reason. Reason in its most serious sense is 'the capacity of personal insight into reality – of all kinds, and most of all whatever is highest and most inclusive as reality'.[3] It is the 'personal capacity of *beholding* wisdom and truth'.[4] This vision of reason fits snugly with a hierarchy of truths. 'Truth of course is manifold and multiform. There

---

[1] R. C. Moberly, *Atonement and Personality* (London: John Murray, 1901).
[2] *Ibid.* p. 234.   [3] *Ibid.* p. 234.   [4] *Ibid.* p. 234, italics mine.

are truths of material fact: truths of abstract statement; truths of historical occurrence; truths of moral experience; truths of spiritual existence; and that truth is deepest and truest which most includes and unifies them all.'[5] It also fits snugly with the clear remnants of an Idealist metaphysics which are peeping through the surface of his thinking.[6]

Building on this metaphysical foundation, Moberly proceeds to develop his own account of the exercise of reason in theology, perhaps the only place where the highest and most inclusive kind of truth is to be found. In this arena, moral and spiritual experience is essential. More precisely, perception of the truth about God requires self-surrender (mirroring and engendered by the self-surrender of Christ on the cross) and spiritual regeneration through the work of the Holy Spirit.

It is not indeed that the powers of human intellect are contemptible. The powers of human intellect are transcendent, beyond all capacity of utterance. But the condition of the development of the transcendent powers of human intellect is its self-surrender, and through this self-surrender, transformation, from its first nakedness of separate self-sufficiency – to the humblest and most dutiful communion with God. By sacrifice of what seemed to it to be its very self, its essential independence of prerogative, it arises purified: the scales dropped off; the mote and beam alike gone: the eyes of the Spirit really opened; the vision of God unveiled. It had been trying to read the secret of wisdom through methods and under limitations which made any real apprehension thereof impossible. Vainly, to the end of time, will human wisdom that has passed through no regenerating process, – spirit-humbling at once, and eye-opening; vainly, that is, will philosophy, otherwise than in conscious and open dependence upon theological truth, attempt to read the riddle of existence, whether in external phenomena, or in man, or in God.[7]

For Moberly, then, human beings can transcend their natural powers of perception and come truly to see spiritually when they are transformed by self-surrender to the work of the Holy Spirit. Given access to the truth thereby discerned, they can then begin accurately to see the deep truth about ultimate reality.

The end of such experience is the capacity to perceive God rightly both in creation and in Christ.

---

[5] *Ibid.* p. 234.

[6] See esp. *ibid.* p. 235: 'the minds of individual persons realize truth, not in proportion as they are independent of, but rather as they perfectly correspond with and reflect that *larger truth of Mind*, which is itself equally true whether reflected in individual apprehension or no. Obviously, in this case at least, *the personal perfectness depends not on its diversity from, but its identity with, a certain larger whole of which the personal perfectness is at most but a part*'. Italics mine.

[7] *Ibid.* p. 242. Note here (and in the next quotation) the critical appearance of the language of sight that is at the heart of Moberly's position.

To see, in the white, worn, bleeding flesh of a crucified convict, the Lord of Life and of death, was no exercise of ordinary, or scientific, reason in the mind of the penitent thief. But it was true insight, into truth as true, not the less but the more, for that. To see God in every common sight: to see Christ above all in the daily experience of the Christian life; to see the majesty of His presence in the person of the poor and sordid sufferer; to see the Glory of His Spirit in little efforts for good for which the world, if it saw them at all, would resent or despise: this requires indeed conditions and faculties of insight which we sometimes, by perfect antithesis, are ready even to contrast with 'rational'; and yet it is, after all, a true insight into truth of Divine fact, in the highest conceivable plane of Divine truth.[8]

It is clear that Moberly was developing a vision of the spiritual perception or discernment that was foundational to his epistemology of theology. Failure to take this up in a book on atonement would have left it with a massive lacuna; understanding what God did in the death of Christ required properly attuned spiritual perception. It is equally clear that this whole approach was swept away at the beginnings of analytic philosophy in the first quarter of the twentieth century. The marriage to Idealism, so characteristic of a golden period in Anglican theology in England into the 1930s, turned out to have been a fateful one.[9] Idealism was utterly undermined by the devastating attack launched against it in terms of theories of meaning as verification by sense-experience; so much so that the kind of moves envisaged here by Moberly simply became unintelligible. The irony of the situation a century later is that the kind of position represented by Moberly is now a live option within analytic philosophy. To be sure, the Idealism is gone; but the fundamentals of the epistemology visible here in Moberly have gained a new lease of life. Indeed, we are in the surprising position of having various ways of articulating what Moberly was after, epistemically speaking. Interestingly, some of the problems that are immediately visible in Moberly also haunt the discussion today. So after reviewing the current state of the discussion, I shall circle back to Moberly en route to a brief final commentary.

There is no need to rehearse in detail the revolution in philosophy that Moberly was not equipped to challenge. Beginning with A. J. Ayer's brilliant *Language, Truth, and Logic*,[10] the positivists turned Moberly's position on its head. Ayer championed a vision of reason that focused

---

[8] *Ibid.* p. 239.
[9] There were problems, of course, from the beginning, for Idealists like Bradley posed a serious challenge to Christian theology on several fronts.
[10] A. J. Ayer, *Language, Truth, and Logic* (New York: Dover, 1952). It was originally published in 1936.

resolutely and exclusively on sense-experience; he made Moberly's bottom tier of truth (that available to observation by sense experience) the only form of truth; he interpreted (or dismissed) moral claims as expressions of emotion; and he systematically rejected all reference to the transcendent as literally meaningless. The result was a radical cleansing of the metaphysical stables that swept theology aside as a form of nonsense.

Many theologians inspired by Karl Barth took refuge in a world of divine revelation insulated from philosophical scrutiny; his disciples and the ingenious innovations they have developed continue to flourish to a third and fourth generation. Those who were more hospitable to the positive significance of philosophical reflection on religion as represented by the analytic tradition endured life in the wilderness for a generation. The initial efforts to turn back the tide of positivism eventually bore fruit in the late 1960s, by which time the acknowledgement of theological discourse as inescapably factual made it possible to reopen the older questions about the justification of religious belief that had been the heart of philosophy of religion even for sceptics like David Hume and for fideistic accommodationists like Immanuel Kant. In turn a quiet revolution in epistemology, represented by the collapse of classical foundationalism, a fresh encounter with John Henry Newman and the rediscovery of Thomas Reid, opened the door for a whole new raft of options in the epistemology of theology. What emerged was a revolution in epistemology that created space for a fresh start in which the rehabilitation of an appeal to the spiritual senses became not only possible but attractive.

I take the spiritual senses tradition to be minimally constituted by the thesis that perception of the divine can be a legitimate ground of theological assertion. It is nicely captured in the beatitude 'Blessed are the pure in heart for they shall see God' (Matt 5: 8). More generally it posits that the reality, activity and nature of God are visible in, say, creation, the life of Jesus of Nazareth and the lives of the saints. So the core claim hinges on the possibility of perception of the divine. This then is extended into the denser claim that human agents are equipped by appropriate senses that discern the truth about God accurately. Note that neither the minimalist claim nor its denser forms involve any claim to self-authentication, or infallibility, or incorrigibility. Nor do they rule out the possibility of other kinds of legitimate grounds for theological assertions, like, say, deduction, cumulative case arguments, inference to the best explanation or special divine revelation. Indeed, one of the important questions raised by claims about perception of the divine is precisely how these claims relate to other potential warrants in theology.[11] This in turn hinges on how the idea of perception of the divine is unpacked epistemically.

One philosopher who took up the appeal to perception of the divine in the teeth of the positivist veto was John Hick. Hick looked to verification in the life to come to meet the positivist demand for verification. In the life to come it was potentially possible to verify Christian theistic assertion about the nature of God; but this was not the case in our present life. In this life, Christians lived by faith, a form of knowledge represented by *seeing* the world as a whole as created, directed, redeemed and brought to its proper end by God. Atheists, of course, see the world differently. However, this is no deterrent to the Christian theist's position. 'All conscious experience of our environment is in terms of the concepts by which we apprehend (or of course misapprehend) objects and situations as having this or that character or meaning. In other words, all experiencing is . . . experiencing-as. The (theistically) religious mind experiences life as being lived in the unseen presence of God and within the sphere of an on-going purpose.'[12] This experience could then be confirmed in the life to come; indeed it could be confirmed to the point of cognitive conclusiveness, that is, verification. This being so, it was a very small step to say that such a way of perceiving the world could be confirmed in this life, a step taken by Basil Mitchell in *The Justification of Religious Belief*.[13] Having pioneered a tradition of cumulative arguments in favour of Christian theism, Mitchell, unlike Hick, was not content to let experience of God stand alone without additional support.

A similar judgement shows up in the work of Richard Swinburne and Caroline Franks Davis.[14] Swinburne takes claims to awareness of God as instantiations of the more general claim to perceive God or divine activity. Perception of God should in turn be seen in terms of a causal theory of perception. 'S perceives X (believing that he is so doing) if and only if an experience of its seeming (epistemically) to S that X is present was caused by X's being present.'[15] This theory of perception is then applied across the

---

[11] This issue is taken up by William Wainwright in Chapter 13 above.

[12] J. Hick, 'Eschatological Verification Reconsidered', *Religious Studies*, 13 (1977), 200–1. Hick developed a full-scale vision of such faith as knowledge in his *Faith and Knowledge* (Ithaca, NY: Cornell University Press, 1957; 2nd edn, Cornell University Press, 1966).

[13] B. Mitchell, *The Justification of Religious Belief* (London: Macmillan, 1973).

[14] R. Swinburne, *The Existence of God* (Oxford: Clarendon Press, 1979); C. F. Davis, *The Evidential Force of Religious Experience* (Oxford: Clarendon Press, 1989). J. Gellman, *Mystical Experience of God: A Philosophical Inquiry* (Burlington, VT: Ashgate, 2001) is also worth consulting. So too is W. J. Wainwright, *Mysticism: A Study of its Nature, Cognitive Value, and Moral Implications* (Madison: University of Wisconsin Press, 1981).

[15] Swinburne, *The Existence of God*, p. 247.

board to religious experiences, that is, to experiences that seem to the subject to be experiences of God. Some of these are public in that they are shared with others ('I perceive God present in creation'); others are private in that they are relative to the subject ('God told me in a dream to take Mary as my wife'). Either way the subject is entitled to take them as veridical unless there is good evidence to believe otherwise. This entitlement is sanctioned by a very general principle of rationality enshrined in the Principle of Credulity: 'How things seem to be is good grounds for a belief about how things are.'[16] For Swinburne, the only alternative to this is scepticism. The Principle of Credulity is a basic principle of rationality; every effort to find a warrant for it, say, by induction already presupposes its validity; the only real alternative is a sceptical bog.

What this means for the epistemology of theology is this: if we find ourselves aware of God (say, perceiving God in creation or in this or that religious experience) we should take that awareness as veridical unless we have good reason to believe otherwise. The defeaters that overturn veridicality are obvious: we show that the subject is unreliable, that the awareness arises in unreliable circumstances, that the claim is overridden by relevant background circumstances or that there are causes of the experience other than God. Until such defeaters are supplied the subject's interpretations should be taken as veridical; they are innocent until proven guilty. Moreover, the principle of credulity is complemented by the principle of testimony. 'Other things being equal, we think that what others tell us they perceived, probably happened.'[17] Clearly this extends the range of evidence derived from perception of the divine; but the appeal to testimony, of course, is parasitic on the principle of credulity, for reports of our perceptions are secondary to those perceptions. Moreover, Swinburne is well aware of the minimalist epistemic role this latter move involves.[18] Thus he appeals to religious experience only after a long and complex cumulative case argument for theism. The appeal to religious experience comes in at the very end to tilt the scales decisively in the direction of generic theism.[19]

One of the striking features of Swinburne's proposals is the resolute rejection of any effort to drive a wedge between our perception of ordinary objects of sense and our perception of the divine. The standard move on

---

[16] *Ibid.* p. 254.   [17] *Ibid.* p. 271.

[18] The very way in which Swinburne names his principle of rationality, that is, as one of 'credulity', alerts us to the stark minimalism involved, for it suggests that the mere appearing of p to be true gives initial ground for p being true. This is the lowest of the low (if it is anything) in epistemology.

[19] The overall structure of Swinburne's strategy is worth noting here. He begins with purely secular understanding of concepts and argument and then applies them to theological issues. His work as a whole is a brilliant, relentless exhibition of this strategy.

this score was to accept the Principle of Credulity as applied to, say, tables and chairs but to reject it once the description became more ramified and contested. It did not apply to cases where the subject claimed to see angels, demons or divine activity in creation or Christ. The latter were seen as involving interpretations of experience rather than experiences *simpliciter*. This worry was taken up by Caroline Franks Davis in terms of the status of the interactive nature of concept formation as applied to all experience. The crucial worry can be captured nicely in terms of the problem of vicious circularity. Given that experience of God involves interpretations of experience in terms of religious doctrines, any appeal to these experiences to justify the relevant doctrines must be viciously circular. Prior evidence that the doctrines are probably true needs to be in place before we are entitled to place a religious interpretation on our experience. Clearly, if this holds, the appeal to perception of divine collapses immediately.

Franks Davis takes this worry head on by arguing that this line of argument depends on a network of indefensible assumptions

which can be expressed as: (i) the idea that one can distinguish between 'the given' and 'interpretation', so that a religious experience is 'an interpretation of an experience' in a way that sensory perception of material objects is not; (ii) a linear, foundationalist view of the relationship between beliefs and experiences, and a naïve 'associational' view of concept formation; (iii) a rigidly non-cumulative view of the justification of perceptual claims; and (iv) ignorance of the principle of credulity.[20]

She proceeds to make good on the indefensibility of these assumptions by providing an unusually dense and sensitive account of concept formation and of incorporated interpretation as applied to religious experience. Her conclusion provides a sophisticated reiteration of Swinburne's central claim: 'Religious incorporated interpretations, like all incorporated interpretations, must be regarded prima facie as probably trustworthy, but challenges are always possible.'[21]

A very different but equally thorough effort to establish epistemic parity between ordinary sensory perception and perception of the divine within the context of a cumulative case argument for Christian theism has been developed by William P. Alston (1921–2009).[22] His *Perceiving God: The*

[20] Davis, *The Evidential Force of Religious Experience*, pp. 143–4.
[21] *Ibid.* p. 165. The rest of her book is a concerted effort to deal with the challenge of conflicting claims and the challenge of reductionistic redescription.
[22] The crucial elements in the cumulative case for Alston are tradition, divine revelation, natural theology and the internal structure of Christian belief.

Epistemology of Religious Experience[23] represents one of the most important texts in analytic philosophy of religion in the last generation. The background music in play in this case is reliabilist in orientation, that is, Alston insists that our standard sources of belief as represented by perception, introspection and memory should be accepted on trust as reliable until particular instances of these have been shown otherwise by appropriate internal challenges. Conventional efforts to ground these sources in something deeper fail for one reason or another. We do not need to provide a rationale for their reliability before we take them as grounds for the beliefs that they generate. He then uses this epistemic framework (itself worked out with characteristic felicity and rigour in his more general work in epistemology) to explain how our perceptual beliefs about God can be justified.

Alston develops his own technical vocabulary to explore and explain both the epistemology of sensory perception and the epistemology of perception of the divine.[24] What is at issue in both cases is not an argument to the effect that the existence of perceptual objects or the existence of God provide the best explanation for sensory experience or religious experience but that people perceive both perceptual objects and God and thereby acquire justified beliefs about perceptual objects and God. There is here in play a full-blooded realist perspective licensed by a Theory of Appearing in which perception of something's appearing *as such-and-such* is taken as basic and unanalysable. There is no effort here to prove the genuineness of perception of God; rather there is the defence of the claim that the construal of experience of God as perception can be defended on the basis of a more general account of perception. For S to perceive X is simply for X to appear to S as so-and-so. Read in terms of an externalist account of perception, this means that for S to perceive X, in an experience E, X figures in an appropriate way in the causation of E, and/or E leads to beliefs about X or tendencies to beliefs about X. Thus those who undergo experiences in which God (or God's actions and activities) appears to them are entitled to believe that they really have perceived God (or God's actions and activities).

Alston defends the claim to entitlement in terms of a carefully mapped account of epistemic justification as applied to perception that cannot be pursued in detail here. Both sensory perception and Christian Mystical

---

[23] W. P. Alston, *Perceiving God: The Epistemology of Religious Experience* (Ithaca, NY, and London: Cornell University Press, 1991).
[24] Given that Alston does not work with any idea of cognitive faculties, he does not delineate what does the perceiving (e.g., ordinary senses, ordinary senses illuminated, the heart and the like). It would suffice to say that the human agent does the perceiving.

Perception are doxastic practices that are firmly established, psychologically and socially. They involve the non-reducible, autonomous exercise of a system of belief-forming habits or mechanisms, 'each realizing a function that yields beliefs with a certain kind of content from inputs of a certain type'.[25] Doxastic practices utilize appropriate conceptual schemes. They also provide *prima facie* justification for the beliefs generated. Given that the beliefs generated are in turn subject to overriders that can be sustained, rebutted or undermined, justification can be of a lesser or greater degree. While doxastic practices are subject to epistemic circularity, this is not a vicious circularity for they are well-established, have significant self-support and cohere with other firmly established doxastic practices and their output. Indeed there is no escaping epistemic circularity in the case of our basic doxastic practices; either we trust them or we do not. Such justification as they can have is a practical justification, that is, it is reasonable to engage in them given our aims and situation.

It is crucial to Alston's analysis that we note the significant differences that exist between the doxastic practices related to sensory experience and those related to experience of God. This is where the differences from Swinburne are clear. Swinburne's Principle of Credulity is a very general principle where you can take beliefs individually when it comes to their assessment. Alston operates with the notion of socially established practices. This constitutes a much richer account of belief formation and its internal mechanisms, say, for overriding different kinds of beliefs. This latter move allows him to provide a skilful rebuttal to a serious difficulty that is not as easy to handle with the epistemic apparatus given by Swinburne.[26] The difficulty in mind is this: the doxastic practice deployed in perception of the divine is partial in its distribution compared with the doxastic practice deployed in cases of ordinary perception. Thus there is much greater consensus about the deliverances and reliability of ordinary perception than shows up in the case of perception of the divine. To use Alston's language, the Christian Mystical Perceptual Doxastic Practice (CMP) does not match the standard at play in the case of sense-perception (SP).

Alston's rejoinder to this is that this way of thinking about perception ignores the fact that our doxastic practices come in systems; while there are significant formal similarities across these systems, they are not identical. It is the systems as whole that are the target of assessment rather than singular perceptual claims normed by a universal standard or by a standard derived

---

[25] Alston, *Perceiving God*, p. 155.
[26] However, Davis's elaboration of Swinburne's basic moves goes a long way to taking care of the charges identified in what follows.

from one system. Hence to denigrate perception of the divine because it does not fit exactly the practices related to sensory perception is a form of epistemic imperialism; it involves taking the standards of one doxastic practice and making them normative for all doxastic practices. What matters is the attending to the particularities of our varied, autonomous doxastic practices rather than the eliminating of one on grounds that it does not fit the standards internal to another. Equally unacceptable is the move to deploy a double standard. In this instance the objector unwarrantedly makes requirements of one practice which are then set aside in other cases where they should apply. For example, the doxastic practice of perception of the divine is not allowed because it is restricted, while other doxastic practices of perception, which are restricted, like wine-tasting, are allowed. In short, the objector fails to note that there is an irreducible pluralism to our doxastic practices that must be respected.

Alston's conclusion is both substantial and cautious. The CMP doxastic practice is a fully fledged socially established doxastic practice; it has its own distinctive input–output functions; it has its own distinctive conceptual scheme; it has a functioning overrider system; it lacks sufficient reasons to take the practice as unreliable; and it enjoys a significant degree of self-support. 'As such, it possesses a prima facie title to being rationally engaged in, and its outputs are thereby prima facie justified, provided we have no sufficient reason to regard it as unreliable or otherwise disqualified for rational acceptance.'[27] Hence our perceptual beliefs about God, as they show up in the Christian tradition, are justified and can be deployed in a wider cumulative case argument for Christian theism.

In moving from Swinburne to Alston the target of our enquiry has shifted. We have moved from a justification of mere theism to a justification of Christian theism. The move to develop a robust account of Christian, as opposed to generic theism, is also at the heart of Alvin Plantinga's vision of the spiritual senses tradition in recent analytic philosophy of religion. One crucial difference between Plantinga and Alston is that while Plantinga holds that there are lots of good arguments in favour of Christian theism, he rejects the view that these are in any way necessary for establishing the rationality or the positive epistemic status of Christian belief. Christian beliefs can properly be held without propositional evidence; they can be construed as properly basic beliefs. We can see immediately that we are about to encounter a radically different way of thinking about the spiritual senses.

---

[27] Alston, *Perceiving God*, p. 225. Alston goes on to consider alleged reasons for disqualification and seeks to undermine their cogency.

Plantinga introduces his central proposals with a quotation from Paul: 'The Spirit testifies with our spirits that we are God's children' (Rom 8: 16).[28] Plantinga signals in this text both that he is interested in the deep content of Christian belief and that he sees in the work of the Holy Spirit a vital element in constructing a far-flung vision of the epistemology of theology. His aim is to provide a model, 'for warranted *Christian* belief: a model in which full-blooded Christian belief in all its particularity is justified, rational, and warranted'.[29] According to this model, human agents were created with knowledge of God and his glory. Regrettably, they fell into sin; but God instituted a plan of salvation centring in the life, death and resurrection of Jesus Christ, the Son of God. In order to inform the world of this, God inspired the scriptures (functioning as its author), making available the good news of the gospel. Correlative with scripture, God sent his Holy Spirit to repair the ill effects of sin, including its cognitive effects, and to enable hearers to embrace and enjoy the great truths of the gospel. So folk come to believe in Christ's reconciling work for the sins of the world. In and through this the Holy Spirit generates faith in a process of regeneration in which believers 'come to commit themselves to the Lord, to conforming their lives to his will, to living lives of gratitude'.[30]

How does this help in dealing with issues of epistemology?

The answer is simplicity itself. These beliefs do not come to the Christian just by way of memory, perception, reason, testimony, the *sensus divinitatis*, or any other cognitive faculties with which we human beings were originally created; they come instead by way of the work of the Holy Spirit, who gets us to accept, causes us to believe, these great truths of the gospel. These beliefs don't just come by way of the normal operation of our natural faculties; they are a supernatural gift. Still, the Christian who has received this gift of faith will be *justified* (in the basic sense of the term) in believing as he does; there will be nothing contrary to epistemic or other duty in so believing (indeed, once he has accepted the gift, it may not be within his power to withhold belief).[31]

It might be objected that I am misreading Plantinga's account if I take it as a variation of the spiritual sense tradition. I agree that there is a slight stretching of Plantinga's position here, but it is a stretching that is not

---

[28] A. Plantinga, *Warranted Christian Belief* (New York: Oxford University Press, 2000), p. 241. This book is extraordinary in its philosophical range and theological depth. It will become and remain a classic, a landmark contribution to philosophy in the analytic tradition. Reading and rereading it is like immersing oneself in an ocean of felicitous prose, fascinating theological ruminations and rigorous philosophical reflection; the chapter on the cognitive effects of sin is a brilliant theological tour de force that should be required reading for all theology students.

[29] *Ibid.* p. 242, italics in the original.   [30] *Ibid.* p. 244.

[31] *Ibid.* pp. 245–6, italics in the original.

without support in his work. Plantinga's central moves are in the area of the spiritual senses tradition in two ways. First, for him the work of the Holy Spirit enables sinners to *perceive* that scripture is authored by God, that God was in Christ engaged in a great work of salvation and that the gospel applies personally to them.[32] Second, we can surely interpret Plantinga's proposals in the direction of a radical repairing of the *sensus divinitatis* that has been damaged by the ravages of sin. Thus he is happy to allow for a resemblance between the way belief in the gospel is instigated with memory, perception, reason, testimony, induction and other standard belief-producing processes.[33] Even more interesting is the claim that 'the *restoration and healing* induced by the work of the Holy Spirit also counters [the] noetic effect of sin. It *restores* us to a position of seeing that we have been created in God's image'.[34]

All this may still seem a long way from epistemology. On the contrary, it lands us full square in the arena of epistemology, for Plantinga sees in this process of belief-production an instantiation of epistemology as it should be conceptualized, articulated and defended.[35] For Plantinga the crucial epistemic desiderata, such as rationality and warrant, come by way of the proper functioning of our cognitive faculties. Thus Plantinga's account of the epistemic status of Christian belief fits neatly into his wider account of epistemology.

First, they [the great truths of the gospel] will be internally rational: they will be an appropriate doxastic response to what is given to the believer by way of her previous belief and current experience. That is, the believer's response is such that a properly functioning person with the same current experience and antecedent beliefs could form the same or similar beliefs, without compromising proper function. But the beliefs in question will also have *external* rationality. There need be no cognitive

---

[32] 'The believer encounters the great truths of the gospel; by virtue of the activity of the Holy Spirit, she comes to *see* that these things are indeed true.' *Ibid*. p. 256, italics mine. The analogy with perception is well brought out when he notes that belief is not a matter of argument from religious experience. 'It is rather that (as in the case of perception) the experience is the *occasion* for the formation of the beliefs in question, and plays a causal role . . . in their genesis.' *Ibid*. pp. 258–9, italics in the original. Plantinga goes on to quote Jonathan Edwards: 'They believe the doctrines of God's word to be divine, because they *see* divinity in them.' *Ibid*. p. 259, italics mine. There are also several quotations from Paul and John Calvin where the language of perception is naturally deployed. See *ibid*. pp. 171, 174. One might say that Plantinga's position is an elaboration of the spiritual senses tradition rather than a straight articulation of it.

[33] *Ibid*. p. 245–6.   [34] *Ibid*. p. 282, italics mine.

[35] Plantinga has supplied a full-dress, comprehensive treatment of central topics in epistemology and his own positive contribution to the field in his *Warrant: The Current Debate* (New York: Oxford University Press, 1993) and *Warrant and Proper Function* (New York: Oxford University Press, 1993). His *Warranted Christian Belief* is a sequel to these volumes; they provide the epistemic framework for his account of the epistemic status of Christian belief.

malfunction downstream from experience, in believers, but there need be none *upstream* either: all their cognitive faculties can be functioning properly. Finally, on this model, these beliefs will also have *warrant* for believers: they will be produced in them by a belief-producing process that is functioning properly in an appropriate cognitive environment (the one for which they were designed), according to a design plan successfully aimed at the production of true beliefs.[36]

If we allow Plantinga's position as a variation or extension of the spiritual senses tradition, we can see immediately that it is difficult to cut our accounts of the spiritual senses loose from their embeddedness in a wider theological system. Clearly Swinburne seeks to avoid this in that his position works from a generic, universal principle of rationality enshrined in the Principle of Credulity. Franks Davis's proposals move beyond this in her account of concept formation, so much so that theological doctrines become incorporated into the description of religious experience, thus requiring her to deal at length with the charge of circularity.[37] In Alston's case Christian doctrines come into play in the overrider system governing his Christian mystical doxastic practices. 'CMP takes the Bible, the ecumenical councils of the undivided church, Christian experience through the ages, Christian thought, and more generally the Christian tradition as normative sources of its overrider system.'[38]

What we see here is the tendency to develop an account of perception of the divine and divine activity that moves deeper and deeper into biblical and theological categories. Drawing on the pregnant epistemic comments of Paul in his famous account of the foolishness of the gospel in 1 Corinthians 1–3, Moberly captures this element of the discussion in two ways. First, he insists that there is 'a transformation, of a moral and spiritual order, without which the intellect must still remain disordered and incompetent as intellect'.[39] Second, without this and without access to the knowledge of God unveiled in the gospel, the Christian faith will appear to be utter foolishness. Not surprisingly, he then quotes Paul with approval, insisting that there is no knowledge of God without the work of the Holy Spirit, who supplies the wisdom needed to articulate the things freely given by God. So the reason that knows the truth of the gospel is a reason that can be attained only when we become 'the property of Christ, – wholly dependent on Christ, as Christ is dependent on God'.[40]

---

[36] Plantinga, *Warranted Christian Belief*, p. 246, italics in the original.
[37] This represents a significant improvement on Hick, who tries to deal with the role of thick descriptions of religious experience in terms of the inevitability of seeing-as in all experience. Given that Hick has moved away from his earlier theological commitments I shall set him aside for now.
[38] Alston, *Perceiving God*, p. 193.   [39] Moberly, *Atonement and Personality*, p. 243.
[40] *Ibid.* p. 244.

WILLIAM J. ABRAHAM

With the move into theology proper, epistemologists are caught between a rock and a hard place. On the one side, perception of the divine will take its initial cues from the epistemology of sensory perception. This is the rock. The hard place is furnished by the fact that it is very difficult to assimilate *simpliciter* perception of the divine to ordinary sensory perception.[41] We can all agree that we have sense organs; we simply do not agree that we have spiritual senses. So the differences between the two are going to require the kind of enrichment supplied in different ways by Franks Davis in her account of incorporated interpretation of religious experience, by Alston in his account of Christian mystical doxastic practices and by Plantinga in his vision of the work of the Holy Spirit in proper function. Another way to identify the hard place is to note that perception of the divine requires massive support from cumulative case arguments, as we can see in the cases of Mitchell, Swinburne, Franks Davis and Alston. Alternatively, where it is allowed to stand alone, as happens in the case of Plantinga, it requires deep embedding in an original and dense vision of warrant that is supernatural and theological in orientation.[42]

One of the ways to address the problem in view here is to exploit the tacit assumption of Moberly that our conception of reason undergoes significant transformation in the very process of coming to faith. As we grow into the world of divine revelation in the church then we extend our cognitive resources in terms of both the capacities and the data deployed. Thus in order to do justice to both an appeal to ordinary perception and to the additional epistemic desiderata required we need to take into account not just synchronic but also diachronic considerations in epistemology. Coming to know a host of significant propositions involves a complex journey where we have to take into account what is gained en route to our search for knowledge. This would enable us to deal more forthrightly with the place of divine revelation in knowledge of God and take much more seriously the foolishness of the faith to outsiders noted by Paul and reiterated by Moberly.[43]

---

[41] I leave aside here queries about perception of the divine that arise from the side of scripture and theology. See S. T. Davis, 'Eschatology and Resurrection', in J. L. Walls (ed.), *The Oxford Handbook of Eschatology* (Oxford University Press, 2008), pp. 394–6.

[42] For a defence of the claim that Plantinga's epistemology can still be construed as a form of naturalism see A. Plantinga, '"Respondeo" to Earl Conee', in J. L. Kvanvig (ed.), *Warrant in Contemporary Epistemology: Essays in Honor of Plantinga's Theory of Knowledge* (London: Rowman & Littlefield, 1996), pp. 352–7.

[43] This is the direction of my own thinking in the epistemology of theology. See W. J. Abraham, *Crossing the Threshold of Divine Revelation* (Grand Rapids, MI: Eerdmans, 2007). I deploy there the language of *oculus contemplationis* as the best way to draw on the spiritual senses tradition. See

However we deal with this unfinished business, it will be clear that Christian philosophers in the analytic tradition will be drawn to various options as they seek to give an account of the knowledge they believe they have gained through perception of the divine. There is no agreement in sight on this score. Yet we should see this diversity and fecundity as natural in that the Christian faith originally did not canonize any one way of resolving the epistemic queries evoked by the gospel and by the development of Christian doctrine. In fact over the last fifty years we have had a golden period in the field of analytic philosophy of religion, so much so that it has now spawned the development of analytic theology.[44] This latter development dovetails nicely with the tendency we have noted in this chapter, that is, philosophers have found that they cannot reach their goals without entering deeply into the actual content of Christian theology. Thus philosophers have found themselves doing theology in the course of doing philosophy; they have now taken to doing theology for themselves. The old boundaries between the two disciplines that were championed by the positivists and the pioneers of the analytic tradition have disintegrated.

Given both the quality and the quantity of work even on such a singular topic as the spiritual senses, many analytic philosophers continue to be myopic in their reading of the current landscape. John Gray's summary statement is not untypical. 'Contemporary philosophy is a discipline in which religion hardly figures. A subject called philosophy of religion exists and has some devoted practitioners, but in the discipline as a whole inquiry into religion is a marginal activity.'[45] Gray goes on to tell the standard story of the success of positivism and logical empiricism in privileging scientific method in epistemology and in undermining metaphysics. Neither the move to make philosophy closer to arts and literature nor the rise of phenomenology has made any difference, for in the end ' . . . religious experience has rarely been given much attention, and aside from a few who devote themselves to antireligious polemics it seems tacitly agreed by most philosophers that religion is not a worthwhile subject of inquiry'.[46] Gray may well be misled at this point by his conviction that 'metaphysics and religious apologetics have never been far apart'.[47] This was certainly true of the work of Moberly, as we already noted. What Gray fails to

---

ibid. p. 66. I propose that there is a basic capacity to perceive God in creation. This capacity can be supported by evidentiary considerations, and it is deepened as one crosses over into the world of divine revelation.

[44] See O. D. Crisp and M. C. Rea (eds.), *Analytic Theology: New Essays in the Philosophy of Theology* (Oxford University Press, 2009).

[45] J. Gray, 'A Rescue of Religion', *New York Review of Books*, 55.15 (9 October 2008), p. 43.

[46] *Ibid.* [47] *Ibid.*

see is that the demise of Idealist metaphysics did not at all mean the end of penetrating work in epistemology as this relates to the Christian religion. On the contrary, positivism and logical empiricism, even as they cleared the decks of metaphysics, dissolved from within through internal criticism and even failed to prevent the revival of metaphysics.[48] In time this has allowed philosophers and theologians to become clearer about the distinction between metaphysics and theology, allowing theology a life of its own.

In the meantime a significant network of philosophers working on issues on the nature and justification of religious belief now find themselves doing theology in their work as philosophers. Historians of the analytic tradition have a lot of catching up to do at present, if they are to do justice to this recent development in philosophy of religion. In turn philosophers of religion must now take more seriously the content of their theological commitments as they show up in their work. Theologians for their part can make pertinent assessments of these theological elements in philosophy, and they can surely make their own important contribution to debates about the epistemology of their own discipline. We have come full circle: the kind of multi-tasking that we encountered in the work of Moberly is certainly now needed more than ever if we are to make progress on the nature and significance of the spiritual senses.

[48] For a brilliant paper that draws on the great genius and pioneer of analytic philosophy, Ludwig Wittgenstein, in relation to the spiritual senses see S. Coakley, 'The Resurrection and the "Spiritual Senses": On Wittgenstein, Epistemology and the Risen Christ', in her *Powers and Submissions: Philosophy, Spirituality and Gender* (Oxford: Blackwell, 2002), pp. 131–52.

Select bibliography

Abraham, William J., *Crossing the Threshold of Divine Revelation* (Grand Rapids, MI: Eerdmans, 2007).

Adams, Robert, *A Theory of Virtue* (Oxford University Press, 2006).

Adnès, Pierre, 'Gout spirituel', *DS*, vol. VI (1967), pp. 626–44.

Agus, Aharon R. E. and Jan Assmann, *Ocular Desire* (Berlin: Akademie, 1994).

Allers, Rudolf, 'The *Vis cogitativa* and Evaluation', *The New Scholasticism*, 15 (1941), 195–221.

Alston, William P., *Perceiving God: The Epistemology of Religious Experience* (Ithaca, NY: Cornell University Press, 1991).

  'Perceptual Knowledge', in John Greco and Ernest Sosa (eds.), *The Blackwell Guide to Epistemology* (Oxford: Blackwell, 1999), pp. 223–42.

  The Reliability of Sense Perception (Ithaca, NY: Cornell University Press, 1993).

Andia, Ysabel de, *Denys l'Aréopagite: Tradition et metamorphoses* (Paris: J. Vrin, 2006).

Armstrong, Arthur Hilary, *The Architecture of the Intelligible Universe in the Philosophy of Plotinus* (Cambridge University Press, 1940).

  Cambridge History of Later Greek and Early Medieval Philosophy (Cambridge University Press, 1967).

Ayer, Alfred Jules, *Language, Truth, and Logic* (New York: Dover, 1952).

Azkoul, Michael, *God, Immortality, and Freedom of the Will According to the Church Fathers: A Philosophy of Spiritual Cognition* (Lewiston, NY: Edwin Mellen Press, 2006).

Baillie, John, *The Sense of the Presence of God* (New York: Charles Scribner's Sons, 1962).

Baker, Sylvia, *Seeing and Believing: Evolution, the Eye and Sight* (Leicester: Genesis Agendum, 2004).

Balthasar, Hans Urs von, *Cosmic Liturgy: The Universe According to Maximus the Confessor*, trans. B. Daley, SJ (San Francisco: Ignatius Press, 2003).

  Herrlichkeit: Eine theologische Ästhetik, 3 vols. (Einsiedeln: Johannes Verlag, 1961–9). In English as *The Glory of the Lord: A Theological Aesthetics*, trans. Erasmo Leiva-Merikakis, Andrew Louth, Brian McNeil et al., 7 vols. (San Francisco: Ignatius Press, 1982–9).

Balthasar, Hans Urs von (ed.), *Origen: Spirit and Fire: A Thematic Anthology of his Writings*, trans. Robert J. Daly (Washington, DC: Catholic University of America Press, 2001).

Barbet, Jeanne, *Le commentaire du Cantique des Cantiques 'deiformes animae gemitus'* (Paris and Louvain: Béatrice-Nauwelaerts, 1972).

Thomas Gallus: Commentaires du Cantique des Cantiques (Paris: Vrin, 1967).

'Thomas Gallus', *DS*, vol. xv (1991), pp. 800–16.

Barnes, Michel R., 'The Polemical Context and Content of Gregory of Nyssa's Psychology', *Medieval Philosophy and Theology*, 4 (1994), 1–24.

Baudouin, Charles (ed.), *Nos sens et Dieu* (Paris: Les études Carmélitaines, Desclée de Brouwer, 1954).

Beare, John Isaac, *Greek Theories of Elementary Cognition from Alcmaeon to Aristotle* (Oxford: Clarendon Press, 1906).

Becker, Aimé, 'Poésie et mystique: Le thème claudélien des "sens spirituels"', *RSR*, 43 (1969), 118–48; 44 (1970), 33–48.

Beeley, Christopher, *Gregory of Nazianzus on the Trinity and the Knowledge of God: In Your Light We shall See Light* (New York: Oxford University Press, 2008).

Beierwaltes, Werner, '*Visio facialis* – Sehen ins Angesicht: Zur Coincidenz des endlichen und unendlichen Blicks bei Cusanus', in Rudolf Haubst (ed.), *Das Sehen Gottes nach Nikolaus von Kues: Akten des Symposions in Trier vom 25. bis 27. September 1986, Mitteilungen und Forschungsbeiträge der Cusanus-Gesellschaft*, 18 (Trier: Paulinus-Verlag, 1989), pp. 91–118.

Bell, David N., *The Image and Likeness: The Augustinian Spirituality of William of Saint Thierry* (Kalamazoo, MI: Cistercian Publications, 1984).

Benson, Bruce Ellis and Norman Wirzba (eds.), *Words of Life: New Theological Turns in French Phenomenology* (New York: Fordham University Press, 2010).

Benson, Joshua C., 'Identifying the Literary Genre of the *De reductione artium ad theologiam:* Bonaventure's Inaugural Lecture at Paris', *Franciscan Studies*, 67 (2009), 149–78.

Blackburn, Lee, 'Sensing the Love of God: The Anthropology of Richard Rolle's *Incendium amoris*', unpublished student seminar paper, University of Notre Dame, 2005.

Blowers, Paul M., *Exegesis and Spiritual Pedagogy in Maximus the Confessor: An Investigation of the Quaestiones ad Thalassium* (South Bend, IN: Notre Dame Press, 1991).

Boersma, Hans, *Nouvelle Théologie and Sacramental Ontology: A Return to Mystery* (Oxford University Press, 2009).

Bond, Lawrence H., 'The "Icon" and the "Iconic" Text in Nicholas of Cusa's *De visione Dei* I–XVII', in Thomas Izbicki and Christopher Bellitto (eds.), *Nicholas of Cusa and his Age: Intellect and Spirituality* (Leiden: Brill, 2002), pp. 177–95.

Bonnefoy, Jean-François, *Le Saint-Esprit et ses dons selon saint Bonaventure*, Études de philosophie médiévale, 10 (Paris: J. Vrin, 1929).

Les trois voies de la vie spirituelle (Montreal: Éditions Franciscaines, 1945).

Bougerol, Jacques Guy, *Introduction to the Works of Bonaventure*, trans. J. de Vinck (Paterson, NJ: St Anthony Guild Press, 1964).

'La perfezione cristiana e la strutturazione delle tre vie della vita spirituale nel pensiero di S. Bonaventura', *Incontri bonaventuriani*, 6 (1970), 69–84.

'Sensus spirituales', *Lexique saint Bonaventure* (Paris: Éditions Franciscaines, 1969), pp. 117–18.

Une somme bonaventurienne de théologique: Le 'De triplici via' (Paris: Librairie Saint-François, 1934).

Bourke, Vernon J., 'Intellectual Memory in the Thomistic Theory of Knowledge', *The Modern Schoolman*, 18 (1941), 21–4.

Bowker, John, *The Religious Imagination and the Sense of God* (New York: Oxford University Press, 1978).

Bradshaw, David, *Aristotle East and West: Metaphysics and the Division of Christendom* (Cambridge University Press, 2004).

Brennan, Robert E., 'The Thomistic Concept of the Imagination', *The New Scholasticism*, 15 (1941), 149–61.

Breton, Valentin-M., *La triple voie de saint Bonaventure* (Paris: Éditions Franciscaines, 1942).

Brewer, Bill, *Perception and Reason* (Oxford University Press, 1999).

Brown, Frank Burch, *Good Taste, Bad Taste, and Christian Taste: Aesthetics in Religious Life* (New York: Oxford University Press, 2000).

Bruyne, Edgar de, *Études d'esthétique médiévale* (Bruges: De Tempel, 1946).

Bulgakov, Sergei, *Svet Nevechernii* (Moscow: Respublika, 1994).

Bull, Michael and Back Les (eds.), *The Auditory Culture Reader* (New York: Berg, 2003).

Bynum, Caroline Walker, 'The Female Body and Religious Practice in the Late Middle Ages', in Michel Feher et al. (eds.) *Fragments for a History of the Human Body*, 3 vols. (New York: Zone, 1989), vol. I, pp. 160–219.

Holy Feast and Holy Fast: The Religious Significance of Food to Medieval Women (Berkeley: University of California Press, 1987).

Canévet, Mariette, 'Sens spirituel', *DS*, vol. XIV (1990), pp. 598–617.

Capellino, Mario, *Tommaso di S. Vittore, abate vercellese* (Vercelli: Società Storica Vercellese, 1978).

Carton, Raoul, *L'expérience mystique de l'illumination intérieure chez Roger Bacon* (Paris: J. Vrin, 1924).

Cary, Phillip, *Augustine's Invention of the Inner Self: The Legacy of a Christian Platonist* (New York: Oxford University Press, 2000).

Certeau, Michel de, 'The Gaze: Nicholas of Cusa', *Diacritics*, 17.3 (1987), 2–38.

Chase, Steven, *Angelic Wisdom: The Cherubim and the Grace of Contemplation in Richard of St. Victor* (University of Notre Dame Press, 1995).

Chenu, Marie-Dominique, 'Pro fidei supernaturalitate illustranda', in Sadoc Szabo (ed.), *Xenia Thomistica* (Rome: Polyglottis Vaticanis, 1925), vol. III, pp. 297–307.

Chidester, David, *Word and Light: Seeing, Hearing, and Religious Discourse* (Urbana: University of Illinois Press, 1992).

Chrétien, Jean-Louis, *The Call and the Response*, trans. Anne A. Davenport (New York: Fordham University Press, 2004).

Clapper, Gregory, *John Wesley on Religious Affections: His Views on Experience and Emotion and their Role in the Christian Life and Theology* (Metuchen, NJ, and London: Scarecrow Press, 1989).

Clark, Francis, *The Pseudo-Gregorian Dialogues* (Leiden: Brill, 1987).

Classen, Constance, 'Foundations for an Anthropology of the Senses', *International Social Science Journal*, 153 (1997), 401–12.

Worlds of Sense: Exploring the Senses in History and Across Cultures (London and New York: Routledge, 1993).

Classen, Constance (ed.), *The Book of Touch* (Oxford: Berg, 2005).

Coady, Mary, *The Phantasm According to the Teaching of St. Thomas* (Washington: Catholic University of America, 1932).

Coakley, Sarah, 'On the Identity of the Risen Jesus: Finding Jesus Christ in the Poor', in Beverly Roberts Gaventa and Richard B. Hays (eds.), *Seeking the Identity of Jesus: A Pilgrimage* (Grand Rapids, MI: Eerdmans, 2008), pp. 301–19.

Powers and Submissions: Philosophy, Spirituality and Gender (Oxford: Blackwell, 2002).

'The Resurrection: The Grammar of "Raised"', in D. Z. Phillips and Mario von der Ruhr (eds.), *Biblical Concepts and Our World* (Basingstoke: Palgrave, 2004), pp. 169–89.

Coccia, Antonio, 'S. Bonaventura e il problema critico della conoscenza', in Francisco de Asis Chavero Blanco, OFM (ed.), *Bonaventuriana: Miscellanea in onore di Jacques Guy Bougerol, OFM*, 2 vols., Bibliotheca Pontificii Athenaei Antoniani, 27–8 (Rome: Edizioni Antonianum, 1988), vol. I, pp. 257–76.

Colish, Marcia L., *The Stoic Tradition from Antiquity to the Early Middle Ages*, 2 vols., 2nd corrected printing (Leiden: Brill, 1990).

Coolman, Boyd Taylor, *Knowing God by Experience: The Spiritual Senses in the Theology of William of Auxerre* (Washington, DC: Catholic University of America Press, 2004).

'The Medieval Affective Dionysian Tradition', *Modern Theology*, 24.4 (2008), 615–32; reprinted in Sarah Coakley and Charles M. Stang (eds.), *Re-Thinking Dionysius the Areopagite* (Oxford: Wiley-Blackwell, 2009), pp. 85–102.

Cooper, Adam, *Body in St Maximus the Confessor: Holy Flesh, Wholly Deified* (Oxford University Press, 2005).

Cottingham, John, *The Spiritual Dimension* (Cambridge University Press, 2005).

Crivelli, Riccardo, *L'esperienza cristiana: Figura, senso, e logica secondo S. Bonaventura* (Vicenza: LIEF, 1996).

Crossnoe, Marshall E., 'Education and the Care of Souls: Pope Gregory IX, the Order of St. Victor and the University of Paris in 1237', *Mediaeval Studies*, 61 (1999), 137–72.

Crouzel, Henri, *Origéne et la connaissance mystique* (Paris: Desclée de Brouwer, 1961).

Dähnert, Ulrich, *Die Erkenntnislehre des Albertus Magnus gemessen an den Stufen der 'abstractio'* (Leipzig: Gerhardt, 1933).

Daley, Brian E., '"The Human Form Divine": Christ's Risen Body and Ours According to Gregory of Nyssa', *Studia Patristica*, 41 (2006), 301–18.

'The *Nouvelle Théologie* and the Patristic Revival: Sources, Symbols and the Science of Theology', *International Journal of Systematic Theology*, 7 (2005), 362–82.

Dancy, Jonathan (ed.), *Perceptual Knowledge* (Oxford University Press, 1988).

Daniel, E. Randolph, 'Symbol or Model? St. Bonaventure's Use of St. Francis', in Francisco de Asis Chavero Blanco, OFM (ed.), *Bonaventuriana: Miscellanea in onore di Jacques Guy Bougerol OFM*, 2 vols., Bibliotheca Pontificii Athenaei Antoniani, 27–8 (Rome: Edizioni Antonianum, 1988), vol. I, pp. 55–62.

Daniélou, Jean, 'La chronologie des œuvres de Grégoire de Nysse', *Studia Patristica*, 7 (1966), 159–69.

'Introduction', in Herbert Musurillo (ed.), *From Glory to Glory: Texts from Gregory of Nyssa's Mystical Writings* (New York: Scribner, 1961), pp. 3–78.

Platonisme et théologie mystique: Essai sur la doctrine spirituelle de saint Grégoire de Nysse (Paris: Aubier, 1944; 2nd edn, 1954).

Davis, Caroline Franks, *The Evidential Force of Religious Experience* (Oxford: Clarendon Press, 1989).

Davis, Stephen T., 'Eschatology and Resurrection', in Jerry L. Walls (ed.), *The Oxford Handbook of Eschatology* (Oxford University Press, 2008), pp. 601–34.

Déchanet, Jean M., 'Guillaume de Saint-Thierry', *DS*, vol. VI (1967), pp. 1241–63.

Deck, John N., *Nature, Contemplation, and the One: The Study in the Philosophy of Plotinus* (University of Toronto Press, 1967).

DeCorte, Marcel, 'Notes exégetiques sur la théorie aristotélicienne du *Sensus communis*', *The New Scholasticism*, 6 (1932), 187–214.

Del Zotto, Cornelio B., 'La sistematizzazione dell filosofia e teologia del cuore in S. Bonaventura', in G. Beschin (ed.), *Antonio Rosmini, filosofo del cuore? 'Philosophia' e 'theologia cordis' nella cultura occidentale* (Brescia: Morcelliana, 1995), pp. 113–46.

La teologia dell'immagine in San Bonaventura (Venice: LIEF, 1977).

Demacopoulos, George E., *Five Models of Spiritual Direction in the Early Church* (University of Notre Dame Press, 2007).

'Leadership in the Post-Constantinian Church According to St. Gregory Nazianzen', *Louvain Studies*, 30 (2005), 223–39.

'The Soteriology of Pope Gregory I: A Case against the Augustinian Interpretation', *American Benedictine Review*, 54 (2003), 312–27.

Demacopoulos, George E. (ed. and trans.), *St Gregory the Great: Book of Pastoral Rule* (Crestwood, NY: St Vladimir's Seminary Press, 2007).

Dieu, Jean de, 'Les trois voies de la vie spirituelle', *Études Franciscaines*, 42 (1930), 481–90.

Dillon, John M., 'Aisthêsis Noêtê: A Doctrine of Spiritual Senses in Origen and in Plotinus', in A. Caquot, M. Hadas-Lebel and J. Riaud (eds.), *Hellenica et Judaica: Hommage à Valentin Nikiprowetzky* (Leuven and Paris: Peeters, 1986), pp. 443–55.

'The Knowledge of God in Origen', in R. van den Broek (ed.), *Knowledge of God in the Graeco-Roman World* (Leiden: Brill, 1988), pp. 219–28.

Dobbins, Dunstan, *Franciscan Mysticism: The Mystical Theology of the Seraphic Doctor* (New York: J. F. Wagner, 1927).

Dölger, F.-J., 'Das Segnen der Sinne mit der Eucharistie', *Antike und Christentum*, 3 (1932), 230–44.

Doyère, Pierre, 'Ste. Gertrude et les sens spirituels', *RAM*, 36 (1960), 429–46.

Drage, Rosemary Hale, '"Taste and See, for God is Sweet": Sensory Perception and Memory in Medieval Christian Mystical Experience', in Anne Clark Bartlett (ed.), *Vox Mystica: Essays on Medieval Mysticism in Honor of Professor Valerie M. Lagorio* (Cambridge and Rochester, NY: D. S. Brewer, 1995), pp. 3–14.

Dretske, Fred, *Knowledge and The Flow of Information* (Cambridge, MA: MIT Press, 1981).

Perception, Knowledge and Belief (Cambridge University Press, 2000).

Seeing and Knowing (University of Chicago Press, 1969).

Drobnick, Jim (ed.), *The Smell Culture Reader* (New York: Berg, 2006).

Duffy, Stephen, *The Graced Horizon: Nature and Grace in Modern Catholic Thought* (Collegeville, MN: Liturgical Press, 1992).

Edwards, Elizabeth and Kaushik Bhaumik (eds.), *Visual Sense* (New York: Berg, 2008).

Endean, Philip, *Karl Rahner and Ignatian Spirituality* (Oxford University Press, 2001).

Ernest, James D., 'The Patristic Inheritance in Calvin's Understanding of Sin as an Obstacle to Theological Knowledge', *Reformation and Revival*, 13.4 (2004), 95–109.

Evans, Ashley S., 'The Mind Sees: Spiritual Senses in Gregory of Nyssa's *De anima et resurrectione*', undergraduate dissertation, Harvard College, Cambridge, MA, March 2002.

Everson, Stephen, *Aristotle on Perception* (Oxford: Clarendon Press, 1997).

Falque, Elena, 'Vision, excès et chair: Essai de lecture phénoménologique de l'oeuvre de saint Bonaventure', *Revue des sciences philosophiques et théologiques*, 79 (1995), 3–48.

Festugiere, Andre Marie Jean, *Le Dieu inconnu et la gnose* (Paris: J. Gabalda, 1954).

Fields, Stephen, 'Balthasar and Rahner on the Spiritual Senses', *Theological Studies*, 57 (1996), 224–41.

Fiorenza, Francis Schüssler, 'The New Theology and Transcendental Thomism', in James Livingston et al. (eds.), *Modern Christian Thought: The Twentieth Century*, 2nd edn (Upper Saddle River, NJ: Prentice Hall, 2006), vol. II, pp. 197–232.

'Rahner on Method', in Declan Marmion and Mary E. Hines (eds.), *The Cambridge Companion to Karl Rahner* (Cambridge University Press, 2005), pp. 65–82.

Foster, John, *The Nature of Perception* (Oxford University Press, 2000).

Fraeters, Veerle, 'Gender and Genre: The Design of Hadewijch's *Book of Visions*', in Thérèse de Hemptinne and Maria Eugenia Góngora (eds.), *The Voice of Silence: Women's Literacy in a Men's Church* (Turnhout: Brepols, 2004), pp. 57–81.

Fraigneau-Julien, Bernard, *Les sens spirituels et la vision de Dieu selon Syméon le Nouveau Théologien* (Paris: Beauchesne, 1985).

Frank, Georgia, '"Taste and See": The Eucharist and the Eyes of Faith in the Fourth Century', *Church History*, 70 (2001), 619–43.

Fulton, Rachel, '"Taste and see that the Lord is sweet" (Ps 33: 9): The Flavor of God in the Monastic West', *Journal of Religion*, 86.2 (2006), 169–204.

Fumerton, Richard, *Metaepistemology and Skepticism* (Lanham, MD: Rowman & Littlefield, 1995).

Gaffney, Mark, *The Psychology of the Interior Senses* (St Louis: Herder, 1942).

Gannon, Mary Ann Ida, 'The Active Theory of Sensation in St. Augustine', *The New Scholasticism*, 30 (1956), 154–80.

Gasson, John A., 'The Internal Senses: Functions of Powers?', *The Thomist*, 26 (1963), 1–14.

Gavrilyuk, Paul, 'Baptism in Pseudo-Dionysius's *Ecclesiastical Hierarchy*', *Studia liturgica*, 39.1 (2009), 1–14.

'Did Pseudo-Dionysius the Areopagite Live in Constantinople?', *Vigiliae Christianae*, 62 (2008), 505–14.

Gellman, Jerome, *Mystical Experience of God: A Philosophical Inquiry* (Burlington, VT: Ashgate, 2001).

Gendler, Tamar Szabo and John Hawthorne (eds.), *Perceptual Experience* (Oxford University Press, 2006).

Gersh, Stephen, *From Iamblichus to Eriugena: An Investigation of the Prehistory and Evolution of the Pseudo-Dionysian Tradition* (Leiden: Brill, 1978).

Gerson, Lloyd, *Aristotle and Other Platonists* (Ithaca, NY: Cornell University Press, 2005).

Gilson, Étienne, *The Philosophy of St. Bonaventure*, trans. Dom Illtyd Trethowan and Francis Joseph Sheed (London: Sheed & Ward, 1940).

Goldman, Alvin, *Epistemology and Cognition* (Cambridge, MA: Harvard University Press, 1986).

Golitzin, Alexander, 'Dionysius Areopagites: A Christian Mysticism?', in Basil Lourié and Andrei Orlov (eds.), *The Theophaneia School: Jewish Roots of Eastern Christian Mysticism* (St Petersburg: Vizantinorossika, 2007), pp. 128–79.

Gondreau, Paul, *The Passions of Christ's Soul in the Theology of St. Thomas Aquinas* (Münster: Aschendorff, 2002).

Gooday, Frances, 'Mechthild von Magdeburg and Hadewich: A Comparison', *Ons Geestelijk Erf*, 48 (1974), 305–62.

Gray, John, 'A Rescue of Religion', *New York Review of Books*, 55.15 (9 October 2008), 43.

Greco, John, *Putting Skeptics in their Place: The Nature of Skeptical Arguments and their Role in Philosophical Inquiry* (Cambridge University Press, 2000).

Gregoric, Pavel, *Aristotle on the Common Sense* (New York: Oxford University Press, 2007).

Griffin, David Ray, *Reenchantment without Supernaturalism: A Process Philosophy of Religion* (Ithaca, NY: Cornell University Press, 2001).

Guardini, Romano, *Die Sinne und die religiöse Erkenntnis: Zwei Versuche über die christliche Vergewisserung* (Würzburg: Werkbund Verlag, 1950). In French as *Les sens et la connaissance de Dieu: Deux essais sur la certitude chrétienne*, trans. Thomas Patfoort (Paris: Éditions du Cerf, 1954).

Haddock, Adrian and Fiona Macpherson, *Disjunctivism: Perception, Action, Knowledge* (Oxford University Press, 2008).

Hadot, Pierre, *Philosophy as a Way of Life: Spiritual Exercises from Socrates to Foucault*, ed. A. Davidson, trans. M. Chase (Oxford: Blackwell, 1995).

Hain, Rodolphe, 'De vi cogitative et de instinctu hominis', *Revue de l'Université d'Ottawa*, 2 (1933), 41–62.

Hambrick-Stowe, Charles E., *The Practice of Piety: Puritan Devotional Disciplines in Seventeenth-Century New England* (Chapel Hill: University of North Carolina Press, 1982).

Hammond, Jay M., 'Dating Bonaventure's Inception as Regent Master', *Franciscan Studies*, 67 (2009), 179–226.

Hammond, William A., *Aristotle's Psychology: A Treatise on the Principles of Life (De anima and Parva naturalia)* (London: S. Sonnenschein & Co., 1902).

Hancock, John C., 'The Nexus in the Eye: Physical and Spiritual Vision in Dante's *Divina commedia*', Ph.D. thesis, Brigham Young University, 2003.

Harl, Marguerite, 'La "bouche" et le "cœur" de l'Apôtre: Deux images bibliques du "sens divin" de l'homme ("Proverbes" 2, 5) chez Origène', in *Forma futuri: Studi in onore del Cardinale Michele Pellegrino* (Turin: Bottega d'Erasmo, 1975), pp. 17–42.

Harrison, Carol, *Beauty and Revelation in the Thought of Saint Augustine* (Oxford: Clarendon Press, 1992).

Haug, Walter and Dietmar Mieth (eds.), *Religiöse Erfahrung: Historische Modelle in christlicher Tradition* (Munich: Fink, 1992).

Hayes, Zachary, 'Christology and Metaphysics in the Thought of Bonaventure', *The Journal of Religion*, 58, suppl. (1978), 82–95.

Heinzmann, Richard, *Die Unsterblichkeit der Seele und die Auferstehung des Leibes: Eine problemgeschichtliche Untersuchung der frühscholastischen Sentenzen- und Summenliteratur von Anselm von Laon bis Wilhelm von Auxerre*, Beiträge zur Geschichte der Philosophie und Theologie des Mittelalters, Texte und Untersuchungen, 40.3 (Münster: Aschendorff, 1965).

Helander, Birgit H., *Die visio intellectualis als Erkenntnisweg und -ziel bei Nikolaus Cusanus* (Stockholm: Almqvist & Wiksell, 1988).

Henry, Michel, *The Essence of Manifestation*, trans. Girard Etzkorn (The Hague: Nijhoff, 1973).

Hick, John, 'Eschatological Verification Reconsidered', *Religious Studies*, 13 (1977), 189–202.

Faith and Knowledge (Ithaca, NY: Cornell University Press, 1957).

Hollywood, Amy, *Soul as Virgin Wife: Mechthild of Magdeburg, Marguerite Porete, and Meister Eckhart* (University of Notre Dame Press, 1995).

Hopkins, Jasper, *Nicholas of Cusa's Dialectical Mysticism: Text, Translation, and Interpretive Study of* De visione Dei (Minneapolis: Arthur Banning Press, 1985).

Horn, Gabriel P., 'Le miroir et la nué: Deux modes de connaissance de Dieu chez saint Gregoire de Nysse', *RAM*, 8 (1927), 113–31.

'Les sens de l'esprit d'après Diadoque de Photicé', *RAM*, 8 (1927), 402–19.

Howes, David (ed.), *The Empire of the Senses* (New York: Berg, 2004).

The Sixth Sense Reader (New York: Berg, 2009).

The Varieties of Sensory Experience: A Sourcebook in the Anthropology of the Senses (University of Toronto Press, 1991).

Howle, David Wilcox, 'Seeing and Being Seen: The Motif of Sight as a Narrative Tool in Deuteronomy and the Former Prophets', Ph.D. thesis, Golden Gate Baptist Theological Seminary, 1993.

Humphrey, Edith McEwan, *And I Turned to See the Voice: The Rhetoric of Vision in the New Testament* (Grand Rapids, MI: Baker Academic, 2007).

Hütter, Reinhard, 'Transubstantiation Revisited: *Sacra doctrina*, Dogma, and Metaphysics', in Reinhard Hütter and Matthew Levering (eds.), *Ressourcement Thomism: Sacred Doctrine, the Sacraments, and the Moral Life: Essays in Honor of Romanus Cessario, O.P.* (Washington, DC: Catholic University of America Press, 2010), pp. 21–79.

Ivánka, Endre von, *Plato Christianus: Übernahme und Umgestaltung des Platonismus durch die Väter* (Einsiedeln: Johannes Verlag, 1964).

Janicaud, Dominique, *Phenomenology and the Theological Turn: The French Debate* (New York: Fordham University Press, 2000).

Johansen, Thomas K., 'In Defense of Inner Sense: Aristotle on Perceiving that One Sees', *Proceedings of the Colloquium on Ancient Philosophy*, 21 (2005), 235–76.

Jütte, Robert, *A History of the Senses: From Antiquity to Cyberspace* (Cambridge, MA: Polity Press, 2005).

Kennedy, Leonard A., 'The Nature of the Human Intellect According to St. Albert the Great', *The Modern Schoolman*, 37 (1960), 121–37.

Kilby, Karen, *Karl Rahner: Theology and Philosophy* (New York: Routledge, 2004).

Kitanov, Severin Valentinov, *Beatific Enjoyment in Scholastic Philosophy and Theology: 1240–1335*, unpublished doctoral thesis, Faculty of Theology, University of Helsinki, 2006.

Klubertanz, George P., *The Discursive Power; Sources and Doctrine of the 'Vis Cogitativa' According to St. Thomas Aquinas* (St Louis: Modern Schoolman, 1952).

'The Internal Senses in the Process of Cognition', *The Modern Schoolman*, 18 (1941), 27–31.

Knowles, David, *The English Mystical Tradition* (London: Burns & Oates, 1961).

Koenigsberger, Dorothy, *Renaissance Man and Creative Thinking: A History of Concepts of Harmony, 1400–1700* (Atlantic Highlands, NJ: Humanities Press, 1979).

Korsmeyer, Carolyn (ed.), *The Taste Culture Reader* (New York: Berg, 2005).

Krebs, Engelbert Gustav Hans, *Theologie und Wissenschaft nach der Lehre der Hochscholastik*, Beiträge zur Geschichte der Philosophie und Theologie des Mittelalters, 11 (Münster: Aschendorff, 1912).

LaNave, Gregory F., 'Knowing God through and in All Things: A Proposal for Reading Bonaventure's *Itinerarium mentis in Deum*', *Franciscan Studies*, 67 (2009), 267–99.

Landsberg, Paul Ludwig, 'Les sens spirituels chez saint Augustin', *Dieu vivant*, 11 (1948), 83–105.

Lang, Albert, *Die theologische Prinzipienlehre der mittelalterlichen Scholastik* (Freiburg: Herder, 1964).

Die Wege der Glaubensbegründung bei den Scholastikern des 14. Jahrhunderts, Beiträge zur Geschichte der Philosophie und Theologie des Mittelalters, 30 (Münster: Aschendorff, 1930).

Lauer, Rosemary Z., 'St. Albert and the Theory of Abstraction', *The Thomist*, 17 (1954), 69–83.

Lawell, Declan, 'Affective Excess: Ontology and Knowledge in the Thought of Thomas Gallus', *Dionysius*, 26 (2008), 139–74.

'*Ne de ineffabili penitus taceamus*: Aspects of the Specialized Vocabulary of the Writings of Thomas Gallus', *Viator*, 40.1 (2009), 151–84.

'*Qualiter vita prelatorum conformari debet vite angelice*: A Sermon (1244–1246?) Attributed to Thomas Gallus', *Recherches de théologie et philosophie médiévales*, 75.2 (2008), 303–36.

'*Spectacula contemplationis*: A Treatise (1244–1246) by Thomas Gallus', *Recherches de théologie et philosophie médiévales*, 76.2 (2009), 249–85.

'Thomas Gallus's Method as Dionysian Commentator: A Study of the *Glose super angelica ierarchia* (1224), Including Considerations on the Authorship of the *Expositio librorum beati Dionysii*', *Archives d'histoire doctrinale et littéraire du Moyen Âge*, 76 (2009), 89–117.

Leclerq, Jean, *La spiritualité du Moyen Age* (Paris: Aubier, 1961). In English as *The Spirituality of the Middle Ages*, trans. F. Vandenbroucke and Louis Bouyer (London: Burns & Oates, 1968).

Lochbrunner, Manfred, *Hans Urs von Balthasar und seine Philosophenfreunde* (Würzburg: Echter Verlag, 2005).

Longpré, Ephrem, 'Bonaventure', *DS*, vol. 1 (1937), pp. 1767–843.

'La théologie mystique de S. Bonaventure', *Archivum Franciscanum historicum*, 14 (1921), 36–108.

Lossky, Vladimir, *The Vision of God* (Leighton Buzzard: Faith Press, 1973).

Lottin, Odon D., 'Les dons du Saint-Esprit chez les théologiens depuis Pierre Lombard jusqu'à S. Thomas d'Aquin', *Recherches de théologie ancienne et médiévale*, 1 (1929), 41–61.

Psychologie et morale aux XIIe et XIIIe siècles (Louvain: Abbaye du Mont César, 1960).

Louth, Andrew, *Maximus the Confessor* (London: Routledge, 1996).

Origins of the Christian Mystical Tradition from Plato to Denys (Oxford University Press, 2007).

Lubac, Henri de, *Corpus Mysticum: The Eucharist and the Church in the Middle Ages* (University of Notre Dame Press, 2007).

Luby, Daniel Joseph, *Perceptibility of Grace* (Rome: Pontificia Studiorum Universitas A. S. Thomas Aquinas in Urbe, 1994).

Maddox, Randy, *Responsible Grace: John Wesley's Practical Theology* (Nashville: Kingswood, 1994).

Malevez, Léopold, 'La doctrine de l'image et de la connaissance mystique chez Guillaume de Saint-Thierry', *RSR*, 22 (1932), 178–205, 257–79.

Mann, Friedhelm, *Lexicon Gregorianum: Wörterbuch zu den Schriften Gregors von Nyssa*, vol. 1 (Leiden: Brill, 1998).

Maranesi, Pietro, *Verbum inspiratum: Chiave ermeneutica dell'Hexaëmeron di San Bonaventura* (Rome: Istituto storico dei Cappuccini, 1996).

Maréchal, Joseph, 'Application des sens', *DS*, vol. 1 (1937), pp. 810–28.

Marion, Jean-Luc, *The Visible and the Revealed*, trans. Christina M. Gschwandtner (New York: Fordham University Press, 2008).

Markschies, Christoph, 'Innerer Mensch', in Ernst Dassmann et al. (eds.), *Reallexikon für Antike und Christentum* (Stuttgart: Anton Hiersemann, 1998), vol. XVIII, pp. 266–312.

Marxer, Fridolin, *Die inneren geistlichen Sinne: Ein Beitrag zur Deutung ignatianischer Mystik* (Freiburg: Herder, 1964).

Matthews, Rex, '"Religion and Reason Joined": A Study in the Theology of John Wesley', Th.D. diss., Harvard University, 1986.

McGinn, Bernard, *The Essential Writings of Christian Mysticism* (New York: Random House, 2006).

'The Language of Inner Experience in Christian Mysticism', *Spiritus*, 1 (2001), 156–71.

The Presence of God: A History of Western Christian Mysticism, 4 vols. (New York: Crossroad, 1991–2006).

Mealey, Mark T., 'Taste and See that the Lord is Good: John Wesley in the Christian Tradition of Spiritual Sensation', Ph.D. diss., University of St Michael's College, Toronto, 2006.

'Tilting at Windmills: John Wesley's Reading of John Locke's Epistemology', *Bulletin of the John Rylands University Library of Manchester*, 85.2–3 (2003), 331–46.

Merton, Thomas, *Mystics and Zen Masters* (New York: Dell, 1967).

Mettepenningen, Jürgen, *Nouvelle Théologie – New Theology: Inheritor of Modernism, Precursor of Vatican II* (New York: T. & T. Clark, 2010).

Meyendorff, John, *Christ in Eastern Christian Thought* (Crestwood, NY: St Vladimir's Seminary Press, 1975).

Michaud-Quantin, Pierre, 'Albert le Grand et les puissances de l'âme', *Revue du Moyen Âge latin*, 11 (1955), 59–86.

'La classification des puissances de l'âme au XIIe siècle que résument ces lignes', *Revue du Moyen Âge latin*, 5 (1949), 15–34.

Miles, Margaret, 'Vision: The Eye of the Body and the Eye of the Mind in St. Augustine's *De trinitate* and *Confessions*', *The Journal of Religion*, 63 (1983), 125–42.

Milhaven, John Giles, *Hadewijch and her Sisters: Other Ways of Knowing and Loving* (Albany: SUNY Press, 1993).

Millar, Alan, 'The Scope of Perceptual Knowledge', *Philosophy*, 75 (2000), 73–88.

Mitchell, Basil, *The Justification of Religious Belief* (London: Macmillan, 1973).

Moberly, Robert Campbell, *Atonement and Personality* (London: John Murray, 1901).

Modrak, Deborah K. W., *Aristotle: The Power of Perception* (University of Chicago Press, 1987).

Moore, Thomas, 'The Scholastic Theory of Perception', *The New Scholasticism*, 7 (1933), 222–38.

Moser, Paul K., *Knowledge and Evidence* (Cambridge University Press, 1989).

Mouroux, Jean, *L'expérience chrétienne: Introduction à une théologie* (Paris: Aubier, 1952).

Naab, Erich, *Augustinus: Über Schau und Gegenwart des unsichtbaren Gottes* (Stuttgart and Bad Cannstaat: Frommann-Holzboog, 1998).

Nancy, Jean-Luc, *Noli me tangere* (Paris: Bayard, 2003).

Noli me tangere: On the Raising of the Body, trans. Sarah Clift, Pascale-Anne Brault et al. (New York: Fordham University Press, 2003).

Nash, Ronald H., 'Illumination, Divine', in Allan D. Fitzgerald (ed.), *Augustine through the Ages: An Encyclopedia* (Grand Rapids, MI: Eerdmans, 1999), pp. 438–40.

The Light of the Mind: St. Augustine's Theory of Knowledge (Lexington: University Press of Kentucky, 1969).

Nautin, Pierre, *Origène: Sa vie et son œuvre* (Paris: Beauchesne, 1977).

Nellas, Panayiotis, *Deification in Christ: The Nature of the Human Person* (Crestwood, NY: St Vladimir's Seminary Press, 1987).

Newman, Barbara, *From Virile Woman to Woman Christ: Studies in Medieval Religion and Literature* (Philadelphia: University of Pennsylvania Press, 1995).

Nichols, Aidan, *Byzantine Gospel: Maximus the Confessor in Modern Scholarship* (Edinburgh: T. & T. Clark, 1993).

The Word has been Abroad: A Guide through Balthasar's Aesthetics (Edinburgh: T. & T. Clark, 1999).

Nicolò Cusano agli inizi del mondo moderno, Congresso Internazionale Nicolò Cusano (Florence: G. C. Sansoni, 1970).

Nightingale, Andrea Wilson, *Spectacles of Truth in Classical Greek Philosophy: Theoria in its Cultural Context* (Cambridge University Press, 2004).

Noble, Henri D., 'Note pour l'étude de la psychophysiology d'Albert le Grand et de S. Thomas: Le cerveau et les facultés sensibles', *Revue Thomiste*, 13 (1905), 91–101.

Notopoulos, James A., 'The Symbolism of the Sun and Light in the *Republic* of Plato', *Classical Philology*, 39 (1944), 163–72.

Nuttall, Geoffrey, *The Holy Spirit in Puritan Faith and Experience* (Chicago and London: University of Chicago Press, 1992).

O'Daly, Gerard, *Augustine's Philosophy of Mind* (Berkeley: University of California Press, 1987).

O'Donnell, James, *Augustine: Confessions*, 3 vols. (Oxford: Clarendon Press, 1992).

Osborn, Eric, *The Beginning of Christian Philosophy* (Cambridge University Press, 1981).

Ottaviano, Carmelo, *Guglielmo D'Auxerre (–1231): La vita, le opere, il pensiero* (Rome: Biblioteca di Filosofia e Scienze, 1931).

Outler, Albert et al. (eds.), *Bicentennial Edition of the Works of John Wesley* (Oxford: Clarendon Press, 1975–).

Pasnau, Robert, 'Henry of Ghent and the Twilight of Divine Illumination', *The Review of Metaphysics*, 49 (1995), 49–75.

Peghaire, Julien, 'A Forgotten Sense: the Cogitative, According to St. Thomas Aquinas', *The Modern Schoolman*, 20 (1943), 123–40.

Pelikan, Jaroslav, *The Light of the World: A Basic Image in Early Christian Thought* (New York: Harper, 1962).

Penco, Gregorio, 'La dottrina dei sensi spirituali in Gregorio Magno', *Benedictina*, 17 (1970), 161–201.

Pépin, Jean, 'Augustin et Origène sur les *sensus interiores*', in Massimo L. Bianchi (ed.), *Sensus–sensatio: VIII colloquio internazionale del Lessico Intellettuale Europeo* (Florence: Olschki, 1996), pp. 11–23.

Perreault, A. M., 'Senses', *New Catholic Encyclopedia*, 2nd edn (Detroit: Gale, 2003), vol. XII, pp. 911–14.

Piazza, Leonardo, *Mediazione simbolica in San Bonaventura* (Venice: LIEF, 1978).

Plantinga, Alvin, '"Respondeo" to Earl Conee', in Jonathan L. Kvanvig (ed.), *Warrant in Contemporary Epistemology: Essays in Honor of Plantinga's Theory of Knowledge* (London: Rowman & Littlefield, 1996), pp. 307–78.

  Warrant and Proper Function (New York: Oxford University Press, 1993).

  Warranted Christian Belief (New York: Oxford University Press, 2000).

  Warrant: The Current Debate (New York: Oxford University Press, 1993).

Pouillon, Henri, 'La beauté, propriété transcendentale chez les scholastiques (1220–1270)', *Archives d'histoire doctrinale et littéraire du Moyen Âge*, 15 (1946), 263–329.

Poulain, Augustin, *Des grâces d'oraison*, 10th edn (Paris: G. Beauchesne, 1922). In English as *The Graces of Interior Prayer*, trans. L. L. Yorke Smith from the 6th edn, and corrected to accord with the 10th French edn (London: Kegan Paul, Trench, Trübner & Co., 1950).

Principe, Walter H., *The Theology of the Hypostatic Union in the Early Thirteenth Century*, vol. IV: *Philip the Chancellor's Theology of the Hypostatic Union* (Toronto: Pontifical Institute of Mediaeval Studies, 1975).

Prini, Pietro, *La scelta di essere: Il 'senso' del messaggio francescano* (Rome: Città Nuova, 1982).

Rahner, Hugo, 'Die Anwendung der Sinne in der Betrachtungsmethode des hl. Ignatius von Loyola', *Zeitschrift für katholische Theologie*, 79 (1957), 434–56.

Rahner, Karl, 'Der Begriff der Ecstasis bei Bonaventura', *Zeitschrift für Aszese und Mystik*, 9 (1934), 1–19.

'Le début d'une doctrine des cinq sens spirituels chez Origène', *RAM*, 13 (1932), 113–45. In English as 'The "Spiritual Senses" According to Origen', in *Theological Investigations*, vol. XVI, trans. David Morland (New York: Seabury Press, 1979), pp. 81–103.

'La doctrine des "sens spirituels" au Moyen-Âge, en particulier chez saint Bonaventure', *RAM*, 14 (1933), 263–99. In English as 'The Doctrine of the "Spiritual Senses" in the Middle Ages', in *Theological Investigations*, vol. XVI, trans. David Morland (New York: Seabury Press, 1979), pp. 104–34.

'Experience of Transcendence from the Standpoint of Catholic Dogmatics', in *Theological Investigations*, vol. XVIII, trans. Edward Quinn (New York: Crossroad, 1983), pp. 173–88.

Foundations of the Christian Faith: An Introduction to the Idea of Christianity, trans. William V. Dych (New York: Crossroad, 1982).

Geist in Welt: Zur Metaphysik der endlichen Erkenntnis bei Thomas von Aquin (Innsbruck: Rauch, 1939). In English as *Spirit in the World*, trans. William Dych (New York: Herder & Herder, 1968).

'Die Lehre von den "geistlichen Sinnen" im Mittelalter', in Karl Neufeld, SJ (ed.), *Schriften zur Theologie*, vol. XII: *Theologie aus Erfahrung des Geistes* (Zürich: Benziger Verlag, 1975), pp. 137–72.

Rappe, Sara, *Reading Neoplatonism: Non-Discursive Thinking in the Texts of Plotinus, Proclus, and Damascius* (Cambridge University Press, 2000).

Rea, Michael and Oliver Crisp (eds.), *New Essays in Analytic Theology* (Oxford University Press, 2009).

Reypens, Léonce, 'Ruusbroec-Studien, I: Het mystieke "gherinen"', *Ons Geestelike Erf*, 12 (1938), 158–86.

Riehle, Wolfgang, 'The Experience of God as a Spiritual Sense Perception', in Wolfgang Riehle (ed.), *The Middle English Mystics* (London: Routledge & Kegan Paul, 1981), pp. 104–27.

Rist, John, 'A Note on Eros and Agape in Pseudo-Dionysius', *Vigiliae Christianae*, 20 (1966), 235–43.

Roberts, Robert and Jay Wood, *Intellectual Virtues: An Essay in Regulative Epistemology* (Oxford: Clarendon Press, 2007).

Rorem, Paul, *Pseudo-Dionysius: A Commentary on the Texts and an Introduction to their Influence* (Oxford University Press, 1993).

Rosen, Stanley, *The Quarrel between Philosophy and Poetry* (New York: Routledge, 1988).

Rudy, Gordon, *Mystical Language of Sensation in the Later Middle Ages* (New York and London: Routledge, 2002).

Ruh, Kurt, 'Beguinenmystik: Hadewijch, Mechthild von Magdeburg, Marguerite Porete', in *Kleine Schriften*, 2 vols. (Berlin: Walter de Gruyter, 1984), vol. II, pp. 237–49.

Geschichte der abendländischen Mystik, 4 vols. (Munich: Beck, 1990–).

Russell, Norman, *The Doctrine of Deification in the Greek Patristic Tradition* (Oxford University Press, 2004).

Russo, Renato, *La metodologia del sapere nel sermone di S. Bonaventura 'Unus est magister vester Christus': con nuova edizione critica e traduzione italiana* (Grottaferrata: Collegium Sanctae Bonaventurae ad Claras Aquas, 1982).

Ryan, Edmund J., *The Role of the 'sensus communis' in the Psychology of St. Thomas Aquinas* (Carthage, OH: Messenger Press, 1951).

Santinello, Giovanni, *Il pensiero di Nicolò Cusano nella sua prospettiva estetica* (Padua: Liviana, 1958).

Sastri, Martin, 'The Influence of Plotinian Metaphysics in St. Augustine's Conception of the Spiritual Senses', *Dionysius*, 24 (2006), 99–124.

Scaramelli, Giovanni Battista, *Il direttorio mistico, indirizzato a' direttori di quelle anime, che iddio conduce per la via della contemplazione* (Venice: S. Occhi, 1754). In English as *A Handbook of Mystical Theology: Being an Abridgment of Il direttorio mistico*, trans. D. H. S. Nicholson (London: John M. Watkins, 1913).

Schmidt, Margot, 'Elemente der Schau bei Mechthild von Madgeburg und Mechthild von Hackeborn', in Peter Dinzelbacher and Dieter R. Bauer (eds.), *Frauenmystik im Mittelalter* (Ostfildern: Schawabenverlag, 1985), pp. 123–51.

'Versinnlichte Transzendenz bei Mechthild von Magdeburg', in Dietrich Schmidtke (ed.), *'Minnichlichiu gotes erkennusse': Studien zur frühen abendländischen Mystiktradition* (Stuttgart and Bad Cannstatt: Frommann-Holzboog, 1990), pp. 61–88.

Schneider, Arthur Carl August, *Die Erkenntnislehre des Johannes Eriugena: Im Rahmen ihrer metaphysischen und anthropologischen Voraussetzungen* (Berlin: de Gruyter, 1921).

Die Psychologie Alberts des Grossen (Münster: Aschendorff, 1903).

Sciamannini, Raniero, *La contuizione bonaventuriana* (Florence: Città di Vita, 1957).

Sellars, Wilfred, *Empiricism and the Philosophy of Mind* (Cambridge, MA: Harvard University Press, 1997).

Sheehan, Thomas, *Karl Rahner: The Philosophical Foundations* (Athens: Ohio University Press, 1987).

Sileo, Leonardo, *Teoria della scienza teologica* (Rome: Pontificium Athenaeum Antonianum, 1984).

Smith, Arthur David, *The Problem of Perception* (Cambridge, MA: Harvard University Press, 2002).

Smith, J. Warren, 'Macrina, Tamer of Horses and Healer of Souls: Grief and the Therapy of Hope in Gregory of Nyssa's *De anima et resurrectione*', *Journal of Theological Studies*, 52 (2000), 37–60.

Solignac, Aimé, 'Application des sens', *Nouvelle revue théologique*, 80 (1958), 726–38.

'Oculus (animae, cordis, mentis, etc.)', *DS*, vol. XI (1982), pp. 591–601.

Stead, G. Christopher, 'The Concept of Mind and the Concept of God in the Christian Fathers', in B. Hebblethwaite and S. Sutherland (eds.), *The Philosophical Frontiers of Christian Theology: Essays Presented to Donald MacKinnon* (Cambridge University Press, 1982), pp. 39–54.

Steneck, Nicholas H., 'Albert the Great on the Classification and Localization of the Internal Senses', *Isis*, 65.2 (June 1974), 193–211.

'The Problem of the Internal Senses in the Fourteenth Century', unpublished Ph.D. diss., University of Wisconsin, 1970.

Stock, Alex, 'Die Rolle der "icona Dei" in der Spekulation "De visione Dei"', *Mitteilungen und Forschungsbeiträge der Cusanus-Gesellschaft*, 18 (1989), 50–68.

Studer, Basil, *Zur Theophanie-Exegese Augustins: Untersuchung zu einem Ambrosius-Zitat in der Schrift De videndo Deo* (Rome: Herder, 1971).

Suarez, Armando, 'Los sentidos internos en los textos y en la sistematica tomista', *Salmanticensis*, 6 (1959), 401–75.

Swinburne, Richard, *The Existence of God* (Oxford: Clarendon Press, 1979).

Taylor, Charles, *Sources of the Self: The Making of the Modern Identity* (Cambridge, MA: Harvard University Press, 1989).

Tedoldi, Fabio Massimo, *La dottrina dei cinque sensi spirituali in San Bonaventura* (Rome: Pontificium Athenaeum Antonianum, 1999).

Théry, Gabriel, 'Commentaire sur Isaïe de Thomas de Saint-Victor', *La vie spirituelle*, 47 (1936), 146–62.

'Critique du thème vercellien', *La vie spirituelle*, 37 (1933), 163–78.

'L'éloge de S. Antoine de Padoue par Thomas Gallus', *La vie spirituelle*, 38 (1934), 22–51.

'Formation du thème vercellien', *La vie spirituelle*, 37 (1933), 94–114.

'Thomas Gallus: Aperçu biographique', *Archives d'histoire doctrinale et littéraire du Moyen Âge*, 12 (1939), 141–208.

Thunberg, Lars, *Microcosm and Mediator: The Theological Anthropology of Maximus the Confessor*, 2nd edn (Chicago: Open Court, 1995).

Torrell, Jean-Pierre, 'Le savoir théologique chez saint Thomas', *Revue Thomiste*, 96 (1996), 355–96.

Théorie de la prophétie et philosophie de la connaissance aux environs de 1230: La contribution d'Hugues de Saint-Cher (Louvain: Spicilegium Sacrum Lovaniense, 1977).

Turner, Denys, *Eros and Allegory: Medieval Exegesis of the Song of Songs* (Kalamazoo, MI: Cistercian Publications, 1995).

Vance, Eugene, 'Seeing God: Augustine, Sensation, and the Mind's Eye', in Stephen G. Nichols, Andreas Kablitz and Alison Calhoun (eds.), *Rethinking the Medieval Senses: Heritage, Fascinations, Frames* (Baltimore: Johns Hopkins University Press, 2008), pp. 13–29.

Vanni Rovighi, Sophia, *San Bonaventura* (Milan: Vita e Pensiero, 1974).

Vasaly, Ann, *Representations: Images of the World in Ciceronian Oratory* (Berkeley: University of California Press, 1993).

Wagner, Michael F., 'Sense Experience and the Active Soul: Some Plotinian and Augustinian Themes', *The Journal of Neoplatonic Studies*, 1.2 (1993), 37–62.

Wainwright, William J., 'Jonathan Edwards, God, and "Particular Minds"', *International Journal for Philosophy of Religion*, 68.1 (2010), 201–13.

Mysticism: A Study of its Nature, Cognitive Value, and Moral Implications (Madison: University of Wisconsin Press, 1981).

Reason and the Heart (Ithaca, NY: Cornell University Press, 1995).

Waldstein, Michael, 'An Introduction to von Balthasar's *The Glory of the Lord*', *Communio*, 14 (1987), 12–33.

Wallis, Richard T., 'The Spiritual Importance of Not Knowing', in Arthur Hilary Armstrong (ed.), *Classical Mediterranean Spirituality* (New York: Crossroad, 1986), pp. 460–80.

Walsh, James, 'Guillaume de Saint-Thierry et les sens spirituels', *RAM*, 35 (1959), 27–42.

Sapientia Christianorum: The Doctrine of Thomas Gallus Abbot of Vercelli on Contemplation (Rome: Pontificia Universitas Gregoriana, 1957).

Walton, Brad, *Jonathan Edwards*, Religious Affections *and the Puritan Analysis of True Piety, Spiritual Sensation, and Heart Religion* (Lewiston, NY, Queenston, Ont., and Lampeter: Edwin Mellen Press, 2002).

Watson, Nicholas, *Richard Rolle and the Invention of Authority* (Cambridge University Press, 1991).

Wesley, John (ed.), *A Christian Library: Consisting of Extracts from and Abridgments of the Choicest Pieces of Practical Divinity which have been Published in the English Tongue*, 50 vols. (Bristol: Farley, 1749–55).

Willaert, Frank, *Hadewijch: Visioenen* (Amsterdam: Uitgeverij Prometheus, 1996).

Williams, Rowan, 'Macrina's Deathbed Revisited: Gregory of Nyssa on Mind and Passion', in *Christian Faith and Greek Philosophy in Late Antiquity: Essays in Tribute to George Christopher Stead . . . in Celebration of his Eightieth Birthday, Vigiliae Christianae*, 19 (1993), 227–46.

Wolfson, Harry Austryn, 'The Internal Senses in Latin, Arabic, and Hebrew Philosophical Texts', *HTR*, 28 (1935), 250–314.

'Maimonides on the Internal Senses', *The Jewish Quarterly Review*, new series, 25.4 (1935), 441–67.

Woolgar, Christopher M., *The Senses in Late Medieval England* (New Haven, CT: Yale University Press, 2007).

Wynn, Mark R., *Emotional Experience and Religious Understanding: Integrating Perception, Conception, and Feeling* (Cambridge University Press, 2005).

Zeegers-Vander Vorst, Nicole, 'La création de l'homme (Gn 1: 26) chez Théophile d'Antioche', *Vigiliae Christianae*, 30.4 (1976), 258–67.

Ziegler, Joseph, *Dulcedo Dei: Ein Beitrag zur Theologie der griechischen und lateinischen Bibel* (Münster: Aschendorff, 1937).

General index

Index of select biblical references

58563796R00188

Made in the USA
Lexington, KY
13 December 2016